Advance Praise

"I was fascinated by Gordon Lore's account of UFO history and NICAP's ceaseless struggle to uncover and reveal the truth. Working with highly-charged, up-to-the-minute material, the author invokes military and civilian aviators, police officers, trainmen, abductees, scientists, CIA moles, gold miners, FBI bureaucrats and the everyday people whose sightings are the backbone of the UFO phenomenon. If a book dedicated to evidence-based research can be thrilling, *Flying Saucers From Beyond the Earth* is it."

—**David J. Hogan**, author of *UFO FAQ: All That's Left to Know About Roswell, Aliens, Whirling Discs, and Flying Saucers.*

"Gordon Lore provides us with a marvelous look at the Golden Era of flying saucers and UFOs, giving us an uncommon look at the past from the perspective of one who actually lived it as an official of NICAP in Washington, D.C. This inside look at many classic saucer sightings comes from the time when UFOs made national headlines, were the subject of official Air Force investigations, and were targeted for two Congressional hearings in 1966 and 1968. It is pure nostalgia for those curious about the controversy over life in space."

—**Barry J. Greenwood**, co-author of *Clear Intent: The Government Coverup of the UFO Experience.*

"Gordon Lore has given us a careful, comprehensive and honest reportage of the UFO phenomenon based on his many years of investigating the phenomenon. He is neither an alarmist nor a radical in his conclusions. The reader will find this an essential counterweight to distortions that sometimes muddy this ever-timely subject."

—**Neil Earle**, author of *The Wonderful Wizard of Oz in American Popular Culture*.

"As the author of the classic works *Mysteries of the Skies: UFOs in Perspective* (1968) and *Strange Effects From UFOs* (1969), Gordon Lore finds himself back on familiar ground with this book. He brings a fresh perspective to a subject that has become increasingly relevant even in the mainstream press, giving us a clear, objective view based on years of research and experience."

—**Alan Doshna**, co-author of *Richard Anderson. At Last… A Memoir From the Golden Years of M-G-M and the Six Million Dollar Man to Now*.

"This valuable addition to the canon of UFO works is told from the author's unique perspective as a key member of NICAP during its most successful years and its controversial closure. Replete with insights and accounts of a vast number of important cases, this book should be on the shelves of all serious researchers."

—**Lindy Powell**, author of *The Disclosure Man*, a forthcoming biography of Major Donald E. Keyhoe.

"Part candid memoir, part historical treatise, this fast-moving read succinctly examines the landmark cases and seminal events in UFO history as viewed through the lens of a veteran saucer sleuth. A timely return to form for a versatile author, *Flying Saucers From Beyond the Earth* is a must-read for anyone seeking new insights into that age-old, ever-mysterious phenomenon."

— **D.H. Mintz**, screenwriter of *The Reluctant Daughter of Mr. Flying Saucer*, a film based the life of Major Donald E. Keyhoe

FLYING SAUCERS FROM BEYOND THE EARTH

A UFO Researcher's Odyssey

By Gordon Lore

Flying Saucers From Beyond the Earth: A UFO Researcher's Odyssey
© 2018. Gordon Lore All rights reserved.

All illustrations are copyright of their respective owners, and are also reproduced here in the spirit of publicity. Whilst we have made every effort to acknowledge specific credits whenever possible, we apologize for any omissions, and will undertake every effort to make any appropriate changes in future editions of this book if necessary.

No part of this book may be reproduced in any form or by any means, electronic, mechanical, digital, photocopying or recording, except for the inclusion in a review, without permission in writing from the publisher.

Published in the USA by:
BearManor Media
P O Box 71426
Albany, Georgia 31708
www.bearmanormedia.com

Printed in the United States of America
ISBN   978-1-62933-343-4 (paperback)

Book & cover design and layout by Darlene Swanson • www.van-garde.com
Front cover design provided courtesy of Michael Riley

Dedication

A very special thanks to my stepson, Junius Adam ("Jay") Triche III, whose patience with my lack of technical expertise is unending and very much appreciated. He has always been there for me with constant love and support when I have needed him. He also provided valuable technical assistance with the photographs, sketches and illustrations.

I also honor the memory of the spirits of my departed friends and UFO colleagues **Major Donald E. Keyhoe, Richard H. Hall**, and **Dr. James E. McDonald**. They have made lasting contributions to the ongoing scientific investigation of Unidentified Flying Objects.

Acknowledgements

As the author of this book, I am very grateful for a wide number of other well-qualified individuals other than those on the Dedication page for their help throughout my career and beyond researching, investigating, and reporting reliable UFO reports from around the world.

These individuals include (in alphabetical order): Robert ("Bob") Barrow, Robert ("Bob") Barry, Noel J. Becar, Howard Benedict, Melvin Carmichael, Paul Cerny, Pearl Christiansen, J.D. Collner, William Curry, Alan Doshna, Ann Druffel, Neil Earle, Frank Edwards, Claude L. Elmes, Idabel Epperson, Edward Evers, Doris R. Fickelsher, Donald E. Flickinger, Raymond F. Fowler, Stanton Friedman, John G. Fuller, Tony Goudie, Jeffrey J. Gow, John Gray, Barry J. Greenwood, Henry C. Hawecki, Julian A. Hennessey, Ion Habana, Dr. J. Allen Hynek, David J. Hogan, R. Conway Jones, Rose Marie Julig, Bruce J. Kennedy, Her Majesty's Seaman Ian Kinsey, Diana Knopp, Dennis Leatart, Martha D. ("Marty") Lore, Erica Lukes, Joan Lusby, John Lutz, Robert Mattingly, Clark C. McClelland, Lex Mebane, John Meloney, Clay T. Miller, Daniel Mintz, Willard D. Nelson, Simon Oakland, Dr. Lincoln La Paz, Lindy Powell, Ralph Rankow, C. Reed Ricks, Francis Ridge, Wiley Robinson, Congressman J. Edward Roush, Dr. David R. Saunders, Terri Smith, Ray Stanford, Leonard H. Stringfield, Hugh Tapping, Dr. Jacques Vallee, Walter N. Webb, Agnes M. Wehrle, Lieutenant Colonel E. Garrison Wood, and Ruth A. Ziegenfuss.

Author's Note

Many of the UFO sighting reports and related incidents in this book do not include possible follow-up investigations that were conducted years later while others do. As the author, I was actively involved with certain UFO sighting reports during my stints as a staff member and later assistant director/vice president of the National Investigations Committee on Aerial Phenomena (NICAP) from 1965 to 1970 and as the president of my own UFO Research Associates (UFOR) from 1970 to 1980.

I particularly want to thank **Barry J. Greenwood**—the co-author with Lawrence Fawcett of *Clear Intent: The Government Coverup of the UFO Experience* with a Foreword by Dr. J. Allen Hynek—for his gracious help in providing me with his insight into the famous Roswell, New Mexico, so-called crash-and-retrieval case of July 1947, and the MJ-12 controversy. I also want to thank **Francis Ridge**, the founder and webmaster of the fact-loaded NICAP website, for his help and support. Both of these long-time investigators have made lasting contributions to the more than half-a-century of ongoing scientific investigations of what may eventually turn out to be the most incredible event in world history… *proof of actual contact with extraterrestrial beings!*

My thanks also goes to a new friend, **Erica Lukes**, host of a global radio talk show on which I, as of this writing, am slated to appear. Her knowledge of significant events in the more than sixty years of serious scientific investigations of flying saucer reports is also truly impressive.

After more than six decades of investigating UFO reports from reliable witnesses in virtually every scientific and other fields of endeavor, many UFO researchers and investigators believe that contact with extraterrestrial beings may have already been made and we have benefited from it.

Table of Contents

Acknowlegements vii
Author's Note ix
Introduction *Eyes in the Skies* xiii

Part One: The NICAP Years

Chapter 1	Incidents at Loch Raven Reservoir and Carl Jung. 3
Chapter 2	The UFO Invasion of West Texas 13
Chapter 3	The Killian Case 21
Chapter 4	Aliens in Socorro and J. Edgar Hoover 33
Chapter 5	The Rex Heflin Photos 45
Chapter 6	The "Baby UFO" and A Landing in South Hill 53
Chapter 7	The *Morgantown Victory* and Other Sightings at Sea. 65
Chapter 8	From Joe Franklin to the King Shot Effect 77
Chapter 9	From a Congressional Hearing to the D.C. Area Sightings 87
Chapter 10	*2001: A Space Odyssey*, The Titusville Humanoid and Beyond. 97
Chapter 11	The Carmichael and Becar Encounters 109
Chapter 12	"Liar! Liar! Pants on Fire!" The University of Colorado UFO Project 117
Chapter 13	The Bismarck Area Sightings 131
Chapter 14	The U.S. Air Force Grudge and Blue Book Reports 137
Chapter 15	The Colorado UFO Report is Published 147

Chapter 16	UFOs in Rumania	157
Chapter 17	The Strange Effects	163
Chapter 18	The McDonald Factor	227
Chapter 19	The CIA Connection	235
Chapter 20	The Keyhoe Factor: An Homage	241

Part II: The UFOR Years

Chapter 21	The Mantell Tragedy	251
Chapter 22	The Wood River Junction and Spanish Peakes UFOs	261
Chapter 23	Flying Saucers Pace Trains	267
Chapter 24	Bizarre Alien "Claim Jumpers" and the Happy Camp Sightings	277
Chapter 25	Incident in Colusa	291
Chapter 26	UFO Zaps Car in Georgia, and Jimmy Carter	297
Chapter 27	From a Witness in the Light to a Housebound UFO	303
Chapter 28	Flying Disc Causes Physiological Effects	309
Chapter 29	Flying Saucers Pace Planes and Trains	315
Chapter 30	The Humming UFO and Sightings in Pennsylvania and Maryland	321
Chapter 31	From NASA to a Silver UFO	327
Chapter 32	UFO "Retrievals of the Third Kind" and the Roswell Incident	335
Chapter 33	The Syracuse UFO Flap	355
Chapter 34	UFOs Cavort Over Pittsburgh	369
Chapter 35	The AATIP Program	375
Epilogue	Celebrity Quotes	381
References		405
Index		423
About the Author		439

INTRODUCTION

Eyes in the Skies

It was the long hot Summer of 1955 in my little hometown of Solomons Island, Maryland, a pleasant little seafaring hamlet tucked neatly in the mouth where the Chesapeake Bay meets the Patuxent River. To me, it was as if the mighty jaws of the Chesapeake—a prime sailing and harvesting spot for mariners from Hollywood celebrities to seafood planters and packers like my father and grandfather—had belched the river up onto its curving path as a watery backyard to Washington, D.C., the same route the British took during the War of 1812 when His Majesty's forces attacked and burned the President's House and other federal buildings in August 1814. During this humid and quiet summer night, my eyes were on the skies.

I had just finished a fascinating book by Major Donald E. Keyhoe (USMC-Ret.)—the man who had written the first book on the UFO, or flying saucer, phenomenon in 1950—and I was a convert. Little did I know that, on that evening, the conversion would take on real meaning both then and ten years later. It was during that night that I would have my own first experience with a flying saucer.

I had walked to nearly the end of the Chesapeake Biological Laboratory's half-mile long pier stretching far out into the calm river and aimed in the direction of the Patuxent Naval Air Station (PAX River) directly across the moon-drenched river in St. Mary's County. The air was still and there were few visible stars.

The pier was my favorite spot on the little half-mile-long island. I reached what I called the visitor's alcove where a wooden awning hung overhead and the hard cement benches were a welcome relief for the weary walker.

The Silver Disc

In the middle of my usual young reverie, my attention was drawn to what at first appeared to be a faint light in the distance quickly approaching from the jaws of the Chesapeake. With wide-open eyes and a vivid imagination, I strained to see what it was. Then the light grew brighter and illuminated a large silvery disc-shaped object that appeared to be about half the length of a football field. In clear view, I watched as the UFO suddenly dropped down into the water and disappeared for perhaps twenty seconds, then reappeared as I saw streams of water fall from its bottom.

I grabbed tightly onto one of the pier poles as the object approached me. Then, as it was close enough to the pier to scare the living hell out of me, a large panel at its bottom opened and what seemed like several tons of water splashed close enough to my spot on the pier to pepper me with a Patuxent shower. I sat down with my eyes still on the object as it swiftly glided silently overhead and disappeared out of sight heading north.

I had recently seen *The Day the Earth Stood Still* (1951) for the second time and wondered if this was the real thing. Had the robot Gort come to destroy the warmongers who threatened the earth's destruction and those inhabited planets in our solar system with nuclear bombs and weapons? It was a fanciful thought. Or was it?

It was the beginning of my start into the fascinating world of Unidentified Flying Objects (UFOs) and my years of work with the man who had already become my hero. Two more personal encounters with strange objects in the sky were still to come before I had my chance to work with Major Donald E. Keyhoe, already known as "Mr. UFO."

The Mother Ship

At 8:15 p.m., April 2, 1959, I was returning to my home on Solomons Island. It was dark and foreboding on that lonely stretch of road between Prince Frederick, the Calvert County seat, and my home facing my father's marina set in a watery alcove in the middle of the attractive harbor sporting the tree-shadowing effects of tiny Mile Lakes Island. I was returning home from the Peabody Conservatory of Music in Baltimore, where I was a piano and voice student. Suddenly, I looked up and saw a white light considerably brighter than the planet Venus hanging over a barn on the left side of the road.

For about three minutes, the light remained in its stationary position. Then it started to blink on and off while moving slowly toward Solomons, about five or six miles away. The light appeared to follow my car for about a mile or more. Then it stopped once again, this time behind some trees, and was lost from view.

I continued south. When I got to within a mile or so from home, the UFO stopped once more and hovered over another barn. *What was this attraction to barns?* I wondered. There was no question about it.... The object had been following my car. As I purposely slowed down several times, then suddenly accelerated to a fast drive home, the UFO followed suit, keeping me in sight.

Suddenly, I was startled when the strange object began blinking its light on and off. Then it performed some fantastic maneuvers. In what seemed like only an instant, it appeared at one end of the sky and, only a split second later, reappeared at the other end. I couldn't believe something could move that fast, almost quicker than the eye could see. It obviously wasn't a conventional aircraft or a jet from PAX River. Nothing that I knew of could move that fast! Nothing, perhaps, than a possible alien craft from some other place in our galaxy or beyond....

After the object had completed its incredibly fast maneuvers five or six times, it stopped once more. Then, as I strained to watch in a shocked and bewildered state, a large, brilliant red light descended nearly faster than the eye could see and merged with the much larger white light. It appeared that the larger object had swallowed the smaller one. It was then that my car radio—which had been operating normally playing classical music from Baltimore—began emitting a loud screeching noise, which continued to the end of the strange and startling encounter.

The blinking white light followed my car. As I approached the Patuxent River on the right side of the road, the light slowed, but continued to follow my automobile until it slowly crossed the river and headed south until it disappeared.

Cigars Over the Patuxent

Nearly seven months later, on November 20, 1958, I was only twelve days away from reporting for duty as a U.S. Army draftee on December 2. I was working at my father's oyster house, J.C. Lore & Sons, which directly faced the expansive Patuxent River, one of the largest tributaries of the Chesapeake Bay.

It was 5:15 p.m. I had just finished my shift cleaning freshly shucked oysters and had moved outside with several other shuckers on the road overlooking the river. Suddenly, I could see a red streak of light that was hanging over the river. Several of the others were starting to head home when they also saw the sharp and clear light.

"Look!" someone yelled, excitedly pointing at the sky. "What the hell is that?"

"Maybe it's a flying saucer!" someone else piped in.

As I quickly focused on the light, it suddenly changed to what appeared to be three slender, cigar-shaped objects that resembled narrow cloud formations hanging over the river in a direct line with the oyster house. Then the UFOs moved slowly across the river into St. Mary's County.

Suddenly, quicker than my eyes could follow, a fourth object seemed to spring out of nowhere. This UFO was so large that it literally dwarfed the other three objects. As we all watched in stunned disbelief, the larger UFO began an elongated expansion from both ends at the same time. The objects appeared to be only a few hundred feet away. Meanwhile, an additional fifteen or so shuckers had joined our small group.

Now, all four of the objects were in clear view over the river, where they remained for about ten minutes. Then, the larger object began slowly ascending into the sky. It came to a stop at what I roughly estimated to be about 20,000 feet altitude. A few seconds later, quicker than my eyes or mind could comprehend, the UFO changed its color and shape to a silver, round disc that suddenly disappeared at a tremendous speed high in the northeastern sky.

A few days later, I sent both of these sighting reports to the National Investigations Committee on Aerial Phenomena (NICAP) at its headquarters office on Dupont Circle in Washington, D.C. Little did I know then that I would spend nearly five years working with NICAP Director Major Donald E. ("Don") Keyhoe, Richard H. ("Dick") Hall, then the Assistant Director, and other staff members. It was to be one of the most rewarding and, at times, most frustrating experiences of my life.

PART ONE

The NICAP Years
Introduction

About two years after leaving the Army in December 1960, I moved from my boyhood home on Solomons Island and began my career as a writer-editor in Washington, D.C. This was the time of the nationwide folksong craze. While I was a piano, guitar and voice student at the Peabody Conservatory of Music, I also became a folksong enthusiast and singer.

I even set to music a poem by Supreme Court Chief Justice Oliver Wendell Holmes that he wrote as a tribute to his dog entitled "The Pedigreed Piddlin' Pup in Ten Piddles and a Puddle." It was a hit at the Unicorn Coffee House, where I frequently performed. During one session, Peter Yarrow—of the famed Peter, Paul and Mary folksong trio—showed up and was in the small audience when I sang it. Following my short time on stage, Peter stood up and started clapping loudly. This prompted the other denizens of the Unicorn to do the same.

During one of my performances during the summer of 1965, Dick Hall showed up and was impressed. He invited me to his apartment, where I entertained a small group of his friends. I told him about my abiding interest in UFOs and clued him in on the two sightings I had made in 1958, which I had sent to NICAP.

Before the evening was over with yet another rendition of the Piddlin' Pup, we had become fast friends and Dick had quickly hired me to join the NICAP staff. Two days later, I gave my resignation as a minor editor at a U.S. News and World Report subsidiary and was on my way to a new life with Keyhoe, Hall, and their crack NICAP staff. It was to become a dream job mixed with more than a little anxiety about keeping the organization afloat during the next five years.

CHAPTER ONE

Incidents at Loch Raven Reservoir and Carl Jung

When I joined the NICAP staff, I knew I had a lot of catching up to do. It had been eighteen years since private pilot Kenneth Arnold spotted nine disks flying in formation over Mt. Rainier in Washington State on June 24, 1947. Arnold described them as "like pie plates skipping over the water." This report is regarded as the jumping-off point to the so-called modern era of UFO reports, but I also knew that people around the world had been seeing unexplained phenomena in the skies for untold centuries.

As a quick catch-up, I began receiving first-hand information from Keyhoe and Hall, both of whom assured me that not everyone was buying the Air Force rant. One of the first articles I read came from the *Charleston Evening Post* in South Carolina with the following interesting teaser from Air Force Regulation 200-2.9: "Information regarding a (UFO) sighting may be released to the press or the general public… only if it has been positively identified as a familiar or known object."

My antennae took a quick leap into outer space on that one. It sure as hell sounded like the Air Force was not releasing any UFO reports that it could not explain. Don Keyhoe and Dick Hall, of course, knew this first-hand and I was just beginning to get into that frame of mind based on reliable investigations from the crews of NICAP's field subcommittees around the world.

Is Something Going On "Up There"?

The author of the Charleston newspaper article called the Air Force to task when he or she wrote:

> Without meaning to alarm the children, we would suggest ever so cautiously that another 15 or 20 years will see an explanation for the common phenomena known as Unidentified Flying Objects or, to some, "flying saucers." The Air Force says it is not alarmed. Neither are we. But the fact remains that something is going on "up there", and we rather suspect that the Air Force knows it.
>
> The latest rash of UFO reports from scientists and others in Asia, Europe, Latin America and the Antarctic is really nothing unusual. Reputable scientists and equally reputable nonscientists have been watching UFOs perform [around the world] for many years. One or two of the earthlings, moreover, were sober at the time.
>
> The most perplexing part of the whole business is not the UFO reports; UFOs, whatever they are, exist, and it is not unnatural that people have reported seeing them. Some have even photographed them. What is hard to understand is the attitude of the Air Force.
>
> Confronted by a UFO report, the service immediately begins to crank out of the wild blue yonder the same pre-recorded announcement it has been playing for 20 years: "scratch, scratch, the Air Force has no evidence, scratch, scratch, the Air Force has no evidence…." It all depends, of course, on what is meant by evidence. If our courts shared the Air Force's professed suspicion of credible witnesses, our jails would be empty.
>
> But in another 20 years or so…, the full story will be told. By that time, one of these unidentified objects will have set down politely beside a television crew and had its image, in living color, flashed around

the world. When that happens, the second most interesting story of the year will be the Air Force version of why for 40 years it kept the public in the dark.

Unexplained Reports Continue

Now, of course—as I write this fifty-two years later—that prediction has still not become a reality. Nor am I holding my breath that it will happen any time soon. The Air Force, along with other government investigating agencies, would have too much explaining away to do. In this 21st Century period, reliable and unexplained UFO reports from around the world from highly qualified witnesses continue. The availability of the Internet and e-mails have provided a wealth of information—both positive and negative—about UFOs and their continued sightings from every corner of the world.

Soon after joining the NICAP staff, I asked Richard Hall for some UFO reports he investigated himself as part of a quick catch-up on the wealth of sightings the organization had in its files. Dick handed me a detailed report on a case he personally investigated. It involved an encounter in Towson, Maryland, a suburb of Baltimore, near where I had spent four years in high school and the Peabody and was a favorite shopping place for my family during my childhood and teen years.

Encounter at Loch Raven Reservoir

At 5 p.m., October 26, 1958, Philip Small dropped his wife off at work and drove back to their home on Reisterstown Road just outside Baltimore. From six to seven p.m., he sat and talked with a friend, Alvin Cohen. Then both men decided to "go for a ride" through downtown Baltimore. They seemed to somehow be drawn toward Loch Raven Reservoir. Small said that he and Cohen just had "a feeling" that they had to go there. He said they were only driving around waiting to pick up their wives. Mrs. Small was at her job while Mrs. Cohen was bowling.

The two men headed for the first bridge over the reservoir. As they approached a bend in the road, they saw a tremendous, white, egg-shaped object about 100 feet long and seventy-five feet high. It was glowing, and it appeared to be about 100 feet over the bridge around 300 yards away.

The E-M Effects

Philip and Alvin cautiously and slowly approached the object. As they came to within 100 feet of it, Small's car headlights and motor conked out. The driver slammed on the brakes and stopped. Small attempted to turn the ignition on, but nothing happened.

"This damned car won't start!" he cried out. "Did that thing cause my car to conk out? What the hell is it anyhow? Jesus, man, I'm really starting to get scared!"

The automobile's entire electrical system had ceased functioning. Both men sat scared for a short period before deciding to quickly leave the car.

"Let's get the hell out of here!" the frightened Alvin exclaimed.

"No Place to Run"

Crouching down beside the car, the men quickly saw that there was nowhere to run. They were hemmed in by the reservoir on one side of the road and a steep embankment on the other. Now, they were face-to-face with the strange object. It was not a friendly feeling as the two friends stayed close to each other.

As the men fearfully watched, the UFO glowed much more brightly, then flashed brilliantly. They felt a wave of heat beat against their faces and heard a thunderous explosion. Then the object ascended like a shot and disappeared.

Philip and Alvin jumped back into the car. Small turned the ignition key. The engine started. He pushed the accelerator to the floor and quickly tore away from the area. The car with the still badly shaken men screeched to a halt in front of nearby Loch Raven Inn. While they were at the inn, Small called the Ground Observer Corps (GOC) and told them what they had seen. A GOC official said they had probably encountered a Navy blimp that could still be cruising around in the area.

There was no way that explanation would pass muster, the men thought. A blimp simply could not have made a sound like a thunderous explosion, then disappear into the sky like a shot. The GOC guys would have to do better then that.

The men decided to call the nearby Towson Police Station and report the incident. At 11:05 p.m., approximately thirty minuets after the object zoomed away, a police car with Officers Kenneth Hartmann and Richard Fink stopped in front of the inn. Inside, they found that both of the witnesses were still scared. The policemen noticed that the faces of the two men were parched, as if they had been sunburned.

"These men appeared to be sober, but they were scared to death," Corporal Hartmann later confirmed. "I can tell you that!"

A Return to Loch Raven

The UFO sighting report at Loch Raven Reservoir that Dick Hall investigated wasn't the first such report at that location. Nor would it be the last. Nearly five years earlier, another encounter with a strange aerial intruder was reported to the Towson Police Department.

It was about 7:45 p.m., at an unspecified day in May 1953. Two young men (who wished to remain anonymous) were heading toward the reservoir on their way to meeting two women from Towson State College for a date. They were nearing one of the bridges spanning the area encompassing the reservoir when their car quickly and inexplicably came to an abrupt halt. While the driver vainly attempted to restart the automobile, the car headlights and radio also ceased functioning. The driver made repeated attempts to restart the car, but to no avail.

"How are we going to pick up the girls if we're already out of gas?" the passenger jokingly asked, nudging his friend.

"Damned if I know!" the driver responded.

"Lip-to-Lip" Saucers

The two men were an estimated seventy-five feet from the bridge when they spotted what they described as "an orange glowing object with an ultraviolet band which divided what appeared to be two saucers lip-to-lip." The UFO appeared to be about 300 feet away.

The two friends were quickly terrified by the intruder. They bolted from the car and ran for cover.

"I think we need to get the hell out of here!" the driver shouted. "You go right. I'll run to the left."

The driver made a beeline to the left, then scrambled up an embankment into a wooded area. The passenger headed to the right, diving into a ditch next to a sharp drop-off into the lake.

The huge UFO was at an estimated height of 275 feet above the water. It looked to be about 175 feet wide and fifty-five or so feet in height. It hovered over the water for a short while, during which a column of fog or haze or mist was seen by a light located in the center of the UFO between the object and the surface of the water. There appeared to be a conical shape of the column below the intruder. The object rose another 100 feet or so into the air as the fog/haze/mist disappeared. Then it disappeared so quickly that the men were unable to determine its direction.

The "Operation Blue Book" Men

The entire incident lasted about ten minutes. Both men also said the craft made a strange *mum-mum-mum*-type noise that sounded like cicadas or locusts.

The observers returned to their car in a vain attempt to restart it. They had to wait until a police car returned and escorted them back to Towson, where they filed a report.

The next day, both men were interrogated by four men in civilian clothes. The witnesses were told the men were from Operation Blue Book. They interrogated the men for about one hour and were given what amounted to make-believe scenarios of what they had seen. They were then released with the threat that if they didn't remain silent about this incident, their jobs would be in jeopardy.

Letters From Dr. Carl Jung

Shortly after studying the Lock Raven Boulevard sightings, I came across in the NICAP files two letters from famed psychologist Dr. Carl Jung to Major Keyhoe. Jung's teacher and mentor was Dr. Sigmund Freud, the father of psychology. In 1958, Jung had published his own UFO book, *Flying Saucers: A Modern Myth of Things Seen in the Skies*.

In his book Jung praised Keyhoe.

"I would like to call the reader's attention to Keyhoe's books, which are based on official material and studiously avoid the wild speculation, naivety, or prejudice of other publications," Jung wrote.

Both letters are reproduced here in Jung's less-than-perfect English spelling and grammar. Both were written from the psychologist's home in Zurich, Switzerland. The first letter was dated August 16, 1958:

Dear Major Keyhoe,

Thank you for your kind letter! I have read all you have written concerning UFOs and I am a subscriber to the NICAP-Bulletin. I am grateful for all the courageous things you have done in elucidating the thorny problem of UFO-reality.

The article in [the] APRO [Aerial Phenomena Research Organization]-Bulletin July 1958, which caused all that stir in the press, is unfortunately inaccurate. As you know, I am an alienist and medical psychologist. I have never seen an UFO and I have no first hand information neither about them nor about the dubious attitude of the A.A.F. On account of this regrettable lack I am unable to form a definite opinion concerning the physical nature of the UFO-phenomenon. As I am a scientist, I only say, what I can prove and reserve my judgment in any case where I doubt my competence. Thus I said: "Things are seen, but one does not know what." I do neither affirm, nor deny. But it is certain beyond all possible doubt that plenty of statements about UFOs are made and they are of all sorts. I am chiefly concerned about this aspect of the phenomenon. It yields a rich harvest of insight into its universal significance. My special preoccupation does neither preclude the physical reality of the UFOs nor their extraterrestrial origin nor the purposefulness of their behavior etc. But I do not possess <u>sufficient</u> evidence, which would enable me to draw definite conclusions. The evidence available to me, however, is convincing enough to arouse a continuous and fervent interest. I follow with my greatest sympathy your exploits and your endeavour to establish the truth about the UFOs.

In spite of the fact that I keep my judgment concerning the nature of the UFOs—temporarily let us hope—in suspence, I thought it worthwhile to throw a light upon the rich phantasy material, which has accumulated itself around the peculiar observations in the skies. Any new experience has two aspects: 1) the pure fact and 2) the way one conceives of it. It is the latter I am concerned with. If it is true that the A.A.F. or the Government withholds telltaling facts, then one can only say, that this is the most unpsychological and stupid policy one could invent. Nothing helps rumors and panics more than ignorance. It is self evidence, that the public ought to be told the truth, because ultimately it will nevertheless come to the daylight. There can be hardly any greater shock than the H-bomb and yet anybody knows of it without fainting.

As to your question about a possible hostility of the UFOs I must emphasize, that I have no other knowledge about them, than that, which everybody can get out of printed reports. That is the reason that I am still far from certainty about the UFOs physical reality.

Thank you for your kind offer to send me clippings. I got enough of them. It is a curious fact, that whenever I make a statement, it is at once twisted and falsified. The press seems to enjoy lies more than the truth.

I remain, dear Major, yours

(s) C.J. Jung

Nearly two months later, on October 13, 1958, Jung sent a second much shorter letter to Keyhoe:

Dear Major Keyhoe,

My recent experience with APRO shows me that I must be careful in getting mixed up with UFO-organisations. Although I am vividly interested in these questions, I prefer to detach my name from organizations of this kind. This does not mean, that I am not perfectly willing to contribute whatever I can, to the research-work, such organisations are concerned with. If I am able at all [to] help in psychological matters, I am glad to do so, but I prefer it in an in-official way.

I enclose a report in the "Neue Zurcher Zeitung" of Oct. 1st 1958, which is unfortunately inconclusive.

Sincerely yours,

[s] C.G. Jung

CHAPTER TWO

The UFO Invasion of West Texas

During my first few weeks at NICAP, I continued to ask Dick Hall for a series of reports he and other staff members of the organization had investigated and found to be authentic. The second heavily-ladened file he laid on my desk was a stunner. I sat and read it with marked enthusiasm. The chief NICAP investigator was Walter N. Webb, the lead Astronomer with the Charles Hayden Planetarium in Boston, Massachusetts.

In November 1957, a huge wave of UFO reports came from virtually every corner of the United States. Newspapers, magazines, radio and television accounts highlighted flying objects that caused a plethora of special circumstances such as physiological and electro-magnetic (E-M) effects, animal reactions, badly frightened witnesses, and radioactivity.

Many of the most heavily reported sightings came from West Texas, particularly in Levelland, a cotton and oil town of around 10,000 people thirty-two miles west of Lubbock—where another sighting known as the Lubbock Lights was seen and photographed years earlier—in Hockley County. It was the night of November 2-3, 1957.

Heavy E-M Effects

"Something happened near the town that night that could have come straight out of a science fiction tale or a wild nightmare except that it was not imaginary, but very real if we believe the testimonies of persons who [saw] a brilliant, glowing, red, egg-shaped object some 200 feet long sitting on the road and cutting off the automobile engines and headlights," Webb stated in his report. "When the thing took off, engines and lights functioned normally. At least ten [car] motors were affected around Levelland."

At 10:50 p.m., November 2, the first call of a strange flying object came in to the Levelland Police Station. The officer on duty was A.J. Fowler. He listened as the terrified witness, Pedro Saucedo, 30, a farmhand and barber, related the strange story. Pedro said he and a friend, Joe Salaz, were about four miles west of Levelland on Route 116 when they spotted a torpedo-shaped UFO that was about 200 feet long.

"We first saw a flash of light in the field to our right and we didn't think much about it….," Saucedo explained. "Then it rose up out of the field and started toward us, picking up speed. When it got nearer, the lights of my truck went out and the motor died. I jumped out and hit the deck as the thing passed directly over the truck… with a great sound and a rush of wind. It sounded like thunder and my truck rocked from the blast. I felt a lot of heat. Then I got up and watched it go out of sight toward Levelland."

As the object left the area, the truck lights resumed functioning and Saucedo was able to restart the engine. When it left the area, the driver said: "It sounded like an ear-splitting clap of thunder, as if something had exploded." Patrolman Fowler, however, initially shrugged off the report because he thought the caller was drunk.

Return Engagements

About an hour later, just before midnight, the police station phone rang again. The caller, Jim Wheeler from Whitharral, said he was driving around four miles east of Levelland on the Lubbock Route 116 highway when he came across a brilliant 200-foot egg-shaped object sitting on the road. His car lights went out and the motor died. The [UFO] was lit up like neon lights and [it] cast a bright glare over the entire area. As Wheeler began exiting his automobile, the object rose to an altitude of about 200 feet. Then its brilliant light went out and Wheeler's lights came back on.

At about the same time that evening, Jose Alvarez, of Whitharral—eleven miles north of Levelland—said he was driving on Route 51 when he approached the same or a similar 200-foot glowing object on the road that apparently caused his automobile motor and lights to cease functioning. One account of the incident said that Alvarez saw the object circle a cotton field.

Small Object Lands on Road

At 12:05 a.m., November 3, Newell Wright, Jr., 19, a Texas Tech freshman, was driving from Lubbock back home to Levelland. He was approximately nine miles east of his destination on Route 116 when he noticed that his 1952 Ford was not running right. His ammeter jumped to "discharge," then went back to normal. The motor began running down like it was out of gas and the car rolled to a stop. Then the lights dimmed and went out.

The puzzled and concerned freshman exited the car, raised the hood, checked the motor, battery and wires, but could find nothing wrong. As he was closing the car hood, he saw an oval-shaped object he estimated to be about 125 feet long sitting on the highway. The UFO had a flat bottom and resembled a loaf of bread. It also had a glowing blue-green light. The intruder seemed to be made of an aluminum-like material.

By now, Newell was very panicky. *Had aliens from space landed?* he wondered. He jumped back into his car and tried once more to fire up the engine. No luck. Frightened, he slid down in his seat but continued watching the object sitting on the highway for several more minutes. Suddenly, it took off in a split second, raising straight up, then veering slightly to the north and disappearing from sight. The young student was then able to frantically restart his car and drive home. It was an experience he would remember for the rest of his life.

"A Bat Out of Hell!"

Less than ten minutes later, at 12:15 a.m., Frank Williams, from Kermit, called in his sighting report to police headquarters from a phone booth near Witharal. He said he came upon the "egg" sitting at the intersection of a dirt road and Route 51 an estimated nine miles north of Levelland.

As soon as Williams caught sight of the object, both his car engine and headlights stopped functioning. Then the UFO, which had been glowing, rose straight up to about 200 feet. Its light went out and Frank's car lights and motor returned to normal functioning.

"When it took off, it sounded like thunder," the driver told Webb. "It just blasted off like a bat out of hell!"

By this early morning hour, the local police knew "there was something being seen around the town." Sheriff Weir Clem, along with some police officers and highway patrolmen in the area, took to the roads in search of the hedge-hopping egg.

A Ball of Fire

At 12:45 a.m., about the time Sheriff Clem began his investigations, Ronald Martin, 18, was heading east on Route 116 around six miles west of town when he suddenly spotted a big orange ball of fire hovering in the sky an estimated mile-and-a-half ahead. The object, he said, stopped about 200 feet off the ground, came straight down and landed on the highway about 300 to 400 yards in front of his truck.

"I was scared as hell!" Ronald admitted. "I had heard about flying saucers and this looked like the real thing. *Damned if it didn't!*"

When the object landed, the witness continued, it changed to a bluish-green color and then changed back to its original shade when it took off. Martin said it was a round object and was about as wide as the paved portion of the highway. The UFO was approximately the size of two cars. And there was such a strong glow from the craft that it lit up the inside of his truck cab. There were also E-M effects to his motor, headlights and radio during the object's presence.

"I Was Scared as Hell!"

It was now 1:15 a.m. in Levelland. The next witness, James Long, became a badly frightened truck driver from Waco. He was driving about four and one-half miles northwest of town on the Oklahoma Flat Road when he suddenly approached a brilliant egg-shaped mass that was an estimated 200 feet long and intermittently glowed like a neon sign.

Following the lead of previous encounters that same night, Long's truck engine and lights failed. He quickly exited his vehicle at the same time that the object suddenly rose straight up and streaked away.

"No question about it...," James remarked. "I was scared as hell!"

"A Brilliant Red Sunset"

About fifteen minutes later, at 1:30 a.m., Sheriff Clem and his deputy were patrolling south along the Oklahoma Flat Road about four-and-a-half miles from town. Suddenly, they saw an oval-shaped object that resembled a brilliant red sunset over the highway about 300-400 yards to the south.

"It lit up the whole pavement in front of us for about two seconds," Clem remarked. "It was beautiful, really...."

Meanwhile, two highway patrolmen a few miles to the south of the Sheriff and his patrolman along with Constable Lloyd Ballen of Anton, also spotted the UFO which was traveling so fast that it appeared only as a flash of light moving from east-to-west.

The sightings continued north of town. Levelland Fire Marshall Ray Jones was on patrol searching for the object when his lights dimmed and his car engine almost died, then started up again. He saw a brilliant streak of light north of the Oklahoma Flat. Jones briefly and nervously wondered if extraterrestrial aliens had invaded.

Grain Combines Are Silenced

James Lee, from Abilene—who was conducting his own personal investigation of the Levelland sightings—reported on two more cases in which two grain combines, each with two engines, were operating at night near Pettit, northwest of Levelland, when "both were silenced by a passing object."

At about the same time, approximately ninety miles to the southwest, an unidentified motorist—who was driving from Hobbs to Carlsbad, New Mexico—was attempting to outrun an approaching UFO and reached ninety miles per hour before the object passed overhead and cut off his engine and lights. It was the continuation of a startling night of flying saucers and E-M effects. And it wasn't over yet....

The Fog-Enshrouded UFO

At 8 p.m. on November 3, a close-up view of a UFO was observed around 100 miles north of Levelland. An unidentified couple were returning to Amarillo from Palo Duro Canyon when they approached a brightly glowing object in the middle of the road. The intruder was surrounded by a fog. As they drove into the fog, the [car] motor died and the battery went dead. A passing motorist managed to push the badly shaken couple into town where the battery was recharged.

Sheriff Weir Clem—who had been the Hockley County Sheriff for more than five years—was impressed by the frightened witnesses' accounts.

"I definitely knew there was something really strange going on," he remarked. "I knew it from not having any controversy between those who saw it. Their stories fit to a T."

The Air Force Investigates

During the afternoon of November 4, Air Force officials announced that a special team of investigators would conduct a preliminary investigation of the Levelland object. That special team consisted of a lone investigator who arrived in Levelland the next day. He interviewed only three witnesses and left about six hours after his arrival.

On November 15, the Air Force released its official evaluation of the Levelland-area sightings: "Weather phenomenon of electrical nature, generally classified as 'Ball Lightning' or 'St. Elmo's Fire,' caused by stormy conditions in the area, including mist, rain, thunderstorms and lightning.... Preliminary reports have not revealed [the] cause of 'stalled' automobiles..., although rain and electrical storms at the time of the reported sightings, affecting wet electrical circuits, could be [the] cause."

The NICAP investigator, Walter Webb, wasn't buying it. He said:

This so-called 'explanation' for what observers actually claimed to have seen and generally agreed upon—a brilliant egg-shaped object some 200 feet long squatting on roads, killing engines and lights, and then rising up and away at great speed, an obviously solid, material craft of some kind under control—this profound 'explanation' is certainly one of the sloppiest and most preposterous answers the Air Force has yet concocted in its attempts to brush off the better UFO sightings.

CHAPTER THREE

The Killian Case

Another UFO sighting report Dick Hall wanted me to study involved a small formation of UFOs in the skies over Pennsylvania that was seen by several airline pilots, crews and passengers on February 24, 1959. The sighting stirred up a mountain of controversy with the U.S. Air Force on one side of the ledger and at least three airline pilots, their crews and passengers, and Major Keyhoe and NICAP on the other.

The report was not particularly among the stronger ones because of the possibility that it could be explained as an in-the-sky refueling by Air Force planes. On the other hand, other possibilities pointed out by Keyhoe were possible. Hall wanted me to begin becoming familiar with some cases that could be either explained as something other than a true unidentified flying object... or not. Both Keyhoe and Hall leaned toward the true UFO side of the fence. They wanted to know what I thought about the case. So, I sat down at my desk for another dive into the ocean of one of the more intriguing cases in the NICAP files.

The Orion Factor

Around 8:45 p.m., Captain Peter W. Killian, a veteran pilot with American Airlines, said he saw "three lights off my left wing in the vicinity of Bradford, Pennsylvania, and west of Williamsport." He was flying at 8,500 VFR on top of broken clouds. Visibility was unlimited with no upper clouds observed... The lights had a yellow to a light orange color and their intensity changed from dim to a bright brilliant. Sometimes the interval of the three lights were identical to the belt in the constellation Orion. Occasionally, the red lights lagged somewhat behind.

The lights also changed altitudes. Killian, his co-pilot, crew and passenger saw them for fifty minutes. During that time, the rear lights lagged somewhat behind and changed altitudes. They also occasionally came forward from a 9 o'clock position to an 11 o'clock position and then fell back to the original 9 o'clock position. At times, they also extinguished completely, alternating from one to another. At other times, all three of the lights went out at once. Besides Killian, four crewmembers and some passengers aboard the craft also saw the lights. And the pilots of two other planes in the area said they observed the strange lights.

A Refueling Operation?

At first, Killian speculated that he may have observed a jet tanker refueling operation, but was not sure. Later, he seemed certain it was not an aerial refueling. His air speed during the flight was 250 knots. He also said: "It was difficult for me to believe they were jets because of low speed and configuration."

Killian said he could not see any size or shape to the lights. They were seen "30 degrees above my horizon."

The pilot added that "the objects were first sighted at an 8 o'clock position, behind our left wing" and were moving in a parallel position. The lights appeared to be moving around each other at times and then were going back-and-forth.

"As we approached Chardon, the lights would go off one at a time, or two at a time, then all three would go out," Killian remarked. "There was no pattern to the lights going on and off."

The pilot was positive that he was not observing an atmospheric condition or refraction. By the time the aircraft reached Chardon, "the lights were at our 11 o'clock position."

Killian thought the candlepower of his DC-6 was around 15,000 and speculated that it would have to be ten times that at least for the three lights. He added that his flight experience was about 3500 hours in piper cubs up through military jets during a twelve-year period.

Lex Mebane Joins the Fray

Quick to investigate was Lex Mebane, the Administrative Vice-President of Civilian Saucer Intelligence of New York. He interviewed Killian, who said the lights fluctuated in brightness.

There was a report that Killian had been "shut up" on what he saw and was told not discuss it, even with his wife.

On the evening of February 26, Lex Mebane talked by phone with Killian for about thirty minutes. Mebane said the pilot was extremely friendly, polite, helpful, cooperative, and unstandoffish, not at all inclined to resent the quizzing even though he admitted that this was by no means the first time he'd been button-holed by saucer people since the story hit the press.

Air Force officials had wanted the pilot to submit a complete questionnaire, but, other than that, there was no personal grilling.

Mebane's notes made the following observations: The three objects were only star-like bright lights. He said they were not sharp, like a searchlight, but irregular, like a fire at a distance… They were arranged much like the belt of Orion. At first he thought they may have been just that. But he soon realized Orion was right above him. The objects were seen to his left at the nine o'clock position as he maintained his course on a 300-degree heading. The lights were definitely brighter than the stars of Orion's belt. The so-called "number one boy" located to the right "was slightly lower than the others… Number Three moved about quite a lot—more than the others. However, they generally maintained a constant spacing and were never seen to interchange positions."

Orion's Belt

Killian added that the angular elevation of the UFOs was probably closer to fifteen or twenty degrees than the thirty degrees he had estimated.

Also, the orientation of Orion's Belt was sloping upwards to the right, with the star on the right being the highest. This [was] opposite to the orientation observed for the three UFOs. This differentiation from Orion "is important because the Air Force's explanation is apparently that the UFOs were... the stars of Orion's Belt. What struck their attention about the objects was their variations in brightness. Mostly they were of a yellowish-white or even orange color, but they would irregularly brighten up and dim out. The intensity varied tremendously... Sometimes all three would brighten or fade in synchronism... Several times [all] three went out," but later reappeared "in approximately the same positions. The objects... generally maintained a straight-line arrangement. However, the whole group also moved with respect to the plane... He had the impression that their speed was much greater than his own at such times." When they were first seen, Killian reported, they were five-to-eight miles away.

As he started to fly over Lake Erie, he called to other planes that might be in the vicinity so he could ask them if they also had spotted the flying objects. Two other pilots in American Airlines planes replied. The pilot who "was near the radio fix point called 'Dolphin'... somewhere over the northern shore" of the lake said he had been watching the objects for ten or fifteen minutes. The UFOs were directly south of his location.

The second pilot in the other aircraft that was over Toledo or Sandusky said he had not seen them at first, but spotted them when alerted by Killian. This pilot said he saw the UFOs in the southeast. They were also "higher than I am" at about 14,000 feet. At that time, Killian was flying at 8,500 feet "and saw them to his 10 o'clock position."

Lights Out!

The forty or so passengers also saw the UFOs and seemed to enjoy watching them. Killian even ordered the cabin lights to be turned out so everyone could get a clearer view of the objects. He thought that this might help bolster his own case about seeing the objects.

One of the passengers, a man, was apprehensive.

"Don't worry," Killian told him. "If they were going to do anything to hurt us, they would have done it before now."

The careful pilot wanted to fly closer to the lights in order to see them more clearly, but didn't. He was afraid the passengers might panic. And he figured he probably couldn't fly fast enough to catch them.

"As I began my descent over Lake Erie and entered the haze over Cleveland, I lost sight of the objects," Killian remarked.

Later, Lex Mebane obtained a taped interview with James John Dee—the co-pilot from Nyack, New York—from Bob O'Connor, apparently a reporter from WLNA Radio. On Thursday morning, February 26, it was played on the Long John Program. Two days later, on the 29th, a statement on the radio from the Air Force attributed the sighting to the Orion constellation.

More than a month later, on April 2, Lex called Captain Killian to ask him about a rumor of him being silenced.

"Let's put it this way...," the pilot responded. "My company doesn't want me to talk about it no more."

Killian apparently didn't want to elaborate and Mebane ended the conversation. On April 16, however, Lex tried calling the pilot again. He was determined to somehow get him to say more about any attempt to silence him.

"Mrs. Killian answered the phone and recognized my voice," Lex reported. "I asked if the Captain was at home and she told me he was in Washington. I... asked whether or not the imposed silence upon the Captain was still in effect."

"I Can Talk!"

"The Captain has been getting a few calls and he has referred them to the Public Relations of American Airlines," she answered. "He is not talking. What do you want to know? Perhaps I can answer. *I can talk!*"

Lex asked Mrs. Killian if the Captain or the other pilots could ascertain whether the three objects may have been positioned *between* the planes. Mebane also asked if he could quote her.

"Yes, you may quote me," she answered. "But I can't answer that question truthfully as it is a technical one. I do know, however, that the Captain radioed the other planes in the area and a triangulation was done by a United Airlines plane. I can ask the Captain and perhaps he will give me the answer, if he knows, and you can call me again another time and I can let you know."

The Silence Mongers

Lex pressed on, asking her if officials at American Airlines had been approached by representatives of the Central Intelligence Agency or the Air Force, telling her that the Captain had to remain silent. She responded that her husband's company was approached by someone requesting her husband's silence. Apparently, it was more than just a request because both Captain and Mrs. Killian felt they had to comply.

"I told her that it had been rumored that, perhaps, American Airlines might have feared that the publicity of Captain Killian repeating his story would harm a reported eight million dollar sale of some of its aircraft with an overseas airline, especially if word got out that they sanctioned the Captain's repeating of the report," Lex explained. "Therefore, the company may have imposed the silent treatment themselves."

Mrs. Killian, however, wasn't buying that explanation.

"Don't believe it," she remarked. "The sale has already been made."

Mebane felt it would be utterly futile to silence Captain Killian due to the all the publicity given in the newspapers and the tapes that had been made. He told her he thought it was really silly.

"Oh, yes, definitely," she agreed. "Very much so. It really makes me boiling mad!"

Lex then asked her if her husband would be willing to travel to Washington to tell his story to members of the Space Committee hearings on Capitol Hill.

"Definitely," Mrs. Killian replied. "One Senator did ask the Captain to come to Washington and tell his story. He said he would go, but they would have to subpoena him. *Then* he could talk."

Additional Witnesses

"We are trying to locate ground observers who might have seen those objects that night as well," Lex explained.

"We have gotten some letters, even from England, and one from a New Jersey woman who saw three lights in the sky that very same night," Mrs. Killian stated. "I will mail you the names and addresses. Call me again if you wish."

By April 21, however, Mebane had not received word from Mrs. Killian that contained the names and addresses of those who had written the Captain about his sighting. Lex called her again that day, saying: "I did want so much to contact any ground observers that might have seen these objects." Mrs. Killian, however, said she didn't have the names and addresses because "any mail that doesn't require a reply is thrown out… I am sorry. But I did ask the Captain if the three objects were positioned *between* the planes. He said: 'No. They were not. The objects were flying off my left wing…' They seemed to be right alongside at 8,500 feet and maintained that position until he descended for a landing."

Shortly after that, sometime in May, there was a rumor that Captain Killian and his wife had been placed under an imposed silence. But who had shut them up? No one seemed to know.

Earlier, on Saturday, February 28, another investigator, Mrs. Gladys Fusaro from Huntington, New York, had a telephone interview with Mrs. Killian. More detailed information came out during this phone call.

An Amazing Encounter

"The Captain was so amazed at what he saw at first that he couldn't actually believe his eyes," Mrs. Killian explained. She elaborated further:

> Then he called attention to the crew and passengers... He knew he wasn't just seeing things by himself. These objects played with the airliners for forty-five minutes. There was plenty of time to observe them. The Captain tried to get the three objects in the radarscope, but that didn't do any good because it was only a weather radar and trying to obtain contact by radio was an impossible task. There were just too many different bands.
>
> The Captain contacted two other American Airlines planes flying in the vicinity. Both Captains of these planes also saw the three objects. There was an estimate of 15 miles distance between Captain Killian's plane and the nearest UFO. The estimated size of the UFO was about 300 feet. This was much, much bigger than the DC-6, which is 90 feet.
>
> The Captain was very thankful that the passengers did not at any time get panicky. Panic was what he feared most of all and he assured them that there was no danger. They also seemed too interested to think of doing anything rash.

Mrs. Fusaro then asked Mrs. Killian if the captain thought the UFOs were remotely controlled.

"It would be impossible to control UFOs remotely due to a number of factors," she replied. "During the time the UFOs were in view, the Captain had a strong feeling that eyes were following every move that was being made by both the plane and the crew! The formations just had to be done by human brain and hand! He believes the objects were humanly manned!"

The "Playing Along" UFOs

The pilot's wife added that the nearest UFO traveled at speeds up to 1,000 miles per hour. Then it slowed down and lagged back to pace the airliner. The unknown aerial craft was merely playing along with the airliner until all of the objects disappeared from view.

On February 28, Gladys Fusaro called Mrs. Killian again.

"The Captain was so amazed at what he saw at first that he couldn't actually believe his eyes," Mrs. Killian remarked. "Then he called attention to the crew and passengers… These objects just played with the airliner… The Captain tried to get [the three objects] in the radar scope, but that didn't work."

Captain Killian then contacted two other nearby American Airlines planes and both pilots said they also encountered the three objects. The closest UFO was estimated to be about 300 feet long… about three times the length of the DC-6.

Mrs. Fusaro asked Mrs. Killian if the Captain thought the UFOs were remotely controlled.

"It would be impossible to control the UFOs remotely due to a number of factors," Mrs. Killian answered. "During all the time the UFOs were in view, the Captain had a strong feeling that eyes were following every move that was being made by both the plane and the crew…"

Mrs. Killian also said her husband believed the nearest object flew at speeds up to 1,000 miles per hour and then it would lag back and pace the airliner, as if it were playing along with it.

The Keyhoe Factor

The phone calls between the two women continued. On March 16, Mrs. Killian said that the Captain gave a talk at a NICAP meeting at a hotel in New York City on March 12 during a bad storm. More than 200 people attended the lecture. Another NICAP talk was slated for Captain Killian at the Hotel Diplomat in New York, which Major Donald Keyhoe was slated to attend.

Gladys then asked Mrs. Killian how her husband reacted to the Associated Press story from Washington entitled "Saucers or Stars?"

"The article didn't bother the Captain at all," she replied, "but Major Keyhoe really got boiling mad at a similar article in the *New York Herald Tribune* written by a Ralph Chapman. The Major got real upset over it. And the opinion about seeing stars will never be accepted by the Captain... He will never forget what he saw and nothing can ever change that."

The Air Force Explanation

On March 20, Mrs. Fusaro also talked with Captain Killian. She asked him what he thought about the Air Force explanation for the sighting that jet bombers were refueling.

"Someone from the Long Island *Daily Press* called yesterday and told me about it," Captain Killian said. "I told him that I have seen jet bombers refueling and I can tell what a B-47 looks like at night. What I saw was *not* any jet bomber... I will not change my story even though they try to say... we were looking at Orion and stars. I saw the objects as well as the stars and Orion at the same time... I know what I saw."

On March 24, 1960, Richard Hall, then the NICAP Secretary and Assistant Director, received a letter from Major Lawrence J. Tacker of the Air Force Public Information Division. Tacker said that "this sighting turned out to be B-47 type aircraft accomplishing night refueling from KC-97 tankers... A KC-97 tanker has several groups of lights which at a distance would appear to be one or more lights." Tacker concluded that "the airline pilots saw a night aerial refueling operation."

Air Force Major General W.P. Fisher, the Legislative Liaison Director, backed up Major Tacker in his letter to New York Congressman Howard W. Robison: "The investigation of this incident revealed that an Air Force refueling mission, involving a KC-97 and three B-47 aircraft, was flown in the vicinity of Bradford, Pennsylvania, at the time of the sighting by Captain Killian. That refueling operation was conducted at 17,000 feet altitude at approximately 230 knots true air speed for a period of approximately one hour."

Captain Killian, however, wasn't buying it. Neither was NICAP. Keyhoe was quick to denounce the Air Force explanation in the *U.F.O. Investigator*.

"In an attempt to discredit six airliner crews who recently reported a UFO formation, an AF Headquarters spokesman has publicly ridiculed all 'flying saucer' witnesses," Keyhoe wrote. "Some were sarcastically labeled as persons who 'can't remember anything when they sober up [the] next day.' The rest, implied the official spokesman, either were deluded by ordinary objects or were outright liars."

Keyhoe and Killian

Keyhoe stood solidly on the side of Killian, who had been a pilot for twenty years, fifteen of them logged in airliners, for a total of more than four million miles. Keyhoe reported that Killian, after alerting First Officer Dee to the UFOs, also told the thirty-five passengers about the objects. The two stewardesses, Edna LaGate and Beverly Pingree, turned out the cabin lights for a better view, and in the next forty minutes, all aboard saw the mysterious objects.

One of the passengers, N.D. Puncas, had an aviation background as the General Manager of Curtiss-Wright's Utica Division.

"I looked out and saw the objects in precise formation," Puncas stated. "Every now and then one would glow brighter than the others, as if it moved closer to the plane. I have never experienced anything like it before."

The United Airlines Encounters

At least three United Airlines flight crews observed the UFOs. In one case, according to Keyhoe, "Capt. A.D. Yates reported the objects were tracked from 8:40 to 9:10 p.m. between Lochaven, Pennsylvania, and Youngstown, Ohio. This was confirmed by Flight Engineer L.E. Baney."

Crew members of United Flights 937 and 321 flying west from Newark, also saw the UFOs. All the pilots and flight engineers agreed that the lights were on separate vehicles which were holding a formation.

Keyhoe vs. the Refueling Tag

Keyhoe also made it clear he wasn't buying the Air Force refueling explanation, saying that a check after Killian and his crew landed disclosed there had been no such flights involving refueling operations. Also, in an interview with Lex Mebane, Killian said that not only had the color of the UFOs altered at times from yellow to bluish-white, their intensity had also varied from extreme brilliance to temporary fade-outs.

The speed of the UFOs also varied, according to Captain Killian. At times, the objects would quickly pull ahead, then seemed to lag behind as if they were waiting for Killian to catch up with them.

Don Keyhoe was convinced that Killian and the other pilots, their crews and passengers, had seen real UFOs, not an Air Force refueling operation or the Orion constellation. He said "the Air Force tactics in the recent airlines case may backfire on the censors… If the majority of airline pilots who have seen UFOs unite in self-defense, their combined testimony will have a powerful impact on Congress."

CHAPTER FOUR

Aliens in Socorro and J. Edgar Hoover

During my first few weeks at NICAP, I continued to ask Dick Hall for a series of reports he and other staff members of the organization had investigated. The second bulky file report he gave me was incredible. I sat at my cluttered desk and read it with marked enthusiasm.

The Policeman and the Grounded Aliens
On the clear, sunny Friday of April 24, 1964, Police Officer Lonnie Zamora was on duty in his patrol car about a mile north of Socorro, New Mexico, when he heard a roaring noise, which he thought might have been an explosion at a nearby dynamite shack. Lonnie thought there also could be a car in trouble or worse. Perhaps it had overturned in a gully or was somehow abruptly drawn off the nearby highway.

Zamora hurried to the scene and quickly saw what appeared to be a white or gleaming metallic object on the ground in the gully. Two stilt or girder-like legs could be seen on the sides of the UFO.

Near the object, the startled policeman observed two small figures dressed in what appeared to be white coveralls. At first, he thought they may have been children playing in the area. But there was something weird about them, a certain thing that didn't seem to be human in a Planet Earth manner. Then the figure standing furthest from Lonnie suddenly turned and faced him with piercing eyes that emitted a fierce, dagger-like look.

At the same time, the startled police officer noticed some red markings on the side of the craft. A sketch of these markings was later given to an Army officer at White Sands Proving Grounds.

UFO Takes Off in "a Cloud of Dust"

As Zamora slowly walked toward the object, he could no longer see the humanoid figures. They had apparently entered the craft. Lonnie was puzzled, however, since he could not see any doors or openings through which the occupants could enter. Then a sudden roaring sound came from the UFO, which slowly kicked up a cloud of dust.

The frightened witness quickly turned and ran, but looked back as the noise stopped and he saw the object quickly take off and fly over the nearby dynamite shack, just missing it at an estimated altitude of twenty feet. As the astonished policeman continued to watch, the craft maintained this low altitude until it disappeared from view.

Zamora grabbed his car phone and called the New Mexico State Police, who immediately contacted the local Federal Bureau of Investigation (FBI) office at nearby White Sands. Sergeant Sam Chavez from the State Police quickly arrived on the scene and began inspecting the landing site. He was joined by other investigators, who noticed that the craft had left a burned area under the spot where it stood and there were also four wedge-shaped impressions in the hard desert floor where the legs of the object had been.

Socorro in the Limelight

Word of the sighting quickly spread via newspapers, radio and television accounts. Reporters, scientists, UFO investigators, and members of the public descended on Socorro and singled out Zamora, who was overwhelmed by all the sudden attention.

Enter Dr. J. Allen Hynek, the astronomer who was then the official Air Force debunker. He quickly appeared on the scene accompanied by a

Sergeant Moody from the Aerial Phenomena Branch at Wright-Patterson Air Force Base in Dayton, Ohio. Hynek spent a day examining the landing scene, talking with Zamora and describing the incident as "puzzling." He was also apparently impressed by Zamora himself and considered him a reliable witness. This was confirmed by Dr. Lincoln La Paz of the University of New Mexico, who had known Zamora for about sixteen years. The police officer was highly regarded in the area and wasn't the type to invent tales or be easily confused. And officials at White Sands and other bases in the area stated that they had no devices which would answer the description of what Zamora saw.

The debunkers, however, continued their work. Some military officials said Zamora may have seen one of the balloons which commonly inhabited the New Mexico sky, but this could hardly explain the figures, scorched area or depressions in the ground. Still other doubters said it may have been a rancher's helicopter. But the NICAP New York Subcommittee, whose members also investigated the incident, countered: "It does not seem too likely that an experienced police officer could mistake a helicopter for the object described, especially since Zamora was about 100 feet away and did not notice any windows or doors. And 'children do not fly helicopters.'"

More Sighting Reports Pour In

The subcommittee report also said that, shortly after Zamora's sighting, six more UFO incidents were filed with the local authorities. One of these involved a youth who reported that he fired at a strange aerial object near Moriarty. There was also a report from Montana by four children of a landing by a craft of the same size and appearance as the one Zamora saw. Some investigators speculated that this was the same object that the police officer observed since it included the details of impressions of four legs and a burned area on the ground. Five members of an Air Force investigating team reportedly took soil samples, photos and measurements from the Montana landing site.

In early June, the U.S. Air Force circulated its short report on the Zamora incident. It added that, at one point, the officer believed that the object was about to explode and he became frightened, turned, and ran back to shield himself behind the police car, bumping his leg and losing his glasses on the way. He said that he crouched down, shielding his eyes with his arm while the noise continued for another ten seconds. As the object slowly rose, Zamora reportedly saw a design on the object which he described as markings in red about one-to-one-and-a-half-feet in height. It was shaped like a crescent with a vertical arrow and horizontal line underneath.

Enter J. Edgar Hoover

On April 25, only one day after Zamora saw the UFO and its occupants, famed Federal Bureau of Investigations (FBI) Director J. Edgar Hoover received a report on the incident from Strategic Air Command headquarters in Albuquerque. It didn't specifically denounce Zamora or his sighting. It did, however, mention that the military was conducting an operation known as Cloud Gap which could possibly explain the incident, but it was not known if the incident was related to Cloud Gap.

The FBI Director may well have been far more interested in UFOs and their origins than anyone outside his agency or elsewhere in the U.S. Government realized. He apparently wanted in on the action.

Hoover threw his towel into the UFO ring early on… less then six weeks after the famed UFO crash-and-retrieval case in Roswell, New Mexico, on or about July 2, 1947. On July 15, five days after receiving a copy of an Office Memorandum from E.G. Fitch to D.M. Ladd—in which Fitch recommended that the FBI not investigate UFO reports—Hoover, in his wobbly handwriting, scribbled at the end of the memo the following to his second-in-command Assistant Director Clyde Tolson: *"I would do it but before agreeing to it we must insist upon full access to discs recovered. For instance, in the LA case the Army grabbed it & would not let us have it for cursory examination."*

The Hottel Memo

A couple of years later, on March 22, 1950, Guy Hottel—the Special Agent in Charge of the FBI's Washington Field Office, wrote the following astounding Office Memorandum to Hoover:

> *An investigator for the Air Force stated that three so-called flying saucers had been recovered in New Mexico. They were described as being circular in shape with raised centers, approximately 50 feet in diameter. Each one was occupied by 3 bodies of human shape but only 3 feet tall, dressed in metallic cloth of a very fine texture. Each body was bandaged in a manner similar to the blackout suit used by speed flyers and... pilots.*
>
> *According to [the] informant, the saucers were found in New Mexico due to the fact that the Government has a very high-powered radar set-up in that area and it is believed the radar interferes with the controlling mechanism of the saucers.*

This stunning memo was about as close as it comes to the government admitting that, not only were UFO reports authentic, they were also obviously visitors from somewhere in space. But top-level government officials still wanted to play the game that negated that hypothesis.

Truman vs. Hoover

There was little question that Hoover wanted to stay on top of the UFO reports and investigations, but he wasn't getting from-the-top input about the sightings. That was probably because Harry S. Truman, the President, had no love for the FBI Director. He thought Hoover had the capability of becoming a petty dictator. In a private letter to his wife, Bess, the First Lady, Truman wrote: "If I can prevent [it], there'll be no NKVD [Soviet Secret Police] or Gestapo in this country. Edgar Hoover's organization would make a good start toward a citizen spy system. Not for me." Truman even threw a cold blanket on Hoover's attempt to "send him dirt via techniques like wiretapping and ordered it stopped in no uncertain terms."

Obviously Truman, like subsequent Commanders-in-Chiefs, knew about UFOs surveiling earth and he wasn't going to share that information with Hoover. The President had only met directly with Hoover once, about a month after he took up residence in the White House.

Mining the Vault

The controversy about possible in-the-field-investigations of UFO reports, particularly the crash-and-retrieval cases, continues to this day. UFO aficionados continue to flock to the FBI Vault, the electronic reading room containing numerous bureau records that were released under the Freedom of Information Act. By far, the most viewed document over a two-year period (2011-2013) from the Vault's opening has been a March 22, 1950, memorandum by Guy Hottel, the Special Agent in Charge of the FBI's Washington Field Office. Nearly one million people had viewed the one-page document addressed to Hoover.

The subject of the blockbuster memo said that an Air Force investigator alleged that three flying saucers had been recovered in New Mexico. A specific time and location were not disclosed. Could they have been talking about Roswell? Probably not…

Alien Bodies Recovered

In this case, there were apparently three UFOs involved. The memo continues: "They [the saucers] were described as being circular in shape with raised centers, approximately fifty feet in diameter. Each one was occupied by three bodies of human shape but only three feet tall, dressed in metallic cloth of a very fine texture. Each body was bandaged in a manner similar to the blackout suits used by speed fliers and test pilots." The memo ends with: "No further evaluation was attempted."

Matters concerning the possibility of crashed saucers now seemed to be more confusing than ever. The controversy continues… to this day.

The Gallegos Encounter

Hoover, however, did continue receiving flying saucer reports. One of these came from Air Force officials in Albuquerque describing an encounter at La Maderia, New Mexico, around seventy miles north of Santa Fe, on April 26, 1964, more than thirty hours after Lonnie Zamora's encounter. NICAP also received a report on the incident.

Orlando Gallegos, 35, and his family were visiting his father, Frank, just north of the town. At about 12:45 a.m., Orlando left the house to chase some noisy horses from the cattle corral.

Suddenly, he observed a bright, metallic, egg-shaped object resembling a butane gas tank resting in the dry bed of Vellecitos Creek approximately 300 feet from the house. The witness said it was as long as a telephone pole and appeared to be about fourteen or fifteen feet high. He approached to an estimated 200 feet of the UFO, but was too frightened to get any closer.

As the startled Gallegos watched, the object emitted a ring of blue fire from jets at the bottom. At first, the fire burned and glowed brightly. Then it was extinguished.

Too shaken to see what else might happen, the witness ran back into the house. His wife said he was badly shaken as he frantically burst through the door.

The next day, Gallegos found that the landing site was [still] smoldering and rocks in the area were scorched. Several markings on the ground were also discovered.

Gallegos reported the incident to law enforcement officials in nearby Espanola. State Police Captain Martin E. Vigil dispatched Officer Albert Vega to the scene with the witness. After carefully examining the area, Vega called in and requested that Captain Vigil and Officer David Kingsbury hurry to the scene.

"Officer Vega advised that he had observed four depressions on the ground," Vigil stated in his official report, "one of which was quite clear, the other three having been obliterated due to windy weather conditions. Officer Vega stated that the [clear] depression was approximately eight-by-twelve inches in size, about three or four inches deep, and sort of 'V'-shaped at the bottom."

"There were also numerous oval-shaped, or 'cat-paw-like' markings around the scorched area. They were approximately three and one-half inches in diameter. Upon arrival at the scene, I personally interviewed Mr. Gallegos.... [He] is obviously not the type of person that would make up such a story."

Captain Vigil told NICAP that none of the Gallegos family knew about the earlier Socorro sighting. The police reported the results of their investigation to both officials at Kirtland Air Force Base, Albuquerque, and the FBI. Major William Connors, from Kirtland, interviewed Gallegos at the landing site.

Return to Socorro

Fadeout and a quick return to the Lonnie Zamora case in Socorro.... At NICAP headquarters in Washington, D.C., Richard Hall announced that one of his investigators, Ray Stanford, from Phoenix, Arizona, was at the landing site with Dr. J. Allen Hynek and had gathered samples and other evidence for NICAP. He was also making tests with a Geiger counter. Hall added that, on April 28, 1964, NICAP conducted a phone interview with Zamora and confirmed the main points of his report.

The day before, Hall phoned Coral Lorenzen, Director of the well-respected Aerial Phenomena Research Organization (APRO) in Tucson, Arizona. Lorenzen had been at the landing site on Sunday, April 26. Hall said that Coral was convinced, after examining the site and interviewing Zamora, that an alien vehicle had landed there. She obtained soil samples for analysis, but NICAP apparently never received a report on what may have been found.

"We are completing a detailed documentary report this month which will show that hundreds of similar reports by equally reliable witnesses have been played down by official investigators," Hall announced. "The public is being misled about UFOs."

"A Reliable Witness"

Meanwhile, Lonnie Zamora continued to be recognized as an honest reliable witness. Those who shouted his praises included Charles Richards at United Press International (UPI), who reported that police and military men seemed inclined to believe him. Among them was Army Captain Richard T. Yolder, Uprange Commander at White Sands' Stallion Range, who said that Zamora is a "very reliable witness."

Even Dr. Hynek remained impressed by Zamora and his sighting. This was one report he could not say with any degree of certainty was a hoax.

"It is one of the soundest, best substantiated reports as far as it goes," Hynek told the Associated Press as reported in the *Salt Lake Tribune*. "Mr. Zamora's story is simply told, certainly without any intent to perpetuate a hoax. The story… was told by a man who obviously was frightened badly by what he did see. He certainly must have seen something."

An Astronomer is Impressed

On November 4, 1964, NICAP Advisor and Astronomer Walter N. Webb from the Charles Hayden Planetarium in Boston wrote his own fifteen-page report with sketches.

"The observation at Socorro satisfied enough requirements to make it one of the best authenticated UFO sightings on record," Webb wrote.

The astronomer added that the landing spot was approximately thirty-eight miles northwest of the Trinity Site, where the world's first atomic bomb was exploded in July 1945. He said that the figures the police officer saw were approximately four-to-four-and-a-half-feet tall. Zamora also said he heard two metallic bangs that sounded like doors slamming shut. Approaching to within 100 feet of the saucer, the witness estimated the UFO to be twelve-to-fifteen feet long, about four feet thick, and was supported by girder-like legs or stilts.

Webb also remarked that Zamora appeared incredulous as the UFO took off and barely cleared the dynamite shack by an estimated three feet. After flying at a low altitude toward the southwest for two or three miles, it ascended rapidly over a perlite mine and disappeared into the distance in the direction of Black Mountain and Six-Mile Canyon.

Physical Traces Found

Only minutes after the UFO departed from the site, Zamora was joined by Sergeant Chavez. Both men examined the landing ground and discovered apparent physical traces that they thought were left by the craft. This included several clumps of grass and the ground that were scorched at the landing area. They were still hot and smoking. Only the sides of the plants facing in toward the center of the site were burned, suggesting an intense heat source had emanated from the center. Green greasewood does not burn easily. And branches were broken on one of the bushes.

There were also indentations found in the soil where the object landed. These holes were about twelve inches long and six inches wide. There was no question about it… Something alien had landed there.

Zamora Impresses Other Officials

Webb said that J. Allen Hynek had been his boss when Webb was a member of the Smithsonian Astrophysical Observatory's Satellite Tracking Program. He confirmed that the astronomer was greatly impressed by Zamora and his sighting, which Hynek described as "unique" among all the UFO reports he had investigated up to that point.

Other influential individuals were also impressed by the Socorro policeman. These included famed fireball and meteorite expert Dr. Lincoln LaPaz of the Institute of Meteoritics at the University of New Mexico in Albuquerque, who said: "I… have had contacts with Mr. Zamora for sixteen years in my work and he is a thoroughly dependable observer."

Later, sometime between 11:30 a.m. and 12:15 p.m., radar operators at the Stallion Site tracked two UFOs over the range north of the station. The objects flew side-by-side. Then they maneuvered up and down, separated, and rejoined each other. A trained radar operator saw the saucers visually, describing them as brown and football-shaped.

Webb concluded his report by saying that all the information gathered from the Socorro case "adds up to a highly advanced technology utilizing methods of travel presently unknown to us."

Separating the Wheat From the Chaff

After reading the report on the Socorro case Dick Hall had given me, I was blown away by it, but soon realized that it was only one such report in what seemed to be a mountain of saucer sightings reported by reliable witnesses of every conceivable stripe.

I soon learned that the trick was to quickly and thoroughly separate the honest UFO witnesses from what we termed "the kooks." These included George Adamski, whose books claimed such absurdities as riding to and from Venus with lovely Venusian beauties in flying saucers. The fact that Venus has a surface temperature of around 900 degrees Fahrenheit didn't seem to bother him.

Other individuals who continued to muddy the waters of scientific investigation when I was an involved investigator were Orfeo Angelucci, Daniel Fry and Truman Bethurum. Their welcome mats were not displayed in front of the NICAP or UFOR doors.

CHAPTER FIVE

The Rex Heflin Photos

After studying the file on the Lonnie Zamora encounter in Socorro, New Mexico, I realized I still had a lot of research to do if I had any chance of catching up to the expertise that many of the NICAP investigators possessed. I had finally realized my dream of being a part of the world's largest and most respected UFO organization and I wanted to digest as many of the most significant sighting reports that I could before being sent out on my first field trip. Firing up my pipe with circling rings of smoke, I also read the reports from the various investigating teams among the thirty-five or so field subcommittees around the world.

During the first week of my tenure at NICAP, I discovered that the most impressive and researched photo case to come into our office occurred when Rex E. Heflin, a road maintenance supervisor from Santa Ana, California, saw and photographed a UFO on August 3, 1965. A lengthy investigation would show that it was, at the time, the most reported and well-researched case of a UFO photograph (see photo section).

"I was heading north on Myford Road at 11:30 a.m. . . . and was attempting to make radio contact with the Orange County Road Maintenance Superintendent (Mr. Art Ashcroft) regarding tree limbs growing as to obstruct the view of the crossing sign at the rail crossing nearby," Heflin wrote in his report to NICAP on or about September 26, 1965.

Heflin's attempt to contact Ashcroft failed because his radio went completely dead. He reported that, "at this time, I became aware of the UFO. However, I thought it was a conventional aircraft."

Disc Hovers in Front of Truck

The supervisor continued his report:

> The UFO moved from my left to in front of me and momentarily hovered there.... I grabbed my camera (semi-automatic—Model 101 Poloroid) from the seat of the truck and took the first photograph through the windshield of the truck.
>
> The object then moved slowly off to the Northeast. Then I snapped the second picture through the right door window.... This is when I saw the rotating beam of light emitting from the center of the UFO on the bottom side.... The UFO positioned itself to another angle of view and I snapped the third picture through the same side window as in picture two....
>
> As the UFO traveled, it maintained a relatively low altitude (150 feet) in relation to the flat terrain. However, the UFO acted similar to a gyroscope when losing its stability. The UFO continued moving, slowing gaining altitude. [Then it] tipped its top toward me slightly. It seemed to gain stability, then it increased its velocity... and altitude more rapidly, leaving a deposit of smoke-like vapor.

Shortly after the sighting, the Air Force got into the act and immediately blasted the report. Heflin was not happy about being called an unreliable witness. Idabel Epperson and NICAP's Los Angeles Subcommittee were quick to follow up.

Muddy Waters

"This case has become so involved and controversial that I hardly know what to tell you about it....," Epperson lamented in her letter to Richard Hall dated September 24, 1965. "I have not even made up my own mind as yet. Ed Evers, who is conducting an investigation, is an engineer with North American (working on the Apollo Moon Shot) and is usually a cool-headed, objective person....

"The story, as we get it from Ed…, is that Heflin was a skeptic—never heard of NICAP and didn't seem to know any of the crackpots. At the time Heflin saw the UFO and took the pictures, he thought it was something that [was] sent up at the Marine Base.…"

Heflin told Evers that "they tried to make me feel like a crackpot." Epperson added that John Gray, an engineer with North American, did some very important preliminary work on the case.

Meanwhile, NORAD officials retrieved the photos from Heflin and soon began its debunking, but Idabel Epperson wasn't to be shunted aside.

"The pictures were returned to Heflin by an officer from NORAD," she wrote. "Air Force officers tried to belittle Keyhoe, saying that they were told that Keyhoe 'had received a medical retirement from the Marines.'"

Heflin Versus the Air Force

Epperson said that Heflin was furious at the Air Force statement that the UFO was only three feet in diameter and fifteen feet in altitud and "he now feels that [a fourth] photo showing [a] smoke ring shows a high wire and trees and gives the lie to that statement.…"

"Heflin wants to tear his phone off the wall and forget the whole thing….," the equally frustrated Epperson continued. "He seems to be ready to leave town or do most anything to get out of it.…"

But somehow, Heflin continued to forge ahead.

"Mr. Heflin seems to have recovered from whatever it was that was bothering him following the Air Force blast in the newspapers and again seems to want to cooperate with us completely….," Epperson wrote to Hall in her letter dated October 7, 1965.

Blue Book Cries "Hoax"

In its October 27, 1965, issue, the *San Jose Mercury* reported that Air Force Major Hector Quintanella, Director of Project Blue Book, classified the event as "a photographic hoax on the basis of extensive photographic analysis."

On September 30, 1965, Ralph Rankow, the owner-operator of Photographic Ilustrations in New York City, wrote to Dick Hall: "The photos definitely show an object. If this is a hoax and the object is a model which was sailed into the air and then photographed, a second person would have been required. It would have been very difficult for him to sail an object into the air and then get back into the truck and take the picture before the object hit the ground...."

Rankow sent a more detailed report to NICAP on October 29, 1965:

The Air Force's [A.F.] 'explanation' of the Rex Heflin photos [was] obviously designed for those who have never had the opportunity to view the enlargements of the full photo which Mr. Heflin took through the windshield of his truck.... The A.F. tells us that 'the center white stripe on the road and the object appeared to have the same sharp image.' The truth is that the only thing in the picture which is [a little] blurred is the UFO and this was caused by the movement of the object....

The A.F. tells us [that] the terrain background was blurred in all three photographs. The truth is that the background is so sharp that even the thin telephone lines—which are strung from pole-to-pole—are visible along the San Diego Freeway, which runs across the picture in the distance. To be sure, the background is hazy, but this has nothing to do with sharpness or blurriness. The pictures were taken on an overcast day, and there was haze off in the distance....

Completely ignored by the Air Force is the fact that Heflin was in the midst of using his two-way truck radio when the UFO came upon the scene and completely knocked out all signals....

The Air Force conclusion insinuates that Mr. Heflin is a liar and a hoaxter. For what motive, they don't bother to explain. This is the sort of treatment at the hands of the A.F. which anyone can expect when they report a UFO.... And, unfortunately, this is the sort of treatment which has discouraged the reporting of vast amounts of UFO data. This is what the A.F. calls their "scientific investigation" of UFOs. Frankly, I feel it is high time that the Air Force was made to answer [to] the American people about their very unscientific UFO explanations if not their investigations.

Congressman Questions NORAD

The sighting as well as Heflin's photographs were brought to the attention of Congressman James B. Utt (R-CA), who contacted the North American Air Defense Command (NORAD) Center in Colorado. On November 9, he received a reply from NORAD Chief of Staff Major General M. M. Magee:

> During the period of approximately 15 September to 22 September, Mr. Heflin supplied the pictures to the local Santa Ana newspaper, the UPI and U.S. Marine representatives from El Toro Marine Station. In each case, the pictures were returned to Mr. Heflin. On 22 September, he received telephone calls from persons representing themselves as responsible people from Boeing Aircraft and NORAD respectively. Both persons told him to make no further comments regarding the UFO for security reasons. On the evening of 22 September, a person in civilian clothes representing himself as a member of NORAD requested the UFO pictures for study by NORAD. He identified himself with an ID card, the description of which sounds like a gasoline credit card. Mr. Heflin gave this person the pictures without obtaining his name or a receipt....

> NORAD does not have the responsibility for evaluation of UFOs and therefore would not knowingly be in the business of collecting UFO pictures for evaluation. In addition, the office of primary interest for UFO matters is the Department of the Air Force.

On New Year's Eve, 1965, Clay T. Miller, Chief Photographer for *The Register*, Santa Ana, California, wrote NICAP: "When Heflin brought the photos to *The Register* office, they caused much interest. Everyone crowded around to look at them. To me, the photos looked clear with all parts of the picture[s] being in focus.... Under much questioning, Heflin gave the same answers and said he really did see the UFO and did take a picture of it. He did not seem to want to dodge any issue that was brought up and had a complete answer for each question. In my opinion, he appeared to be a sincere, honest person. As far as I could tell, the photos were authentic and had not been altered in any way whatsoever."

Battle For the Photos Continues

My own direct involvement with the Heflin photos didn't come until I received a letter from Idabel Epperson on November 30, 1967:

> On October 11, 1967, at about 8 p.m., Mr. Heflin called me... to describe a visit he had just received from a gentleman attired in the uniform of an Air Force officer. He identified himself as Captain C. H. Edmonds stationed at the USAF Space Systems Division in Los Angeles and displayed his credentials, which Mr. Heflin said he examined to his satisfaction.

> The main points of the ensuing conversation, according to Mr. Heflin, were the inquiries by the visitor as to whether he (Heflin) had any intentions of attempting to retrieve his missing photographs and whether he was a member of any UFO organizations. Mr. Heflin's response was in the negative to the first inquiry and in the affirmative to the second since he had just previously joined NICAP. He related he thought he detected in the visitor's manner of phrasing the first question the hint of a threat to the effect: "You'd be better off to forget the photographs" and that he perceived an expression of relief from the visitor upon hearing the negative reply.

During the course of the interview…, Mr. Heflin detected on his hi-fi musical program three distinct and unusual 'pop' sounds separated by periods of several seconds duration…. Also during the investigation, he observed in the rear seat of the visitor's late model sedan, parked in front at the curb, movements that appeared occasionally to obstruct his view of a violet light within.

Since he was standing on his front porch, he was in full view and about 25-30 feet from the auto while the visitor stood on the steps below and to one side of him. The duration of the conversation… was approximately fifteen minutes.

To date in the year 2018, the Heflin case remains one of the most heavily investigated UFO sightings involving photographs. Both Heflin's reports and the four photographs have never been convincingly denied by serious UFO investigators.

CHAPTER SIX

The "Baby UFO" and A Landing in South Hill

The first UFO sighting and reported landing I was able to personally investigate with Richard Hall soon after becoming a NICAP staff member occurred on October 16, 1965. On Halloween Eve, Hall and I interviewed the main witness, a personable fourteen year-old boy named Dwight Myers near his home in Spring Grove, Pennsylvania. Joining us in the field were Bob Barry, of WGCB A.M. & F.M. Radio in Red Lion, Pennsylvania, and Joan Lusby, a local businesswoman from Southern Maryland.

Back at NICAP headquarters on November 1, 1965, I wrote the following account of the interview entitled "A Reported Landing in Spring Grove, Pennsylvania, Saturday, October 16, 1965":

Abstract

A group of about eight young children, the oldest fourteen, playing at the local school yard at about 7:30 p.m.... saw a small, luminous object land on the macadam road and parking lot adjacent to the school. The object remained about thirty seconds during two approaches, then skimmed along the macadam and took off at a shallow angle.

Minutes later, as the children walked in the area, the same or a similar glowing object came overhead from the departure direction and continued in a straight line out of sight over a small stand of trees. Some children who did not observe the landing and had been skeptical were among the witnesses of the second pass.

Background

NICAP first learned of the report in a letter from Bob Barry, received on October 28. Mr. Barry was on the staff of WGCB AM & FM in Red Lion, Pennsylvania. Upon receiving the report, Barry interviewed the oldest witness and aired the story as well as an editorial about it....

On October 29, NICAP phoned Mr. Barry and made arrangements to drive to the site and talk with the children. On October 30, Richard Hall, Gordon Lore, and Joan Lusby drove to York, Pennsylvania, then to nearby Yoe, where Mr. Barry resided. He drove us to the Spring Grove Elementary School, about seven miles from York and the residence of the Myers family, located about 150 yards from the school. Dwight D. Myers, 14, and his younger brother, Dan, were two of the witnesses.

We walked to the school grounds, where several children were playing. Dwight pointed out the apparent landing spot on the macadam lot adjoining the school. We paced off distances, took photographs, and drew a sketch map of the site. One of the young girls playing nearby was... one of the witnesses. We tried to question her, but she seemed intimidated when four adults crowded around her. She did confirm seeing a strange object (which she called a "flying saucer") in the sky on the night in question, but further information could not be elicited. According to Dwight, she had been badly frightened by the sighting. At least one of the investigators felt her reluctance to talk was based on a desire not to think about the event.... She was more interested in getting back to her game of hopscotch which we had somewhat rudely interrupted.

Dwight took us to a nearby house just past the Spring Grove Junior High School in the direction of the paper mill, where more of the witnesses lived, but they were not home. It was a pleasant, sunny Saturday afternoon. When we first arrived at the Myers home, Dwight and some other children were playing catch with a football in the yard. The school and the Myers home are situated among rolling hills and small stands of trees.

The Story

On the night of October 16, at about 7:30 p.m., Dwight Myers and eight other children between the ages of seven and thirteen were playing in the schoolyard. It was dark, but the school lights partly illuminated the area.... One of the children, Robert Kirshner, was so badly frightened by the sighting that Mrs. Myers had to drive him home....

The children became conscious of a glow in the sky above the area of the flagpole. Then they looked up and saw the UFO moving from right to left above the school. It descended with a back-and-forth ("falling leaf") motion as if to land on the rooftop, then descended quickly straight down onto the macadam-covered lot. [In an aside, Dwight whispered to me that the object looked to him like "a baby UFO."] The area is in a corner formed by a school wall to the left and a concrete retaining wall with a wire fence on top.... Behind the fence rises a steep grassy knoll. Dwight and the children were standing near one of many green stakes (spaced along the lot and driveway) approximately forty-five feet from the landing point. With these reference points, Dwight originally estimated the UFO's size to be about twenty inches in diameter and six inches deep. We asked Dwight about the size.

"It looked like a bicycle wheel," he responded.

In the air, the UFO appeared as a brightly glowing bluish-white light with a trail of equal width and about five feet long, with the blue portion turning to orange at the trailing end. While descending, the "trail" swirled around the object. On the macadam, it was seen to be elongated and symmetrical.... Upon questioning, it was determined that this was the only outline Dwight had seen—a roughly elliptical face. At no time had it appeared circular. The ends were pointed and a darker line across the center suggested a rim....

After resting on the macadam for about thirty seconds, during which time neither pulsation nor any change in appearance was observed, the UFO suddenly began skimming along the surface of the lot toward the entrance, rose at a shallow angle and disappeared over trees to the right of the Junior High School in the direction of the paper mill. As it started to move, a scraping sound like metal against macadam was heard. Asked whether the UFO had tipped up or remained horizontal when it took off, Myers replied that he did not recall seeing it tip up.

Dwight said he later noticed that a light sprinkling of sand on the macadam was swirled around where the object had been. No other evidence of its presence was found.

The children went to the Junior High School building and told some others what they had seen. As the group walked back from the school, a glowing light came overhead from the direction of the paper mill and continued on in a straight line, disappearing over a small stand of trees behind the Myers home.

Measurements

The landing spot—as reconstructed for us by Dwight Myers—was about forty-five feet from his vantage point fifty feet from the grass patch in the corner formed by the concrete retaining wall and the school building, ten-to-fifteen feet out from the wall. The short retaining wall had drainage holes evenly spaced along its length about six inches above the pavement. The landing spot was in line with the sixth drainage hole from the school building and the flagpole [was] visible towering above the grass knoll....

Character

The NICAP investigators and Bob Barry were very favorably impressed with young Dwight Myers (see photo section). He was friendly, intelligent and cooperative, giving careful and thoughtful answers to all our questions. There was no apparent guile in his manner.

Some of the other children at the schoolyard were ribbing him about his experience, but this did not seem to bother him. When questioned about his friends' reactions and whether they believed him, he replied:

"Some do and some don't." He freely admitted having read news stories about UFOs during the year. When asked if he ever heard Bob Barry's radio report on UFOs, he replied, "Oh, sure," in complete innocence and matter-of-factly, with no apparent awareness that such an admission might incriminate him. Many of the children, including Dwight, were well aware of the term "flying saucer."

Bob Barry said he had talked with the school principal, who said Dwight was a reliable and intelligent boy, not likely to make up such a story. NICAP had written to the principal for a character statement.... Mr. Barry is satisfied that the report is authentic after interviewing the parents, the children, and hearing the children's comments and questions at length. The children were extremely curious to understand what they had seen.

The stereotype of a "flying saucer" or UFO is not as [what was] described by Dwight. It seems likely that, if he were to make up a story, it would not be of a small UFO (rarely reported and not generally known) nor one of the shape described. Nor is it likely that so many young children could be involved in a hoax without giving themselves away.

The Bob Barry Report

Bob Barry was also quick to publicize his own report on the incident via a newscast he made in the WGCB, Red Lion, Pennsylvania, studio on October 16, 1965. He said "the object was first seen coming from the general direction of the P.H. Gladfelter Paper Mill. It first appeared as a bright object flying an erratic course.... [Several minutes later], "the mysterious craft stopped and hovered. Then it moved in swiftly to the area where the children were playing and came straight down, making a touch landing on the parking area of the Spring Grove Elementary School for a period of about thirty seconds."

Dwight Myers said that object, described as about twenty inches around and approximately six inches in height at the center, was very bright and appeared like highly polished chrome. The youths were less than 100 feet from the little UFO when it landed. Suddenly, the object departed, going straight up while spewing out a lengthy flame of blue and orange. No sound was heard at anytime with the exception of a scraping noise as the object left the parking area of the school.

Myers said he received a slight headache while watching the UFO after it landed. The object was described… as two plates, one introverted on top of the other. One of the youngsters (Robert Kirshner) became frightened as the result of the experience. Eugene Gruver, Principal of Spring Grove Elementary School, said the youngsters had been talking about the incident… of a strange visitor indeed to Spring Grove, Pennsylvania.

The Interview

During our interview with Dwight Myers and the rest of the children who saw the UFO land on the macadam parking lot, Richard Hall asked Dwight: "This trail that was coming out of it…. You say it was kind of bluish. Was it visible because of the school lights, do you think? Were you able to see the trail or was it glowing?"

Dwight was quick to answer the question: "No…. Well, yeah, it might have been because of the school lights. We seen [sic] it coming down the road. I think it was fully as bright as it was before." He added that he and the other witnesses "ran down there near the see-saws" when it was apparent that the small object was about to land nearby. He added that, when the object suddenly took off, it made a disturbing scraping sound.

The object didn't stay away for long. It quickly came back in view of the young witnesses.

"It disappeared and my brother and a neighbor boy across the hill here [saw it]….," Dwight continued. "He had gone for BBs at the store and they were coming back and we were sitting up there at the other school, the junior high, and we told them this and they didn't believe us. We… showed them where it landed and they still didn't believe us until we were going down the road and then it sort of buzzed us. Then they believed us."

The personable Dwight added that the UFO "made half of a dish and then it disappeared behind a barn and a house." He added that, when he and the other witnesses were watching the object on the macadam of the school parking lot, it was "giving out its own light." It was a glowing light and the rim around the light could be clearly seen. Richard Hall suggested that the object, instead of being round, could have been cigar-shaped or like a hot dog. Myers agreed.

Dwight Myers added that he and rest of the witnesses became alarmed when the object suddenly started to move, scraping itself against the macadam surface. The object took off rather fast, Dwight added. Then it flew off toward the mill.

Myers added that they saw what looked like smoke being emitted from the baby UFO.

"It took off and it got up in the sky," the boy said. "Then we saw the flame and that was it.... I couldn't see any smoke. Just a little flame...."

Dwight added that the object emitted the blue flame "when it took off.... When it got up higher, it was still a little blue there, but it turned to orange."

"About the noise you heard, was it more of a whirring sound or did it sound like metal scraping against the cement?" I asked Dwight.

"Yeah," Dwight responded. "Like metal scraping against cement."

The boy also said the flame from the object was still apparent after it returned for a second visit. When the UFO left for the final time, the witnesses scurried away to inform others at the junior high school as they sat huddled in a corner of the building.

Back at NICAP headquarters, Dick Hall and I discussed the small size of the object. Could it be a much smaller scout ship that was being controlled by a much larger mother ship-type UFO in the sky? It was a possibility, we agreed, perhaps even a certainty, since it was clear to us that the much smaller object was not at its landing place on its own.

A Landing in South Hill

Another significant sighting I was able to personally investigate occurred at approximately 9 p.m. on April 21, 1967, in the small town of South Hill, Virginia, a few miles above the North Carolina border. Dick Hall had received the initial report from a NICAP member and investigator in Richmond, Virginia, and quickly summoned fellow NICAP staffers Leon Katchen, Donald Berliner, and I. He asked if we could put everything else on hold and start out early the next morning to South Hill with a quick stop in Richmond to discuss the incident with our sighting coordinator. We all eagerly agreed and scrambled to get what we needed ready for the trip. This included taking my tape recorder.

Soon after arriving in South Hill, we were joined by William Powers, an assistant to Dr. J. Allen Hynek at Dearborn Observatory at Northwestern University in Chicago. At the time, Hynek was still the Air Force's official spokesman. After we completed our investigation, we learned that Hynek later stated that the sighting by Clifton Crowder, a fertilizer warehouse manager and the main witness, "simply defies explanation." We were beginning to wonder if the man known among UFO buffs as "Mr. Swamp Gas" himself was starting to turn his thinking around to a more objective viewpoint. We were later to learn that he was.

The Main Witness Talks

When we arrived in South Hill, we interviewed Crowder, who said he had been working late. After closing and locking the warehouse doors, he jumped into his car and drove the few hundred feet to the tarred macadam road that ran through the town.

"When I got on this hard surface road…, I saw this object, which appeared to be approximately twelve feet in diameter," he explained. "It was circular [and made] of some form of metal… It was sitting up on legs about three feet high…"

Crowder remarked that the UFO was sixteen or seventeen feet tall and was "shaped like a water tank standing on end. No windows or other physical characteristics were observed." The startled witness told us he continued to slowly drive to within 250 or so feet of the craft that was resting on the macadam surface of the road.

The Object Takes Off "Like a Flash"

The witness then shined his night lights on the object and briefly saw the landed craft for an estimated five seconds. Then it rapidly took off and disappeared "just like a flash." Crowder told us he watched as the road burned for several seconds after the UFO took off. He added that he lost sight of it when it got to an estimated altitude of 200-300 feet.

Meanwhile, Norman Martin, a tobacco farmer who lived just off Route 747, where the object landed, told us he watched as a bright light rose from the ground and lit up "a whole tree… just as bright as day" at the same time as the Crowder encounter. He added that he could not make out the object's shape or the flame on the road from his farmhouse, which was located across a tall wheat field from the landing site.

The strange object left a fairly wide burned-out area on the inch-and-a-half thick tarred road. Around the burned spot were four holes that measured up to three-quarters of an inch deep and one-half an inch wide. There was also a nearly exact spacing of the holes. (See the photo section.)

Samples Are Taken

After our initial interview with Crowder, we headed for the location of the landing. After thoroughly circling and investigating the burned area in the road, we determined that it measured around three feet wide. At about the same time, we watched as members of the Virginia Highway Department took core samples of both the burned and unburned sections of the road, along with three of the holes intact, for analysis by NICAP through our chemical laboratory contact members. The final results, however, were apparently inconclusive.

Further investigation revealed that several members of the Fort Lee Fire Department observed two blinking and revolving red lights for five-to-six minutes. One witness, James Hajacos, said he and several others saw the lights coming straight at them at 9:15 p.m. Then the lights suddenly stopped, turned at a ninety-degree angle, hovered, then slowly disappeared toward the northeast. Hajacos said he estimated that the lights flew at an altitude he estimated to be under 600 feet. He added that Fort Lee was around fifty miles northeast of South Hill.

The Following Evening...

Later, we learned from the South Hill Police Department that there were several sightings of unidentified flying objects on the following evening, April 22. At about 9:45 p.m., Police Chief Bill Williams and several of his officers saw strange lights that spread through the area "like lightning." Williams reported that he watched as three lights rose from the ground very quickly and were followed by two more lights. All five of the lights formed a diamond formation. One light left the formation and moved very fast toward the northeast and away from South Hill.

While closely keeping a keen eye on the UFOs, Chief Williams shifted his patrol car into high gear and followed the lights at breakneck speeds up to seventy-five miles per hour. He nervously watched as the diamond-shaped object "dipped up and down, occasionally disappearing behind trees and rising up again." Then it instantly turned and headed back toward the town. Suddenly, it came to an abrupt halt and remained stationary. Williams said he had never seen anything like it. The light was still hovering in the night sky when he left the scene.

CB-ers Join the Chase

We also learned that around five South Hill residents with citizens-band (CB) radios in their cars saw what they described as "strange lights" at 9:30 p.m. The CB-ers had what they said was "a running commentary of the sightings" back-and-forth between them.

Other witnesses—including William Brooks, Melvin W. Cage, Thomas G. Cliburne and Roy Edmonds—reported seeing a red ball that changed to an orange-yellow color. The unidentified object descended to tree-top level, then disappeared below tree-top level. When it reappeared, it had apparently divided into two separate objects, one of which seemed to be far away from the other. Then the UFOs came back together and again disappeared below the trees. When they rose into the air once more, the witnesses saw what they described as "three objects about one-half the size of the full moon."

An E-M Effect?

Roy Edmonds, who was nearly trembling with fright, quickly floored his accelerator and sped home so he could call the police, but the phone was dead." *Could the UFOs have zapped my phone?* he wondered. Later, we labeled this incident as a possible electro-magnetic (E-M) effect that often occurred in sighting reports. When Roy looked outside again, he saw a cluster of lights that was moving up and down.

An hour or so earlier in the evening, South Hill Police Dispatcher Norman Ball and four others observed a "pinkish ball of fire" they estimated to be the size of a grapefruit at tree-top level. The object was stationary at first. Then it slowly moved and disappeared behind a hill.

Both Clifton Crowder and another witness, Norman Thomas, told us that they believed what they saw was probably a helicopter or a secret weapon, but neither of them heard a sound. Later, Crowder told us he believed that someone may have staged "an elaborate hoax," but added that these theories were "just supposition on my part."

CHAPTER SEVEN

The *Morgantown Victory* and Other Sightings at Sea

Sometime during my first year at NICAP, I came across a UFO encounter at sea from a contact I had at the Patuxent Naval Air Station in Lexington Park, Maryland. It involved a sighting by the captain and crew of the SS *Morgantown Victory*—one of the 534 Victory Ships built by the U.S. Maritime Commission during World War II—that was on a routine cruise in the North Atlantic. The sighting was reported in the June 1966 issue of *Sealift Magazine*.

Captain Petrie Reports Sighting

My informant told me that the ship's skipper, Captain Glynn Petrie, gave a detailed summary of the events to the publication. These events began playing out when Able Seaman Robert J. Claunch, the bow lookout, first saw a "large glowing object coming from the horizon on the starboard beam."

At this point, Captain Petrie took up the narrative:

Just prior to 2200, ship time, January 11, 1966, I was in my bunk when I heard a hurried clatter of feet on the bridge grating over my head.... The phone rang and Mr. Richard M. Anderson, third mate, reported what appeared to be a plane afire on the post quarter. I ran to the bridge, but could see nothing. The information given me indi-

cated a plane in trouble had headed for the ship and [had] ditched on the port quarter.

At 2201, the vessel [turned]. The bow lookout was doubled and a search was made utilizing the vessel's searchlight. During the search, I realized that I had heard no sound such as a plane would have made. I questioned Robert Claunch, A.B., on bow lookout, and learned that the object had maneuvered approximately 180-degrees about the vessel without sound.

At 22:38, [the] vessel executed another... turn and resumed her original course and continued [the] search. At 2300, I took statements from each of the witnesses....

Captain Petrie said that the weather was very clear with a mild south-southwest wind. He continued his report:

There were two phone calls from the bow. [The first came] when [the] object was on [the] starboard quarter. The third mate ran to [the] starboard wing and looked forward, seeing nothing. Another phone call from the bow was to have the bridge look on the port quarter. The third mate and Fache... saw the object....

Meanwhile, the statements obtained from the three sailors under Captain Petrie's command were made by "mature seamen with [a] combined sea-time of seventy-nine years."

Able Seaman Claunch's Statement

Claunch's statement came next:

At a little before 2200..., I was [the] bow lookout in clear, fine weather. I sighted a large glowing object coming from the horizon on the starboard beam. It approached to within one mile at a height of about 400 feet. It then altered course to a position off the starboard quarter, where it hovered for thirty seconds. It appeared to be cigar-shaped with a bright light at its head, a glowing body with a duller light aft and a fiery tail. It was silent and I saw it for about thirty minutes…. I first thought it was a plane in trouble and looked for running lights, but saw none. It did not flare or light up the surroundings. The lights were steady. This definitely was not a meteor. I… have been at sea for twenty-five years and have never seen anything like it.

Helmsman Fache Pipes in Next

Fache said:

> …I was at the wheel steering 257 gyro. When the lookout reported a flying object, I looked out and saw what appeared to be a plane on fire on the port quarter. I watched it for over a minute when it showed a bright flash and went out. The ship was steering well and making [a] steady course. I have never seen the likes of this before. I [have] seventeen years sea experience.

Richard Anderson Weighs In

Anderson, the Third Mate on watch, reported:

> [The] lookout phone from [the] bow to [the] bridge [reported] a flying object low on [the] starboard side. I glanced out starboard forward and did not notice anything. [The] lookout called again and said it was on the port quarter. I glanced out and saw an orange glow-like fire trailing behind a flying object streaming out behind for what appeared to be about fifteen or twenty feet. [This] disappeared in about a minute heading in an easterly direction approximately three or four degrees above the horizon. [I] pointed out the object to [the] helmsman and phoned Captain Petrie, notifying him…. I hold a second mate's license and have been to sea for 37 years.

* * *

Having been raised in a maritime environment on the Chesapeake Bay in Maryland, I was anxious to learn of other sightings of strange aerial craft that mariners may have witnessed during the last several centuries. Some of the following reports were used in my book *Mysteries if the Skies: UFOs in Perspective* (1968).

The *Santa Maria*

It was around 10 p.m., October 11, 1492. Admiral of the Ocean Sea Christopher Columbus was making his rounds on the deck of his flagship, the *Santa Maria*—off the coast of the land he would discover only a few hours later—when he observed "a light glimmering at a great distance." He quickly yelled for his most trusted crewmember, Pedro Gutierrez, known as "a Gentleman of the King's Bedchamber," who also saw the light.

A short time later, the light disappeared, then was seen bobbing up and down "in sudden and passing gleams." The light was first spotted about four hours before land in the New World was sighted.

At first, Columbus and Gutierrez thought they may have seen a foolhardy fisherman a long way from shore during a midnight-style hunt for food. This did not seem likely, however. The rough water would preclude such foolhardy action. The next morning, October 12 (annually celebrated as Columbus Day), land was discovered and the beginning of foreign occupation of the North American and parts of the South American continents had begun.

John Winthrop's Journal

It was 265 years before the Wright Brothers made heavier-than-air history when they flew their plane over the sand dunes at Kitty Hawk, North Carolina, ushering in the era of flight as a major mode of transportation. In 1638, colonial Massachusetts was the scene of a UFO sighting when a mysterious aerial display was observed around the harbor in Boston. John Winthrop, a Governor of the Massachusetts Bay Company, wrote an account of the event in his journal dated January 18, 1644.

Winthrop wrote that James Everell and two other mariners were on a barge heading down the Muddy River during the night when they saw a huge light swoop down on them. Frightened and bewildered, the men found that they were being incredibly drawn upstream against the tide by an unknown powerful force. The object then quickly disappeared and the astonished trio rowed frantically to shore, where a number of people also gave accounts of the remarkable light. Some observers said the light sometimes shot out flames and sparks.

John Winthrop continued his search for permanent settlements in the New World. In 1630, he "headed the great emigration to Massachusetts, landing at Salem [site of the infamous witch trials in the 1690s] and settling in Boston."

The *Victoria* Encounter

It was around 9:30 p.m., June 18, 1845. The British brig *Victoria* was en route from Newcastle, England, to Malta. The weather was calm at a location the crew guessed was less than 100 miles north of Malta. Suddenly, the brig's "topgallant and royal masts… went over the side as if carried away by a squall."

A strong, violent wind from the east laid siege to the ship, but the brig withstood the battering. Then the wind ceased and, once more, the ship was becalmed. At the same time, some of the crew members were feeling sick from air that had become almost unbearably hot with a strong stench of sulphur let loose in the atmosphere.

Then, without any warning, three bright, shining objects rose from the ocean approximately one-half mile from the ship. The crew kept the strange aerial crafts in sight for about ten minutes before they disappeared. A short time after the sighting, a strong wind once more began to blow, driving the brig and its crew into a current of cold air.

A Dutch Bark Experience

Another reported sighting at sea occurred around 5 p.m., March 19, 1887, in the Atlantic Ocean. Captain Swart was the commander of *J.P.A.*, a Dutch bark. He and his crew's encounter with strange objects at sea came when the ship was sailing the Atlantic about 900 miles east of New York City. The captain suddenly spotted two aerial objects that were quickly approaching.

Captain Swart wrote:

It looked like two balls, one very black, and the other brightly illuminated. The latter fell and, as it seemed that it would strike the vessel, she was hove to under storm sails. The meteor dropped into the sea close alongside, making in its flight a tremendous noise.

Before reaching the water, the upper atmosphere was darkened while below and on board everything appeared like a sea of fire. The force of the meteor in striking the water caused heavy breakers, which washed over the vessel making her roll in a tremendous matter.

Some of the crewmembers said a suffocating atmosphere accompanied the huge waves that were breaking over the ship, causing "the perspiration to pour from the faces of all on board, rendering fresh air a necessity." There was also "a strong smell of sulfur."

Captain Swart continued his sea log:

Immediately afterwards, solid lumps of ice fell on the decks, and the decks and rigging became coated with an icy crust, caused by the immense evaporation. The barometer during the phenomenon oscillated so violently that no reading could be taken.... On the side, where the meteor fell into the water, the ship appeared all black and some of the copper sheathing was blistered.

The catch was that the thermometer registered only sixty-six degrees Fahrenheit!

Some have argued that the roaring noise and the sulfuric smell were indicative of a large meteor. But what of the ice forming on the decks and rigging in a temperature thirty-four degrees above freezing? And what about the barometer's violent oscillations, which indicated sudden changes in atmospheric pressure?

Doris and Cape Hatteras

Nearly three and a half years later, on August 29, 1890, *Doris*, a German ship, was near the infamous graveyard of ships, Cape Hatteras, North Carolina, "when an object was sighted about five degrees above sea level." Captain Ohling said "the object stood perfectly still for about one minute and then slowly rising to twenty degrees above [the] horizon, it separated into two parts and disappeared."

Other sightings continued to occur on the world's seas.

A "Spheroidal Mass" Over the Wellington Channel

It was May 24, 1850. The Henry Grinnel Expedition set sail from English waters with the *Advance* and the *Resolute* in a frantic and prolonged search for the pioneer Arctic explorer Sir John Franklin, who had sailed with two ships in search of a northwest passage in 1845. There had been no word from the ill-fated expedition since July of that year, nearly five years before the expedition began its search. There was little hope that anyone would be found alive.

Dr. Elisha Kent Kane was the Senior Medical Officer of the expedition on board the *Advance* in Wellington Channel, a part of the Queen Elizabeth Islands, Canada's northernmost extremity. He noted an account of an object seen at sea on September 15, 1850:

> *This afternoon..., a large spheroidal mass was seen floating in the air at an unknown distance to the north. It undulated for a while over the ice-lined horizon of Wellington Channel and after a little while, an-*

other [object], smaller than the first, became visible a short distance from it. They receded with the wind from the southward and eastward, but did not disappear for some time.

At first, Captain De Haven thought it was a kite, but, independently of the difficulty of imagining a kite flying without a master, and where no master could be, its outline and movement convinced me it was a balloon.... The balloon was to leeward, nearly due north of us.... Its appendage [was] larger than an ordinary dinner plate. This incident interested us much at the time, and I have not seen anything in the published journals... that explains it.

Elisha Kent Kane was a native of Philadelphia. He was born there on February 3, 1820. He graduated as an M.D. at the age of twenty-one, then enlisted in the U.S. Navy as a surgeon. The doctor enjoyed extensive travel and served in the Army during the War with Mexico in 1848. In February 1849, he was presented with a sword by the city of Philadelphia.

Following more travel and close calls at sea, Kane became the surgeon for the Grinnel Expedition. At one time during a later and again unsuccessful attempt to search for Franklin, he collected valuable data later published in Volumes Ten to Thirteen of the *Smithsonian Contributions to Knowledge* in 1858. In October 1855, suffering from poor health, he was advised by his doctor to travel to the warm climate in Cuba. He died in Havana in 1857.

Lady of the Lake

On March 22, 1870, the American bark *Lady of the Lake* was sailing near the equator about halfway between Senegal on the East African coast and Natal, Brazil, when its Captain Frederick William Banner and crew spotted a strange object in the south at 6:30 p.m. The wind was blowing from the north-northeast. The witnesses described what they saw as a circular-type cloud, which appeared to have a semicircle near its center. There were also four arm-like appendages stretching from the center to the edge of the circle.

"From the center to about six degrees beyond the circle was a fifth ray, broader and more distinct than the others, with a curved end....," Captain Banner entered in his ship's log.

The light-gray UFO flew considerably lower than the clouds. It moved from the southeast to the northeast. Captain Banner added that the craft "came up obliquely against the wind and finally settled down right in the wind's eye."

Operation Mainbrace

In 1952, a NATO exercise called Operation Mainbrace—composed of numerous ships, planes and personnel—was north of Bornholm Island, Denmark, on September 13 when crew members of the *Willemoes*, a Danish destroyer, spotted a triangular-shaped UFO that was moving at high speed.

A week later, on September 20, crewmembers aboard the aircraft carrier U.S.S. *Franklin D. Roosevelt* spotted a silver spherical object that was photographed by them. Officials kept the color photos hidden. Air Force Project Chief Captain Edward J. Ruppelt, who later wrote his own UFO book, managed to obtain the photographs and said they were "excellent."

A Royal Navy Intruder

It was an unspecified month and day in 1963 off the coast of Norway. Tom Preston (not his real name), a twenty year-old British Royal Navy Lieutenant, was a navigator and radar-sonar operator on fleet exercise duty with the Navy. Suddenly "a large object descended on them."

The UFO, which appeared on the radar screen, moved extremely fast. Then it stopped almost instantly. The intruder seemed to watch the fleet maneuvers for several minutes before plunging under the surface of the water. The sonar detectors on board Preston's ship managed to locate the submerged object. He was later reminded that he had signed the Official Secrets Act and was forbidden to discuss the sighting with anyone.

It would seem that America was not the only country with something to hide when it came to reporting certain UFO sightings.

The *Tiro* and the Football Field UFO

It was an unidentified date in 1966. The U.S.S. *Tiro* SS-416 submarine was moored to a pier in Seattle, Washington, for public touring during the Rose Festival. The captain and crew were tired and trying to get some shut-eye. Their trip to the mainland, however, had hardly been routine.

During the long trip from Pearl Harbor in the Hawaiian Islands to Seattle, a lookout on the port side of the sub noticed a strange object that was about two miles away. He called for other sailors and they all saw a metallic craft that appeared to be larger than a football field. The UFO flew into the sea. Then it suddenly and quickly emerged and sped up into the clouds.

The Underwater UFO

In 1968, the Panama Bulk Carrier *Grichuna* was loaded with coal when it left its moorings in South Carolina en route to Japan. A second officer was pacing the deck on night watch as the vessel sailed off the Florida coast. The sea was calm as the ship plowed along at fifteen knots.

The officer was on the port side of the vessel watching the lights emanating from Palm Beach. Then he became distracted by strange lights under the water. He saw a spherical-shaped object with windows. He reported that the underwater UFO "moved faster than a sub could move."

E-M Effects Aboard an Oil Tanker

On an unspecified date in 1969, a British Grenadier oil tanker crew sailing the Atlantic saw "an arrow-shaped UFO… hovering above the ship." The object continued to be seen around the vessel for three days. On the first day, as the UFO was in sight, "the ship's engines abruptly stopped."

As the flying object was still in sight on the second day, the onboard food storage refrigeration unit suddenly sparked out. No reason was found for the outage. There were more electrical problems on the third day, when the engines failed again. Then all the systems returned to normal function on the third day as the UFO vanished from view.

Objects Over the North Sea

In July 1977, Flight Lieutenant A.M. Wood was on duty at RAF Boulmer in Northumberland, England, when he spotted bright objects that were hanging over the North Sea. He later said the UFOs appeared to be about three miles off Britain's northeastern coast at an estimated altitude of 5,000 feet.

The brightly luminous objects were about five times larger than a Whirlwind helicopter. The official report said that two other officers also saw the UFOs, which were visible for more than ninety minutes. The operators at the radar installation at the base also registered the objects on their scope.

The Cape Hatteras UFOs

At about 11 p.m. on a clear night sometime during the summer of 1986, the U.S.S. *Edenton* was maneuvering about fifty miles off Cape Hatteras, North Carolina. The crewmember on watch that eventful evening spotted four red circular lights that formed a square in the sky about a mile or so away.

As the sailor watched, the lights appeared to suddenly break off from the square formation and speed away. Later, the radiation detection system on the bridge of the ship began making a loud clicking sound. This was a clear sign that crewmen who were in the area had taken a radiation hit. A presence of radiation was also detected by other instruments on the ship.

CHAPTER EIGHT

Joe Franklin to the King Shot Effect

The flurry of many thousands of UFO reports from around the world in 1965 and into 1966 and 1967 was adding a lot of weight to NICAP's plea for a no-nonsense reliable scientific investigation of the subject. For several months, Keyhoe and the NICAP staff were ecstatic. Maybe our efforts were beginning to pay off. It seemed that everyone wanted to hear more about those strange objects seen in the skies in virtually every country in the world. This was borne out by the all-nighters I pulled in the NICAP office fielding calls from around the world.

It was also now my turn to relieve the Major from the flurry of requests for interviews on radio, television and speeches in schools, universities and other venues around the country. I was a novice at it, but I quickly learned. My own book, *Mysteries of the Skies: UFOs in Perspective* (1968) was about to be published and I would have to be comfortable with the round of television, radio and lecture appearances that would be forthcoming. One interview I really enjoyed was as a guest of famed television host Joe Franklin in New York City.

The Joe Franklin TV Show

I was to appear on Franklin's very powerful and highly-rated talk-show with a fellow author and UFO colleague, John G. Fuller, who had published two popular best-sellers on the subject, *Incident at Exeter: The*

Story of Unidentified Flying Objects Over America Now and *The Interrupted Journey: Two Lost Hours "Aboard a Flying Saucer,"* both released nearly back-to-back in 1966. These cases had been thoroughly investigated by NICAP and were deemed to be extraordinary events experienced by believable and reliable witnesses. And John himself had made a UFO sighting, which spurred his interest in delving more deeply into the subject.

Simon Oakland

Another guest on the same show who was slated for his own segment was the actor Simon Oakland. Simon was a flying saucer fan who talked briefly with John and I before the cameras started rolling. He told us he began his career as a violinist. He loved great music and would follow this avocation throughout his acting career. In the late 1940s, he began acting with a long number of stage, screen, television and radio appearances. I particularly remembered him as the journalist who befriended the convicted murderess Barbara Graham, played by Susan Hayward, in *I Want to Live!* (1958). Susan went on to win her only Oscar for the part. I also fondly remembered Simon as Dr. Fred Richmond, the psychiatrist who explains Norman Bates' murderous behavior in Alfred Hitchcock's horror classic *Psycho* (1960).

As Joe Franklin came in with his winning personality to shake our hands, Simon was quick to briefly corner him.

"Joe, I've got to be on with these guys!" he exclaimed, grabbing the host's arm.

"You're scheduled for a separate segment, Simon," Franklin replied. "I don't know if we can rearrange things like that."

"Oh, sure you can, Joe. I have every confidence in you. This is a damned important subject! People want to know more about it. Hell's bells, *I want to know more about it!*"

"OK, Simon. We're scheduled to hit the airways in a few minutes, but I'll work it out somehow."

Work it out he did. Oakland asked a lot of questions through my own presentation covering the history of UFOs prior to the so-called modern era beginning with the Kenneth Arnold sighting of nine discs flying in formation over Mt. Rainier in Washington State in June 1947.

John Fuller and *The Interrupted Journey*

It was when John Fuller, the popular *Trade Winds* columnist for *Saturday Review*, started talking about his very recent books about the series of extraordinary reports in New Hampshire that Oakland really came alive. He was particularly blown away by the Betty and Barney Hill case, described so vividly in *The Interrupted Journey*. On the night of September 19, 1961, the couple was driving to their home in Portsmouth when they spotted a flying saucer. Suddenly, they both experienced a blackout. Two hours later, when they regained full consciousness, they were shaken and discovered that two hours had passed since they had stopped their car.

What followed was an incredible story the Hills had of being abducted on board a UFO and examined by otherworldly beings. It left an indelible mark on both their lives. The abduction was not fully revealed until Dr. Benjamin Simon, a psychiatrist, hypnotized them. Besides the psychological and physiological repercussions, perhaps the most incredible aspect (to me, at least) was the fact that Betty correctly described a configuration of planets in a galaxy far away that was not even known to the general public until years after their discovery in the distant skies.

"Irrefutable Points"

While Joe Franklin, Simon Oakland and I listened attentively, John Fuller outlined what he called in his book eight "irrefutable points" concerning the Hills' incredible encounter with outer space alien beings:

> Number One: *There is no doubt in my mind or those who have investigated the case that a sighting of some sort took place.*

Two: The UFO or alien craft was similar to many others that have been reported during the last two hundred or so years. The book *Mysteries of the Skies* by my colleague and current co-guest on your show, Gordon Lore, has adequately shown that such sightings have been made for centuries.

Three: The Hills had what I would call "a severe emotional reaction" to their encounter with humanoid-like aliens. These included frequent nightmares as well as physical abnormalities that were revealed under hypnosis by Benjamin Simon, M.D., a highly qualified psychiatrist.

Four: I have no doubt that Betty's and Barney's emotional responses to the incident were heightened by a certain amount of racial insensitivity. Barney is black and Betty is white.

Five: One of the main points that impressed me was the fact that both Betty and Barney had no ulterior motive in fabricating their sighting and apparent abduction. They had confined their experience to a small group of friends and relatives for over four years.

Six: There were several scientific and technical persons who investigated the case and who, I believe, support the possibility of the reality of the experience.

Seven: There is also a certain amount of physical circumstantial evidence that tends to support the validity of the Hills' experience. These included a bright, shiny spot on their car trunk that apparently caused the compass to oscillate. Also, the watches they both wore failed to run following their encounter.

Eight: Under hypnosis by Dr. Simon, both Betty and Barney gave nearly identical accounts of their abduction.

"No Final Answers"

"So, what's the answer to this incredible, even unbelievable case?" Franklin asked.

"Perhaps there are no final answers," Fuller replied. "I would think that, even if we believed for one second that the Hills' experience is true, there could be far-reaching implications concerning the history of Planet Earth. It would promote a reexamination of our religions, politics, scientific efforts, and literature. We would have to reevaluate our international relations with an urgent need for a continuous scientific examination of the UFO phenomenon. Even today, the United Nations Secretary-General and others are talking about a major scientific probe. It was Tennyson who said: 'Maybe [our] wildest dreams are but the needful preludes of the truth.'"

NICAP had thoroughly investigated the case, but Keyhoe—while he was impressed and was prone to believe the Hills' incredible encounter—put a lid on revealing it to his members. He was concerned that the respected organization he co-founded would get a black eye from the scientists and lawmakers he was trying to persuade to take a closer look at the many thousands of reliable reports that kept coming into the NICAP offices and its global scientifically-oriented field subcommittees.

UFO Lands and Frightens Boy

Soon after I returned to NICAP headquarters following my appearance on *The Joe Franklin Show*, I received a report from our friend and tireless investigator, Dr. James E. McDonald. At 11:45 p.m., December 20, 1965, he reported, Edward A. Bruns was driving his father's 1962 Ford pickup truck home. As he was heading west, south of Route 27, near Herman, Minnesota, he observed a bright, oval-shaped object hovering several feet above the road. The large UFO covered the entire road and was shaped like two saucers with a dome on top. What was described as a window-like structure surrounded the dome. A green light glowed from the window.

Suddenly, the truck's engine lost power. The headlights went out and the vehicle was spun violently to the right.

"[Bruns] thinks the truck began to coast to a stop….," stated McDonald, who interviewed the witness by phone. "It ended up on the south side of the road, whereas he had been heading west."

Bruns reported that the truck touched down lightly into a ditch. The ice around the vehicle was left unbroken. Stunned, the boy stared at the UFO. Then, with a whistling sound and emitting sparks from its underbelly, the object quickly ascended and disappeared.

Badly frightened, young Bruns ran the mile-and-a-half distance to his home. His startled mother said he was "white as a ghost and wringing wet." She added he was also "very nervous and disturbed about the whole event."

The boy's father scurried to the site. He attempted to drive the four-wheeled drive truck out of the ditch, but was unsuccessful. Later, a flashlight examination of the area revealed no tire tracks around the immediate area.

McDonald is "Impressed"

Jim McDonald was obviously impressed by the witness' account.

"I phoned [*Herman Review*] reporter Willis Klason…," the physicist told NICAP. "He confirmed that he found the truck in the ditch with [a] complete absence of skid marks in the snow to account for how it got there…. He said Edward was known as a reliable boy with no negative reports from anyone in town. He took photos of the truck in the ditch…. It seems like a strong case to me."

The King Shot Effect

A little more than three months after the Edward Bruns encounter, John King, 24, of Newport, Maine, was driving on Mount Hope Avenue in nearby Bangor at 11:50 p.m. on March 23, 1966. The stars were clearly visible and the moon was shining. King initially saw two solid objects in the sky with a light source coming from within both UFOs. He also reported that the undersides of the objects were revolving. They had a blue bubble on top and emitted bluish-green, yellow and red colors.

King said that, at the time of the sighting, he saw two jets from Dow Air Force Base (AFB) fly over nearby Old Town. He estimated the objects were approximately 200-to-400 feet away from him. He added that Mrs. Robert Collins, Orono, Maine, two Bangor police officers and seven other unidentified persons also saw the UFOs. These included a Dow AFB Captain.

King told NICAP investigator Robert Mattingly: "I had been coming home after bringing my fiancée home. I drove down Interstate 95 toward Bangor, took the Hogan Road exit, then made a right turn on the Mount Hope Avenue road. The Bangor State Hospital is located on the left-hand side of the road as you would travel towards Bangor...."

"I was... Scared as Hell!"

The witness added that, as he approached a second entrance to the hospital, he noticed "an object in the field just past a patch of small bush-trees to my right. I slowed my car down to get a better glimpse of whatever it was about 200 feet in the area from the roadside...." The UFO was approximately two cars in length and was sitting between two telephone poles.

The object was about ten feet high "with a small bluish dome-like canopy on top. It resembled a deflated football, but was more rounded on top than on the bottom. I emerged from my car and took off my glasses to get a better look at it. Then I noticed that the object had a orangey light… in the center." There was also "a bluish light on the right and a white light on the left," both of which exhibited "a frosty or hazy hue."

"The body or fuselage was an awful yellowish color....," the witness added. "I could distinctly see some sort of metalwork in [a] small ribbed form on this thing. From the underside, it looked as if it had a reddish effect which readily changed to a pink, orange and then back to red."

Frightened, King grabbed his .22 magnum automatic pistol from under the seat of his convertible and grabbed the clip from the glove compartment. In a highly emotional and frightened state, he loaded and cocked the pistol, then stood over the left fender of his car, waiting for whatever else might happen. He was not going to let "that damned thing get him."

"I was scared, though," King admitted. "Scared as hell!"

"I Was… Ready For Anything"

King said the object, which was about 200 feet out in the field, "then moved slowly and stealthily about 150 feet vertical with the road."

In a solemn voice tinged with a hint of fright, the witness reported:

> *I was about ready for anything at this time, even dying. I could hear the scraping of the undercarriage of the object on the small elderberry bushes and pine trees that were in its path. It then stopped and started toward me, quickly at first, then slowly, like a tank would approach its target. I aimed the pistol at the orange 'light' in the middle, which kept getting lighter and darker…. Then, when the thing was about 100 feet from me, I broke the silence with a shot from my pistol…. Nothing happened. This thing just kept coming at me slowly.*

> *When it was about forty feet away from me, it stopped. The car lights dimmed and the radio went out. I was listening to music from WKBW in New York. I lost the station completely….*

> *I shot the pistol once more and still there did not seem to be any reaction. The object was hovering then over a large puddle about fifty feet away and I could see rotating lights or windows underneath the craft. The only noise was a light humming electrical sound like [an] ohm voltage current.*

> *I fired once more and it started to glow a little brighter… and took off at a tremendous rate of speed. I fired again as it left. I heard a noise like a recoil from a spring….*

> *I thought I saw another thing take off at the same speed and direction at the same time. This [object] seemed to be smaller.... As I got back in my car, I saw it vanish from the area but observed it high above the city. It was very high and gleaming.*
>
> *I had a little trouble [starting] the car, but finally started it. This should not have happened for it is a fairly new car.*
>
> *I immediately went to the Bangor Police Station and told them what I saw. I was very shaken up. I learned at that time that two Bangor policemen saw something hovering over the city of Bangor at about 10:30 p.m. and described it as [like]"100 police spotlights rotating and hovering in the sky."*

Other Witnesses Log In

Shortly after King filed his report, a caller phoned in to the police station identifying himself as the Captain at Dow AFB. King said he only heard snatches of the conversation, but it was enough to hear the Air Force officer say that four others had also seen something in the sky. King reported that:

> *Another woman called... and said that she and her husband, a music teacher at the University of Maine, and a student also saw something in the sky bobbing up and down and moving from right to left in the sky. The color was a bluish green, orange and red and white. Earlier in the evening, a prominent Bangor woman spotted what seemed to match the description of exactly what I saw over Garland Street Junior High School. This she saw at 9:30....*
>
> *A twelve year-old Bangor girl and her mother [also] witnessed a shiny object at 6:15 p.m. the following night over a wooded section near their home. A family on Indian Island in Old Town... said they saw a bright orange object hovering over their home [that] was much 'bigger than any star'.... It displayed other colors as it rotated.... Two*

policemen in Skowhegan, Maine, reported seeing an object with an orange glow moving at a high rate of speed and stop.

E-M and Physical Effects

In her letter to Major Keyhoe on March 28, 1966, Mrs. Robert L. Mattingly, North Anson, Maine, said that the engineer at WLBZ Channel 2 in Bangor encountered E-M effects when he lost audio and picture information at eleven minutes before midnight for two-to-three seconds. This was just after John's strange object took off and headed in the general direction of the WLBZ tower. In his response to Richard Hall on April 6, 1966, Rudolph C. Marcoux, Station Manager at WLBZ Television, said the outing was traced to a mechanical failure within the station.

Mrs. Mattingly said John told them: "We went back the next morning to investigate and found broken bushes along the same path taken by the object as it approached me...." John measured the distance from his car to the object.

"The thing was fifty-three feet from me when it took off," he logged in. "There were also several sets of holes or depressions found in the earth. Each set was exactly the same and contained three holes which formed a shape."

Mattingly said John estimated the size of the object to be about forty feet across, ten feet thick, and had a hazy blue bubble on top. A number of other people also saw the object in different parts of the city and their descriptions were the same as John's.

CHAPTER NINE

From a Congressional Hearing to the D.C. Area Sightings

The first real sign we at NICAP realized that things may be going our way came early during the second quarter of 1966. On April 5 of that year, Congress held a one-day closed hearing (which turned to an open session halfway through the proceedings) on the subject. The session was officially titled "Unidentified Flying Objects: Hearing by Committee on Armed Services of the House of Representatives, Eighty-Ninth Congress, Second Session."

Six men with impressive scientific credentials were tagged to testify before the august body of national leaders: Dr. Carl Sagan, a world-famous astronomer, astrophysicist and member of NASA's Planetary Atmospheric Study Group; Dr. Bryan O'Brien, a National Academy of Sciences member; Dr. Robert W. Porter, an authority on satellites and guided missiles; Dr. Lauris S. Carter, former U.S. Air Force Chief Scientific Adviser; Dr. Willis H. Ware (no title was indicated); and Jesse Orlansky, Industrial Psychologist with the Institute for Defense Analysis. Congressman E. Mendel Rivers chaired the event.

For the first time, Major Keyhoe and the NICAP staff were beginning to think that, at last, a serious scientific probe of UFOs may be in its infancy. After all, how could serious lawmakers fail to at least consider the overwhelming body of significant sightings from around the world, many of them reported by qualified no-nonsense observers such as airline and military pilots, scientists, radar operators, police officers, and scientists from every field of endeavor?

Keyhoe is "Guarded"

For a brief period following the hearing, it was beginning to appear that our efforts were beginning to pay off in the scientific and other areas that really mattered. Don Keyhoe, however, told me that he was "guarded." He had been disappointed too many times by so-called official announcements from prominent individuals that later turned out to be negative takes on the subject. The feisty major sat down at his typewriter in his home in the beautiful boondocks of Luray, Virginia, to write the page one article, "Air Force Admits Faulty UFO Investigation" in the May-June 1966 edition of NICAP's *The U.F.O. Investigator*.

"The Air Force has admitted to a Congressional committee that it has not properly followed up [on] unexplained UFO reports," he gleefully wrote.

Keyhoe was enthusiastic that the open Congressional session had automatically put all Air Force statements and submitted documents on public record, including:

- "Some UFOs the Air Force publicly claimed were identified actually are unexplained";

- "The Air Force hypothesis that all UFOs have ordinary explanations may be an error, causing new scientific information to be overlooked"; and

- The six scientists on the hearing panel "criticized the Air Force for not scientifically exploring unexplained sightings. The panel urged that teams of non-Air Force scientists fully investigate such cases, with detailed reports to Congress and the public."

But the feisty Major wasn't about to cater to a whole-hog belief that a complete turnabout by the U.S. Air Force or other branches of the government was in the making.

"At first glance, these admissions might appear to indicate an about-face in [the] Air Force 'explain-away' policy," he lamented. "Instead, Air Force Secretary Harold Brown and his advisers added the usual debunking claims: No evidence of UFO reality, no witnesses ridiculed, no information withheld."

Keyhoe was also quick to point out in his article that Chairman Rivers told Secretary Brown: "We can't just write them [UFOs] off. There are too many responsible people who are concerned."

"UFOs Posed No Threat"

In his prepared statement, Brown said that "UFOs posed no threat, were not extraterrestrial, and were ninety percent explained." Then he put on the public record an Air Force memorandum addressed to the Air Force Scientific Advisory Board that was signed by Major General E.B. LeBailly, Director of Information, that said, in part: "Many of the reports that cannot be explained have come from intelligent and technically well-qualified individuals whose integrity cannot be questioned." Then, the icing on the cake: "LeBailly asked for a scientific panel to review Project Blue Book," the Air Force entity that, through the years, had constantly rejected reliable sighting reports from both the general public and highly qualified scientifically-oriented witnesses. But there was apparently no official pressure to hold Blue Book accountable for its wholly negative stance.

At one point in the proceeding, Chairman Rivers "asked if anyone in authority [had] alleged that UFOs come from other planets." Secretary Brown responded that he knew of no one associated with the Air Force who expressed that belief. Keyhoe was quick to respond that Colonel Joseph Bryan (USAF-Ret.), later chairman of NICAP's Board of Governors; Lieutenant Colonel Howard Strand, an Air National Guard base commander; and "other Air Force officers have publicly stated this belief."

Hynek Begins a Turn-Around

Even the official Air Force spokesman, Dr. J. Allen Hynek—Mr. "Swamp Gas" himself—was beginning to back-pedal. He said he had attempted to be open-minded about UFOs and his own tenure as the Air Force spokesman even though, overall, the UFO subject "seemed utterly ridiculous" at the time.

During my visit with Hynek and his aide, Dr. Jacques Vallee—who, at this writing in May 2017, is still active in trying to foster a continued scientific investigation of UFOs—at Northwestern University in Chicago in 1969, told me that Hynek was trying, under repeated pressure, to come to a more scientific public stand on the subject. There was just too much significant evidence for the objective scientific community to ignore.

In the hearing, Hynek admitted that the Air Force was going on the "working hypothesis" that "all UFO reports were errors, hallucinations or hoaxes." His approach had been "very successful," but it could throw the proverbial monkey wrench into the vast amount of information that still needed to be investigated.

Hynek said that the Air Force's official stand may well have thrown up roadblocks to research.

"If one digs too intently for coal, he is apt to miss diamonds....," Hynek aptly put it. "And in dealing with truly puzzling cases, we have tended either to say that, if an investigation had been pursued long enough, the misidentified object would have been recognized, or that the sighting had no validity to begin with."

No doubt about it. It appeared that the official AF "debunker" was beginning to change his stance. During the hearing, he admitted telling AF officials that Blue Book had not been fully investigating "UFO unknowns."

"Enough puzzling sightings have been reported by intelligent and often technically competent people who warrant closer attention than Project Blue Book can possibly encompass," Hynek remarked.

Stirring "the Pot of Public Interest"

The hearings had come in the midst of one of the most significant waves of UFO reports from around the world. These proceedings and the sighting reports had stirred the pot of public interest and its acceptance of reliable, well-documented sightings. One of those who believed in the existence of flying saucers and their occupants was syndicated columnist Roscoe Drummond, who was also a friend of Keyhoe and NICAP. He quickly called for a scientific investigation, adding that "history is littered with examples of the most eminent scientists who were dead certain that things couldn't be done, that they would never come to pass—and wrote with great displays of scientific evidence to prove that they couldn't be wrong. But they *were* [wrong]."

Meanwhile, Hynek was continuing to make inroads in his break with the Air Force. In a series of public statements which Keyhoe called "surprising," the Director of Dearborn Observatory at Northwestern University admitted the existence of unexplained UFO photos and radar trackings and called for an end to the ridicule of reliable witnesses.

A Physicist and the D.C. Area Sightings

Later, as blistering heat continued to plague the Washington, D.C., area, Dick Hall approached my desk at NICAP and told me he had just received reports that a series of sightings had blanketed the area the night before. The witnesses had included a prominent physicist and a number of police officers.

Dick said he would investigate the case himself. He wanted me to stand by and coordinate with him if he asked for information we may have in our headquarters office and UFO sighting reports room he could possibly use.

The case would be a stunner that took place right there in our backyard. During the late evening and early morning hours of July 31 and August 1, 1966, scores of witnesses—including a physicist, a radar operator from Andrews Air Force Base, and numerous policemen—reported seeing multi-colored UFOs that emitted beams of light, traveled at fantastic speeds in the sky, and closely approached the ground in and around Washington, D.C. This series of reports turned out to be one of the most significant round of concentrated sightings during my tenure at NICAP. It would also be a prime example of a case Dick Hall had me study as a way of continuing my lessons in the proper way to conduct a sighting report investigation.

In his report to our Connecticut Avenue headquarters, Dr. Vasil Uzunoglu, a Physicist and Microelectronics Consultant with the Aeronautical Radio Research Corporation, Inc. (ARINC), in Annapolis, Maryland, said he saw an unidentified object at 10:55 p.m., July 31, as he was traveling north on the Capital Beltway. It appeared to be at an altitude of about 19,000 feet with red, yellow and green revolving, or scanning, lights and was in sight for about five minutes.

The "Eye-Like Object"

The physicist elaborated:

> *I first observed it when it crossed the Beltway and hovered [about 100 feet over] the roof of [a] house fifty feet away from the Beltway. I saw its arrival [and] noticed some kind of an action underneath it when it first arrived which I cannot clearly identify.... I could clearly see the top of the body, which was a dark, non-shiny material with no sharp edges. The most striking part was the eye-like object off-center to the right with two distinct yellow regions. The upper region was a very bright yellow color, which was prominent in its intensity and the lower portion [was] darker..., but changing intensity in a regular pattern....*
>
> *When I looked back..., the object was moving away toward [the] south at a very high speed [at a] comparatively low elevation.*

Air Force officials also got wind of the Uzunoglu sighting and sent him their own U.S. Air Force Technical Informatio report form so he could provide "as much information as possible concerning the unidentified aerial phenomenon that you have observed." In his report, the physicist said that "the lower part of [the] yellow light" he saw on the UFO "gave me the impression that a scanning process was in progress. First, the eye-like yellow part was directed toward the houses, then it was directed toward the Beltway and towards [the] north. It hovered over the tops of the houses."

Impressive Credentials

In his report to the Air Force, Vasil, 41, also elaborated on his impressive credentials: "I am a physicist and an engineer in semiconductors, microelectronic circuits, and systems. I have published a book entitled *Semiconductor Network Analysis and Design* through the prestigious McGraw-Hill publishing company. He added that he had also published more than thirty articles on these subjects in the last six years.

Dr. James E. McDonald was also impressed by the fellow physicist, his credentials and his sighting. In his call to Uzunoglu at the witness' residence in Baltimore, McDonald said the mathematician's account was "straightforward and unembellished."

"A Strange Object"

One of the most detailed reports during the entire series of sightings that night that were sent to NICAP came from Officer Frank L. Dowling of the Prince Georges County Police Department. At 12:40 a.m., August 1, he received a call from a Mr. Wagner in Lanham, Maryland, who said a strange object was hovering near his home.

Officer Dowling sped to Wagner's home and immediately saw an object with red, green and white pulsating lights hovering over the College Park, Maryland, area, not far from the University of Maryland campus.

The UFO remained stationary in the north-northeastern area of the sky for about fifteen minutes. Then it began moving toward the north. Dowling quickly restarted his patrol car and began chasing it.

"It Went By Like a Shot"

As he pursued the UFO, he said it started moving back and forth and up and down. Very soon after that, the UFO went straight down toward the ground and disappeared behind some trees. Almost immediately afterward, it ascended and sped faster than a jet in an easterly direction. In a state of near panic, Officer Dowling quickly grabbed his steering wheel, swirled his car around on Glendale Road and chased the object at speeds up to ninety miles per hour.

"It went by like a shot," the startled policeman said. "*Whoosh!*... I mean, it was hairy! Scared the hell out of me!"

Dowling added that the object seemed to be over the Powder Mill Road area. He turned left on Soil Conservation Road and continued the chase. The now thoroughly rattled officer called his office for assistance. Officer William L. Smith responded to his colleague's frantic telecon.

Meanwhile, Dowling continued watching the UFO through a pair of binoculars. He saw a shaft of light or something very brilliant come from underneath the craft as it headed behind the trees. Then it reappeared and once more emitted a combined red, white and green beam of light. It was hovering in the sky as both officers left the sighting area.

Toward sunrise later that same morning, Dowling returned to the site and observed four slowly moving multi-colored objects. Suddenly, another UFO sped up from behind a clump of trees. Grabbing his binoculars, he saw solid white light rise "almost straight up.... Then it veered off and kept going up to the right. It went awfully high and sat there until the sun came up."

Officer E.V. Beall, from the Seat Pleasant Police Station, and a U.S. Park Police patrolman also witnessed the UFOs.

Andrews AFB Joins the Act

Meanwhile, Dowling called nearby Andrews Air Force Base (AFB) and later told NICAP he was informed that a jet would be scrambled to investigate the report, but there was no further confirmation of this.

An official from the College Park Post of the Maryland State Police reported to NICAP that, during his own call to Andrews, he was told that a control tower operator at the base had seen a fast-moving light in the sky but was not able to track it on radar. Along with another dispatcher, Sue Crawford, Rupprecht saw what they thought was the same light outside their own station.

An official from the College Park Post of the Maryland State Police reported to NICAP that, during his own call to the AFB, he was told that a control tower operative at the base had seen a fast-moving light in the sky but was not able to track it on radar.

"Hell-Bent for Election"

Later, at 4 a.m., Corporal Lee Carpenter from the Prince Georges County Police Department, said he watched a white light traveling quickly from south-to-north "across the sky, hell-bent for election." Meanwhile, an incredulous Friendship Airport tower operator in Baltimore said they had received what he incredibly called "millions of calls" from individuals seeing strange lights in the sky.

"Well, I don't know if it was millions of calls, but it was a hell of a lot," the tower operator admitted. "I had never experienced anything like that before."

Police stations in Seat Pleasant, Rockville, Takoma Park, Beltsville and Bladensburg, Maryland, monitored many calls about the UFOs. So did police barrack members in Annapolis and Fairfax and Alexandria, Virginia.

"It put goose bumps all down my arms," a Prince Georges County policeman who saw one or more objects with his binoculars, told NICAP.

And State Police officers at the College Park Barracks said they received "quite a few calls" throughout the night about the UFOs. Some witnesses remarked that the objects they saw appeared to be "darting around the sky" while others reported that their sightings were of nocturnal objects that "just hovered."

CHAPTER TEN

2001: A Space Odyssey, the Titusville Humanoid and Beyond

As the calendar pages of 1966 flipped over to the cusp of Summer 1967, many other reports flooded the NICAP coffers. As the new Assistant Director, I was responsible for farming out the good sightings worthy of further action by our investigating subcommittees.

2001: A Space Odyssey

But first... Sometime during the Spring of 1967, I received a call at NICAP headquarters from Dr. Frederick ("Fred") Ordway III. He told me he was working with famed space pioneer Wernher von Braun at NASA's Marshall Space Flight Center. (Later, he would play an important part with the Apollo space-flight teams that would send astronauts to the moon.) Now, he told me, he was the technical advisor with famed director Stanley Kubrick on what was destined to become a ground-breaking film that would redefine Hollywood's conception of science-fiction movies, *2001: A Space Odyssey* (1968). He also said he was a friend of Arthur C. Clarke, whose writing inspired the film. Clarke was also working with both Kubrick and Ordway on the project.

Ordway said that he and Kubrick were familiar with the work and books by Major Keyhoe and quickly asked if I would have lunch with him the following day to discuss his work on the film. I quickly agreed.

Early the next afternoon, we met at a restaurant near the Dupont

Circle headquarters of NICAP. Ordway was impeccably dressed in a sparkling light blue suit as we ordered drinks and lunch.

Fred told me that Kubrick was a stern taskmaster and put everything he had into one of his films. He expected those who worked with him to do the same. Ordway told me that he and his family had moved to near the huge studio in England where Kubrick was filming the movie on a mammoth, elaborate set.

"Every detail of the movie has to be as near to perfect as it can possibly be, " Ordway said, sipping his cocktail.

Fred added that he, Kubrick and Clarke had been interested in UFOs and the possibility that some of the reports may constitute alien beings surveying earth. He added that he and Kubrick had read one or more of Keyhoe's books and would have liked to have met him. I told him that Keyhoe lived in Luray, Virginia, and was not a regular visitor to NICAP headquarters.

Ordway said he and Kubrick wanted to garner some thoughts about how astronauts could survive years-long journeys to other planets or star systems. I answered that my own theory had to do with the possibility of cryonic internment. This was in vogue at the time with experiments in Southern California and elsewhere. In theory, astronauts could be frozen in coffin-like containers and later thawed out and revived when they were nearing a distant planet or star system.

While the successful outcome of cryonic internment had never been perfected then or now, some people had been cryonically frozen, including baseball great Ted Williams. The theory was that those who died of a particular fatal disease could later be revived and survive once a cure for that disease could be found. I knew that Dr. Leslie Kaeburn, a scientific member of NICAP's Los Angeles Subcommittee, had done some research on the subject. I referred Ordway to him.

Following further discussion, Fred Ordway thanked me and left. I later learned that he had seen Dr. Kaeburn and the cryonic internment of astronauts was depicted in the early scenes of the film, which was released in April 1968.

The work Kubrick, Clarke and Ordway did on providing as accurate as possible details in the film placed *2001: A Space Odyssey* far above most other sci-fi films of that or any other era and many still consider it to be the best such film of all time. The cinematic epic made its debut in April 1968. Exactly fifty years later, in April 2018, it once more came to the foreground and is still considered to be the king of science fiction movies. I was proud to have played a small part in its birth.

An Animal Reaction in Minnesota

Not long after my visit with Fred Ordway, a report from a NICAP investigator that more than a decade later reminded me of the huge UFO that amazed witnesses at the Devil's Tower in the Steven Spielberg blockbuster *Close Encounters of the Third Kind* (1977) was dropped into my mailbox. It was around 11:50 p.m., on Thursday, June 15, 1967. A farmer—who asked to be assured of complete anonymity—in Herman, Minnesota, was awakened by the high-pitched barking and whining noises of his coon dog. *Was the dog hurt or bitten by some animal?* he wondered.

The witness—who was also employed by a local railroad—quickly got partially dressed, grabbed his loaded 30-30 Remington rifle, and cautiously but quickly walked downstairs. He thought for a moment to awaken his wife, but didn't since she "had been very ill for the past five months."

"I Don't Believe It!"

The witness carefully opened his back door and was immediately confronted by his frightened dog, "who was now whimpering softly and hugging the ground as he walked, half crawling, to his master." Both the farmer and dog walked casually and slowly toward the southwest corner of the barn. Then the shocked witness came to an abrupt halt.

"I don't believe it! *I don't believe it!*" he exclaimed over and over as he was transfixed by what he saw. Around the corner of the barn he saw an object that "appeared solid as a rock." It was "completely round, showing mostly the bottom portion, which had a row of pulsating in-and-out red lights giving off a tremendous red glow, bathing the whole back area… red…." On top of the uninvited visitor, there was what looked like "a dome on top of a dome."

"The top portion of the dome was a brilliant… white soft light which stood off from the red underneath area, [which was] bathed in red," the NICAP investigator added.

The farmer and his dog stood by the corner of the barn for about five minutes in a transfixed state of mind. He didn't feel threatened, only amazed by what he was experiencing.

Previously, the farmer had considered UFO reports to be "hogwash," but now he wasn't at all sure of that assessment. According to the investigator, the sight of the object just seemed to take everything out of him at the time.

About five minutes after it was first spotted, the UFO suddenly shot straight up into the air and disappeared. The farmer, stumbling at first, ran to his back porch while trying to be calm and not wanting to awaken his wife. As he settled down on the porch, the coon dog appeared happy and crawled up near his master.

"I had tears in my eyes," the farmer said. "It was so beautiful. I didn't feel it was going to harm me or my dog."

Loud UFO Causes Dogs to Bark

Meanwhile, the sighting reports continued to flood into NICAP headquarters. On the first day of Summer, June 21, 1967, Shirley M. Moody, a cashier at the Miller & Rhoads Department Store in Mechanicsville, Virginia, was awakened with a headache. She got out of bed at 2:45 a.m. and walked into the kitchen to take some aspirins.

While she was in the kitchen, Shirley noticed a bright light outside with a loud noise that sounded like the roaring of a rocket or a jet exhaust. She quickly moved to her screen door and saw a large light ascending from the woods approximately 1,000 feet from her home. The UFO moved slowly at first. Then, as it moved faster up, its roaring increased.

Mrs. Moody said the object's lights were a brilliant bluish-white color with other lights at the rounded bottom. The object also had a dome on the top. She said the aerial craft was about the length of two houses.

Shirley added that the noise from the UFO "hurt my ears and was very high pitched. The neighborhood dogs barked wildly, which many of the neighbors heard...." She added that the noise from the object was "as frightening as the sight of it. When last seen, [it] was as big or bigger than the moon."

Shortly after the encounter, Shirley's husband examined the nearby woods and spotted several trees that were bent over and others that appeared to be broken off at the top.

The Titusville Humanoid

During this wave of sighting reports, I found that one of the most interesting and compelling cases came from Clark C. McClelland, Co-Chairman of NICAP's Florida Subcommittee Unit 3 in Indian River City. It added to our growing collection of reliable witnesses who were having encounters with humanoid-like flying saucer occupants.

It was 9:15 p.m. on July 20, 1967. Mrs. Elizabeth L. Douglas, 49, was returning to her home in Titusville, Florida, after retrieving an article from her automobile parked in front of her property. She inadvertently tripped over part of the wide fence that had been scattered on the grass by a neighborhood boy who had mowed her lawn. While she was still lying prone on the grass, she reached up to grasp an overhanging branch of a tree to assist in regaining her footing.

Elizabeth glanced beyond the tree to the north and was startled to view an oddly-designed craft with five square windows or portholes that seemed to be floating very slowly and soundlessly from north-to-south. The UFO was about 200 feet away and was sixty-to-seventy feet high. Mrs. Douglas said the ship was an estimated fifty-to-sixty feet long with a bell-shaped exterior design. She added that the width of the object was "bigger than the house across the street."

"A Strange and Frightening Form"

As the UFO passed slowly over the street opposite the Douglas home, a strange and frightening form made an appearance through the fourth window.

"There were [also] other forms moving about, but I did not notice this as much as the form [that was] close to the window," Elizabeth said in her report to NICAP. "I could not tell if this form was trying to look out of the window or if he was doing something else. But I did notice that [he] looked very lean and the arms were very long.... I called my daughter [outside] to see the object."

Mrs. Douglas told McClelland that "the humanoid form appeared to be leaning forward with one or both hands pressing against the transparent glass-like window. She said it may have been looking out of the craft, observing the surrounding... terrain."

"The Creature Had Rubbery Arms"

Now, in a thoroughly frightened state, Elizabeth saw that "the creature had rubbery arms that seemed to be longer than those normally observed on mature men or women. The torso was slim and showed no mid-section or chest structure. The head of the entity was egg-shaped and no facial features such as eyes, nose, mouth or ears were visually evident." There were also "shadowy movements" that were noticed in "other window areas, indicating... that other life forms were engaged in motion somewhere inside... the strange craft."

Mrs. Douglas said she saw the entity for an estimated two minutes. She added that not all of the five windows glowed evenly from the intense neon white lights. The window farthest south was almost dark. Windows three and four were much brighter.

The craft itself appeared to be a dull finished metal with the base and top section being of a darker pigment than the center portion. The witness said "the light of the four brighter windows could be seen reflecting on the base section… of the bell-shaped craft."

"What is That?"

By this time, Elizabeth's daughter, Ingrid, 20, had arrived outside. She had also called to her son, Steven, 15, but he was inside watching television and did not respond. After quickly joining her mother, Ingrid looked up and saw the grayish UFO.

"What is *that*?" she asked, startled.

Her mother, however, was too frightened to reply. Ingrid said she observed the object for about five minutes. Elizabeth quickly scurried back into the house and called the Titusville Police Department. She reported the UFO's direction, approximate speed and current location. She was told that an officer would be sent to investigate.

Meanwhile, Steven was still watching television when he suddenly noticed horizontal wave lines passing through the picture tube. The location of the sighting was about twenty-five miles from the Kennedy Space Center located east of Titusville.

Both Elizabeth and Ingrid Douglas were subjected to numerous questions during several interview sessions. McClelland and other members of the NICAP Subcommittee were impressed.

"It is the opinion of this investigative unit that, due to the sincerity of each witness, this incident should be considered factual as far as personal observation and understanding of the unidentified object [are] concerned by those involved," McClellan added in his report. "There has been no concrete evidence found to prove this case to be a perpetrated hoax."

The Road-Pacing Finale

About three weeks after the Titusville Humanoid case, on the evening of August 10, Richard Malone (not his real name) and his son had a strange, frightening encounter near Harrisburg, Pennsylvania. They were heading home on Strites Road after spending a couple of hours hunting groundhogs. The boy glanced at his watch and saw that it was 9:40 p.m. as they approached Chambershill Road. The son looked over into a field and faced his dad with a puzzled look.

"When did they put a street light in that field, Dad?"

"Damned If I Know…"

"I hadn't heard that they had, son" Richard replied. "Damned if I know what it is."

Malone looked out into the field. At about one-half mile away, he saw a bright white light on an object hovering about 125 feet off the ground. At first Richard thought it may have been a helicopter, but the thing, whatever it was, just sat there.

Dad slowed down to make the right-turn onto Chambershill Road. He looked around and saw that the UFO was pacing them just twenty-five or so feet above the trees near Hershey Road. Malone then spotted two lights at either end of the object. *It couldn't be a conventional aircraft,* he reasoned to himself. *Then, what the hell is it?*

The UFO continued to pace the Malones as they approached Hershey Road. When Richard came to Swatara Creek Bridge, however, "the object crossed over [the] highway and was now paralleling the other side of Hershey Highway." Malone gently applied the brakes and slowed down to about twenty miles-per-hour. The object was now about seventy-five feet above the ground.

The Road-Sky Pacing Continues

According to a Pennsylvania Subcommittee member's report, Malone "now saw a red light on [the] side of [the] craft in addition to white lights on either end...." Meanwhile, the UFO continued gliding along with the car down Hershey Highway until they had nearly arrived at Hummelstown. Then—two blocks on the far side of what the locals called the Hob Nob—the aerial craft stopped and hovered directly over and close to a power line.

Richard again floored the brakes with his foot. He pulled the car to the side of the road and parked. Inside, his son was so shaken by the event that he was crying and trembling.

Diamond in the Sky

Again, the witnesses looked up into the sky and saw the object prominently displayed there. It had a diamond shape and looked to be about seventy-five feet long. The UFO was huge and there was a white light on the front point and a white light on the rear point.

The local NICAP investigator takes up the narrative:

> *There was a red light on the right side point and a blue-green light on the left.... There appeared to be a girder-type shape through the middle [that was] approximately fifteen feet wide. [Malone] saw a clear outline of [the] craft.... It was definitely diamond-shaped.... Then Richard noticed another car pulling up and stopping a short distance from him.*

As he got out of the car, the object started to move and made a 180-degree turn and headed in the direction of Harrisburg. He lost sight of it about thirty seconds later. A few minutes after that, he saw what appeared to be... "a red sky rocket in [the] vicinity of [the] power generating station, but [he] didn't know if it had anything to do with [the] UFO."

Both Richard and his son "were still both very shaken" when they arrived home.

The investigator's report adds the finale to the incident:

In talking with Mr. Malone, we found him to be a very intelligent and rational person, not at all inclined to hallucinations. He told us that he had always been skeptical of... UFOs, but he said that he stood there and witnessed this craft on a clear night with perfect visibility... and he knew what he saw. It was... definitely not an aircraft, but it was there, and it was solid.... He could make out every detail. It had to be intelligently controlled to pace them and turn as it did.

An Encounter Down Under

The virtual flood of UFO reports from around the world continued to inundate NICAP headquarters. No question about it... Nineteen sixty-seven was a big year for global encounters with unknown flying objects. I was beginning to wonder if we were going to make direct contact with the occupants of these aerial craft by the year's end.

At first it was a lonely drive for Alexander Roy Spargo, 37, at about 9:35 p.m. on Monday, October 30, 1967. Spargo was a Shearing Contractor for the Great Southern Shearing Company in Cannington, South Western District, Australia.

The professional sheepshearer was driving his 1967 Valiant Utility toward Boyup Brook from Kojonup at about sixty-five miles per hour. His headlights were on high beam and illuminated the road in front of him.

At a distance he estimated to be ten miles from Myanup, his automobile suddenly came to a complete stop. Both the motor and headlights went out. Alexander repeatedly tried the ignition, but the van wouldn't move. Looking up, he saw what he described as "a tube of light" about two feet in diameter descend close to his windscreen. Johnson looked up the tube and could not see anything, but felt he was being observed.

UFO "Shaped Like a Football"

The object that emitted the tube was "shaped like a football." It had an irredescent blue color with a pulsating glow. The tube appeared to be about thirty feet in diameter.

The shearer said he sat back in a state of bewilderment while he watched the object and the light tube for an estimated five minutes. He admitted he was greatly surprised and, for a while, could not believe his own eyes.

Am I watching an alien craft from another planet or solar system? he wondered. He didn't know, but he was beginning to think he was.

Suddenly, the UFO moved off very quickly and disappeared in a flash. After the object could no longer be seen, the witnesses' van motor began running again. The lights came on and he found that, strangely, he was still traveling at sixty-five miles per hour. He had not stopped the vehicle himself. The only answer was that the UFO had maintained control of his movements and that of his Valiant. He could hardly believe what was happening.

Spargo quickly headed toward Boyup Brook, where he called the police station and reported his roadside encounter.

UFO Joins Thanksgiving Football Game

Less than a month later and half-a-world away, the players and fans at a football game in Florida were rudely interrupted by a UFO. On Thanksgiving evening, November 23, at the Clearwater High School Stadium, William Curry, the Sports Editor at *The Clearwater Sun*, sat in the open grandstand seat next to Ed Haver, his Assistant at the *Sun*; Earl Emmons from the Largo *Sentinel*; and Bill Robinson from *The St. Petersburg Independent*. The Largo football team was playing the Clearwater boys.

In his report to NICAP, Curry provided a detailed account:

> *I was seated in the west grandstand with a group of other sportswriters. At first my attention was attracted to a bright yellow light, far to [the] south, high in [the] sky, approaching slowly. The yellow light*

came up over the south goal posts, moving slowly and steadily due north.... It looked unusual and, as it approached us, we all grew very curious.

During the many minutes it took to pass slowly over the eastern part of the city..., the yellow light grew huge and brighter. While it was still south of our stadium, I raised my powerful binoculars and focused my zoom lens. Immediately, the formless yellow light resolved itself into a sharply defined, rectangular, upright, solid structure resembling a giant box kite.

The source of the yellow light was inside the bottom square, which was... of an opaque material. Although directed downward, the light was so strong that it illuminated the structure above it by natural diffusion. I distinctly saw the gleaming or glinting of four metallic rods holding the unlighted upper square aloft in a vertical position, exactly like a big box kite of brightly reflecting metal rods instead of the usual wooden slats.

The UFO's proportions were... not tilted or swaying.... My impression was—and I am a trained observer with Navy experience—that the UFO was a very large construction, immensely large.... It must have been flying at a great altitude, and its yellow light—to appear so big and bright—must have been enormous....

The sportswriters and many of the fans in the stadium saw the nocturnal visitor for about fifteen minutes before it disappeared from sight. Curry was certain it was a true unidentified flying object, not a box kite. Its movements were too structured for that. It also appeared to be intelligently controlled.

Marshall Cleaver and Robert Spencer Carr, of NICAP's Florida Subcommittee, sent us the report.

CHAPTER ELEVEN

The Carmichael and Becar Encounters

Soon after Richard Hall left NICAP in mid-1967 for a more lucrative position with a publishing firm in Washington, D.C., I took his place as Assistant Director. The sightings—some containing decades-earlier encounters with unknown aerial objects—continued to make their way into our Dupont Circle office.

The first of two older reports that particularly interested me came from Melvin Carmichael in Klamath Falls, Oregon. At 4:50 a.m. in May 1954, he was the fireman on a Southern Pacific freight train on its way to Alturas, California, from Klamath Falls. In the engine cab with Melvin were S.P. Oliver, the Engineer, Glenn Head, the Lead Brakeman, and another brakeman.

Carmichael tells the story:

As we were descending quite a long grade near Canby, California, two large lights in the sky ahead of us caught my attention. They were stationery. Both appeared to be shaped like fat cigars, only slightly tapered at the ends.... They appeared to be about two miles ahead of us, about 1,200 feet above the ground.

The larger of the two lights [were] about the same length as the diameter of a full moon. [The] other light was approximately half that size.

[The] lights were white with a row of seven orange-colored "windows" across the bottom, with another row of three or four above them.

I had been watching them for a couple of minutes, trying to puzzle out what it was I was looking at, when the engineer said: "By God, they're flying saucers!".... I learned then that both he and the head brakeman had been watching them, too.

About that time, both objects made a sidewise leap in space, to a point about 20 miles to the left of their original location. The larger one made the move first, following in a split second by the smaller. The move was... faster than my eyes could follow.... They stayed in this new location only a few seconds..., then "jumped" back to their original location.

All the time we were watching them, our train was moving toward them. They continued to hang there in space as our train went underneath them. I looked back a couple of times and they were still there. Then a curve in the railroad [track] and a large hill east of Canby cut them off from my view.

Carmichael said the UFOs remained visible for about five minutes. He added that, after they reached Alturas, "I learned that one of the three trainmen in the caboose had also observed these lights, but his vision was sometimes obscured by the long string of freight cars in front of him."

On August 20, 1954 (about three months after the train crew in California had their encounter with unknown lights in the sky while they were riding the rails from Oregon to California), Noel J. Becar was an Installation Supervisor with the Western Electric Company in Burlingame, California. He left his job at 4:45 p.m. and headed south toward his home in San Mateo.

"About half an hour later, at around 5:15 p.m., I was traveling down a heavy grade which terminated at the town of Cottonwood, which... was about a half-mile away," Becar related in his report to NICAP.

The supervisor continued his detailed account:

> *Suddenly I caught a flash from the sky in the left side of my left eye. Looking up with the expectation of seeing one of the DC-3's or other airliners being used in the run north at that time, I was astounded to see two U.F.O.'s hovering in a position which looked like they were in the middle of a 45-degree bank to their right, but were actually not in motion. The two objects were fairly close to each other, appearing to be about 80 to 100 feet apart and as near as I could judge from my experience in seeing many, many aircraft over a period of some 36 years..., since 1919, when I first became interested in building and flying aircraft, [it] appeared to be... about the same size as a DC-3.*
>
> *I immediately came to a screeching stop, pulling off the side of the road and got out of the car so... I would be able to view the U.F.O.'s directly without looking through the side window or windshield of the car. As I had been intently interested in the reports of U.F.O.'s..., I had made up my mind that, if I was every lucky enough to actually see one, I would make it my business to take down all of the pertinent facts as soon as possible after the sighting.*
>
> *I also decided in advance to try and time any maneuvers that might be performed such as how long it took [the objects] to disappear from view when they left.... The first thing I did on [leaving] the car was to consult my wrist-watch... in order to time how long they held this hovering position. I estimated about 8 to 10 seconds.... Exactly one minute and 50 seconds later, they "took-off" directly away from me toward the Southwest.... They accelerated at a tremendous rate, becoming smaller and smaller until they disappeared... in exactly 8 seconds.*

The Filling Station Report

Becar jumped back into his car and located a filling station in nearby Cottonwood, "where I wrote down all that had transpired, noting the wind, cloud conditions, temperature, etc...." He mentioned the sighting to the attendant "with the idea that maybe he had noticed them a comparatively short distance north of the station."

What kind of a nut are you? the attendant seemed to ask with his facial expression.

Noel immediately became hesitant about telling many others about his UFO encounter. He would tell his wife, but decided not to relate his experience to his friends because "I didn't know how the people in my work organization might react to this and felt that it might become detrimental to any advancement I might receive."

Noel added that his son, Noel, Jr., dropped by his home to tell his father that he had joined NICAP and the organization would probably be interested in his father's sighting report. Noel said his son was employed with General Electric Company and was well versed with satellite communications for the U.S. Air Force as a civilian employee in the capacity of a project engineer or supervisor.

Keyhoe and Lucky Lindy

Becar also told us at NICAP that, since his retirement on August 1, 1966, "I have been appointed a Regional Representative of the Experimental Aircraft Association [EAA]...." He said that his belief that flying saucers are a real phenomenon "was no doubt influenced partly by the fact that I met Major Keyhoe during the U.S. tour of 'Lindy' in 1927, at which time a friend of mine and myself were assigned as military escorts and helpers during his stay at the Hotel Bellvue (I believe) in San Francisco. My feeling at that time was that Major Keyhoe was a very sincere individual, which in turn gave me confidence in him at the time that he started his crusade against the Air [Force] 'cover-up.'"

When Noel retired following a forty-year stint with Western Electric in early 1967, he said would devote the majority of his time to helping other aircraft builders and to the completion of his own amphibian project. He had been a frequent contributor of technical articles to *Sport Aviation* magazine and was still in demand as a lecturer on such esoteric subjects as "Selecting a Suitable Wing Section," "Selecting Wing Area, Platform and Thickness," and "Sequence of Design."

A Trophy For "Literary Achievements"

In 1963, the Greater Milwaukee, Wisconsin Chapter 18 of the EAA gave Becar a trophy "for his literary achievements in the form of many articles on the design and construction of amateur-built aircraft." This was followed in 1965 by the EAA Dr. August Raspel Memorial Award "for outstanding contributions to the advancement of light aircraft."

As a teenager, Noel had no idea he would eventually become an aeronautical engineer. Back then he was interested in building radios and was one of the first amateurs to build a set in San Jose. Both aviation and radio were still in their pioneering days. After radio became a worldwide commercial enterprise following World War I, Noel lost interest in it. Then he built his first airplane, a glider that he designed himself. In 1919, he joined the 440th Observation Squadron, which became "the first reserve unit boasting actual flying equipment after the war."

"In those days, we had equipment, but no funds for gasoline," Noel related in a *Sports Aviation* article. "So we held dances in the ballrooms of San Francisco's hotels and raised money enough to fly on the weekends from Crissy Field in the Presidio."

In 1923, he began building another glider, but before he could finish, he was hired by Western Electric as a installer of telephone equipment in the San Francisco area. With other colleagues, he constructed several airplanes. The first plane had a small twenty-nine horsepower engine and the takeoff speed equaled its cruising speed of 55 mph. It was flown out of a patch of land that is now a part of the Oakland International Airport.

A Return to Gliders

It was during the mid-1920s that Noel's interest returned to gliders. With his friend, George Wilbur, he built a glider that boasted a fifty-five foot wing span. It carried two people... the pilot in the cockpit and the passenger standing astride the fuselage with his feet on the landing gear axle and his hands holding onto the pilot's shoulders.

Becar was still a flyer in the reserves. Then he transferred to the 381st Service Squadron. As a member of that group, he served as the escort of Colonel Charles Lindbergh in 1927 following Lucky Lindy's historic flight from New York to Paris. Major Donald E. Keyhoe managed and led the historic Lindbergh tour across America (see Chapter Twenty). Noel's friend, George Wilbur, was the other escort for Lindbergh and their duties included opening the hero's fan mail, which came by the sack-full to his hotel room.

From Wings to Dawn Patrol

The Lindbergh tour, under Keyhoe's supervision, was instrumental in having Americans become aviation conscious. The number of air mail routes increased, airlines were formed, and Hollywood made *Wings* (1927) with Clara Bow, Charles ("Buddy") Rogers, Richard Arlen and Gary Cooper in his first starring screen role; *Hell's Angels* (1930), featuring Jean Harlow, Ben Lyon, and James Hall, directed by legendary aviation pioneer Howard Hughes; and *Dawn Patrol* (1938), starring Errol Flynn, Basil Rathbone, David Niven and Barry Fitzgerald.

Many people had become interested in building homebuilt airplanes and gliders. Lindy had fulfilled his promise to instill in millions of Americans a lasting love and respect for aviation.

Buzzing the Golden Gate

Once again, Noel began building airplanes. They were of his own design and the parts were made, begged or borrowed and then assembled in the driveway of his home. Along with Leroy Peters, a friend and colleague, he built a small biplane in 1935 that could fly at 150 miles-per-hour and participate in cross-country flights. The Golden Gate Bridge in San Francisco was then under construction and one of Noel's favorite hops was to inspect it as it was being built. Along the way, he was able to terrify more than one of the bridge's workers as he buzzed close to it.

Becar's regular job was also keeping him very busy. He was instrumental in helping Western Electric "keep up with the population growth in and around Los Angeles, Hollywood and San Bernardino." During the early 1940s, he helped install the long-distance telephone systems through Oregon. In 1943, he traveled north to Alaska and contributed to the installation of the telephone line along the Alaska (then Alcan) Highway from Dawson Creek in British Columbia to Whitehorse in the Yukon. Following a brief stint as an operator for Pacific Telephone, he returned to the Yukon for the completion of the line between Whitehorse and Fairbanks. While he worked on the Alcan job, he "made a motion picture record of the project," which became embedded in the company's official records. Following World War II, Noel did not return to private aviation. It was a full decade before what he called "the old itch" returned sometime after he joined the EAA.

The Pollywog Project

At the time I received his UFO report, Noel and Marion, his wife, lived in San Mateo, where their son and daughter provided them with eleven grandchildren. He intended to continue working on his amphibian project, which was a single-place, twin-engine pusher designated Pollywog BX-8B. A pair of forty horsepower Continental engines were modified and equipped with starters, but Noel made a few changes and planned to use the Nelson H-63C engines. He intended to do most of the work on the professional machine tools which crowded his garage workshop.

Neil said that, "when the amphibian is completed," he hopes "to establish at least six new international records for this type of aircraft.

One will be for altitude, one for flight, and four will be speed records.... Because of people like Noel Becar with his selfless sharing of knowledge with almost everyone who needs it, aviation will continue to make progress on the long road ahead."

Major Keyhoe told me he had the highest regard for Becar and remembered meeting him during the Lindbergh nationwide tour in 1927.

CHAPTER TWELVE

"Liar! Liar! Pants on Fire!" The University of Colorado UFO Project

For a while, at least, things for us at NICAP seemed to be moving along in a positive, if not brilliantly shining, light. Dr. James ("Jim") E. McDonald—the Senior Physicist at the University of Arizona's Institute of Atmospheric Physics in Tucson—had quickly become a NICAP backer. He also became close friends with the author and Richard H. ("Dick") Hall, then the NICAP Assistant Director.

Also, early in November 1967 (a few months after Richard Hall left NICAP and I became the Assistant Director), the previously announced Scientific Study of Unidentified Flying Objects at the University of Colorado in Boulder had begun its preliminary operations. At first glance, it looked promising. The project would be headed by Dr. Edward U. Condon, a noted physicist and former director of the Bureau of Standards. We were told that the project wanted reports from us and that Condon and his team would conduct an independent probe exclusive of any Air Force interference to the contrary.

"Sources at the university have assured NICAP that no stones will be left unturned in regard to obtaining all significant information from the Air Force," Keyhoe told his NICAP members. "The cases listed as 'explained' by the Air Force will be spot-checked where there is any reason to suspect the explanations are not valid. The group will by no means rely solely on Air Force reports and has expressed a desire to examine the best cases NICAP can provide."

The Colorado Investigators

At the time, there was really no known reason for the indomitable Major or the rest of us at NICAP headquarters on the fourth floor high above Dupont Circle in Washington, D.C., to suspect that the new official Congressionally-mandated study would be anything but objective. Besides Condon, a highly respected physicist, the official investigators included four more seemingly well-qualified Colorado University instructors: David R. Saunders, Professor of Psychology; Robert Low, Assistant Dean of the Graduate School; Stuart W. Cook, Chairman of the Department of Psychology; and William A. Scott, Professor of Psychology. The other project members were Franklin Roach, the Acting Director of the Aeronomy Laboratories at the National Bureau of Standards; Michael Wertheimer, a psychologist specializing in perception; and Drs. William Blumen, a meteorologist, and Joseph Rush, a physicist. Through our later admittedly rose-colored glasses, it looked to be a good, objective start to our ongoing effort for a scientific study of UFOs.

"If this project is carried out as an independent probe, as the Air Force has stated it will be, this could emerge as the most important development since the first official UFO reports in World War II," the unusually optimistic Keyhoe was quick to announce to his NICAP members.

It was a start. Maybe. Perhaps. Could it just be what we at NICAP were hoping for? In one of his infrequent visits to NICAP headquarters, Major Keyhoe called a meeting with staff members.

Is It "the Real Thing?"

"Do you really think this may be the real thing?' I asked Keyhoe. "We could really look bamboozled and downright silly if it isn't."

"Dr. Condon has assured us that everything will be on the up-and-up," Don answered. "Other people that matter also seem to think so. We've got to give it a try."

"I agree," Dick Hall piped in. "But Gordon has a point."

We were quickly put to work copying and sending boxes of sighting reports to Colorado. Dick even made two trips there in an effort to keep project members on an objective course of action.

Then—with our six-shooters fully loaded—we began our trip along the road to a high noon showdown in Colorado....

At the beginning of the endeavor, Condon was quick to thank NICAP for its generous contribution of many reliable UFO reports to the project. But it wasn't long before doubts began to creep in. Even a few of the project scientists, especially Dave Saunders, began to be concerned that Condon's initial vow to conduct an unbiased scientific investigation may not be forthcoming. Slowly but surely, Saunders and one or two other project scientists began pulling away from the effort. They even joined with Keyhoe, Jim McDonald and those involved at NICAP, in an attempt to "save" the project from crashing in a non-objective shoot-down.

Early on, it was Condon who was quoted by a newspaper reporter at a talk in New York as saying "the government ought to get out of the UFO business." This was followed by other negative remarks which made it sound as if the project director was pre-judging the subject.

From his home in Luray, Virginia, Keyhoe loaded his pistols, strapped on his gunbelt, and was ready for the showdown. The NICAP Director fired off a letter to Condon demanding an explanation. The project director replied that the newspaper story that had indicated he was conducting a less-than-objective investigation had taken his remarks out of context and made "it sound like I really have my mind made up, but am only pretending otherwise and this is certainly not the case."

It was still a bit too early, however, to shout: *Liar! Liar! Pants on fire!* That would come later.

UFOs and Their Day in Court

"Although we retain some reservations about the impression of Dr. Condon's attitudes conveyed through some press accounts, we find no reason to go along with the skeptics who interpret the project merely as the latest gambit in an Air Force propaganda campaign," Keyhoe told NICAP members. "Having met most of the scientists involved, we are generally satisfied with their fair-mindedness and their thorough plans. They were unwilling to undertake the assignment at the outset until guaranteed total independence from the Air Force and [the] freedom to investigate at will and to say what they please.... All appear quite willing to give UFOs their day in court."

Meanwhile, Dr. Hynek was continuing to slowly pull out the final nails in the umbilical cord still tying him to the negative Air Force UFO stance. It was a definite turnabout from his then famous, or infamous, "marsh gas" explanation for the March 1966 Dexter-Hillsdale, Michigan, UFO sightings, that had garnered worldwide coverage and had "caused unprecedented press and public repercussions."

"A Scientific Problem"

With his protruding pipe intact, the Dearborn astronomer told an estimated one thousand attendees at NASA's 1967 Scientific Colloquim in Greenbelt, Maryland, that UFOs are, indeed, a scientific problem that should be studied and taken seriously by the scientific community. Keyhoe was quick to tell his members that, during the first years of official interest in the sighting reports, Condon's "impression was that the reports would soon die out, but continued reports have convinced him that a phenomenon thus far defying a natural explanation does exist."

Allen Hynek had spent nineteen years as the official Air Force spokesman. Now, was he reversing his stance? It was hard to believe, but there were subtle signs that the astronomer was beginning to feel that he was betraying his objectivity as a scientist and may be ready to do a 360. He admitted that there was a clear enough signal in the so-called signal-to-noise ratio from reliable witness reports to warrant a serious scientific investigation. But he apparently still wasn't quite ready to accept the possibility of an extraterrestrial explanation for some of the sightings. Hynek did, however, point out that, at the beginning of the 19th Century, scientists had adamantly refused to accept the existence of meteorites.

"I would rather believe that two Yankee professors are liars than to believe that stones fall from the skies!" he quoted Thomas Jefferson as saying.

A "Perfect Case?"

In January 1968, Hynek took an even bigger leap toward a positive attitude on reliable UFO cases during an interview with a reporter from the *Richmond News-Leader* in the Virginia capitol. He said he had been working on what he called a "perfect case" involving at least one photograph and was close to confirming it. He indicated he may release it for public scrutiny.

The Northwestern astronomer also confessed to the reporter his former skepticism about UFOs.

"At first, without any question at all, I thought it was stuff and nonsense," he remarked. "But not any more.... My position [has changed] to taking the problem seriously.... We haven't given UFOs a good look.... The Air Force doesn't even have a cross-indexing system. All of this UFO material should go into electronic computers and then correlation studies should be done on the sightings."

On January 9, only days before his visit to Virginia, Hynek told a student audience at Lycoming College in Pennsylvania that the United Nations should create a system through which "countries could compare and coordinate their UFO investigations and profit from each other's discoveries."

Keyhoe Praises Hynek

Keyhoe was impressed and was quick to praise his former adversary.

"Some may still blame him for the role he played in helping the Air Force debunk the UFO reports," the indomitable Major wrote in *The U.F.O. Investigator*. "But far more important is his ability to change after years of skepticism and... official pressure. He did not, like some others, keep a closed mind.... Hynek has emerged as a man of stature. If he continues on this road, he will be hailed as a courageous fighter for the truth."

Meanwhile, Keyhoe had decided to pull the plug on supplying any further UFO reports to the Colorado Project despite earlier letters from both Condon and Project Coordinator Robert Low urging him to continue the flow of sighting reports and other related information.

Dr. Condon was obviously getting "feelers" that NICAP was not happy with the way the project was handling the huge amount of information we were sending them. On December 1, 1967, he wrote a letter to Keyhoe, urging that "we continue cooperation with the project."

"We deeply appreciate the cooperation which has been given to our own scientific study of UFOs from both the central office and field groups of NICAP," he said in a sugarcoated manner. "It is my earnest wish that we can continue to work in full cooperation with NICAP because the help that you have given us so far has been of great importance."

Only one week later, Robert Low opened the entire sugar box and poured it on.

"NICAP's assistance has been invaluable....," he gushed. "Your files, because of the high value of [the] field investigations NICAP has conducted, are of very good quality. Our working relationship with the headquarters office and NICAP members in the field [has] been... excellent, and they have provided valuable support to our research effort. It would be a great pity if they were terminated."

NICAP Breaks With Colorado

Obviously, both Condon and Low had gotten the word that NICAP was unhappy over the direction the project was going and appeared almost desperate to maintain what was their main single source of sighting report information. But Keyhoe wasn't buying it and soon entirely cut off the flow of UFO sighting reports to the university team after seventeen months of cooperation.

On April 30, 1968—in both a press release to NICAP members and the general public and a letter to President Lyndon B. Johnson—the indomitable Major made it official. He gave the following main reasons for the break:

- Dr. Condon "has never made a field investigation of a UFO sighting [and has] not interviewed responsible witnesses, although he is named in the Air Force contract as [the] chief principal investigator."

- Condon "summarily discharged two Project scientists" for revealing the proposal by Project Coordinator Robert Low that they would present to the general public the aura of a "totally objective" stance "when, in fact, it [was] constituted almost entirely of non-believers with an almost zero expectation of finding a saucer."

- Both Condon and Low refused to answer NICAP's questions "as to whether the Project was being conducted in a biased and negative manner." Nor would Condon guarantee that he would examine any of the hundreds of NICAP-investigated UFO reports submitted at the project leader's request.

The "Trick Memo"

It was Robert Low who spilled the beans on what the true direction of the Colorado Project would be in what came to be known as the infamous "Trick Memo."

"Our study would be conducted almost exclusively by nonbelievers who, although they couldn't possibly prove a negative result, could and probably would add an impressive body of evidence that there is no reality to the observations," Low wrote. "The trick would be… to describe the project so that, to the public, it would appear a totally objective study, but, to the scientific community, would present the image of nonbelievers trying their best to be objective but having an almost zero expectation of finding a saucer…." How to do this? Investigate those who report their UFO sightings rather than by a scientific examination of the physical evidence.

To us at NICAP, this memo clearly aimed at discrediting those who reported UFO sightings was despicable. What about all the highly qualified witnesses—scientists, airline and military pilots, radar operators, astronomers, police officers and many others who have reported to NICAP their carefully investigated encounters with unknown objects in the sky and, at times, on the ground?

"If the emphasis were put here," Low remarked, "I think the scientific community would quickly get the message."

It was clear to Keyhoe, Dick Hall, Jim McDonald and myself that the project would indicate to the scientific community that UFO sighting reports were made mainly by individuals lacking the ability to distinguish an unknown object seen in the skies from an easily identified man-made aerial vehicle or a star. This, of course (as I stated above), would completely ignore the well-established fact that a myriad of highly credible individuals in virtually every level of scientific expertise—including at least two U.S. presidents (Ronald Reagan and Jimmy Carter) and Apollo astronauts—have reported their own UFO sightings.

Keyhoe is Hopping Mad!

Condon and his cohorts—including University of Colorado Vice President Thurston Manning—hid their true intentions under the following statement: "The work will be conducted under conditions of strictest objectivity by investigators who, as carefully as can be determined, have no predelictions or preconceived positions on the UFO question. This is essential if the public, the Congress, the Executive and the scientific community are to have confidence in the study...."

Keyhoe was hopping mad! Dr. David Saunders, Manager of the Project Computer Section of the Colorado UFO study, got wind of his intention to withhold any further sighting reports or other cooperation with the project or its top officials. Saunders—who was later discharged by Condon, along with Dr. Norman Levine, for the trumped-up charge of "incompetence"—asked Keyhoe to withhold our knowledge of Low's proposals because he and a few others of the objective project scientists still hoped to persuade Dr. Condon to take a different approach and examine all of the serious evidence.

Saunders and Levine Get "the Sack"

The drama continued. Early in February 1968, Condon and Low learned that Saunders and Levine had given Jim McDonald a copy of Low's nefarious proposals. Condon quickly gave the sack to Saunders and Levine. Even the project's administrative secretary, Mary Louise Armstrong, quickly handed in her own resignation in protest of what she considered to be a totally unfair treatment of two dedicated and objective scientists.

Later in 1968, Saunders quickly laid out his own public views on the study in his well-received book *UFOs? Yes! Where the Condon Committee Went Wrong*. My favorite line from the author is: "Dr. Edward U. Condon had developed a chronic case of psychoceramic itch, and to our growing dismay, he scratched it constantly."

Condon also quickly fired off a threatening letter to McDonald demanding the return of what he called his "stolen" papers. It didn't take our friend more than a split second to refuse the command.

John Fuller—whom I had been a guest with, along with actor Simon Oakland, on the Joe Franklin television show in New York City (see Chapter Eight)—was given the story of Low's proposals. Fuller included the blockbuster proposals in his article about the project in the May 14 issue of the prestigious and widely read *Look Magazine*. A box statement by Keyhoe outlined "NICAP's long cooperation [with the project] and the reasons for the final break."

In his report to the President, Keyhoe asked that Lyndon Baines Johnson himself take up what was becoming a fallen banner:

> *We sincerely regret the failure of the Project, to which so many people looked for a fully impartial evaluation, if not the final answers.... We respectfully suggest... that the void resulting from the Colorado fiasco be filled as soon as possible by creation of a commission of capable scientists, selected by you and completely independent of any military or civilian agencies. We feel sure that scientists of high stature are available, with neither negative nor positive conclusions, but [are] convinced that the UFO situation is serious enough to require total investigation.*

As far as I know, there was no response from President Johnson.

The 1968 Congressional Hearings

As we continued keeping a close watch on the events in Colorado, the year 1968 saw an eventful and promising development in Washington, D.C. On July 29, Congressman J. Edward Roush (D-IN), who was by then a NICAP Board member, became the chairman of more Congressional hearings entitled "Symposium on Unidentified Flying Objects. Hearings Before the Committee on Science and Astronautics, U.S. House of Representatives." Dr. James E. McDonald quickly jumped aboard by helping us scramble for significant reports and discussing the selection of the best panelists to present the positive, unbiased side of the UFO problem.

Keyhoe was ecstatic. This was what he had been aiming for. He put us all to work gathering significant information. Dick Hall contacted his brother, Dr. Robert L. Hall, head of the Department of Sociology at the University of Illinois, who agreed to be one of six panelists. The final pro-UFO panelist was to be Dr. Robert M.L. Baker, Jr., Senior Scientist, Department of Engineering, University of California at Los Angeles.

On the other side of the long table were Dr. J. Allen Hynek; famed astronomer Dr. Carl Sagan, Associate Professor of Astronomy, Department of Astronomy and Center for Radiophysics and Space Research, Cornell University; and Dr. James A. Harder, Associate Professor of Civil Engineering, University of California.

Are UFOs "Rank Nonsense"?

Hynek was the first to speak at the table. He admitted that he initially considered UFOs as "rank nonsense." Now, however, he was climbing the fence to a more positive outlook.

"I have been led to a conclusion quite different….," he began. "The cumulative weight of continued reports from groups of people around the world whose competence and sanity I have no reason to doubt… has led me reluctantly to the conclusion that either there is a scientifically valuable subset of reports in the UFO phenomena or that we have a world society containing people who are articulate, sane and reputable in all matters save UFO reports."

The astronomer indicated that it was now time to stop ignoring the testimony of reliable, honest people who report their sightings.

"By what right can we summarily ignore their testimony and imply that they are deluded or just plain liars?" he asked.

Coming "Out of the Closet"

The astronomer was now clearly coming out of the closet of scientific debunkers. He added that we cannot afford to "overlook something that might be of great potential to the nation.... Can we afford to overlook a potential breakthrough of great significance?"

"Many scientists have expressed to me privately their interest in the problem and their desire to actively pursue UFO research as soon as the stigma is removed," he added.

Hynek also said that a step in the right direction would be a Congressionally-mandated UFO Scientific Board of Inquiry "using all available scientific methods for a complete, serious investigation of reliable reports." Also, the United Nations should consider establishing an international clearinghouse for worldwide UFO reports.

The McDonald Testimony

Congressman Roush next introduced Jim McDonald into the proceedings. The first question came from Congressman Alphonzo Bell (R-CA): "What leads you to believe [that] these phenomena are extraterrestrial?"

"The hypothesis that these are extraterrestrial surveillance [craft] I regard as most likely....," McDonald responded. "They appear to be... machine-like devices.... It is this very large body of impressive witnesses' testimony... that suggests we are dealing with machine-like devices from somewhere else."

Next, the scientist singled out Keyhoe.

"The first open defense of the extraterrestrial hypotheses to be based on any substantial evidence was made by Keyhoe," he remarked. "His subsequent writings, based on far more evidence..., have presented further arguments favoring an extraterrestrial origin...."

McDonald went on to praise the work NICAP had done. He said he had checked on his own many of our compilation of 12,000 or so cases. He told the committee that the NICAP sighting reports "imply a problem that has been… swept under the rug… and now needs very serious and very high-caliber scientific attention."

In his summation, McDonald stepped up to the plate and hit the ball home: "The possibility that the Earth might be under surveillance by some high civilization in command of a technology far beyond ours must not be overlooked."

Carl Sagan and Robert Hall

Carl Sagan was up next. He was no fan of the ET hypothesis.

"There are… people who very much want to believe UFOs are not of intelligent extraterrestrial origins because that would be threatening to our conception of us as being the pinnacle of creation," he remarked. "We would find it very upsetting to discover that we are not, that we are just a sort of two-bit civilization."

Dr. Robert Hall, Dick Hall's brother, was the next panelist at bat. He began by knocking down the belief by some scientists that mass hysteria was the "explanation for solid UFO reports." He said his own investigation of some of the best reports indicated that "there is no resemblance of mass hysteria to the hard-core, well documented cases."

James Harder and Robert Baker

Dr. James A. Harder was the next scientist on the Congressional roster of speakers.

"I think the physical reality of UFOs has been proven beyond a reasonable doubt….," he remarked. "In the UFO phenomena, we have demonstrations of scientific secrets we do not know…. It would be a mistake… to ignore their existence."

Harder "concurred in the need for greatly expanded UFO investigations and scientific studies."

The final panelist—Dr. Robert M.L. Baker, Jr.—said he was involved in projects for NASA, the U.S. Navy and Air Force and had been studying "the UFO problem [for] sixteen years." He also said that some astronomers he knew believed that many of the good, reliable UFO sighting reports may well indicate the reality of "an advanced extraterrestrial civilization." He urged "a long-term investigation program of [the] highest scientific standards."

"The goal of understanding [the impact of an extraterrestrial civilization on earthly endeavors] may be of unprecedented importance to the human race," Dr. Baker concluded.

Congressman Roush is Pleased

Congressman Roush was obviously pleased by the day's proceedings.

"I think that those of you who have sat on this panel today have made perhaps a greater contribution than you realize….," he concluded. "Perhaps we can… cause people to be more responsive and to report what they see. Perhaps we can thereby give an air of respectability to these sightings which will permit people to go ahead without being embarrassed or ashamed of reporting what they have seen."

CHAPTER THIRTEEN

The Bismarck Area Sightings

Several months after the Congressional hearings, a remarkable series of sighting reports came into NICAP headquarters from expert witnesses—including radar flight controllers and pilots—in and around Bismarck, North Dakota. Donald E. Flickinger, Chairman of NICAP's North Dakota Subcommittee Unit #1, quickly assembled his team for an in-depth investigation. The sightings lasted from November 26 to December 6, 1968.

The Flickinger Report

Flickinger managed to quickly hone in on an interview with Alvin Bell, Chief Flight Controller for the Federal Aviation Administration (FAA) in Bismarck. Flickinger's report follows:

> ... An object was sighted at about 5:40 p.m., November 26, by three of the flight controllers in the tower at Bismarck International Airport. The object appeared to be east-northeast of Bismarck [at] a forty-five-degree angle up into the horizon. The object was moving in a northerly direction at a steady speed about that of a piston aircraft and appeared simply as a bright round white light. [Its] brightness [was] compared to that of a bright star....
>
> About this time, the witnesses noticed another object in about the same position... moving to the south. At this point, the tower operators called by radio to an aircraft, which was flying in the area. The

plane was operated by Jack Watts, of Watts Capitol Aviation. Watts radioed back that the objects were visible to him…. They were in a north-northeast direction from him.

The tower operators and the pilot watched the two objects pass in opposite directions. Then—while the one object which was northbound hovered or stopped for a few seconds—the other object suddenly swung upward and reversed course, speeding back into a "side-by-side" formation with the stationary object…. The two [UFOs] then hovered together for about ten seconds, then shot off together at a high rate of speed toward the north or northeast, disappearing in a matter of seconds.

During the first few moments of the sighting…, the tower operators had placed a call to the FAA Flight Control Radar Installation at Malstrom Air Force Base, Great Falls, Montana. The radar facility there reported to the tower operators that they had the objects on radar…, that they were moving erratically at high speeds… and appeared to be about ten miles north-northeast of Bismarck, North Dakota….

Policeman Spots "A Large, Glowing Object"

Flickinger also reported that the next evening, November 27, Joseph Trotier, a policeman in Belcourt, North Dakota, and several other witnesses saw a large, glowing UFO that moved around, then hovered a while, and moved again throughout the Belcourt area. The crack NICAP investigator said he talked with officials at Minot Air Force Base (AFB) who informed him that "one of their F-106's had just landed and reported seeing this object in the Belcourt area…."

The round UFO was "glowing white with 'purple'-colored lights around the top and bottom with a… light that would shine a red-colored beam down toward the ground whenever the object stopped." Trotier was the witness who got closest to the object. He said the UFO was hovering approximately 500 feet above the ground. Trotier aimed his spotlight at it and it "immediately extinguished its lights…." It then disappeared for about five minutes. Then it began moving again. Its lights were on and it flew south toward Minot.

Approximately half-an-hour later, at 7:30, residents of Deering—twenty-five miles northeast of Minot—reported to the FAA tower operators in Minot that there was "a similar object passing towards Minot and just to the east of Deering." Around 8 p.m., two observers—including Will Thompson of Minot—related to Minot City Police "an object they noticed hovering near the Bison Northern States Power Plant at Surrey…."

Newspaper Readers Report

Meanwhile, newspaper readers from the area reported their own sightings. At 5:40 p.m. on November 26, FAA Air Traffic Control employees known as "The Three Jacks"—Jack Wilhelm, Jack Reeves and John ("Jack") Fischer—said they saw two UFOs in the skies for as long as seven minutes. They spotted "bright points of white light" that made sudden maneuvers, then quickly changed direction and disappeared at high rates of speed. One of the objects sped north while the other headed south. Then "the southbound light executed a sudden 180-degree turn, rose and joined the other object." The UFOs hovered in an apparent formation. Then, in a few split seconds, they flew off to the northeast and disappeared.

"We wouldn't have been too concerned about it except for the maneuvers," Wilhelm remarked. "There's nothing that could make a maneuver like the lower one did and at that rate of speed."

Wilhelm added that operators at the Bismarck Air Traffic Control Tower telephoned the Great Falls Air Force Base. Radar operators at the base said they had picked up an "erratic target" about eighty-three nautical miles northeast of Bismarck.

Other witnesses included three cadets from the Civil Air Patrol who told the control tower operators that they had spotted the object while they were between Bismarck and Mandan. They said it flew toward the southeast at a high rate of speed. The cadets also reported that they heard "a sound like they never heard before" from the UFO.

"It was the violent maneuvers, change in course and the apparent cooperation between the two bright objects that made the sighting significant," Wilhelm remarked.

The Gorman Orb

The residents of Bismarck and Fargo, North Dakota, had been no strangers to UFO sightings. They even had a connection with Kenneth Arnold, the private pilot who ushered in the modern era of saucer sightings when he spotted nine discs flying in formation over Mt. Rainier in Washington State in June 1947 while piloting his CallAir A-2 plane from Chehalis to Yakima. Arnold reportedly lived in Minot during the late 1920s and early 1930s. He was a grade and high school student there. North Dakota is where his love of flying developed.

On October 1, 1948, George F. Gorman was piloting an F-51 airplane when he spotted "a small, blinking orb" flying straight at him several times, "breaking away at the last second each time." The UFO was also seen by two other people in another plane flying nearby as well as by two observers in what was then known as the Fargo Air Field Control Tower.

Project Blue Book also got into the act. As usual, it wasn't humming the objective flying saucer tune. Their rather ridiculous explanation was that Gorman had been chasing a weather balloon along with the planet Jupiter. The Air Force didn't bother to explain how a weather balloon or Jupiter could fly directly toward the pilot, then suddenly break away at the last second.

A UFO at Minot AFB

UFOs became regular visitors to North Dakota. On March 2, 1967, a policeman on duty said there were several sightings in Minot. This was followed two days later by witnesses who observed a UFO near the Minot AFB.

The really big sighting near the AFB, however, didn't occur until October 24, 1968, when, for over three hours, a saucer was observed flying over and around the base. It was seen by twenty or more military personnel from ground level. Other witnesses included those in the flight tower and the crew of a B-52 bomber.

What was Blue Book's conclusion? They said the sighting was "a combination of ball lightening and particularly bright stars." Another totally absurd explanation from the boys in blue…

The Abduction

At least one alleged abduction case similar to that of Betty and Barney Hill occurred in the same area and was also investigated by Flickinger and his team. It was August 26, 1975. Sandy Larson, her daughter Jackie, 15, and Terry O'Leary, Jackie's boyfriend, awoke very early that morning.

Sandy, who lived in Fargo, was slated to take a real estate examination in Bismarck around 200 miles away. Sandy, Jackie and Terry headed out early. At 4 a.m., about forty-five miles west of Fargo on Interstate 94, they heard a loud noise similar to a thunderclap. Then they saw "eight-to-ten glowing objects that hovered above a grove of trees" an estimated twenty yards ahead of them. The UFOs apparently had a ring of smoke around them.

One of the objects appeared to be considerably larger than the others and the three witnesses "had the impression that, in some fashion, the other objects had come out of it."

Suddenly, all three of the witnesses reported feeling "an odd sensation, as if they were briefly frozen in time for a second or two." Then the UFOs suddenly disappeared. Terry, who occupied the front seat, suddenly found himself sitting in the back seat with no idea how he got there. All the observers were mystified when they discovered that an hour had mysteriously passed them by.

Later, in December, Sandy and Jackie were submitted to hypnosis by University of Wyoming psychologist and NICAP adviser, Dr. R. Leo Sprinkle. Jackie recalled being outside the car "in a state of paralysis." Sandy said she and Terry had been mysteriously "floated into the UFO..." (However, it was unclear to the investigators as to whether Terry had also been abducted on board the spacecraft.) She related that she was strapped down on what appeared to be an examination table by a six-foot tall robot-like creature with glaring eyes and what appeared to be metal arms. The being "rubbed a clear liquid over her and inserted an instrument up her nose." Other undefined medical procedures were also apparently performed. Then the abductees were returned to their car and all conscious memory of the incident had somehow been erased.

Even today, strange events continue to occur around the Minot-Bismarck area. Residents in nearby Tappen "reported cattle mutilations and possible encounters with aliens." Animal mutilations have been linked by some ufologists and others to UFO encounters.

CHAPTER FOURTEEN

The U.S. Air Force Grudge and Bluebook Reports

In July 1968, NICAP was ready to publish its book on the U.S. Air Force Grudge and Bluebook Reports that we obtained under the Freedom of Information Act. The reports offered some interesting and surprising things for NICAP and Dr. James E. McDonald to consider. McDonald carefully studied the sighting reports and was impressed. It was something neither he nor NICAP had expected. A number of the incidents, at least, seemed to have gotten a fair and thorough hearing and investigation. McDonald was impressed and quickly accepted when we asked him to write an Introduction:

> *Serious students of the UFO problem will... find this compilation of the 1951-53 Grudge and Bluebook reports one of the most significant... of the recent additions to the UFO literature.... The Moss Congressional Subcommittee is to be praised for assisting NICAP in extricating the reports from the Air Force files where they have lain inaccessible for so many years.*
>
> *When one studies the curious history of Air Force handling of the UFO problem, the [period] from October 1951 through September 1953 emerges as a kind of 'heroic period' of Air Force investigations.... That period [was] the one interval during which UFOs were seriously studied and rather vigorously investigated by the U.S. Air*

Force…. Shortly after [that period, there] began a sort of new dark-age when debunking and superficial investigations once again came to characterize Project Bluebook's response to the UFO problem…. After 1953, Bluebook went steadily downhill… and there evolved a steadily more adamant Air Force position that UFOs were only a nonsense problem….

Air Force press statements repeatedly misled the public and the scientific community by conveying a picture [of] Project Bluebook as a high-caliber scientific effort "drawing upon the finest scientific talents and facilities available to the Air Force." As the next effect, the entire UFO question has been swept almost entirely under the rug. Only the efforts of groups like NICAP have prevented complete concealment of the facts about UFOs….

This NICAP publication [is] an outstanding contribution to the UFO literature.

During the two-year period the NICAP book covered, Project Bluebook was helmed by Air Force Captain Edward J. Ruppelt. His book *The Report on Unidentified Flying Objects*, published in 1956, "recounts the history and some of the most important investigations undertaken by Bluebook during his tenure…"

The NICAP staff was quickly rushed into the project. As 1967 began drawing to a close, we contacted the office of Congressman John Moss, Chairman of the Foreign Operations and Government Information Subcommittee of the U.S. House Committee on Government Operations. Back then, this group of U.S. Senators was known as the "Freedom of Information Committee" and they "developed a reputation for freeing previously unavailable Government documents."

The Moss Subcommittee Comes Through

In December, the Moss subcommittee members persuaded the Air Force to make a set of the Grudge and Bluebook Nos. 1-12 available for inspection at the Pentagon and "to permit duplication of these reports in part…" A month or so later, a NICAP staffer paid a visit to the Secretary of the Air Force's Office of Information, "inspected the reports and… made arrangements to obtain the copies" that comprise the NICAP book. For the first time in about fifteen years, it became possible to directly study "the first-hand records of the Air Force investigations, their methods and conclusions."

"During the two-year period covered by these reports, the scope and effectiveness of the Air Force investigation varied widely from one extreme to the other," the publication editors wrote. "NICAP feels that the reports themselves not only add to the general history of the subject, but provide illumination on the many public statements about the subject that issued from the Air Force during that time."

The numerous reports in the 235-page book were marked **SECRET** and **CONFIDENTIAL**, then were relabeled **UNCLASSIFIED** when they were released to NICAP.

The CONFIDENTIAL Reports

- *July 18, 1952.* About 10:45 p.m. Near Patrick Air Force Base (AFB), Florida. Three officers and four airmen reported seeing a series of unidentified lights that were much brighter than a star and amber-red in color. The first light was seen west of the base. It remained still for a minute or so. Then it began to slowly move north. It stopped, then slowly moved south. A short time later, "a similar light was observed… below the first light and [was] moving north at a much higher speed." Suddenly, a third light was spotted heading west, also at high speed. Before that light "had faded in the distance, a fourth light followed it." The first three lights then disappeared when "a fifth light appeared in the west and came directly over the airfield." It made a 180-degree turn and sped west "until it faded from view. This light appeared coming over the base and disappeared in fifteen seconds." Conclusion: "Unknown."

- *July 29, 1952.* 9:49 a.m. Los Alamosa, New Mexico. Several guards and pilots observed a UFO "flying straight and level at high speed north of the Los Alamos landing field." The object was of a shiny metallic color and was observed for thirty minutes with binoculars. Fighter planes in the area "were diverted to the area of the sighting and visually vectored toward the object." The UFO then "disappeared but reappeared in front of the fighters, made a 360-degree turn, came around in back of the fighters, followed for two minutes and disappeared."

- *November 13, 1952.* 2:43 a.m. Glasgow, Montana. A weather observer who was taking a theodolite reading on a weather balloon saw five oval-shaped objects with lights all around them. They were flying in a V-formation. "Each object seemed to be changing position vertically by climbing or diving, as if to hold formation." Their speeds were described as "very fast." The objects were seen for about twenty seconds. They approached from the northwest, went straight over the center of the town, made a ninety-degree turn, and departed toward the southwest. Conclusion: "There are no conclusions as to the nature of the reported visual sighting."

- *November 16, 1952.* McAndrew AFB, Newfoundland, Canada. During the early morning pre-dawn hours, a Technical Sergeant and the base Officer of the Day reported seeing a "large, brilliant object" traveling very fast. It approached from the southwest, made a sharp ninety-degree turn directly overhead and disappeared toward the west. As it left, it gave off a brilliant "cold white light." The sighting lasted only five-to-six seconds. The local radar station was checked, "but they carried no unknown tracks during the period." Conclusion: "Unknown."

The SECRET Reports

The **SECRET** reports included the following:

- *December 6, 1952.* 7 p.m. Angoon, Alaska. An Air National Guard pilot reported seeing "an object consisting of two shiny globes connected by a solid rod" heading toward the south. At times, the object assumed a flattened shape. The pilot compared the UFO's size to a Gruman Goose aircraft. He chased the globes until they accelerated and disappeared "in the sun." Conclusion: "Insufficient data to evaluate."

- *December 19, 1952.* 8:50 p.m. Anderson AFB, Guam. An "unidentified aerial object" was seen by observers from three different locations: (1) Ground crew personnel at the base; (2) a Naval officer fourteen miles south of the base; and (3) the crew of an incoming B-17 115 miles from Guam and heading west. The UFO was reported on a heading of 270-degrees. It was cylindrical in shape [and] had a "silvery color with a bright flame trailing from the rear." Its speed was deemed to be considerably faster than that of a conventional jet. The sighting lasted about forty-five seconds. Conclusion: "Unknown."

- *January 3, 1953.* 4 a.m. Craig, Montana. Three unidentified "sources" reported seeing an aerial object up to forty feet long and twenty-five feet thick "with the appearance of two soup bowls put together. There were several lighted windows with what appeared to be a porthole on the side. The object moved slowly at first, then began a rapid climb." The low-flying UFO first appeared to be 200-to-300 yards away from the observers. Conclusion: "Unknown."

- *February 4, 1953.* 1:50 p.m. Yuma City, Arizona. "A meteorological aide for the U.S. Weather Bureau was searching for a lost weather balloon with aid of a theodolite when he sighted a solid white, oblong object.... The size of the object consisted of one minute of arc. The object appeared to be ascending straight up, then leveled off and at this point was joined by a second object of exactly the same description. The second object left the field of the theodolite twice but returned each time to join the original [UFO]. They both disappeared simultaneously.... The objects remained in vision for five minutes. The observer stated that the objects rose more rapidly than any balloon he has ever seen and... moved against the prevailing westerly winds.... It is concluded that these objects could not have been balloons especially since they were seen to move against the wind.... Because of the maneuvers and the time of day, astronomical activity must be ruled out." Conclusion: "Unknown."

- *March 3, 1953.* Time of sighting not noted. Luke AFB, Arizona. This is possibly the most unusual case in the early Grudge-Bluebook files. An actual UFO was not seen, "but a high altitude condensation pattern was observed. When first sighted, the contrail was approximately 300-500 feet in diameter. The pattern began with a smooth knife-like leading edge, very thin in depth... with an irregular trailing edge."

The contrail was seen by three F-84 aircraft pilots, one of whom decided to break off and give chase to the speedy contrail for fifty-to-sixty miles before breaking away from the chase. During the chase, "the contrail made a slight dip to the northwest and began climbing at twenty degrees." During this maneuver, the pilot "observed the pattern to appear as a sharp-nosed, very thin object about 300-500 feet long with an irregular, wispy trailing edge. Immediately, a heavy condensation trail began to form and extended for approximately 1000 feet back, at which point it separated into a double trail, which again was approximately 1000 feet long, ending abruptly.... The most unusual feature was that the contrail stayed with the unsighted object and did not extend across the sky [like] conventional aircraft contrails." Conclusion: "Unknown."

Could It "Blow the Lid Off?"

Dick Hall, who was back on the NICAP staff as a part-timer, was excited.

"How the hell can the nay-sayers ignore this, Gordon?" he asked. "This could blow the lid off their tightly-bound belief that UFO reports are nonsense."

"I'm excited, too, Dick, but I don't think it will stop the true nay-sayers," I responded. "Maybe a few objective scientists like McDonald will start coming around, but don't expect a full turnaround."

"Have you talked with Major Keyhoe?" Dick asked. "What does he think?"

"He seems to think it's a good start, but 'don't hold your breath' is the way he put it," I replied. "He seems to think that it will take a lot more to convince the true skeptics that a healthy percentage of UFO reports should be considered worthy of full-scale investigation. Even that might not be enough to convince them that even a few of the really good sightings could truly indicate that UFOs are being piloted by beings from outer space and beyond. Still, overall, the Major seems to be mainly happy with the result. He considers the Grudge-Bluebook reports to be a feather in our cap. He was also impressed with Jim McDonald's assertion that the Air Force did a fairly credible job investigating the reports early on before deciding to take their wholly negative stance later."

* * *

Following NICAP's publication of the Grudge-Bluebook sightings, more reports continued to stream into our offices.

UFOs Follow Planes in Florida

A sighting in the skies over Florida I was in charge of coordinating occurred at dusk on November 26, 1968. Flying pilot instructors Lynn Duplantis and Robert Helder were returning from Winter Haven to their home base in Melbourne. Both men had a student pilot with them. Mario Zacchini sat beside Duplantis while Robert Wright occupied the co-pilot's seat next to Holder.

The sky was beginning to darken, but the pilots described the weather condition as "excellent" with maximum visibility. Duplantis was in the lead in a left echelon formation while Holder's plane was about four miles away.

As they were flying over Lake Cyprus, approximately forty-five miles from Melbourne, everyone in both aircraft spotted four unidentified objects to their right at an estimated distance of 2000 yards. The oval-shaped, white and bright UFOs flew in a right echelon formation at approximately the same 1,500-feet altitude as the planes at the same ninety mile-per-hour ground speed. Holder estimated the size of each object to be equal to that of a C-130 Transport with a fuselage they estimated to be about 150 feet long.

"A Vertical Stack"

About ten minutes after the occupants of the two planes first sighted the objects, one of the UFOs left the formation and descended to a point near or on the ground. Then the three remaining objects suddenly stopped and quickly formed "a vertical stack and sped upwards at a great speed until they were completely lost from view."

While watching the three objects carefully as they receded away from him, Duplantis banked steeply to his left so he could follow them. He compared their motion with the climb-out speeds of a B-58 Hustler bomber with which he is familiar. As the UFOs sped away, he estimated their speed to be more than 2000 miles-per-hour, about the same speed as that of a F4H Phantom fighter plane he had observed in vertical flight-testing.

The UFOs had paced the two planes for about thirty minutes. Duplantis and Holder were in radio communications with each about what they were seeing. They had also contacted Kennedy Airport in Melbourne in an attempt to get airport confirmation of the UFOs, but "the airport radar was unable to see them, probably because of the low altitude."

In their report, Wiley Robinson and J.D. Collner—Co-Chairman and Investigator, respectively, of NICAP's Florida Subcommittee Unit 3—said that both Duplantis, 27, and Holder, 26, were employed by the Florida Institute of Technology as full-time instructors for the Florida Air Academy. Duplantis had recently spent four years in the U.S. Air Force with 4200 hours of flying time under his belt while Holder was a veteran of seven years in the U.S. Navy with a total of 3800 hours pilot and aerial observer time on his resume.

"The investigators are in agreement that the objects seen cannot be sufficiently explained by any air device or phenomena known to us," Robinson and Collner concluded in their report.

CHAPTER FIFTEEN

The Colorado UFO Report is Published

A little more than a month after the sightings in North Dakota, in January 1969, what may have been one of the quickest jobs of publishing a nearly one thousand page book in the history of publishing—an incredible twenty-four hours from text to printed page with an immediate release to bookstores and the general public—occurred. A few days before the publication of the so-called *Scientific Study of Unidentified Flying Objects*, Jim McDonald had obtained an advance copy and was quickly on his way to Washington. He spent the night at our home in Bethesda, Maryland, where we pored over the huge document until dawn and well into the early afternoon hours.

It didn't take us long to get the gist. The Introduction by Walter Sullivan, the famed reporter for *The New York Times*, quickly set the negative tone. He wrote that the journal *Science* quoted a statement of James and Coral Lorenzen, the APRO founders, falsely suggesting that NICAP, in conjunction with McDonald, had tried "to control the study. When they found they couldn't control it, they attempted to scuttle it."

McDonald, normally a calm man, was furious and we joined him in his indignation. We were hoping that most readers wouldn't buy it without further corroboration. Sullivan concluded his Introduction by appearing to attack the reports of even the most reliable witnesses.

The Sullivan Factor

"This report—in showing the fallibility of even such sober observers as policemen, airline pilots and radar operators—raises questions as to the role of conditioning in many other fields of human activity….," he wrote. "One wonders to what extent this phenomenon affects such basic attitudes as our nationalism, our theological point of view and our moral standards. Are they really founded on logic and the ultimate truth? One cannot help but view our points of view on a great many things with new skepticism. Anyone who reads this study will, I believe, lay it down with a new perspective on human values and limitations."

For a few brief minutes, Sullivan's comments and the report itself felt like a quick, if not unexpected, knife thrust to the throat, but we also realized it was really no less than what we expected.

Thurston E. Manning, Vice President for Academic Affairs at the University of Colorado, wrote the Preface to the report on Halloween of 1968. He traced the origin of the project. On August 31, 1966, he wrote Colonel Ivan C. Atkinson, Deputy Executive Director of the Air Force Office of Scientific Research (AFOSR), and persuaded him to write to university officials outlining AFOSR's belief that "a scientific investigation of unidentified flying objects conducted wholly outside the jurisdiction of the Air Force would be of unusual significance from the standpoint of both scientific interest in and public concern with the subject."

"The Pros and Cons"

Colonel Atkinson suggested that "the scientists involved will have complete freedom to design and develop techniques for the investigation of the varied physical and psychological questions raised in conjunction with this phenomenon, according to their best judgment." Now it was up to the university administration officials and other faculty members to sit down and discuss the pros and cons of the study project.

"The subject was recognized as being both elusive and controversial in its scientific aspects," Manning remarked, immediately setting the obvious negative tone for the study.

Manning's statement was fodder for the reluctance of a number of scientists to back the study by participating in it. The reason they gave, according to Manning, was that scientists generally hesitate to commit their time and research to a project that does not appear to offer reasonably clear avenues by which definite progress could be made. In addition, the subject had achieved considerable notoriety over the years. Many newspapers, magazines, and books had blamed the Air Force for "not devoting more attention to the subject [while] others criticized the Air Force for paying any attention whatever to UFOs."

Condon Joins the Fray

After mulling over these considerations, university officials concluded that they were obliged to do whatever they could to clarify a tangled and confused issue while being as certain as they could that the highest academic and scientific standards would be maintained. This sentiment was shared by Dr. Edward U. Condon, Professor of Physics and Fellow of the Joint Institute for Laboratory Astrophysics, and may have been the final consideration for his agreement to become the scientific director of the project. Condon then picked Assistant Dean Robert J. Low of the university's Graduate School as the Project Coordinator. The project members also said they would welcome an arrangement that would make it certain that the methods and results of the study would be critically examined at the conclusion of the project.

The official report of the eighteen-month effort seemed determined to deliver an expected knockout punch to such dedicated ufologists as Don Keyhoe, Jim McDonald and Dick Hall as well as to myself and other dedicated NICAP investigators and members.

"New Lines For Research"

Thurston Manning's Preface concluded with: "No one study can answer all questions, but it can point out new lines for research, it can cross off some ideas as not fruitful for further inquiry, and it can lay to rest at least some rumors, exaggerations and imaginings."

It was now time for Condon to take over. On the first page of Section I, Conclusions and Recommendations, he wrote:

> ...The emphasis of this study has been on attempting to learn from UFOs anything that could be considered as adding to scientific knowledge. Our general conclusion is that nothing has come from the study of UFOs in the past twenty-one years that has added to scientific knowledge.... We feel that the reason that there has been very little scientific study of the subject is that those scientists who are most directly concerned, astronomers, atmospheric physicists, chemists, and psychologists, having had ample opportunity to look into the matter, have individually decided that UFO phenomena do not offer a fruitful field in which to look for major scientific discoveries.

The rather laughable (to those who really know the subject) Introduction went on to say that they hoped their conclusion would help other scientists to decide what they have to do and that, "if they agree with our conclusions, they would turn their valuable attention and talents elsewhere...." (As I read this at our conference table, McDonald noticeably winced since his own valuable attention and talents had been drawn to fully investigate the subject, which had quickly grown to a continuous worldwide phenomenon.)

What Should the Government Do?

Further on, Condon ruminated: "The question remains as to what, if anything, the federal government should do about the UFO reports it receives from the general public. We are inclined to think that nothing should be done with them in the expectation that they are going to contribute to the advance of science."

The director also denied that there was any conspiracy by the government to cloak all UFO reports behind a curtain of secrecy. He said: "We concluded otherwise.... What has been miscalled secrecy has been no more than an intelligent policy of delay in releasing data so that the public does not become confused by premature publication of incomplete studies of reports."

Whew! Talk about pouring it on.... The director even decried the fact that many schools were devoting some of their science studies to the UFO phenomenon because they are "educationally harmed by absorbing unsound and erroneous material as if it were scientifically founded." The clear indication was a plea for school teachers not to pollute their children or themselves with those pesky, unscientific flying saucer reports, despite the fact that thousands of scientifically-trained scientists in many fields of endeavor—such as military and civilian airplane, helicopter and other pilots, astronomers, physicists, radar operators, police officers and others—have had their own encounters with sightings of unexplained aerial phenomena. And at least two presidents (Ronald Reagan and Jimmy Carter) had reported their individual UFO sightings (I had seen Carter's report to NICAP when he was the Governor of Georgia). So had several astronauts.

Condon also denied any conspiracy by the government to cloak all UFO reports behind a curtain of secrecy. He said: "What has been miscalled secret has been no more than an intelligent policy of delay in releasing data so that the public does not become confused by premature publication of incomplete studies of reports."

McDonald is Hopping Mad

Jim McDonald could hardly restrain himself and squirmed uncomfortably in his chair as he read Condon's comments. Dick Hall and I had to practically restrain him from blowing his stack, an unusual trait for him.

But Condon still wasn't quite finished with his recommendation that teachers "refrain from giving students credit for school work based on their reading of the presently available UFO books and magazine articles. Teachers who find their students strongly motivated in this direction should attempt to channel their interests in the direction of serious study of astronomy and meteorology and... of critical analysis of arguments for fantastic propositions that are being supported by appeals to fallacious reasoning or false data."

Condon vs. NICAP

The project director still wasn't through with his negative remarks. It was NICAP's turn to be blistered next. He wrote: "NICAP devotes a considerable amount of its attention to attacking the Air Force and trying to influence members of Congress to hold hearings and in other ways to join in these attacks. It maintained a friendly relation to the Colorado Project during about the first year while warning its members to be on guard lest the project turned out to have been 'hired to whitewash the Air Force,'" He added: "When field studies are made by amateur organizations like APRO or NICAP, there are often several members present on a team. But usually they are persons without technical training and often with a strong bias toward the sensational aspects of the subject."

With Keyhoe looking over our shoulders at NICAP headquarters, we quickly published a special January 1969 issue of *The U.F.O. Investigator*. Despite the overall negative conclusions, the report still showed that about twenty percent of the 100 or so cases were listed as unidentified. This was about the same percentage of reports we received at NICAP that we also felt could be legitimate unknowns.

Keyhoe vs. Condon

In his page one article, "The Truth About the Condon Report," Keyhoe was quick to point out that Condon, "although he is named in the Air Force contract as the project's principal investigator, did not make a single field investigation. Nor did he interview even one of the hundreds of pilots, astronomers, aerospace engineers, control tower operators, and other highly competent witnesses whose sighting reports were sent to him by NICAP at his request. Large volumes of case material were apparently completely ignored."

"Dr. Condon stated that there should be no attack on the integrity of persons having different opinions on UFOs," Keyhoe pointed out. "Yet, he ridiculed UFO witnesses, well informed scientists on the subject, and NICAP."

With other factors thrown into the mix, the Condon Report would prove to be the death knell for NICAP in its current form. It only took the rest of the year 1969 for that to happen.

The Buckskin Mountains Encounter

At NICAP headquarters, however, our rapidly diminishing staff was still not ready to throw in the towel. I was determined to keep on top of significant sighting reports.

On May 10, 1969, Jim McDonald continued his tireless investigation of significant UFO sightings by sending a report to me of two pilots who spotted a formation of objects while flying in a small Cessna aircraft over the Buckskin Mountains in Arizona. The pilots were Ben Ripley, 42, and Hermon L. Slater, 41. Both were businessmen from Phoenix. Ripley was a manufacturer of building materials at Universal Wholesale Corporation while Slater operated the Park Central Medical Building barbershop on West Thomas Road. Slater had secured a franchise to distribute the roofing materials that Ripley manufactured. Their flight on March 17, 1969, constituted a business trip to Lake Havasu in connection with the franchise itself.

At 3:20 p.m., after their meeting, the men took off from Lake Havasu for the return trip home in their leased 1969 single-engine, high-wing Cessna 150 in very clear and sunny weather conditions. They were traveling at about 100 miles per hour.

The two men flew over the Jim Williams River, then crossed over the foothills of the Buckskin Mountains southwest of Alamo Dam and east of Planet Peak.

"What the Hell Are Those Things?"

"They had climbed to their cruising altitude of 5500 feet....," McDonald stated in his report. "Ripley suddenly had an urge to loosen his seat belt enough to rise up in his seat, with one hand on the dashboard, and look forward and down to the left. He immediately spotted a formation of objects below them and to their left, coming toward them on a reciprocal heading. Without saying a word, he pointed down over the dashboard.... Slater looked down [and] saw the objects."

"What the hell are those things?" he asked.

Both men spotted about twenty-five UFOs flying in random formation and at about the same altitude, which they estimated to be around 1000 feet or less above the terrain.

"The objects were oval, had a flat white finish, and all had a black band running all around their peripheries," McDonald continued. "The most striking feature that impressed both witnesses strongly was the maneuvers that were made by the objects in perfect unison, as if [they were] under remote control."

Both men continued watching the oval objects as they flew beneath their airplane and a bit to their left. Ripley lost sight of them when they passed behind a portion of the fuselage that blocked his view. Slater, in the left seat, however, could see them somewhat longer.

The objects had the appearance of "mainly a flat white color, definitely not metallic.... A band of black formed a blur all around the periphery of every object."

Both pilots estimated that the UFOs were traveling at a speed of 200- to-300 miles per hour.

"Barrel-Roll" Maneuvers

"There was emphatic agreement... that the single most striking feature of the sighting concerned the perfect unison in which all of the objects executed identical maneuvers," McDonald reported. "These maneuvers were chiefly motions in roll and pitch.... Both men felt that the pitching motion was in response to terrain features over which the objects were flying.... The tilting motions... resembled 'barrel-roll' maneuvers.... Ripley emphasized that he could not imagine any precision aerobatic maneuvers of two dozen aircraft being executed with such perfect precision.... After Ripley lost sight of the objects due to a fuselage panel in his way, Slater continued to watch them below and to his left as they passed aft of the Cessna. The estimated total duration of the sighting they put at about twenty seconds...."

"That was weird!" Slater exclaimed after the men had sat in silence for what seemed to them a long time.

"The meteorological and optical conditions of this sighting are not in accord with any mirage or reflective anomalies, especially since the line of sight is far from the horizontal," McDonald remarked. "Furthermore, afternoon conditions over the Arizona desert at this time of year are incompatible with strong horizontal stratification of the atmosphere. There were no clouds in the area and... any cloud-optical effects such as a sub-sun are out of the question here."

McDonald added: "When I spoke for about forty minutes with Ripley and Slater at [our] May 6 meeting in Scottsdale, I was quite favorably impressed with both."

CHAPTER SIXTEEN

UFOs in Rumania

While the demise of NICAP as Don Keyhoe had led it for thirteen years was imminent, reports still continued to flood into our offices. An international flavor came from the country of Rumania, courtesy of Ion Hobana, our Rumanian correspondent. A science writer for *Ziarul Scuntea* magazine, he unearthed Rumanian sighting reports dating back more than forty years. My friend and fellow staff member, Diana Knopp, helped me prepare the reports for publication in *The U.F.O. Investigator*. The details came from articles by Hobana in *Panorama*, a French magazine.

Farmer Sees "Fiery Light" in 1926

At 1:00 a.m. on an unspecified date during the Summer of 1926, Ion Bunescu spotted "a fiery light" hovering over Cirtsa for about ten minutes. Then, as the frightened farmer watched, the UFO headed directly toward him and was so bright that it illuminated the Olt River.

Suddenly, the object emitted a whistling sound and, as it passed overhead, Bunescu quickly dove into the nearby tall grass and remained hidden there while he watched the aerial object.

"It seemed to be a ship ten feet long, three-to-six feet wide, dark in the middle and as bright as the full moon....," he related. "After staying suspended [for] two or three minutes over my head, it left..., stopped for an instant, returned just over the national highway and passed over a small wood. After this, the light weakened and disappeared."

UFO Appears After a Bomb Raid

During the middle of a Summer day in 1944, Gregore Zmeuranu, an engineer, stood near the Vage Refinery in Ploiesti just after a World War II bombing raid and watched as one of the oil tanks was engulfed in flames. Badly frightened and fearing for his life, he began looking around for a safe place to be when his attention was drawn to the still-smoking sky.

"I noticed a pointed object coming from the north," Zmeuranu reported. "It was yellow… with a whitish tail which, when it met the clouds of smoke, seemed to shorten and vibrate in a strange way."

The engineer said the UFO traveled at a very high rate of speed. Then it turned over the burning refinery, stopped for a moment, then zigzagged toward the north and disappeared.

Hobana told NICAP that Zmeuranu related to him that the object made a sharp 180-degree turn and sped away.

The Blue Saucer

Sometime between midnight and 12:30 a.m. on a Summer night in 1955, Mr. and Mrs. Dumitru Coca spotted a small blue saucer with white beams they estimated to be only five feet in diameter near Faragas.

"It turned very quickly in the direction of the mountain….," Coca remarked. "It moved… to the right with slight oscillations and did not turn on its axis. It projected a bluish light with silver-white rays which turned to blue."

UFO Hovers Over Home

Shortly before midnight on an unspecified day in August 1963, a sighting occurred in the Giulesti District. Virgil Gheorghiu was visiting with his friend, Vasile Storia, when the men saw two very large luminous, round UFOs with sharp contours. The objects slowed down, stopped, then hovered between two chimneys on top of a building nearby. Gheorghiu called for his niece, Cornelia Storia, to come outside and observe the UFOs.

"The one on the right began to move... toward the north... and disappeared to the right of the building," Cornelia reported. "The other, on the left, stayed still. After ten to fifteen seconds, it suddenly went out like an electric bulb. The night was very clear."

A "Zigzagging" UFO

It was about 4 p.m. on March 29, 1967. Batsa Stefan, Chief of the Meteorological Station at Muntele Semenic, was watching a number of skiers through his binoculars when he spotted a brightly shining conical form with the side facing the sun. He observed the object until dusk.

Stefan returned to the site at 7:30 the next morning and saw the UFO again. He observed it until 9 a.m. when it started to slowly zigzag to the southwest. At ten o'clock, Batsa alerted workers at the nearby meteorological stations at Caransebes, Virful, Tsarca and Munte Curtu, who also spotted the object.

"It continued to move slowly and make zigzags [to] the southwest until noon, when it disappeared from my view," Stefan added.

The UFO had not vanished altogether, however. At 1 p.m., it was seen by personnel at the Berzeasco Station. Three hours later, they saw the object once again.

"My colleague, Vasile Cotsci, and I were again able to observe it until just after the sun went down," Stefan reported. "The next day the object reappeared.... [It] was observed from five meteorological stations for about sixty-two hours."

A number of corroborating witnesses said the UFO was tracked by theodolite while they kept a watch on it through binoculars. The saucer had "the appearance of a geometric cone, the top part facing downwards, slightly tilted." It was also observed by witnesses in Resita, around fifteen miles away.

Stefan alerted another witness, who watched the UFO with personnel from the stations at Munte Cuntu and Caransebes.

"The object... at first resembled a sonde balloon," the witness told Hobana. "It had a flat cone shape with rounded angles, shaped rather like an egg. [It] was a flat white color.... The idea that it was a sonde balloon was given up as the reflection of the sun was rather weak, the vertical movements were irregular, and the horizontal movements were against the wind. These were certainly not the characteristic movements of a sonde balloon.... Its movements were alternately slow and fast, then occasionally it stopped completely. I have never seen anything like it in the course of my meteorological career."

A "Butane Flame" Tail

It was the afternoon of September 18, 1967. Valeriu Bitu, an engineer from Bucharest, was standing on the bridge of a boat from Tulcea heading toward Sfîntu Gheorge.

"I saw a very bright object in the shape of a disc which had a tail and which moved to the east," Bitu said in his report. "Suddenly, the disc stopped suspended in the air at 650-to-1,000 feet altitude... and about 1,500 to 1,000 feet from me. The diameter of the object was twenty-to-twenty-five feet and the tail was almost the same length. The sides of the disc were red—almost crimson—while the tail was the color of a butane flame."

After it hovered for an estimated four-to-five minutes, the UFO turned left, stopped again, then rapidly ascended and disappeared into the clouds.

Animal Reactions in Petrila

A UFO that apparently caused chickens to react violently was seen by a farmer at 2 p.m., November 22, 1967, in Petrila.

"I suddenly saw all the chickens in my farmyard running toward me cackling like lunatics and visibly terrified," stated Ladislau Schmit. "They were all flying.... I raised my head and clearly saw a very brilliant object.... It was silver or aluminum, in the shape of a disc. The object bulged slightly and the upper part was dome-like and decorated with small spikes, which made me think of antennae. I called my wife.... The machine was at an altitude of about 16,000 feet.

"At first..., it was completely motionless in the sky, but after about a moment, it began to move slowly. It soon took off at a bewildering speed toward the northwest and disappeared.... Many persons also saw it, including some workers who were fixing the roof of the house in front of us."

Airline Pilots and Crews See Flying Objects

A speeding oval object that radiated an unusually strong green light was observed by an airline pilot and crew of a large IL-18 aircraft over the Oradea Plain very close to the Hungarian border at 8:21 p.m. on an unspecified date in 1967 or 1968.

Captain Benjamin Gabrian was on a direct course for Dusseldorf, Germany, out of Mihail Kogalniceanu Airport at an altitude of around 25,000 feet when he saw the UFO. His crewmen, Alexander Niculescu and M. Constantinescu, also saw the object "speeding in the opposite direction about 1,000 feet above the flight ceiling and half-a-mile to the right of the aircraft." The observers watched as the small object emitted a brilliantly dazzling green light.

"I continued to watch the luminous object for several seconds until, with a sudden increase of speed, it disappeared to the west," Captain Gabrian remarked.

The pilot radioed officials at the Vienna Airport and was told that there were no aircraft within a 250-mile radius. Only a few minutes later, however, someone at the airport in Budapest, Hungary, called to report that another airplane crew saw a similar UFO moving rapidly west about two-and-a-half minutes after the Gabrian observation.

"By making note of the point where it was seen the second time, one can establish that the object was traveling at 7,500 to 8,500 miles per hour, a speed impossible for present means of aerial travel with known sources of propulsive energy," Captain Gabrian stated.

The "Lighted Sea Urchin"

At 7:30 a.m. on December 10, 1967, Adina Paun, a psychologist, was standing outside her home when she observed a bluish-green UFO with "luminous prickles" that resembled "a lighted sea urchin" hovering over Bucharest. Paun said the strange object was between the high and low cloud covers.

Paun's report appeared in the May 23, 1968, edition of *Cutezatorii*.

Tanker Captain and Crew Observe UFO

Captain Nicolae Stefanescu, commander of the *Arges*, an oil tanker, and his crew spotted a UFO at sea at approximately 3:47 p.m. GMT on October 24, 1968. He described the encounter to Hobana, who forwarded his comments to NICAP:

> *We were sailing on a calm sea in the Canal of Mozambique between Madagascar and the east coast of Africa. Suddenly, I heard an astonished cry from the third officer, St. Anton, who... showed me something in the sky. I saw, coming from the southeast, a lighted white object, which was flying... at very great speed. As it came nearer, it became a disc, half the diameter of the moon. It was a very vivid yellow-orange color... emitting bluish-green rays from the center. After some seconds, the object suddenly stopped, rested... for several moments and then suddenly changed direction toward the east, almost perpendicular to our course, and disappeared in space.*

CHAPTER SEVENTEEN

The Strange Effects

One of my main projects during NICAP's last year as a respected, viable UFO organization was finishing, as the author, the special book *Strange Effects From UFOs,* published in 1969. Nearly fifty years later, it is still being sold on e-Bay and Amazon and has gained a respectable position among the pantheon of UFO books. It features an array of well-investigated NICAP cases in which witnesses experienced physiological effects and saw occupants of the craft. There were also a number of incidents involving animal reactions and physical evidence. For me, it was a labor of love.

SECTION ONE
Witnesses Shoot At and Hit UFOs

Case #1: The Booth Incident

It was 11:15 p.m., January 29, 1953. Lloyd C. Booth carefully locked the door of his general store eight miles north of Conway, South Carolina. He jumped into his car and drove to his farm about a mile away. He left a pot of coffee steaming on the stove as he sat down to read the newspaper. Then he began to think of his cow that had died the night before. In his report to NICAP, he said the animal "hadn't been sick at all."

Booth remarked: "Even stranger, in the past few weeks, about twenty cows in the county had met the same unusual death…. Also, hogs were dying in amazingly large numbers. One man lost seventy-five. Nobody could explain the deaths."

As the farmer was still thinking about the strange demise of the farm animals, he heard his own animals outside.

"A bunch of ducks, the chickens, and two mules began making more noise than usual," he related. "I got up and went out to see what was molesting the animals. It was a hell of a thing."

Egg-Shaped Object

Thinking that a prowler might be stalking the farm, Booth quickly grabbed his Harrison and Richards .22 revolver. As he quickly approached the mule stalls, he saw what "looked like an egg cut end-to-end" about ten feet over the treetops.

Booth gave a detailed account of the UFO:

There was a [white] light in the back, but the glass was tinted, smoked, or too thick to see through. The entire body was very streamlined. It was [about twenty-five feet] long and [thirteen feet] broad and [nine feet] deep…. The bottom appeared to be flat except for the protrusion on the bottom which appeared to be three-to-three-and-one-half feet broad extending down to about three and one-half feet from the fuselage or main body and extending about one-half the overall length of the object…. There were two glassed-over areas in front, like cockpits, and light was pouring through what seemed like tinted glass…. Underneath was an opening about three feet wide, and from this protruded a crescent-shaped object that looked like part of a large wheel….

Booth was quick to point out that his training in an Army anti-aircraft unit had taught him to notice the minute details of all types of aircraft.

"I know that the strange craft that hovered over me… was something I had never seen before," he explained. "It was scary."

Strangely, the UFO seemed to be drifting toward the witness from the east. It emitted a slight humming noise. Booth yelled toward the farmhouse, hoping to wake his family. He was unsuccessful.

The object passed overhead toward the west at an altitude of about ninety feet. Keeping a firm and nervous grasp on his pistol, Booth followed the UFO, which was still moving slowly. It passed over the trees as the witness searched for a possible clearing in the woods. He knew there was a swamp ahead. He had gone about as far as he could while still feeling he was on firm ground.

Bullet Strikes Saucer

The object appeared to turn and approach Booth. It flew directly over his head. Badly frightened now, he aimed the pistol directly at the UFO and pulled the trigger. There was loud *ping*! The bullet had obviously struck something metallic. He fired a second time, but heard nothing because the noise from the nocturnal craft increased. It sounded like "a stepped-up electric motor."

"As soon as the [first] shot hit the object…, it seemed to tilt upward… and soared into the air at about a sixty-five degree angle," Booth wrote in his report. "It continued this upward move at about 600 m.p.h. until it vanished…."

The part-time farmer said the UFO disappeared at a far greater speed than any aircraft he knew. He reentered the house and saw that his father, mother and brother had been awakened. His mother said she heard the shots and was wondering what had happened.

Curiosity Seekers and Debunkers

At first, Booth didn't want to report the bizarre incident, fearing ridicule. A week later, however, he told his friend, Reverend Elwell Jones, pastor of the Horry County Carolina Baptist Church. But the Reverend apparently didn't honor Booth's request to keep the story quiet because he carelessly broke the news to the media.

"In a few hours, I was surrounded by curiosity seekers and I found debunkers on all sides," Booth lamented.

One of the debunkers was a Civil Aviation Agency man who said "the witness had shot at one of a fleet of Navy blimps en route from Georgia to North Carolina." Booth wasn't buying it, however.

"I have seen many blimps and I've been in one," he remarked. "I'd certainly know a blimp when I saw one eighty feet over my head!"

An "Honest Christian Man"

Booth had a reputation as an "honest Christian man" in his area.

"I have known Lloyd Booth all my life," Reverend Jones announced. "I have known him to be a good Christian man and when he says he saw something, he did."

A neighbor backed the Reverend up in his praise: "Lloyd Booth is of good character and a truthful man. I have never known him to misrepresent anything." Even a local publication, *The Field*, vouched for him: "There is no doubt in the minds of those who know him well, including ministers, that he is by nature truthful and of high moral integrity. What he saw was no hoax…."

H.B. Ketchum, a writer who reported on the incident in *The Journal of Space Flight*, was also impressed by the sighting and the witness. He wrote: "It is the author's opinion—based upon Mr. Booth's personality and the manner in which the story was told and questions answered—that this is not a hoax. It appears that the man did see a strange craft of a design wholly unfamiliar and with an unknown but powerful means of propulsion."

Finally, our friend and colleague, Dr. James E. McDonald, interviewed the witness and was similarly impressed. He told NICAP: "Booth's account was given to me in a seemingly quite straightforward manner [with] no evident embarrassments or visible dramatization. He sounded like a person of… [an] entirely honest manner."

In his letter to Isabel Davis, a NICAP staff member, in October 1967, McDonald gave further details he obtained from Booth:

The witness had spent about half-an-hour searching for "any marks or identifications" on the craft, but he saw none and realized from his World War II antiaircraft experience that all aircraft, including experimental aircraft, must carry identification marks. When he saw none, he decided to shoot at it to "see what it was made of." I asked him if he thought that was very dangerous and he said that he thought the pistol was so low powered… that he couldn't do much damage to it. He said that, almost as soon as he shot, the object tilted up at an estimated sixty-degree angle and sped off at a great speed, faster than any jet, disappearing from sight… in… ten to fifteen seconds at the most. No one at his home heard the shots…. He said he reported [the incident] to the Air Force at Myrtle Beach. An Army intelligence man came, not a USAF man. He said the man interviewed him very carefully, but never came back…. He answered my question concerning prior or subsequent sightings by remarking that he had never seen anything like it before or since. He said he is still curious about it and asked me to let him know if I ever find out what the cause of it was!

Case #2: Hunter Fires at UFO

Nearly six years later, a similar incident occurred. The skies were clear at 6:15 p.m., October 19, 1959, as teenagers Mark Muza and Harold Moore were on a hunting trip in Big Marsh, an "almost hostile lowland on the fringes of the small town of Poquoson, Virginia." They ignored an ominous sign on the outskirts of the marsh: **WARNING—DANGER AREA. BOMBING RANGE. LIVE AMMUNITION AND BOMBS. WARRANTED FOR TRESPASSING.**

As they entered the marsh, the boys separated. Muza waded through the mud and water, then stopped to inspect his twelve-gauge shotgun. A minute or so later, he heard a sound he described as like a flock of wild birds. Startled, he looked up and saw a circular UFO approximately four feet in diameter coming straight down toward him. He quickly raised his gun, aimed it, and pulled the trigger. A barrel-full of #4 shot blasted out and he heard "the ring of metal striking metal."

The UFO stopped at about a fifty-foot altitude. The frightened teen quickly reloaded the gun and fired again, using a steel bearing. Mark clearly heard a loud ping sound as the slug hit the object.

Meanwhile, Moore, who was about 100 yards away from his friend, saw the UFO as Muza fired the first round. He said he heard a "whirring noise" during the incident. Following a third shot, the object, which was whirling and spinning like a toy top, sped straight up and disappeared in only a few seconds.

NICAP member Larry Bryant investigated the incident and sent us his report.

SECTION TWO
The Occupants

For the first time, Major Keyhoe gave the NICAP staff the go-ahead to begin making public some of the well-investigated UFO cases in which occupants were sighted. We assembled an expert Occupant Panel that included a psychologist, a psychiatrist, an astronomer, a medical doctor, an anthropologist, and a radiation biologist.

Case #1: Incident At Ririe

Willie Begay and Guy Tossie were Navajo Indians who worked on the Earl Hunter farm in Ririe, Idaho. At 9:30 p.m., November 7, 1967, they were traveling south of the town with Begay at the wheel of a 1956 white Buick sedan on State Highway 26. Both men admitted they had been drinking beer, but were not intoxicated and were "in command of their faculties."

Suddenly, without any warning, "there was a flash of white light which startled and temporarily blinded them," according to C. Reed Ricks, a NICAP member who investigated the bizarre incident. At first, Begay and Tossie thought they may have been struck by lightning. They looked up and saw a small UFO hovering around five feet off the ground directly in front of them. Then something stopped their car. Begay later swore he never touched the brake pedal.

The object, with a transparent dome on top, had flashing green and orange lights that were seen through holes in a moving ring at its center joint. The lights on the ring were slowly rotating. Ricks added that "the clear top opened as though hinged at one side."

Humanoid Emerges From the Craft

Suddenly, the men saw two small humanoid figures. One of them virtually floated from the craft "like a bird" and descended to the driver's side of the car as the startled and frightened witnesses cringed inside. The creature, which looked like it had deeply scarred features, was estimated to be three-to-three-and-a-half feet tall and had high, extended ears. The eyes were round like tiny balls and it had no visible nose or lips. The humanoid had a deep chest and tight-fitting clothes that resembled coveralls. The alien being also had what appeared to be "a flat pack on its back [that] protruded above the head and only two fingers were visible on one hand."

Alien Drives the Car

The witnesses quickly moved out of the way as the humanoid "entered the vehicle and grabbed the wheel." Then "the car began to move."

"[The witness] could not explain how he reached the pedal, but further questions revealed the car may have been towed," Ricks stated in his report. "The UFO maintained its fixed position 'like the car was fastened to it.' It was steered across an approach into a wheat stubble field and stopped about seventy-five feet from the highway...."

Begay said the strange creature, who had taken control of the vehicle, briefly spoke in a rapid, high-pitched voice "like a woman [or] bird." The Indian did not respond. He said he was so terrified that he nearly fainted and cringed down deep into his seat trembling.

Then the highly nervous and frightened Tossie managed to open the door, quickly jumped from the vehicle and ran approximately one-fifth of a mile down the highway to the farmhouse of Willard Hammon. Tossie later said he felt the second occupant was chasing him.

Back in the automobile, Begay watched as the creature left the car, then floated up to the UFO and entered it. He watched as the top of the object closed while "its colors brightened." Then it "rose in a zig-zag path" while "a yellow light shot from the bottom center and 'played like a flame.'" The object accelerated and quickly disappeared at a great speed with a whirring sound and a rush of air.

Panic at the Farmhouse

Meanwhile, at the farmhouse, Willard Hammon was startled by the "loud, frantic knocking" at his door. He opened the door and the terrified Tossie bolted inside. Hammon said he saw a trickle of blood flowing from the corner of Tossie's mouth. Bob, the farmer's frightened teenaged son, was standing nearby.

Appearing to be completely disoriented, incoherent and badly shaken, the Navajo blurted something out about "a light that drove their car off the road and a 'dead' friend." Hammon remarked that, perhaps, they should return to the scene of the sighting, but Tossie was too frightened. The farmer persisted, however, and he, his son, and Tossie drove in Hammon's car to the wheat field. The still badly frightened Tossie huddled in the back seat of the car.

Approaching the Buick, the three men saw that the car headlights were still glowing and the motor was still running. Inside, Begay "was trembling beside the steering wheel, his eyes closed. He responded upon recognizing the men and recounted the incident."

The Hammons remained with the Navajos, comforting them until they calmed down and were able to drive home with Willard and his son following close behind. After the Indians were safely home, Hammon "turned back toward town and stopped at a bar where the witnesses may have been drinking." Maybe the bartender could fill him in on what may have happened.

Police Investigate and Cattle React

Hammon and his son were discussing the incredibly weird story over coffee when the county Deputy Sheriff and a policeman came in for a sandwich. They did not have long to wait before Begay and Tossie, who said they were too afraid to go home alone, also entered the bar. Once again, they related their story to the officers who then contacted the State Police. An officer from the State Police Barracks was ordered to investigate.

A little more than one hour after the UFO disappeared, Corporal Tom Harper met the witnesses at the scene of the sighting. The policeman knew that the men had been drinking prior to their encounter with the strange object and the alien beings, but he emphasized that they were *not* drunk and were still obviously scared. Once again, Begay and Tossie related their incredible story. Harper examined the car for possible signs of radiation, dents or burns, with negative results.

Later, Mrs. Rita Barnes, a storekeeper friend of Willie Begay, reported seeing "a number of frightened dogs and stampeded cattle in the vicinity that same night." Also that evening, Mrs. Claude Mann said her cattle had broken through a steel pipe and ran for about two miles. They were rounded up and corralled, but somehow managed to break through the fence and escape once again.

Approximately two hours after the initial observation by Begay and Tossie, Mrs. Elaine Quinn drove from her home in the Snake River Valley, an estimated six miles east of Riri, and headed for a relative's home to pick up some medicine for her sick child. She had driven about two miles from her home when she spotted a rotating, zig-zagging light.

Mr. X and the "Small Man"

As I wrote in my account of the strange and frightening incidents, "the most amazing corroborating evidence of all came from a man who, for fear of ridicule, refused to allow use of his name...."

At 11:30 p.m., around the same time as the sighting by Mrs. Quinn, Mr. X was driving on State Highway 48 between Ririe and Rigby when a small UFO descended in front of his truck, causing it to suddenly screech to a halt. Then Mr. X couldn't believe that he was seeing a small man leave the object and approach his truck. As the terrified and astonished witness watched, the creature tapped on his windshield. X thought he was losing his mind, but "he succeeded in shaking off the weird creature and escape. He lay awake all night, seriously questioning his sanity."

The next morning at seven o'clock, Mr. X showed up at work and told a friend about his bizarre encounter. A few short hours later, an account of the Begay-Tossie encounter was reported over a local radio station and Mr. X "turned white as a sheet," his friend said.

C. Reed Ricks had a clearly favorable impression of X, who "shows the outward signs of an average intellect with average or above average intelligence. He is very afraid that, if his story gets out, he will be ridiculed." The NICAP investigator concluded in his report that the Ririe people were convinced that the encounter related by the two Navajos "was a true experience."

The Occupant Panel Weighs In

Keyhoe, Dick Hall and I were initially skeptical of these occupant reports and were somewhat surprised when our carefully chosen and highly qualified Occupant Panel weighed in on the positive side. The first to submit his report was Dr. Allen S. Mariner, a psychiatrist.

"This... is [a] most convincing case....," he wrote. "The single element which makes it so extremely convincing is the very strong emotional reaction of the witnesses, amounting to panic—surely an appropriate response in such a situation. Their consistency under cross-examination is another convincing element, as is the report of frightened animals in the area... The fact that these witnesses may have had a beer or two does not impress me. Their panic reaction is not all typical of reactions to alcohol; further, for two men to react with panic and to agree about the cause of their fright if the cause is not something real would be virtually unheard-of."

Dr. Mariner added that alcoholic intake "*per se* does not produce hallucinations.... While alcohol does... dim one's faculties and makes one a less reliable observer of things in general, it simply does not produce the sort of phenomena with which were are dealing."

The psychologist on the panel, who apparently wanted to remain anonymous, found the case to be "most credible."

"Because [the witnesses] were observed before and after the sighting and were obviously terrified afterwards, they are credible," he remarked. "The circumstances—one witness running for help, the other terrified, were highly convincing. So was their willingness to talk to police and their later reluctance to be named or sought out.... This is [a] most credible, yet... most fantastic case. The social implications are apparent: an unsuccessful effort at communication, individual terror in reaction, great technological power."

Walter N. Webb, an astronomer with the Charles Hayden Planetarium in Boston, Massachusetts and a good friend of NICAP, was equally impressed, calling the incident "one of the most interesting... on record." Panel Member Dr. Norman S. Wolf, a radiation biologist, called the case "a very convincing report, especially with the indirect confirmation of another contact made that same night. The anthropologist (also anonymous) said the apparent backpacks "may have been life-support equipment feeding directly into their suits or bodies or [they] may have been personal propulsion, testing or communications gear.... The fact that no masks or helmets were present does not... rule out some life-support function for the packs."

Case #2: Fiji Islanders See "the Figure of a Man"

Sometime during the evening of October 8, 1957, four Fiji Islanders in a boat off Nawaka said they were frightened to see a revolving white disc descend to about twenty feet altitude, then stop and hover over them, according to a report we received from a United Press correspondent. As the Fiji natives drew closer, the UFO emitted a brilliant light beam that both "dazzled them and made them feel weak." Then, suddenly, the frightening object ascended straight up and disappeared.

At about the same time in a separate location, a Seventh Day Adventist Church Official, R.O. Aveling, saw what was believed to be the same object swinging in the sky at about 5,000 feet altitude as its color seemed to vary "from white to flashing red."

A separate third independent report from fishermen off Suva reported that they spotted "an object shaped like a jelly fish glowing bright red and fading to a white speck." And "still another report said that the same or a similar object was seen at Korolevu."

Case #3: Humanoids on Top of UFO

Mr. and Mrs. Milin Milakovic, immigrants from Yugoslavia, and their eleven children lived in the small, dank mining town of Hednesford, Staffordshire, England. Sometime during the afternoon of November 20, 1968, the Milakovics and their son Slavic, 11, left home on a house-hunting trip. They traveled through the lovely English countryside to Rugeley, Abbots Bromley, stopping for a visit to Hanbury Hall on the border of Staffordshire-Derbyshire.

On their way home, the Milakovics stopped a little way outside of Hanbury to inspect an old house for sale. Then they continued on the road to home. Between 5:30 and 5:45 p.m., dusky shadows were quickly blanketing the area.

Frightened Rabbits

Suddenly, the couple saw a rabbit quickly racing across the road followed by a number of other rabbits from a hedge on the left side of the road. Then, to their left, they were startled to see a brilliant object resting in the field. Milakovic quickly applied the brakes and brought the car to a screeching halt. At the same time, the UFO slowly rose and glided over the automobile.

Milin and his wife jumped from the car and watched as the UFO moved over a field on the right side of the road. It was heading for a house about 100 yards from the road. It hovered over the house for a short period. Then it quivered "like a jelly."

Doris Milakovic reported to NICAP that the air temperature was much warmer as the UFO flew overhead. As it continued on, however, the temperature dropped. She said the object appeared to be as wide as a house.

"Humanoid Figures" Seen

For several minutes, the three Milakovics spotted what looked like five humanoid figures walking across the bright top of the UFO. A couple of the figures were seen to bend over as though they were looking at something in the part of the object below the rim.

Suddenly, in a pulsating or jerking movement, the craft began moving upward into the sky. The light intensity from the object was greatly increased and Milakovic felt that his eyes were burning. Thoroughly frightened, Milakovic—a normally brave man who was rarely scared of anything—grabbed his wife and son, pushed them roughly into the car, and sped away from the incredible scene.

It was a startling and profound experience the Milakovics would probably remember for the rest of their lives.

SECTION THREE
The Physiological Effects

This section contains five accounts of witnesses who suffered various physiological effects such as mysterious burns, eye injuries, temporary paralysis and shock during their encounters with mysterious objects seen in the skies. At the time I was careful to add the caveat: "We wish to stress… that NICAP has no proof or even convincing evidence that any of these effects were caused as a result of direct hostility. Most appeared to be due to either a somewhat inexplicable natural course of events or the fact that witnesses approached too close to the UFOs."

Case #1: The Businessman and the Spinning UFO

It was late on the evening of June 29, 1964. Businessman Beauford E. Parham was on the road returning home between Carnesville and Lavonia, Georgia, in the northeast corner of the state.

"I spotted a very bright light in the sky… coming directly toward my car," he explained in his letter to a NICAP member. "The next instance, it was directly in front of my headlights spinning like a giant top. It was shaped like a top and made a hissing sound like a million snakes. The top part of the object was moving in a clockwise direction and the bottom part… in a counterclockwise direction."

The UFO appeared to be large enough to hold a man. It was amber-colored, approximately six feet tall and eight feet wide. A tower-like projection with a dark band was seen at the top. Vane-like configurations were also observed. Small portholes dotted the bottom through which flames could be seen.

Object Disappears "in a Flash"

Suddenly, the object disappeared in a flash, then reappeared.

"It stayed directly in front of my headlights for at least a mile, never touching the car but spinning just in front of my lights," Parham said.

Although he was traveling at sixty-five miles-per-hour, the UFO kept an estimated five feet in front of the automobile and only one or two feet above the road. The top part of the object was tilted toward the witness. Parham said he followed in a near trance-like state.

In his report, Parham wrote: "When the object left…, it suddenly went up over the top of my car, leaving a strong odor… like embalming fluid and a very gaseous vapor which left an oily substance all over my car."

E-M and Physiological Effects

The UFO wasn't through with the businessman just yet. It reappeared for a third time and headed straight for the car. The motor began to sputter and miss. Parham slammed on the brakes and stopped the car. He looked up and saw that the object was "spinning like crazy." Then it took off and disappeared in a split second.

"By this time, my arms were beginning to burn…," Parham stated in his report. "My only thought was to get somewhere and let someone know what I had seen."

Parham quickly started the car and drove to Anderson AFB, South Carolina, to report the bizarre and frightening incident to Federal Aviation Administration (FAA) officials and newsmen. T.F. Acker, a reporter, told NICAP that he found Parham to be "intelligent, sincere and sober."

In his own report, Parham stated that he was unable to get rid of the oily marks on his car in spite of repeated cleanings. And the burning sensation also remained even after repeated washing of his arms.

Other Effects

Dan Sheridan, a former Marine Corps pilot and a NICAP advisor, interviewed the witness and found him to be "a very sober individual." Sheridan also discovered that the witness' car hood was in a warped condition and bubbled-up paint was found on the body. Samples were scraped from the car and forwarded to a local college for analysis, but no results were forthcoming. During an interview with a local newspaper, Parham said that his car radiator was eaten away and his water hose had collasped.

Federal Aviation Administration (FAA) officials Dean Carpenter and Albert Myrick also got into the act. They checked for any possible radiation effects. Apparently, some radiation was detected, but the exact amount was not disclosed.

Ball Lightning?

The Air Force was quick to come up with one of its favorite debunking explanations: ball lightning. The witness, however, wasn't about to go along with this explanation.

"There was not a cloud in the sky," he retorted. "Lightning would not rotate at [the] top and bottom as this object did…. It was definitely not that because ball lightning could not have followed my car for at least two miles!"

Also, the physical characteristics of the sighting did not correspond with the ball lightning explanation, according to personnel with the Westinghouse Research Laboratories. And "ball lightning occurs more often on high mountains than in the lowlands."

NICAP supporter Dr. James E. McDonald also gave a thumbs-down to that possibility.

"The most obvious difficulty with the ball lightning hypothesis is that any plasmoids of that type can be naturally generated in the absence of intense electrical storms….," he remarked. "Hundreds of credible observers have reported UFO phenomena without any involvement of power lines (as well as without any involvement with thunderstorms)."

Case #2: UFO Burns Witness' Hand

It was about 9:15 p.m., March 29, 1966. Charles Cozens was walking in a field between the Mountain Police Station and East 9th Street in Hamilton, Ontario, Canada. Suddenly, he spotted what he described as "two white, glowing, oval-shaped objects, one lower than the other, descending on the center of the field." The UFOs landed as the witness cautiously approached. Both of the relatively small objects were estimated to be three feet high, eight feet long and four feet wide.

NICAP Member Investigates

NICAP member Hugh Tapping investigated the incident.

"At about the center (vertically) of both there was a slight indentation which circled the objects," he reported. "In this indentation were lights about one inch in diameter and five inches apart. They flashed red, blue and green with no two lights on simultaneously."

One object had a four-foot long antenna protruding below the lights. Cozens carefully approached. Then he reached out and touched the antenna. It was extremely smooth, almost silky, like a gleaming, highly polished coffee table top. The UFO and the antenna were brightly glowing. As Cozens passed his hand along the projection, he saw a bright flash and heard what he described later as something like a buzzing sound. His hand was "blown off" the object and "knocked back several feet."

"Badly Frightened" Witness

Badly frightened and disoriented, the witness ran home. He sped past the police station, but didn't stop, fearing possible ridicule. Later that night, however, Constable Arnold Read investigated and confirmed the burned hand. Sometime during the following morning, superficial cuts or scratches had appeared along with the burn.

Some three or so months later, the indefatigable Jim McDonald telephoned and interviewed Cozens and his father.

"Both father and son sounded to me to be very careful and reliable persons," the physicist wrote in his report to me. "I am… inclined to take that unusual account very seriously. Charles recounted in a rather convincing manner what had happened with a judicious and basically very conservative attitude toward all that he was describing."

Case #3: Witness "Unable to Move"

A short time after midnight on March 8, 1967, William L. Wallace and his wife were driving to their home in Leominster, Massachusetts, following a pleasant evening observing the snow-laden trees in the country. As they drove southeast on Lancaster Street, they noticed a heavy fog patch surrounding St. Leo's Cemetery that was only seen around the graveyard grounds. There was no fog in the clear night sky. Wallace checked his watch and saw that it was 1:05 a.m. when they drove through the cloudy graveyard.

As they drove away from the cemetery, Wallace saw a bright glow to his left. He thought it may have been a fire and the mysterious fog was smoke from it, but neither he nor his wife smelled any smoke. Wallace quickly turned his 1955 Cadillac around and began heading back, his foot firmly on the pedal. He wanted to get home as quickly as possible. Then both he and his wife saw that the light was hovering about 400-500 feet over the cemetery.

In his report, Raymond F. Fowler, Chairman of NICAP's Massachusetts Subcommittee, said Wallace told him that he stopped his car, placed it in neutral gear and put the emergency brake on while the motor was still running. The driver lowered the windows, then left the car and pointed toward the UFO. As he performed this action, however, his arm was suddenly pulled abruptly against the roof of the automobile. As he grimaced in pain, he saw that his car had stalled, the headlights had gone out, and the radio stopped playing.

"I was unable to move," the witness stated in his report. "My wife was in a panic. My mind was not… affected. I just could not move. It felt like shock or numbness."

In a trembling voice, Mrs. Wallace remarked: "When the car went dead, I was yelling for Bill to get back into the car, but he did not move from where he was standing. I then slid across the seat and reached for him."

Mrs. Wallace clutched onto her husband's jacket and held it tightly. She was worried that Bill might be paralyzed. He was known for having a fearless character, but she became greatly concerned when he did not move. He later said he had been immobile for at least half-a-minute before he felt he could move again. Then, Wallace noticed that the radio and lights came back on. Meanwhile, the UFO was now rocking back and forth. Then it quickly sped upward and disappeared while emitting a humming sound.

Wallace, who was now badly frightened despite his reputation for not being afraid of anything, scurried back into the car and turned the ignition. The vehicle started normally. Still in a state of near panic, he quickly turned the car around and sped toward home. His wife was beside him, hugging and comforting him. Wallace was still in a slow and sluggish state as he turned into his down-graded driveway to the garage. But his reflexes were now very slow. He even had difficulty moving. He tried to stamp down hard on the brakes, but was not successful. He smashed into the garage door with a grounding thud, but he and his wife were badly shaken but not injured.

A little while after arriving home, the couple wanted to call someone, but they didn't have a telephone. After they calmed down, they decided to go out once more. But once again, they seemed inexplicably drawn to the cemetery. The fog was no longer visible when they arrived there. About ten minutes had passed since the object disappeared. The relieved couple drove back home with a piercing memory of the encounter that would last them for the rest of their lives.

Case #4: Justice of the Peace is Pulled Toward UFO

At 7:45 p.m., April 5, 1967, Justice of the Peace John H. Demler, was driving near his home in Jonestown, Pennsylvania, at 7:45 p.m., April 5, 1967, when his car suddenly "missed" three times.

"It then stopped and [the] lights went out," he explained in his report to NICAP. "At the same time, I saw an object coming towards the car about 20 feet above the street."

The justice was clearly shaken, but he still made an effort to observe the slow-moving UFO more closely. He estimated the object to be about thirty feet wide and it appeared to have lights in back of a painted black glass. Then it flew over the automobile as the driver quickly lowered his window and immediately drew in what smelled like oil and sulphur. He also heard a noise from the object that sounded like a running electric motor. This sound grew louder as the UFO left the area. It also shot off sparks similar to that of grinding on an emory wheel.

"A Terrific Burst of Speed"

Then, faster than Demler could comprehend, the UFO quickly approached the car and came to a stop immediately in front of it. After a short period hovering over the automobile, the alien craft started off slowly, then put on such a terrific burst of speed that the driver and his car seemed to be pulled to it. It was as if the object and its inhabitants, if any, wanted to somehow lift the justice into the body of the UFO.

After one or two more attempts, the aerial craft apparently abandoned its attempt to draw the driver and his car to it. Demler felt that the object had actually pulled him and his car a short distance off the ground at one point when they were suddenly released. The vehicle hit the ground with such force and a loud thud that he was flung all the way across his front seat. After taking a brief moment to compose himself, Justice Demler looked out the window again and saw that the unwanted object had changed color to a bluish tinge and was now very far away in the sky.

"My condition was all nerves the next day….," Demler stated in his report. "I was wet with perspiration 'til about 4 p.m.…. [The] skin peeled off my hands and feet…."

We immediately informed Jim McDonald of the justice's encounter. The physicist was quickly on the phone to Demler. The atmospheric physicist was impressed, telling us that the sighting was "one I believe to be fairly strong." He also told me that he had talked with one of Demler's co-workers, who confirmed that his friend was in an obvious state of physical or psychological shock for many hours.

Case #5: UFO Light Beam Hits Boy

It was about 8:40 p.m., March 19, 1968. Young Gregory L. Wells, Beallsville, Ohio, was on his short way home from visiting with his grandmother, who lived next door, when he spotted a red, oval-shaped UFO hovering low over some trees. It was so bright that it completely illuminated the road, stated the boy's mother, Mrs. James E. Wells. Gregory could see what he described as a band of dimmer red lights flashing around its center.

"I stopped," Gregory stated in his report to NICAP. "I wanted to run or scream, but, suddenly, a big tube came out of the bottom which moved from side-to-side until it came to me and a beam of light shot out."

Gregory quickly turned away as the light beam struck the upper part of his arm, knocking him to the ground. The boy's jacket caught fire and he rolled around on the ground, screaming with fright. Both his mother and grandmother ran from their homes to comfort him and help extinguish the flame. Mrs. Wells said she also saw the object, which just faded away.

During the brief encounter with the UFO, a large night light attached to a nearby pole went out, according to Gregory's father, James. Also, there was electro-magnetic interference to a television set. And the grandmother's dog reacted violently.

Boy "Treated for Second-Degree Burns"

Gregory was quickly taken to Beallsville Hospital, where he was treated for second-degree burns. Confirming the burns was Bruce Francis, who reported the near-deadly incident to NICAP. Francis said that the boy's scar was still visible three months later.

Monroe County Sheriff F.L. Sulsberger investigated the incident, but he could find no explanation. He forwarded the jacket to the Ohio Bureau of Criminal Investigation in London for analysis, but no evidence of radioactivity was found. Ward Strickling, the Civil Defense Director, also found no traces of radioactivity after he combed the area with a Geiger counter. However, he was quick to say that there were some types of radioactive beams that leave no detectable traces.

Jim McDonald Investigates

Jim McDonald was also quick to investigate the case.

"In the course of checking this case, I interviewed a number of persons in the Beallsville area, some of whom had seen a long cylindrical object moving at very low altitude in the vicinity of the Wells' property that night," McDonald stated. "My conversations with persons who know the boy, including his teacher, suggest no reason to discount the story, despite its unusual content."

McDonald was also confident enough in Gregory's account that he used it as part of his testimony at the U.S. House of Representatives' Committee on Science and Astronautics' Symposium on Unidentified Flying Objects in Washington, D.C., on July 29, 1968.

SECTION FOUR
The Animal Reactions

Case #1: Australian Cattle React Violently

Charles Brew was busy milking his cows on his Willow Grove, Australia, farm, approximately eighty miles southeast of Melbourne, when he turned his eyes to the sky and saw a UFO descend fast out of the east at about a forty-five-degree angle at 7:10 a.m., February 15, 1963. As the object got to within seventy-five feet—and about the same altitude—of the witness, it stopped and hovered.

The UFO sported a dome that appeared to be made of some kind of glass material. There was a metallic-appearing protrusion estimated to be five or six feet long at the top of the dome. The gray-colored middle section of the object appeared to be metallic and the bottom was rotating in a counter-clockwise direction. There were also scoop-like protrusions around the side, which seemed to be making a swishing noise. The object itself appeared to be about twenty-five feet wide and around nine feet high.

Frightened Cattle

The UFO also apparently caused the cattle to violently react.

"They did everything but turn somersaults....," Brew told Peter Norris, President of the Victorian Flying Saucer Research Society, who sent his report to NICAP.

Then the UFO took off instantly... with a bang!

Brew also said that, as he was watching the saucer, he suddenly got an awful headache. A pain-killing medication was not helpful, but the ailment wore off later that night.

Both Australian Air Force officers and F.A. Berson, of the Division of Meteorological Physics of the official Commonwealth Scientific and Industrial Research Organization, investigated the sighting area. They took rock samples for analysis, but NICAP received nothing further concerning the strange encounter.

Case #2: Bull Bends Metal Pipe

Young Harold Butcher, 16, was at his daily chore milking the cows in his father's barn in Cherry Creek, New York, at 8:20 p.m., August 19, 1965. Outside, close to the barn, a three-year-old bull was tied by the nose to a metal pipe. As he was working, Harold was listening to Radio Station WKBW.

Suddenly, Harold heard the bull make a weird, frightening noise like he had never heard come from an animal before. Rushing outside, he saw that the creature was bending the pipe in an frantic attempt to break loose. At the same time, Butcher saw a metallic-looking football-shaped UFO about fifty feet long and approximately twenty feet thick hovering just above the trees around 450 feet from the barn.

As the boy focused on the object, he saw it descend behind a maple tree. It emitted a red vapor from around its edges along with a beep-beep sound. At the same time, a lot of broken static was coming from the radio despite the fact that WKBW Radio usually had a clear signal in that area.

As Harold quickly approached the struggling bull, the UFO rose to behind some clouds "as fast as a snap of my fingers."

The Bouncing Vapor

Jeffrey J. Gow investigated the sighting for NICAP. He reported: "As it began to rise, the red vapor, which was about fifty inches wide, shot from the edges toward the ground, then bounced back to the ship as it hovered about ten feet in the air." The noise from the object also increased to what sounded like a sonic boom as it ascended. When the UFO disappeared behind some clouds, the clouds themselves mysteriously turned green.

Harold quickly scurried into the farmhouse. Inside, his mother, Mrs. William Butcher, was trying to correct what she called "definite interference" in her radio reception. Harold and his brother, Robert, went outside and were startled to see that the flying object had returned. It was hovering over a pine grove. For the second time, it quickly ascended while emitting the red vapor and turning the color of the clouds green.

Other people in the house included Kathleen Broughman, a friend, and William Butcher, Jr. While they were discussing the incredible event, Mrs. Butcher quickly called the Fredonia State Police Station. She was told that an officer would be sent to the scene. Then everyone but Mrs. Butcher, who was looking after a small daughter, scurried outside to see the object, but they could detect nothing unusual. William, Jr., ran into the milk barn while Harold and Robert returned to the house.

"It's Here Again!"

At 9 p.m., Kathleen Broughman, in an apparent terrified state, ran into the house, nearly tripping over the small daughter.

"*It's here again!*" she screamed in a state of panic.

Everyone but Mrs. Butcher ran outside and saw the UFO hovering overhead while emitting a glowing yellow vapor trail. But the clouds still held their green glow. The witnesses watched as "the object headed southwest toward Jamestown."

"A Pungent Odor" and E-M Effects

A short while later, Trooper C.J. Haas and his partner pulled up to the farmhouse. They joined the others as they walked out to inspect the area of the initial sighting. They noticed a pungent odor. Later, both Harold and the young daughter suffered from upset stomachs. According to Mrs. Butcher, the cows gave only a single can of milk that evening as opposed to their usual two-and-a-half cans.

Meanwhile, at the same time as the sighting encounter, Mrs. Sharon Rouland, Mrs. Butcher's niece, who lived five miles from the scene of the sighting, said that there was significant interference to her television set.

Physical Evidence

Back on the farm, Harold discovered a purple liquid oily-smelling substance and turned it over to the state police who, in turn, gave it to Captain James A. Dorsey—Operations Officer of the 4621st Air Force Group—and five other officers at the Niagara Falls AFB. The next afternoon, these Air Force men arrived at the Butcher home to investigate the sighting report. The NICAP investigator, Jeffrey Gow, also arrived on the scene. He noticed that the foot-tall grass in the area appeared to be bent over in long curved sweeps.

"I picked up plants which seemed to be singed on one side but were still green on the other," Gow stated in his report to NICAP. "I also dug up a one-foot-round area which seemed to be very slightly singed.... We discovered parallel two-inch-wide tracks separated by two inches of sod. The tracks were two inches deep.... In the tracks, the soil had been just recently exposed. The sod that appeared to be scooped out in these tracks could not be found...."

This physical evidence was forwarded to Henry C, Hawecki, a Consulting Engineer and NICAP adviser. He said: "The presence of phosphorous in the grass could have accounted for the odor of phosphene."

Case #3: The Alsatian and the "Flying Cross"

Angus Brooks had served with a Royal Air Force Middle East Command unit as a World War II Photographic Interpreter and was a former Flight Administrative Officer for British Overseas Airways Corporation (BOAC). On October 26, 1967, he was walking his Alsatian and Dalmation dogs in the vicinity of Moigne Downs, Dorset, England. A strong wind was blowing and he was having trouble controlling his animals, constantly pulling and tugging at their leashes as they struggled to break away. At 11:25 a.m.—as he held tightly on to the leashes of the hyper-active dogs—he sat down and rested his head in an indentation on the hill while the animals settled in on a shelter against the blustery weather.

His head had barely touched the ground when he saw what appeared to be a contrail high in the sky. Then the contrail quickly disappeared and was replaced by an unknown object that came down at lightning-like speed to an estimated 200-to-300 feet altitude.

"The shape of the craft prior to leveling out to an hover position was of a central circular chamber with a leading fuselage in the front and three separate fuselages together at the rear," Brooks stated in his report to NICAP. "On slowing to hover position, the two outer fuselages at the rear moved to a position at the side of the craft to form four fuselages at equidistant position around the center chamber.... On attaining hover, the craft rotated ninety degrees clockwise and then remained motionless, unaffected by the very strong wind."

"Distraught" Alsation

For the next twenty-two minutes, the strange object remained completely motionless in the sky. The Alsatian had just returned from foraging for game and stood beside Brooks in a distraught manner.

"The dog was standing here and her ears were pricked straight up like she does when she hears sounds that she was worried about," Angus remarked.

The witness said the UFO appeared to be made of a translucent material with dark shadows that were dotted along the bottoms of the fuselages and center chamber. What looked like nose cones and groove-like fins could be seen along the fuselage bases. The center chamber appeared to be around twenty-five feet in diameter and twelve feet high. Each fuselage was about seventy-five feet long, seven feet high and eight feet wide.

The Flying Cross

Brooks said he guessed that the UFO, which resembled a flying cross, was hovering between the Portland Underwater Defence Station and the Winfrith Atomic Station and about a mile inland from the USAF Communications Unit at Ringstead Bay.

Suddenly, at 11:47 a.m., the object took off toward the east-northeast and disappeared. On future walks in the same area, Brooks' Alsation still appeared to be nervous. About six weeks later, the unfortunate animal died of acute cystitis of the urinary bladder.

Investigating the incident was Julian A. Hennessey, Chairman of the NICAP European Subcommittee Unit #1.

Case #4: Children and Dogs React to Near-Landing

Early on the morning of July 30, 1968, three residents in Claremont, New

Hampshire, who wished to remain anonymous, saw a strange dome-shaped UFO. Shortly after 1 a.m., a worker at a manufacturing plant was carrying two buckets full of water to his garden when he spotted a bright round object that was floating in a gentle arc low in the sky to the northeast. He said it had the look of a full moon at a very low altitude. It quickly disappeared behind some trees.

Not long after that sighting, a land surveyor came into his new home after being hard at work in his rock garden less then two miles from where the plant worker lived. At 2 a.m., he and his wife saw a dome-shaped object that was an estimated twenty feet wide and hovered about ten feet over the ground.

"The object… was moving slowly, causing shadows on some freshly cut hay," the husband said in his report to NICAP. "These shadows had the effects of people moving."

Suddenly, a twenty-foot wide, gray-colored beam of light from the UFO struck the ground. The terrified couple reported that their apparently panic-stricken children and dogs were highly disturbed.

Wife's Account

The wife gave the most complete account of the frightening event:

> *Our children… were very restless. They were moaning as it something was hurting them…. They were actually crying out in their sleep. The children are both very quiet sleepers and once they are in bed, they do not wake up unless they are sick…. Our German Shepard was whimpering and whining as if something was hurting her…. My poodle was most upset. He sleeps in our bedroom… and he pawed the side of the bed until I put him in bed with us. He was actually shaking from being so upset. As soon as the object left, both dogs quieted down and went to sleep….*
>
> *My fear for the children was what upset me the most. I kept saying to*

my husband, what was going to happen to the poor children if someone should come to the house?

Both the husband and wife said they were helpless, isolated and terrified. The husband desperately wanted to drive to find help, but his wife refused to let him leave. Then the couple heard a high-pitched humming sound like that of a utility pole transformer.

Shepherd Dog Whines

A few minutes later, the couple saw the UFO move an estimated twenty-five feet toward the east. It remained there until 4:30 a.m. It was then that the humming sound increased to a very loud volume. At about the same time, the light from the object brightened to a high intensity. Then the disc began moving toward the west, barely clearing the trees and disappearing. Meanwhile, the shepherd dog was whining loudly.

"During this time, I thought of all kinds of things," the wife lamented. "I kept hearing sounds throughout the house. Any other night, they wouldn't have meant a thing, but tonight they were most terrifying."

While watching the UFO, the couple saw a projection from the aerial object descend toward the ground.

"Our experience was very terrifying and I hope that it never happens again," the wife concluded. "However, if it should, I hope that my husband and I will be prepared by then to handle the matter in a better way."

The husband reported the encounter with the strange object to Captain Ernest M. Fausse, of the Claremont Police Department. The captain confirmed to John Meloney, of NICAP's New Hampshire Subcommittee, that the witness appeared nervous and apprehensive.

Case #5: E-M Effects and Animal Reactions

Mrs. Elaine Pelchy had just dropped her husband off at work in Marcellus, New York at 6 p.m., November 25, 1968. Then she picked up her son and drove to the home of Mrs. Oliver Pelchy, her mother-in-law. It was the task of the elder Mrs. Pelchy to baby-sit while her daughter-in-law returned to her home to pack Christmas toys. Her route was to be the Lee-Mulroy Road. This was comprised of a left turn on Route 174, then a right turn on Route 20 and a final left turn on Amber Road.

They had covered about half of the distance they needed to go on Route 174 when Elaine and her son spotted "five round, red blinking lights."

"Then our car radio got very static," Mrs. Pelchy wrote in her report to NICAP.

English Setter and Baby React

The witness thought the UFO was about 100 feet in front of the car and was heading towards the southeast. It was then that her English setter "started crying, fighting, clawing first to get out the window, then in my lap, covering his eyes and ears, falling off the back seat."

Mrs. Pelchy said she began to be really concerned when her two year-old son began to cry, but he was soon silenced with a stern command from his mother. Then the car began acting up like it no longer had power and might be running on two cylinders instead of eight.

"To say the least, I was all over the road… and chugging along," the witness related.

As mother and son watched, the object abruptly executed a U-turn and headed rapidly back toward the northwest. When it turned, its lights changed to a blinking blue and white color "like in a pattern as in a neon light, but not in sequence." Mrs. Pelchy stared in amazement as the object turned and moved "faster than I had ever seen anything travel."

UFO Merges With "Star"

With her eyes set firmly on the aerial intruder, Elaine saw it suddenly stop in mid-air and seemingly change to "a white, dome-shaped object with [another] object like 'a fluorescent star' next to it." She continued to watch as the larger object appeared to merge into the "star" and disappear. Then the star-like UFO grew larger and brighter. Mrs. Pelchy kept her eyes on the unwanted visitor that was now between the hills and the trees.

"At first, I was calm, then apprehensive about having my son and dog involved," she admitted in her report. "Then I was frightened and tense and couldn't wait to get safely home."

The witness quickly dropped her son off at home, but she felt mysteriously drawn to return to the spot where they saw the unsettling UFO. When she returned to the scene of the sighting, she said:

> *I had the feeling that someone was looking over my shoulder when again the car [lost] power and [the] dog started to cry as if in pain again and go through the previous business [of] whining, barking, etc. I looked over my left shoulder. The devil couldn't have startled me more than this huge, bright fluorescent light.... If you looked at it directly, it would have been blinking like a welding torch. It also had these fuzzy lights around it.*

Elaine continued to watch as the UFO got brighter, then duller, then brighter again, then blinding as it seemed to get smaller at the same time. Mrs. Pelchy brought her car to a halt at a stop sign and watched as the object performed a zig-zag circular motion.

The "Inverted Cone"

Immediately after she returned home, Elaine grabbed the phone and dialed her friends, Mr. and Mrs. William King, who also witnessed the phenomenon. Then she called Betsy Paranteau, her next door neighbor, who drove with her back to where she saw the UFO.

When they arrived, the two witnesses saw that the object had suddenly appeared in front of their car. It was at an estimated 100 feet off the ground. Then it performed zig-zag movements like a bird looking for a place to light. As the women continued staring, the UFO changed its shape to what resembled an inverted cone.

"After watching a few more minutes and not seeing the light disappear, we came home with qualmy stomachs," Mrs. Pelchy stated in her NICAP directive. "I would rather escape the whole episode by putting it out of my mind, but the fact is that something very mysterious did happen.... I'll not be driving on that road or area alone at night anymore."

Soon after her encounter, Elaine learned that Joan Nagen, a Lakeland woman, and her husband spotted what they described as "unusual moving lights" at 7:15 p.m. that same evening. This was about the same time that Mrs. Pelchy and Mrs. Paranteu had returned home.

Case #6: "Barking and Howling" Farm Animals

At 2 a.m., April 23, 1969, in Silver Springs, Maryland, a suburb of Washington, D.C., Mrs. Virginia A. Guinn and her boarder were quickly awakened by violent reactions from Virginia's cats and dogs at her farm. Even the boarder's German shepherd was barking in a peculiar manner—a series of short, snappy barks. Mrs. Guinn's four cats were also frantic, loudly meowing, yowling and fighting. They were frantically climbing up the screen door, clawing the thin wire loose in a desperate attempt to get inside. It was something they had never done before.

Both witnesses ran outside and spotted a circular bluish-white UFO that appeared to be as large as two rooms. The light looked like the glow around a welder's arc. The object traveled toward the north-northeast beyond the barn. Then the two wary witnesses heard a humming noise, and the object suddenly went out like a light. Shortly after the UFO disappeared, the animals quieted down.

Later that morning, Mrs. Guinn found that the horses in the barn had broken free of their tie-stalls and had knocked harnesses and other equipment off the walls. She added that the barn of a neighbor was torn up by terrified horses during the sighting.

Karl T. Pflock, NICAP's Capitol Area Subcommittee Chairman, investigated the incident.

SECTION FIVE
The Physical Evidence

Case #1: Seaman Sees Object on Nova Scotia Beach

In late November 1965, two sightings in the Annapolis Valley of Nova Scotia, Canada, created quite a stir and "considerable interest."

On the early morning of November 30, Seaman Ian Kinsey, of Her Majesty's Coastal Service, was on his two-to-four a.m. watch at the Cornwallis Station. His watch entailed making the rounds of one of the barracks and he was to pass by a certain window in the barracks two times between those duty hours. Visible through the window was a small, confined beach approximately 500 paces long and about fifty paces wide at low tide. This particular section of Canada had what were believed to be at the time the world's largest tides.

At 3:30 a.m., Seaman Kinsey passed by the window a second time. As he looked out, he expected to see the usual things, including the eerie pitch-blackness, the lights of the shoreline, the communications station, and radio antennae. But there was something else in the mix of things to see that night. Kinsey saw a sharply oval, yellow object resting on the beach. It was lit up, but not glaring.

About five minutes after the seaman spotted the UFO, a sliding door on its side opened, emitting a white light. Then a smaller, cigarette-shaped UFO entered the larger object through the door. The larger object then rose and slowly cruised over the mountain and was gone for good.

Kinsey said that, as the UFO left the area, it appeared to push rocks, logs and other material away from the center of the beach.

Seaman is Questioned

As the Assistant Director at NICAP, I received a number of letters from Ian Kinsey, who said no one seemed to believe his incredible story. He even said he was sent to several doctors to "test his sanity," but no real tests were made.

"There's a good chance they will give me a medical discharge....," Kinsey told me. "They say I am emotionally disturbed. Since I took no tests, I can't see how they came to a conclusion like this.... They put me in the hospital under treatment.... They say if I stick to my story, I will be thrown out of the Navy."

I became concerned about Kinsey and his situation and wrote to Captain J.M. Paul, his commanding officer.

"I wish to assure you that Ordinary Seaman Kinsey is not being released because he refused to deny the sighting of an unidentified flying object," Captain Paul responded. "This man is... being released, but for reasons which are in no way connected to this incident."

A Corroborating Report

Only a few hours before the Kinsey encounter, late on the evening of November 29, young Kevin Davis and Gary Jardine saw a UFO supporting a blinking red dome near Springhill, stated an article in *The Springhill Record*. The object reportedly had portholes and emitted an exhaust and a humming sound.

Suddenly, as the frightened boys watched, a long bar-like object was emitted from the largest porthole. It reentered and emerged a second time. Then, something resembling smoke came from the large UFO and sparks flew upward. Also, snow covering the area was blown around and some of the bushes were flattened.

Springfield is approximately 125 miles northeast of Cornwallis.

Case #2: Pioneer Woman Encounters UFO

At about the same time this sighting was reported to NICAP in 1968, Mrs. Pearl Christiansen was one of the few still-surviving pioneer women left in the western United States. She migrated to Gleeson, Colorado, in 1920 as a teacher for the children of the mining community settlers. She had gotten used to many things in that sparsely populated area of the country, including droughts and floods, but she had never seen a UFO. That dramatically changed at 7:50 p.m., August 26, 1968.

Mrs. Christiansen was driving back to her ranch from Gleeson and stopped to unfasten the chain protecting her private driveway. That was when she "saw this big, round, silver disk with a trail of flickering lights and haze… which burned out," she remarked in her report to NICAP.

The Brown's Peak UFOs

The retired schoolteacher kept her eyes on the object for about five minutes. Then she spotted a second UFO, which was "very shiny and gold," near the first object. Both glowing objects hovered overhead. The second UFO "was also round and 'rich gold' in color with a pink band."

"It hurt my eyes to look at its brightness," Pearl remarked.

Both UFOs seemed to be sitting on top of 7,200-foot high Brown's Peak. The witness said that, shortly before midnight, the two craft seemed to back off into the valley behind the park and disappear.

Mrs. Willard Mayfield—who managed the Gleeson Museum with her husband—was a corroborating witness. However, she reported seeing three objects.

"They looked like round dimmed headlights….," she told NICAP in her report. "The larger of the three was sitting to the west of the two smaller objects."

A reporter, Cecil James, and Dan Tortorell, a photographer for the *Daily Citizen,* hurried to the landing site. James wrote that "strange fires... had scorched parts of the peak. The burning pattern of cactus and grass was erratic."

APRO Investigates

Among the investigators were James and Coral Lorenzen, the head honchos at APRO. Lorenzen told Cecil James that he believed Mrs. Christiansen probably saw UFOs, but thought the fire may have been set by members of a nearby hippie settlement. Cecil James, however, wasn't buying it.

"I doubt if [hippies] set the fire," he said. "Individual sotol cactus plants... were badly charred at their bases, but not burned at the top. Others were burned by a fierce heat, which left only the blackened base of the plant. A direct row of four plants measuring about four feet in length appeared to have been hit by a flame-thrower. Still, a plant near the fourth one hardly was singed. Also, the peak... had burned spots no more than four to eight inches in diameter. And there were many dead clumps of grass and pieces of drywood, which were not touched at all. [The] rocks showed signs of terrific heat. None of the fires appeared to have resulted from lightning strikes."

Two days after the sighting, Mrs. Mayfield's husband, an unidentified Army major and Mrs. Christiansen inspected the area around the peak. In his report to NICAP, "Mayfield confirmed the physical evidence discovered by the *[Daily] Citizen* employees."

"In the burned area, the rocks... were still too hot to hold my hands on," Mayfield added. "There was a peculiar [acid-like] odor about the place."

Case #3: Car Rocked By "Thunderous Explosion"

It was less than two weeks after the pioneer woman, Pearl Christiansen, saw her UFO. Shortly after 9:30 p.m., September 6, 1968, two friends, John Dow and Paul Franklin, were driving around the town dump in Taradale, New Zealand, about half-a-mile from the Redcliffe Power

Station. The station was where 11,000-volt lines travel from the main East Coast grid supplier, Tuai Station, through the outer fringes of the dump to Taradale, Napier, Pakowhai and Fernhill Stations.

As they sped along Springfield Road, the young men saw twenty-to-thirty red and green lights that were flying aimlessly above the dump. They quickly pulled to the side of the road and watched as a thunderous explosion ripped through the air. Both the ground and the automobile, a 1957 Austin A55, shook and vibrated. In what seemed like a split second, the lights appeared to group up. Then they rose straight up and disappeared into the night sky.

In a completely frightened state, the men told what had happened to the officer on duty at the Taradale Police Station. The duty officer later said that John and Paul had seen flashing power cables that appeared to be impregnated with salt spray. The men seriously doubted this explanation and returned to the dump the following night, but saw nothing unusual.

Other Encounters

Two nights later, at 7:30 on the evening of September 8, Dow and Franklin had another encounter with the same or another UFO. They saw a small light rise from a field to about 1,000 feet altitude, stop, expand, and disappear.

The sightings of strange and unexplained lights continued for the two friends. About twenty-four hours later, on September 9, they were again in the Puketapu area and watched a light for ten minutes.

The following evening, September 10, however, came the terrifying event the boys would never forget. They were heading back to Taradale along the Omaruni road when they were startled to see a circular object with a red and green light that was only a few feet in diameter and was glowing white. As they approached in an apprehensive state, the UFO disappeared, apparently behind a cloud.

Dow turned the wheel of the car onto Highway 50 and crossed the

Tutaekuri River Bridge. It was then that Franklin again spotted the object. It was hovering on the opposite side of the river. It was also glowing very intensely and sped toward the automobile from the rear.

The boys were terrified.

"Bail out! It's got us!" Franklin screamed in terror as he flung the door open.

The car was traveling at around 35 m.p.h. As Franklin flung himself from the vehicle, his feet became tangled with his friend's legs, lifting his feet from the gas pedal and brake. This caused the car to spin out of control. Then Dow also fell through the left door. Franklin struck the ground hard on his back while Dow landed on his chest with a dull, painful thud.

The now brilliantly bright UFO hovered only about two feet over the roof of the car. Franklin, afraid he and his friend were about to be blinded, covered his eyes with his arm.

"The light! The light!" he frantically called out.

Dow began to cautiously get back up on his feet, but his friend stopped him.

"For God's sake, stay down!" Franklin commanded. "They are after us!"

Car Crashes Into Store

The two friends were obviously afraid they were about to be kidnapped by the flying object. At about this time, the car careened to the right and crashed into the store of a fruit dealer on Gloucester Street about 100-to-200 yards away. There was the sound of shattered glass as a window was smashed. The right-side fender was almost completely ripped from the body of the car and the headlight was nearly pulled from its socket.

A crowd began gathering around Dow and Franklin, who were still lying dazed alongside the road. They were trembling with fear. Soon the police arrived followed by a tow truck. The driver later reported that the boys were badly shocked and still cowering with fear. Then Dow's father arrived and drove the boys home.

About twenty-four hours later, on October 12, Dow made a required appearance before the Napier Magistrate's Court with W.K.L. Dougall presiding. He pleaded "not guilty." Constable Barry Martin-Bus, a policeman, testified that, when he arrived on the scene, he found both boys "in an hysterical condition." Dougall dismissed the case, saying that "Dow's state of mind at the time had made him lose control of the car."

Dow's insurance company was also satisfied.

"We [indemnified] Mr. Dow in respect of accidental damage to his motor vehicle and were quite satisfied… that the damage to his car arose from an accident…," the company reported.

Claude L. Elmes, a NICAP supporter and member, investigated the case.

Major Donald E. Keyhoe was the Director/President of NICAP from 1957-1969. *(Photo by the Author from his Collection.)*

Major Donald E. Keyhoe (standing akimbo at far right) managed the 1928 nationwide tour of famed aviator Charles Lindbergh (far left), next to his wife, Anne Morrow Lindbergh. *(Courtesy of Richard H. Hall and NICAP.)*

This was Major Donald Keyhoe's first book, published in 1928 to honor Charles Lindbergh. *(Photo scan by Jay Triche from the Author's Collection.)*

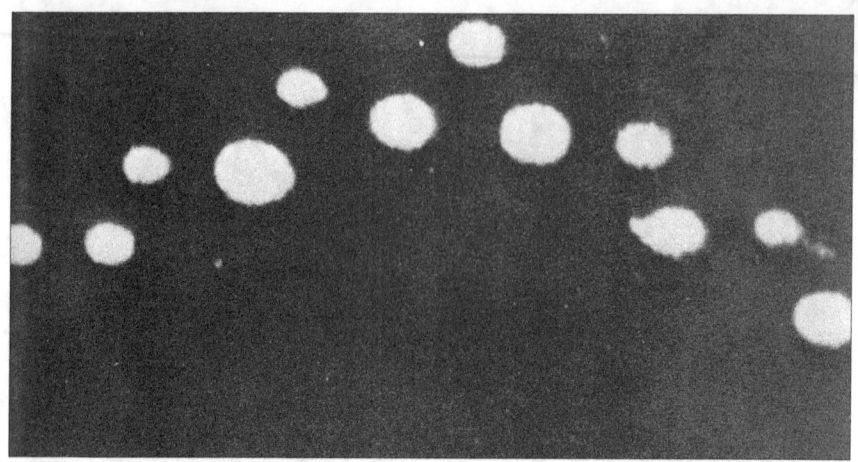

This photo of the famed Lubbock Lights in Texas was taken by Carl Hart, Jr., 18, on the evening of August 30, 1951. *(Courtesy of NICAP.)*

This official U.S. Coast Guard photo was taken by Shell Alpert at the Coast Guard Station in Salem, Massachusetts, on July 16, 1952. *(Courtesy of NICAP.)*

The UFO Evidence (1964), by Richard H. Hall, was a classic early NICAP publication sent to all members of Congress.
(Photo scan by Jay Triche from the Author's Collection.)

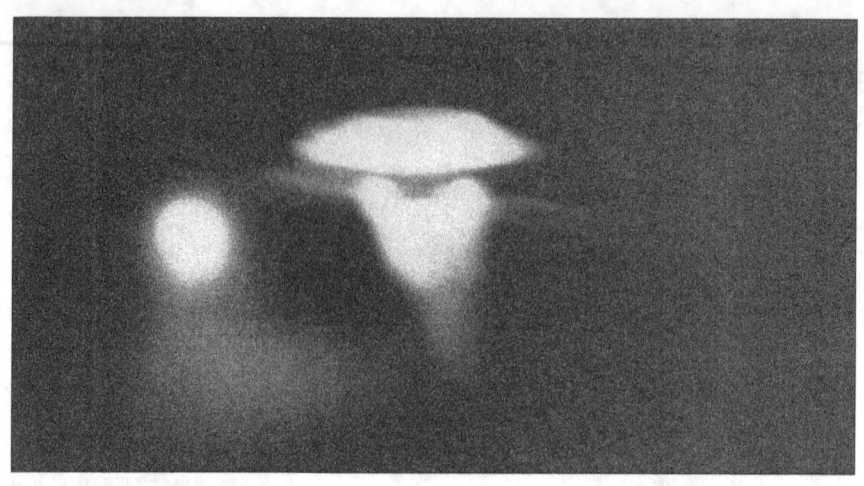

Amateur astronomer James Lucci snapped this photo of a nighttime disc over Beaver, Pennsylvania, on the evening of August 8, 1965. *(Courtesy of James Lucci, NICAP and John Fuller.)*

Rex Heflin, an Orange County, California, highway investigator, snapped this first of several renown photos from his truck's cabin in Santa Ana, California, on August 3, 1965. *(Courtesy of NICAP.)*

Second flying saucer photo taken by Rex Heflin. *(Courtesy of NICAP.)*

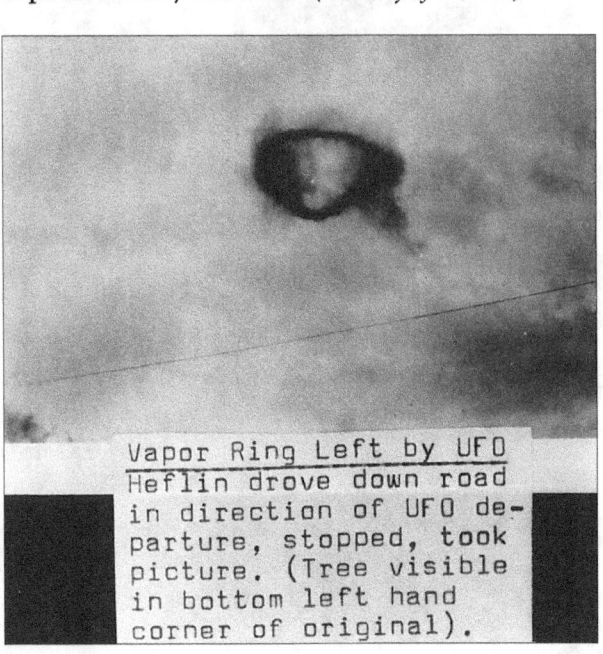

This vapor ring was emitted by the UFO seen and photographed by Rex Heflin. *(Courtesy of NICAP.)*

Vapor Ring Left by UFO
Heflin drove down road in direction of UFO departure, stopped, took picture. (Tree visible in bottom left hand corner of original).

Young Dwight Myers stands at the site of his saucer sighting in Spring Grove, Pennsylvania, on October 30, 1965.
(Photo by the Author from his Collection.)

The author works on his book *Mysteries of the Skies: UFOs in Perspective* (1968) at NICAP headquarters. *(Photo scan by Jay Triche from the Author's Collection.)*

The author, left, and Harold Deneault check UFO sighting locations on the NICAP board. *(Photo scan by Jay Triche from the Author's Collection.)*

Gordon Lore, far right, circles the landing spot on the road where a UFO is believed to have landed in South Hill, Virginia, on April 21, 1967. *(Courtesy of NICAP.)*

UNIDENTIFIED FLYING OBJECTS

HEARING

BY

COMMITTEE ON ARMED SERVICES

OF THE

HOUSE OF REPRESENTATIVES

EIGHTY-NINTH CONGRESS

SECOND SESSION

APRIL 5, 1966

[Pages of all documents printed in behalf of the activities of the House Committee on Armed Services are numbered cumulatively to permit a comprehensive index at the end of the Congress. Page numbers lower than those in this document refer to other subjects.]

U.S. GOVERNMENT PRINTING OFFICE
50–066 O WASHINGTON : 1966

NICAP geared up for its first Congressional UFO Hearing in 1966. *(Photo scan by Jay Triche from the Author's Collection.)*

The author measures the hole that may have been made by one of the object's landing legs in South Hill. *(Courtesy of NICAP.)*

NICAP staff members Gordon Lore, left, and Leon Katchen investigate the possible UFO landing site in South Hill. *(Courtesy of NICAP.)*

An enlargement of a hole in the road at South Hill that may have been made by an alien object. *(Courtesy of NICAP.)*

The author (center) shows NICAP interns a sighting report circa 1967. *(Courtesy of NICAP.)*

The author, second from left, at the bulletin board with NICAP volunteers circa 1967. *(Courtesy of NICAP.)*

Dr. James E. McDonald was a tireless UFO investigator and friend of the author, Richard Hall and NICAP. *(Photo scan by Jay Triche from the Author's Collection.)*

Gordon Lore (left) sits with Dr. James E. McDonald at an undisclosed UFO meeting circa 1969. *(Courtesy of Ann Druffel.)*

UFO enthusiast and actor Simon Oakland was on *The Joe Franklin Show* in New York with the author and journalist John Fuller in 1968. *(Photo scan by Jay Triche from the Author's Collection.)*

Police Officer Lonnie Zamora saw a UFO with three small alien beings land outside Socorro, New Mexico, on April 24, 1964. *(Courtesy of NICAP.)*

Ann Druffel's seminal tribute to Dr. James E. McDonald is a favorite with UFO enthusiasts. *(Courtesy of Ann Druffel.)*

Dr. J. Allen Hynek, left, walks with Dr. Jacques Valle.
(Courtesy of Jacques Valle.)

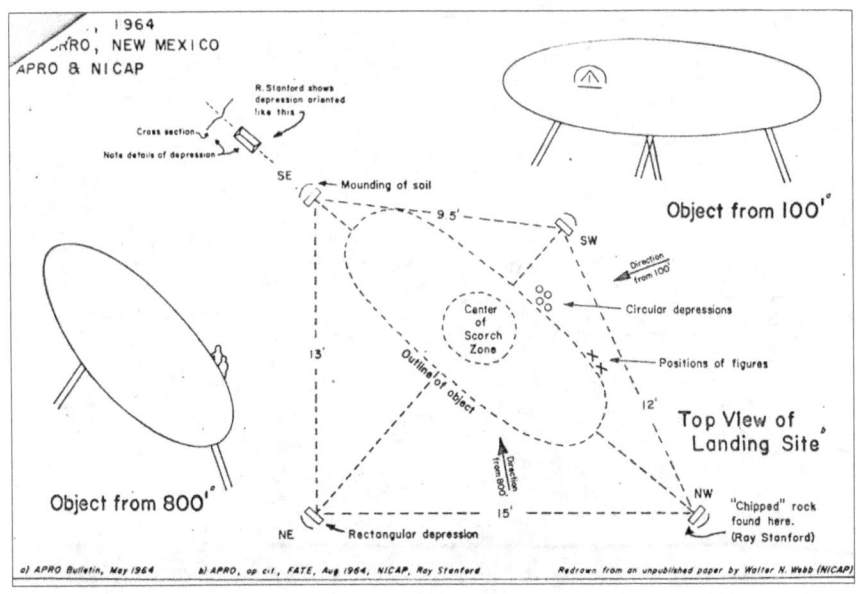

A drawing of the UFO landing site near Socorro, New Mexico, April 24, 1964.
(Sketch by Walter N. Webb. Courtesy of NICAP.)

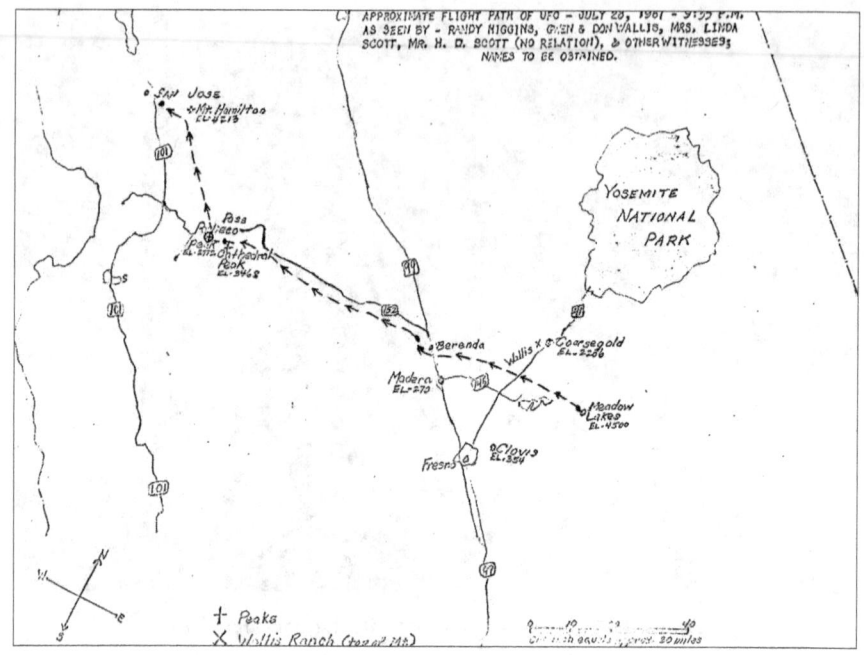

Sketch of flight path of a UFO seen near Yosemite National Park on the evening of July 28, 1967. *(Photo scan by Jay Triche from the Author's Collection.)*

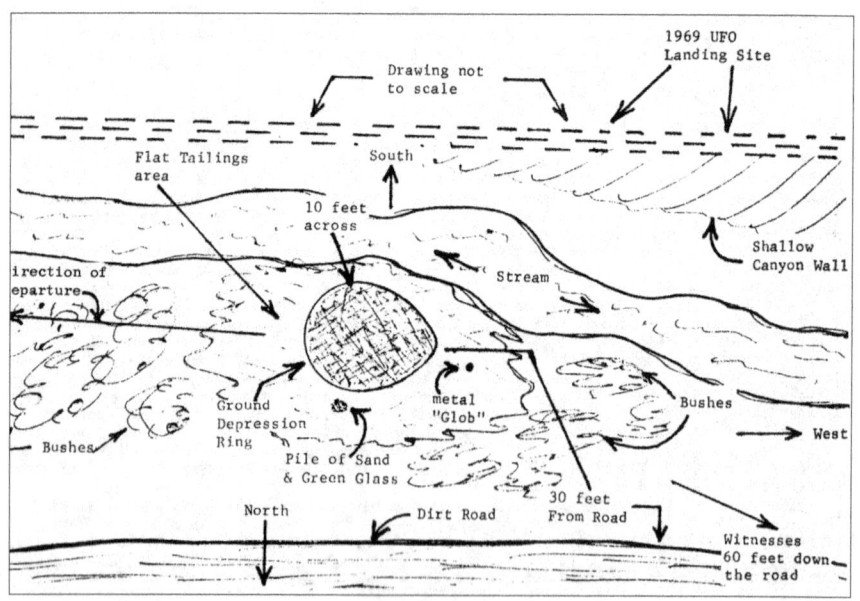

Drawing of UFO landing site near Redding, California, October 30, 1969.
(Photo scan by Jay Triche from the UFO Research Newsletter.)

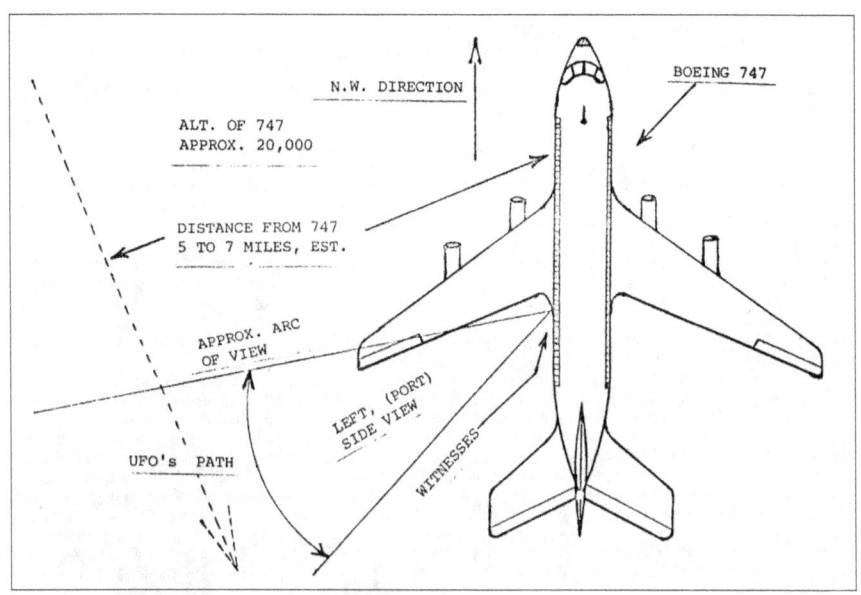

Sketch of the flight path of four aerial objects seen by passengers aboard a Boeing 747 jet plane near Lompoc, California, April 11, 1977. *(Courtesy of Paul C. Cerny. Drawing scan by Jay Triche from the* UFO Research Newsletter.*)*

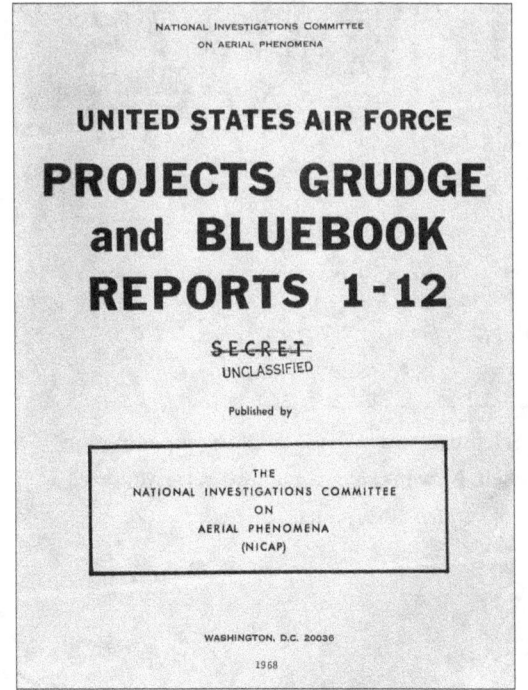

This groundbreaking NICAP publication broke open the lock on SECRET and CONFIDENTIAL Air Force UFO reports through the Freedom of Information Act. *(Photo scan by Jay Triche from the Author's Collection.)*

Flying Saucers: *Four Scientific Papers*

By
Nuclear Physicist Lecturer
STANTON T. FRIEDMAN

31628 Trevor Avenue
Hayward, California 94544
415-471-0160

Page
1. Science Fiction, Science, and UFOs - 1977
2. Fiction, Fact, and Flying Saucers - 1979
6. A Scientific Approach to Flying Saucer Behavior - 1975
23. The Case for the Extraterrestrial Origin of Flying Saucers - 1979

Published by
UFORI, P.O.B. 502, Union City, Ca. 94587   First Printing Jan. 1980

$3.00

Nuclear physicist Stanton T. Friedman was instrumental in reopening the world-famous July 1947 Roswell, New Mexico, crash-and-retrieval case.
(Courtesy of Stanton T. Friedman.)

Congressman J. Edward Roush was a member of the NICAP Board of Governors. *(Courtesy of NICAP and* The U.F.O. Investigator.*)*

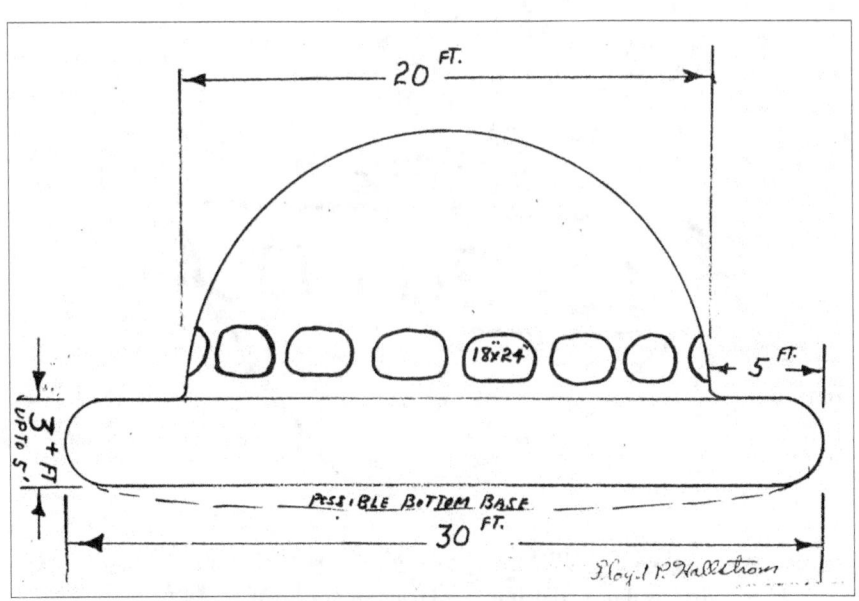

Witness' Sketch of UFO Over Santa Monica, California, January 1, 1978. *(Courtesy of Idabel Epperson. Photo scan by Jay Triche from the* UFO Research Newsletter.*)*

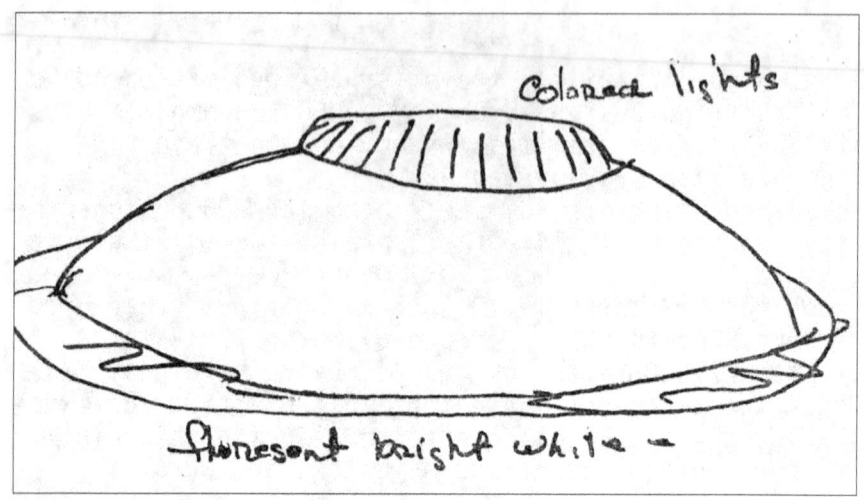

Debbie Ballway drew this sketch of a florescent UFO she observed, near Cazenovia, New York, on May 3, 1978. *(Courtesy of the* Syracuse Post-Standard. *Photo scan by Jay Triche from the* UFO Research Newsletter.*)*

Sketch of UFO with possible occupants that was observed near Baltimore, Maryland, on April 25, 1978. *(Courtesy of John Lutz. Photo scan by Jay Triche from the* UFO Research Newsletter.*)*

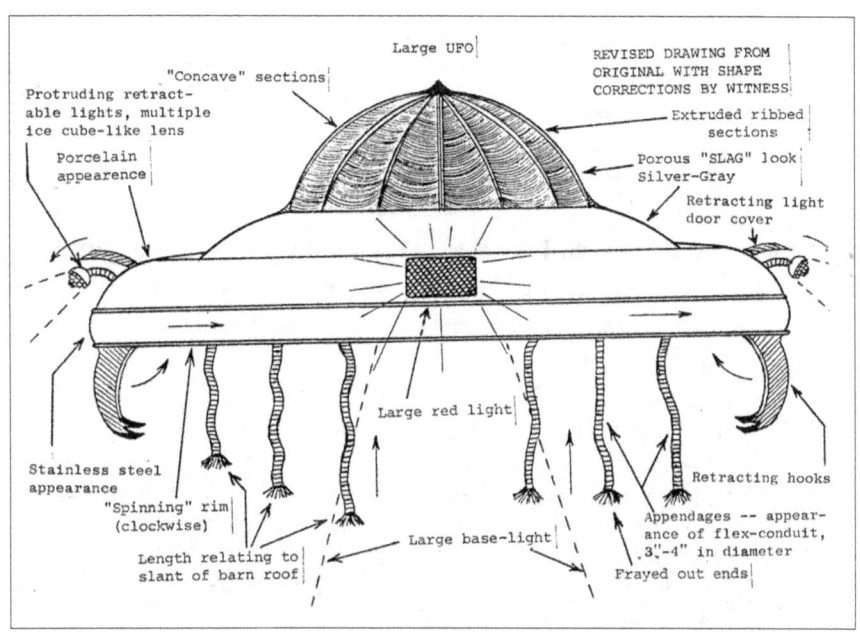

Bill Pecha and others saw this UFO on September 10, 1976, in Colusa, California. *(Courtesy of Paul C. Cerny. Drawing scan by Jay Triche from the* UFO Research Newsletter.*)*

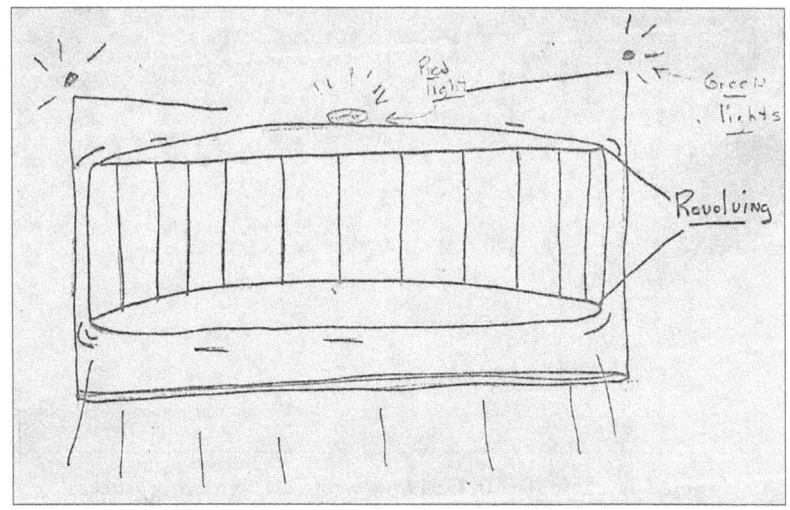

Ellen Roberts, her sister, Jo, and daughter, Laura, spotted this revolving object near San Jose, California, on June 25, 1976. *(Photo scan by Jay Triche from the* UFO Research Newsletter.*)*

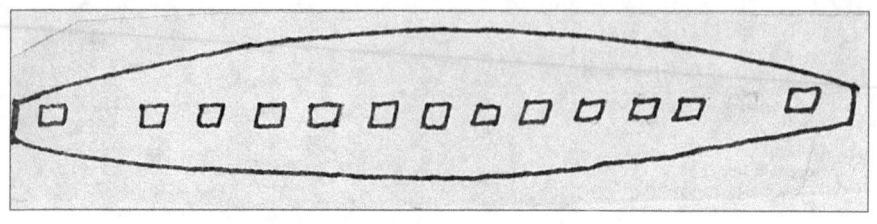

Diane Hickling sketched this object she saw with her son and daughter over Mt. Airey, Maryland, on July 25, 1976.
(Courtesy of Diane Hickling from the UFO Research Newsletter.)

PROF. DR. C. G. JUNG   KÜSNACHT-ZÜRICH
                                              SEESTRASSE 228

                                              October 13th 1958

Major Donald E. Keyhoe
National Investigation Committee
1536 Connecticut Ave N.W.
Washington 6, D.C.

Dear Major Keyhoe,
my recent experience with APRO shows me that I must be careful in getting mixed up with UFO-organisations. Although I am vividly interested in these questions, I prefer to detach my name from organisations of this kind. This does not mean, that I am not perfectly willing to contribute whatever I can, to the research-work, such organisations are concerned with. If I am able at all to help in psychological matters, I am glad to do so, but I prefer it in an inofficial way.

I enclose a report in the "Neue Zürcher Zeitung" of October 1st 1958, which is unfortunately inconclusive.

                          Sincerely yours

                              C. G. Jung

Famed psychologist Dr. Carl Jung wrote his own flying saucer book and corresponded with Keyhoe. *(Courtesy of Major Donald E. Keyhoe. Original letter from the Author's Collection.)*

STRANGE EFFECTS FROM UFOs

A NICAP SPECIAL REPORT

DIRECTOR: **MAJOR DONALD E. KEYHOE**, USMC (RET.)
ASSISTANT DIRECTOR: **GORDON I. R. LORE, JR.**

CHIEF RESEARCHER AND WRITER:
GORDON LORE

NICAP released some of its more controversial encounter and other reports through this book by the author. *(Courtesy of NICAP.)*

CHAPTER EIGHTEEN

The McDonald Factor

Dr. James E. McDonald was an extraordinary scientist who had become both a tireless UFO investigator and a close friend of Dick Hall, my wife and I. The physicist had spent many hours in the NICAP office when I was Assistant Director and Vice President poring over the thousands of reports in our files. During his numerous trips to the Washington, D.C., area, he often spent the nights in our home in Bethesda, Maryland, where we talked into the wee hours of the morning.

McDonald told us that he was getting a lot of negative feedback from U.S. government officials about his probing into many UFO cases. He felt there was a strong feeling from these individuals that he was beginning to sway a number of prominent scientists and others to take a closer more scientific look at the many hundreds of excellent reports from highly qualified witnesses. And these individuals, government and military officials and others, clearly did not want that to happen. We even began to wonder whether or not there may have been a nefarious plot to silence our friend. It was a highly disturbing thought.

The physicist indicated to us that he may have been targeted by stealthy individuals in black vans who were following him around areas close to his home in Phoenix. He added that some of his UFO material had been stolen from his seat on several airline flights. He also related that—during his last visit to our home in May 1971—he had gathered nearly all of the material he needed to write and publish his own book on the phenomenon.

Then... About a month later, his body was found in the desert outside his home with a bullet hole in his head. There was a gun beside him with an apparent suicide note.

A State of Shock

Dick Hall was visiting my wife Marty and I in our home when we got the call that our dear friend was dead. We quickly went into a state of shock and, even, disbelief. It was very difficult, even impossible, for us to believe that our friend would commit suicide only a month after he was in our home, particularly since he appeared very anxious to start work on his own book and showed no sign of being depressed.

Soon after McDonald's death, however, Dick Hall, my wife and I began getting reports that our friend had suffered severe bouts of depression during his life. The fact that his wife, Betsy, had fallen in love with a younger man who was active in the anti-war movement, and had asked for a divorce, hardly helped.

According to Ann Druffel in her excellent book *Firestorm: Dr. James E. McDonald's Fight for UFO Science* (2005)—a superb account of McDonald's life and work—our friend and colleague attempted suicide at his home in the pre-dawn hours of April 9 when he fired a bullet into his head. The missive missed his brain, but hit his optic nerve, causing blindness.

Divorce plans were dropped as Betsy and others helped Jim recover and cope with his loss of sight. But depression is often unforgiving. In early June 1971, he was planning a re-entry into academic life. For a brief period, he accomplished this goal with a renewed burst of positive energy. Betsy, however, was still very worried. She had been warned that her husband might be pretending to handle things well so he could get out of the hospital and try suicide again. Betsy even offered to help him write his UFO book.

On June 12, however, his depression had obviously reached its zenith. He called a taxi and instructed the driver to head for a pawnshop, where he purchased a 0.38 Spanish revolver. Then he asked the driver to head for a nearby desert location, where he disembarked. He told the cabbie that someone would pick him up later. During the middle of the next day, his body was found under a bridge wash where a family was hiking.

Was the U.S. Government Involved?

In an almost desperate attempt to make sense of our friend's apparent suicide, Dick, Marty and I pondered several possibilities. We quickly discovered that his wife had fallen in love with another man and that alone, we reasoned, may have been the impetus for his self-inflicted demise. But we also reluctantly and nervously discussed what we thought could be another possibility: *could it be that some nefarious faction within the U.S. Government wanted his demise?* It was still hard to believe, but we pondered the question.

Jim McDonald had given many speeches (including one at the United Nations) criticizing the government and, like Donald Keyhoe, he was a gadfly to some fellow scientists who believed the subject was not worth investigating. Most of these scientists had not seriously looked at even the basic facts.

"Are UFOs Extraterrestrial Surveillance Craft?"

One of the numerous talks McDonald gave might possibly hold some clue as to why he may have been a target for harm by individuals in the government and/or elsewhere. On March 26, 1968, he gave a carefully prepared lecture before the American Institute of Aeronautics and Astronautics (AIAA) in Los Angeles. Following are excerpts from that speech entitled "Are UFOs Extraterrestrial Surveillance Craft?":

> If it were insisted that I limit my entire talk to a one-word answer to the question posed in [the] title, I should find it hard to choose between the safer answer, "possibly," and the riskier answer, "probably." The ever-increased weight of the evidence I have been examin-

ing would drive me to the latter answer if I had to compress an hour's remarks into a single word.

Surely AIAA members would wholeheartedly agree that if there were even a slim possibility that the earth was under extraterrestrial surveillance in any form, that would be a matter of the greatest scientific importance, warranting the most vigorous investigation. In fact, the evidence that seems to point to the conclusion that UFOs could be such devices is far from negligible; yet because of the history of official and scientific response to the earlier UFO reports, we continue to see mainly neglect or ridicule of this intriguing question.

After nearly two years of intensive study of many facets of the longstanding UFO problem, after examining around a thousand UFO reports and directly interviewing several hundred witnesses in selected UFO cases of outstanding interest, and after weighing alternative hypotheses, I find myself driven steadily further towards the position that the extraterrestrial [ET] hypothesis is the most probable hypothesis to account for the UFO.

That hypothesis, of course, is not original with me. It has been argued for many years by persons knowledgeable with respect to the UFO problem who spoke from outside scientific circles. Our collective failure to examine scientific aspects of the UFO problem will, I fear, be held against the scientific community when the full dimensions of the UFO evidence comes to be recognized. And the latter date may not be far off.

The principal points I wish to emphasize include the following:

1. For the past half-dozen years, our American space program has been keyed to "the search for life in space," yet the now impressive UFO evidence that "life" may, in some sense, already have found us

is either scoffed at or wholly ignored, even within such space-oriented agencies as NASA. I speak from first-hand experience in making that observation.

2. Twenty years of U.S. Air Force [USAF] responsibility in handling UFO reports appear to me to constitute about the same number of years of superficial and scientifically incompetent response to the UFO problem…. USAF investigations of UFO reports have been perfunctory, aimed generally at finding any "explanation," however inadequately it might match the reported facts.

3. The principal reason that no adequate scientific investigation has ever been initiated has been that, despite complete lack of any scientific expertise in the USAF program (Project Blue Book), public pronouncements have repeatedly given strong assurance that the investigations were drawing upon the best scientific talent available to the Air Force. Nothing could be further from [the truth].

4. The present Air Force-sponsored study at the University of Colorado offered promise initially. However, repeated indications of negative bias in public statements by the Project Director [Dr. Edward U. Condon]—combined with a lack of vigorous investigation of the most provocative types of UFO cases reported over the past twenty years—suggest that the Colorado program will fall far short of the required level of investigation. It is very desirable that some program be set up entirely divorced from Air Force affiliation…

5. I have just returned from a visit to Canada where I… emphasized the likelihood that UFO investigatory programs in countries other than the U.S. may have distinctly better chances of making rapid scientific progress towards clarification of the UFO question by virtue of the fact that they'd not be fighting uphill against the kind of thinking that USAF handling of the problem has engendered here….

6. *The types of UFO reports that are most intriguing and point most directly to an extraterrestrial hypothesis are close-range sightings of machine-like objects of unconventional nature and unconventional performance characteristics seen at low altitudes and sometimes even on the ground. The general public is entirely unaware of the large number of such reports that are coming from credible witnesses because ridicule and scoffing have made most witnesses reluctant to report openly such unusual incidents....*

7. *Suggestions that such observations can be explained away in terms of meteorological optics... or in terms of atmospheric plasmas... cannot be supported with cogent scientific arguments....*

8. *Many obvious questions and challenges can be... raised against the ET hypothesis.... To [some of] these... questions that exist [there are] no satisfactory answers to date.*

9. *The first need in accelerating UFO research is for many more scientists and engineers to review carefully and critically the existing evidence in order to design new sensors. (Electromagnetic effects accompanying UFO sightings offer real promise herein.) Also, it is urgently important to exploit already existing radar networks. Data from the latter networks should be brought under scientific scrutiny to search for systematic patterns of UFO appearances and movements. Present anecdotal data, plus fortuitously revealed radar data, are inadequate to define such patterns accurately. Following [the] design of sensor-networks specifically planned for UFO detection, a host of other investigations would naturally follow...*

10. *As a low-cost, minimal-level precursor to such efforts to attain instrumental monitoring of UFOs, it is urged that various organizations and agencies take steps to establish exploratory programs, even if these involve only two or three scientists per organization.... The*

immediate need is to establish a broader base of scientific recognition of the astonishing nature of the existing UFO evidence. Scientific scoffing at UFOs has gone on long enough. Serious attention is long overdue. AIAA could perform a very useful role in stimulating new and vigorous examination of this intriguing yet neglected scientific problem. (I am encouraged to learn that AIAA has... recently formed a UFO Subcommittee and [I] am in touch with it.) Although only a... [percentage] of scientists yet realize it, the past twenty years of yawning neglect of the UFO problem has become a scientific scandal, albeit still well-hidden. The sooner we take a serious new stance and confront the UFO question with adequate scientific talent and manpower, the less embarrassing will be the ultimate admission that we have, for two decades, been overlooking a problem of potentially enormous scientific importance to all mankind.

A Final Tribute

It was Dr. Jacques Vallee who gave Jim McDonald a final and fitting tribute in his Foreword to Ann Druffel's *Firestorm*:

James McDonald's diary makes it clear that he ran into precisely the kind of doctrinaire skepticism about which Allen Hynek had warned him many years before. Perhaps it is to his credit that he still went ahead with his crusade. But his tragic end contains a warning: The notion of academic purity is nothing but a charming myth. We must deal with a scientific establishment that is extremely reluctant to take stock of a new, disturbing phenomena, just as the Church of the Middle Ages refused to consider that the Earth might be revolving around the sun. The learned clerics would not even look through the telescope. Contemporary academics do not behave much better. They refused to study the UFO cases selected by McDonald just as they rejected Hynek's pleas to let him publish his best data in their official journals. A world where people like Allen Hynek are ignored, a world where someone of the caliber of James McDonald is left to die alone and misunderstood is a world crying out for drastic reform of its intellectual institutions. The issue goes far beyond the question of knowing whether or not there are unidentified flying objects, and where they may originate. What is at stake here is our own spirit, and the uncertain future of human intelligence.

CHAPTER NINETEEN

The CIA Connection

Sometime after I became the NICAP Assistant Director during the Summer of 1967, Stuart Nixon, a cocky young man, came to NICAP as a new staff member. (Keyhoe later told me that Nixon had been hired as "a favor" to "a friend." As he continued, I got the idea that the friend may have been Colonel Joseph Bryan, Chairman of NICAP's Board of Governors.)

During his first week at work, Stuart approached my desk and, with a somewhat stumbling aura of authority, announced: "Gordon, I am here to coordinate some changes that will need to be made." Suddenly, he drew back, as if he had said too much.

"What changes are you talking about, Stuart?" I asked. "Who sent you here?"

"Oh, never mind," he nervously replied. "Sorry.... I shouldn't have said anything. I'm just here to help you guys through the rough times."

A red flag had been sent up. Shortly after that, Stuart told me that the NICAP photographer, William ("Bill") MacIntyre—who had also mysteriously come into the picture at about the same time as Nixon—had been shot down in his helicopter in Vietnam in 1965. He was supposedly on a secret mission with the Central Intelligence Agency (C.I.A.), Stuart openly remarked with some degree of admiring glee.

It didn't take me long to wonder if Nixon may have been sent there to recruit me for a possible C.I.A. takeover of NICAP. I had heard from Dick Hall that two of the agency's operatives had visited the NICAP office before I came on board and spent several hours scrutinizing the sighting reports. I soon realized that Don Keyhoe himself may have opened the door for that eventuality by appointing Admiral Roscoe Hillenkoetter, the first Director of the C.I.A., Chairman of the NICAP Board of Governors. The Admiral and Keyhoe had been friends since their days long ago as cadets at the U.S. Naval Academy in Annapolis, Maryland.

Other board members—including Colonel Joseph Bryan and Dewey Fournet—had also been C.I.A. operatives. They were among the many contacts Keyhoe had established in the military, the Pentagon and the intelligence agencies. They would serve him well in obtaining UFO reports he could use in his books and at NICAP. I was also beginning to realize that this infiltration would serve them well if they really had the goal of taking over control of the world's largest UFO organization.

An Early C.I.A. Infiltration?

NICAP may have been infiltrated by the Central Intelligence Agency from its very beginning. According to a UFO Updates article by early NICAP supporter, Jan Aldrich, during the group's first year under the original Director, T. Townsend Brown, "several mysterious persons managed to fit themselves into NICAP's structure." One of these was Nicolas de Rochefort, a Russian immigrant who was a French and Russian script writer for *Voice of America*. Rochefort was also a member of the C.I.A.'s Psychological Warfare Staff. Another earlier NICAP staff member during its first year of operation was Bernard J.O. Carvalho, from Portugal, who was "involved in C.I.A.-owned companies."

By the end of 1956, Brown's leadership came to an end due to his inability to successfully handle the NICAP funds. Don Keyhoe took over as the Director and started to beef up NICAP's prestige by appointing some prominent individuals to the group's Board of Governors. Meanwhile, Admiral Hillenkoetter began making a number of positive statements on UFO reality. Don Keyhoe was happy about this, but Hillenkoetter's position on the board became tentative when Keyhoe became a fierce opponent of government secrecy and pushed for Congressional hearings during the early 1960s.

Hillenkoetter quickly resigned from the NICAP Board. He later said that the group had gone as far as it could and "no further criticism should be aimed at the Air Force for its handling of UFOs." There was also speculation that, as a former Director of the agency, his pro-UFO statements were causing "considerable embarrassment" to the CIA.

Had the stage been set for NICAP's eventual downfall? It seems that was the case.

That evening, I called Don Keyhoe at his home in Luray, Virginia, and told him what Nixon had related to me. There was an uneasy period of silence.

"What do you think, Major?" I asked. "Could Stuart Nixon be a C.I.A. operative?"

"No, he's too stupid for that," Keyhoe told me. "He hasn't got the brains."

I wondered if either Hillenkoetter or Bryan had asked the Major to pipe Nixon aboard the NICAP ship of UFO state. But further pressing by me on the matter yielded nothing more from Keyhoe.

The Final Days

Following the public release of the Condon Report, the prospects for NICAP continuing as a viable UFO organization quickly took a downward spiral. Adding fuel to the fire, unfortunately, was Keyhoe himself. Being an organizational and money manager was not his cup of tea. Some had even compared him to "a second Townsend Brown."

In a secret meeting on December 3, 1969, the NICAP Board with Colonel Joseph Bryan III presiding, fired both Keyhoe and myself. It soon became apparent that I had to be terminated as a convenient "scapegoat." Dick Hall quickly came to my defense. On December 9, he wrote a lengthy letter to the Board of Governors explaining why I had consulted with him in my attempt to help put NICAP back on a safe financial footing. Hall wrote:

Gordon has consulted with me at critical times in taking the steps which have now led to his being summarily fired.... Until now, I have kept silent about internal NICAP matters in the hope that quiet reforms could be made and a constructive program continued. Now I am incensed both by the injustice of what has been done and by the crude manner in which it was done.

On December 5, Gordon was informed by telegram... that his services were no longer required. He was given no advance notice. Furthermore, when he walked into the office to collect his personal effects, he discovered that they had been searched, his desk had been rifled and all the door locks had been changed by Stuart Nixon... allegedly acting under instructions from [NICAP Board Member J.B. Hartranft]. Exposure of such Gestapo-like tactics is sufficient commentary on them.

What grave sins did Gordon commit which resulted in his being treated like a common criminal? Over recent months, quietly to avoid a damaging uproar, he discreetly approached members of the Board to inform them of the seriously deteriorating situation, hoping they would intervene and lead the way in making long overdue reforms. In my view, he was very conscientiously and properly attempting to correct long-standing problems and to save NICAP from the scrap heap....

It is anger over the injustice that has been done, and the fateful decisions made in secret, which now motivate me to alert the entire Board to the tragic state of affairs.

I fought many of the same battles as Gordon... and have some feeling for what he has gone through.... On more than one occasion, I recognized the need for the Board to be kept informed and drafted detailed reports to [them]. These were always pigeon-holed by Major Keyhoe. When that approach failed, I initiated the Affiliate/Subcommittee

Newsletter, with copies to the Board so that you would at least have some general indication of how things were going. But it could not include the same detail as would private reports. Gordon went further because the situation and times called for it, but now he has been made a scapegoat....

I can assure you that both Gordon and I have, on the one hand, been very reluctant to hurt or thwart Major Keyhoe in any way or, on the other hand, to see NICAP reach the state that it presently has. Some present and former staff members have been after Major Keyhoe's scalp, but Gordon and I have always argued for systematic reform through the Board....

Gordon found himself in the unfortunate position of mediating between an unhappy staff and an adamant Major Keyhoe who had lost his grip on things and who remained remote from the office. For the man in the middle, this can be an extremely frustrating position.

As funds declined, staff members were laid off.... As debts increased, office space was cut in half. Virtually all research and writing ground to a halt. Gordon had only two staff members.... The situation became truly critical. The need for rebuilding was obvious, so Gordon approached two members of the Board in confidence and sought their help.... Gordon's role was to alert and involve the Board without causing a panic because he was dedicated to the continuance of NICAP on an improved basis....

I am saddened by the deterioration of NICAP and see no hope for its future. In firing Gordon Lore, the Executive Board has removed the last hope for a gradual change-over to a publications program which might put NICAP back on its feet financially....

A couple of years later, I learned through *Just Cause* that Colonel Bryan was, indeed, an active CIA agent even as he led the charge to fire Keyhoe and I.

To this day, as 2017 draws to a close, I am still saddened by the collapse of NICAP. During its years under Keyhoe's direction, the organization had been responsible for bringing a high degree of scientific credibility to the well-documented and investigated UFO sightings. And it had been the linchpin in persuading many scientists such as Jim McDonald to continue their own efforts in keeping the well-documented and investigated sighting reports in the eyes of both the public and the scientific community.

Additional information concerning NICAP's final year is included in Chapter Four of my book *Connections: A Lifetime Journey Through the World of Celebrity* (2017), also published by BearManor Media.

CHAPTER TWENTY

The Keyhoe Factor: An Homage

During my first visit to Don and Helen Keyhoe's lovely home in Luray, Virginia—not far from the famed Luray Caverns, then the second largest cave formation in the United States—I discovered more about the man I would work with for five years. He seemed willing to tell me about his life and accomplishments. Some of the information here I learned from him and from the investigative work two screenwriters, Daniel Mintz and Blake Cass, did on his life and career in preparation for a screenplay. Some I learned from other sources.

Don was born on June 20, 1897 and raised in Ottumwa, Iowa. He graduated from the U.S. Naval Academy in Annapolis, Maryland, in 1919 and received a commission of Marine Corps Lieutenant. One of his classmates and a friend at the Academy was Admiral Roscoe Hillenkoetter, the first Director of the C.I.A.

There years later, in 1922, Keyhoe's arm was badly injured when he crashed his plane in Guam. He endured a lengthy convalescence, which he used to begin what would turn out to be a long writing career. When he was better, he returned to active duty, but his arm continued to give him persistent trouble. This caused him to retire from the Marines at a young age in 1923. He obtained a position with the National Geodetic Survey, then became the Assistant to the Chief of the Bureau of Aeronautics with the U.S. Department of Commerce.

Lucky Lindy

The indomitable Major's big year in which his writing career would begin to flourish came in 1927. On May 20-21 of that fateful year in the still-early history of aviation, Charles Lindbergh—at the young age of twenty-five—made an historic flight from Roosevelt Field outside New York City to Le Bourget Field in Paris, France, in his jaunty little plane, the *Spirit of St. Louis*. It was not only the first non-stop crossing of the Atlantic Ocean by anyone, it was also the first solo flight, earning him the nicknames "Lucky Lindy" and the "Lone Eagle." At times, Lindbergh had to fly only a scary ten feet above the surface of the churning waves outside his window. His landing at Le Bourget was met by a thunderous, cheering crowd of thousands of people.

Soon after Lindbergh returned home, the crowds in America were no less jubilant. They demanded to see more of Lindy, who had become the most famous and admired person in the world. A nationwide tour was quickly arranged by the Daniel Guggenheim Fund for the Promotion of Aviation. Officials at the fund chose Don Keyhoe to organize and lead the coast-to-coast tour with Lindbergh at the controls of the *Spirit of St. Louis* as the lead plane.

The extensive tour involved daily takeoffs and landings in all kinds of weather at large and small airports. At times, the airfields were so crowded with cheering throngs of well-wishers that Keyhoe had to lead the way and clear the field so the hero could make a safe landing without harming himself or anyone on the ground. As his book reminded us: "It was a journey as fraught with perils as any of [Lindbergh's] flights. How he withstood the dangers of too much homage, of the fatigues and small irritations incident to such an undertaking is written with truth and sympathy by the man who was closest to Colonel Lindbergh through the whole ordeal."

The Freelance Career

Keyhoe knew he had a good book, his first, in the making. By September of the following year, 1928, his first book, *Flying with Lindbergh,* was published and immediately became very successful (see the photo section). This led to Don's freelance writing career. His name as Lindy's tour guide left the front door open for his articles, stories, and short paperback novels to appear in a wide variety of leading publications.

When America entered World War II on December 8, 1941, the day after the Japanese attack on Pearl Harbor, Keyhoe returned to active duty in a Naval Aviation Training Division. After retiring again as a Major after the war, his articles and stories as a freelancer continued to appear in numerous publications, including the *Saturday Evening Post, Reader's Digest* and *The Nation.* Some of his stories had also previously been published in the popular *Weird Tales* magazine.

Then the flying saucer craze ignited the nation's interest immediately on the heels of the sighting of nine disc-shaped objects over Mt. Rainier in Washington in June of 1947. Here was fodder for Don's pen and typewriter.

The timing was perfect. During the Spring of 1949, the U.S. Air Force was releasing misleading and contradictory information about the lightning-quick surge of UFO reports. At the same time, *True Magazine* editor Ken Purdy had been asking Air Force officials for information and kept receiving unclear, misleading data about the saucers. Purdy turned to one of his writers, John DuBarry, who began the project but got nowhere with it. Then he turned to Keyhoe, another of his writers, whom he knew had friends who were important contacts in the military and the Pentagon. At first, Don didn't want to take the assignment, but agreed when Purdy allegedly threatened to sever all ties with him as an important literary outlet for his writing.

"Can You Take Over?"

On May 9, 1949, Purdy sent Keyhoe the following telegram: *Have been investigating flying saucer mystery. First tip hinted gigantic hoax to cover up official secret. Believe it may have been planted to hide real answer. Looks like terrific story. Can you take over Washington end?*

Take it over he did. The result was the article "The Flying Saucers Are Real", which reportedly became one of the two or three most widely read articles in the history of American publishing. That same year, the article was expanded into a book with the same title and hit the bookstores and other venues under the Fawcett Publications banner. According to some sources, it sold over 500,000 copies in its paperback edition.

It was at this point in his story that I asked Keyhoe the all-important question.

Are ETs Monitoring Us?

"Well, Major, what do you think? Have alien beings from other planets been observing and monitoring us all these many years?"

"I have no doubt about it, Gordon," he responded. "By this time, you have seen a lot of information confirming it and will see a lot more, particularly if our work with the Colorado folks continues and is successful."

"But tell me, Major, do you really think that officials at the highest levels of government, including President Johnson, know we are being observed and visited by aliens from God-knows what planet and what galaxy?"

"Yes again. I have no doubt about it."

"Was this confirmed by Admiral Hillenkoetter or anyone else?"

"*Awwwww...,*" the Major murmured with a slight smile. "You're not going to catch me there. I can't say, of course. That would ruin everything. Don't forget that we must have the upper hand in persuading Congress to investigate the sightings while still hoping that the Colorado Project will do a credible job, although, right now, that seems to be questionable."

"Sorry, Major, I didn't intend to make you uncomfortable."

"Don't worry about it, Gordon. I would want to know the same, even if I couldn't get the real facts. I know that, like Dick and myself, you must be frustrated."

"A Gold Medal With a Star"

"Somewhat," I admitted, "but, thanks to you and Dick, just having the opportunity of working with you in this exciting field of endeavor is to me a gold medal of opportunity. And working with the top man in the field is an extra star on that medal."

It wasn't until I was working on this book that I learned about Don Keyhoe's full measurement of devotion to NICAP, the organization he brought to life and kept going through the mire of a large number of financial and other pitfalls for twelve years. At one point—according to Mintz and Cass—when the organization was in danger of closing its doors, Don took the drastic step of curtailing the college education of his two daughters in order to save the money he thought would be necessary to help pull NICAP out of another of its frequent financial crises. It must have been an agonizing decision for him... and one that may have had a lasting negative impression with his daughters.

Conclusion

The last time I saw or spoke with Keyhoe was in 1973, when his final UFO book, *Aliens From Space: The Real Story of Unidentified Flying Objects*, was published. He was holding a press conference at the National Press Club in Washington, D.C., where I was a member, to launch the book. Once again, I asked him if he thought that Stuart Nixon, who had mysteriously appeared as a staff member at NICAP in 1967, may have been a CIA operative. Keyhoe, however, again stated: "No. He's too dumb for that." I gently reminded him that Admiral Hillenkoetter, the first CIA Director, Colonel Joseph Bryan and one or two others on the NICAP Board of Governors had had active ties with the agency. He still demurred and I let it go at that.

Following that day at the Press Club, I had no further contact with Keyhoe. I later learned that he did speak at two or three UFO conferences. In 1981, he even joined the Mutual UFO Network's (MUFON) Board of Directors, but "his membership was essentially in name only due to [his] declining health and he had little to do with the organization."

Los Angeles-based screenwriters Daniel Mintz and Blake Cass have developed a deep personal regard for Keyhoe and have been working on a screenplay about his life. They provided me with a little more personal information about Keyhoe's life during his retirement years at his cherished home in Luray, Virginia:

> *While a lot is known about Don during his UFO tenure, we found [his] life after it... to be particularly fascinating. How does a man like Don, who fought so hard for such extraordinary things, simply just retire to normal life? From our research, we learned that Don appeared to do just that and lived out his golden years rather quietly.*
>
> *The longtime Sheriff of Luray told us that he and his wife Helen would go for coffee every morning at the Intown Motel, [which has] a small restaurant attached to a Best Western-type motel. That was a routine of theirs.*
>
> *[Keyhoe] also drove a big clunky Cadillac from the 1950s (even though this was now the 1970s) and was known for frequent automobile accidents. This may have been due to the fact that he was a short man... and we were told that, when driving in the Cadillac, you couldn't see him behind the steering wheel....*
>
> *We also learned that Don still loved talking about his work and UFOs, even though he had basically retired from "the business" of it all. A clerk at the courthouse told me [that Keyhoe] gave him an autographed copy of [one of] his book[s] and had fond memories of speaking with him.*

Major Donald E. Keyhoe (USMC) passed away at the age of ninety-one on November 29, 1988, and was interred in Green Hill Cemetery in Luray, Virginia, near his beloved Bluemont Home where he had lived with Helen for so many years. Even today, I sometimes fantasize about the indomitable Major cavorting in some heavenly realm with benevolent ET's willing to share with him (and us) their far-away secrets.

PART II

The UFOR Years

CHAPTER TWENTY-ONE

The Mantell Tragedy

About six months after leaving NICAP, my future wife, Marty, and I began our own investigative group, UFO Research Associates (UFOR), which included a monthly publication, the *U.F.O. Research Newsletter*. I still had some contacts from my years at NICAP whom I called on to help us launch our new venture. We operated on a shoestring budget from our homes in Washington, D.C., Bethesda, Maryland, Albuquerque and Taos, New Mexico, and Hollywood, California.

The sighting reports began to flow into our home base. One involved my luck in locating a still-living witness to the tragic Captain Thomas F. Mantell, Jr., case. This startling encounter became the first known and still only incident in which a witness was actually killed while chasing a UFO.

Early in 1971, I received a letter from former Air Force pilot Lieutenant Colonel E. Garrison Wood. The Colonel said he had read the first issue of *U.F.O. Research Newsletter* and was impressed. He added that he was on the site of the Mantell tragedy on that fateful day, January 7, 1948, and was willing to tell me what he knew about the tragic event. Wood even included his phone number. I jumped at the chance and called him for two lengthy interviews. Most of what follows is based on those phone conversations.

The "Flaming Red Cone"

The initial press reports stated that officials at Godman Field located outside Fort Knox, Kentucky, had received a call from Kentucky Highway Patrol officers that they had observed an object estimated to be up to

300 feet in diameter in the sky near Madisonville. Similar reports were received from Irvington and Owensboro.

It was about 1:45 p.m. (according to initial reports, although Colonel Wood told me that his recollection placed the time at closer to 11:30 a.m.) when Sergeant Quinton Blackwell and two other witnesses in the Godman Field control tower spotted what they described as "a white object in the distance," which they estimated to be about one fourth the size of the full moon. One of the observers, Colonel Hix, grabbed his binoculars and saw that the object appeared to have a red border at its bottom. He indicated that he had the stationary UFO in sight for over an hour.

Meanwhile, ground observers at the Clinton County Army Air Field in Ohio saw the same or a similar aerial craft that had the appearance of a flaming red cone trailing a gaseous green mist. They kept their eyes fixed on the UFO for about thirty-five minutes.

Another witness at Lockbourne Army Air Field in Ohio said he was also a witness to the strange craft: "Just before leaving, it came near the ground, staying down about ten seconds, then climbed at a very fast rate back to its original altitude [of] 10,000 feet, leveling off and disappearing into the overcast heading 120 degrees. Its speed was greater than 500 mph in level flight."

Mustangs Join the Hunt

By this time, four F-51D Mustangs from the National Guard's 165th Fighter Squadron had already scrambled to hunt for the object. Mantell joined three other pilots as they were ordered to approach the UFO. One of the pilots, however, found that he was low on fuel and had to return to his home base.

Some sources said that Mantell described the object as "metallic and of tremendous size." Meanwhile, the remaining pilots joined with him in pursuit of the UFO. As he reached the 15,000-foot altitude mark, he radioed back that the object was "directly ahead and above and moving at about half my speed. It appears metallic and of tremendous size. I'm still climbing.... Object is above and ahead moving about my speed or faster. I'm trying to close in for a better look."

As the pilots continued their pursuit at greater altitudes, Lieutenant Albert Clements was the only one of Mantell's wingmen to have an oxygen mask, which was quickly running out. He and the third pilot, Lieutenant Hammond, apparently had the same problem. At 22,500 feet altitude, both pilots had to terminate their pursuit.

Colonel Wood Spots the Object

In his telecon, Colonel Wood told me that it was around 11:30 a.m. when he checked in with the Godman Officer of the Day and received a call that there was "something sighted from the control tower." Wood ran to the tower, where the operator pointed toward a "small pinpoint of light" high in the sky. Someone called the Operations Officer of the Air National Guard fighter group at Standiford Field, Louisville, and asked if he could send up aircraft for the pursuit. The officer said he would initiate an investigation. About ten minutes later, three planes approached the area.

"These three P-51s came directly over the field and I asked the tower operator to try all his VHF channels to see if they could be contacted," Colonel Wood related to me in his telecon.

The Ferry Flight Planes

The flight leader, Mantell, said the three planes were not those that were sent by Standiford. They were returning from a ferry flight from Atlanta to the airfield. Mantell said they would investigate if the flight plans were closed out from Standiford. The plans were closed out and the planes headed toward the object.

There was no more direct radio contact until Mantell called in his final message. Wood told me that he believed his last words were: "I'm not gaining on it!" The deputy commanding officer and others saw the planes disappear, but the object was still in view.

Mantell Crashes to Earth

Mantell continued his pursuit. As he passed the 25,000-foot mark, he apparently was struck with hypoxia (lack of oxygen) and fatally lost consciousness. His plane quickly began spiraling in circles toward the ground. It hit the earth's surface hard on a farm south of Franklin, Kentucky, near the Kentucky-Tennessee state line. Wood told me it wasn't until 7 p.m. that it was discovered Mantell had crashed.

"The UFO was in exactly the same spot the whole time until 7:30 p.m.," the Colonel related to me. "I tracked it by theodolite [a telescope-like instrument used to measure horizontal and vertical angles]. The object did not appear to move at all during the eight or so hours we observed it. [*Author's note: There was controversy as to whether or not Colonel Wood had actually seen the UFO over this long a period. Some NICAP investigators believed that he did not have the object in view for that long.*] It was definitely not a planet, balloon or aircraft. Some idiot officers from Project Saucer [the official Air Force organ investigating UFOs, later renamed Project Grudge and Project Blue Book] came to Godman the next day to investigate. They took the whole damned thing as a joke!"

Colonel Wood told me that this was not the first time that he had seen a UFO. In July 1945—while stationed at the Grand Island, Nebraska, Army Air Corps in the closing days of World War II—he and others observed what he called "something overhead" high in the sky. A P-63 was scrambled aloft to 45,000 feet, but nothing was reported. At the time I talked with him, Wood was a veteran of sixty-five World War II combat missions over Southern Europe with the 376th B-24 Heavy Bomber Group of the 15th Air Force.

Mantell's Body is Retrieved

Later, a ground crew struggled to pull Mantell's mangled body from the wreckage. He had a shredded seat belt and his wristwatch had ceased functioning at 3:18 p.m., the time of the crash. By 3:50 p.m., the aerial object was no longer in sight.

At a rapid-fire pace, the Mantell tragedy was reported by newspaper and magazine articles around the nation. There were also a large number of sensational rumors. Among these were that the object was a Soviet missile or an alien spacecraft had shot down Mantell's fighter plane. Also, the young officer's body was "riddled with bullets; the body was missing; the plane had completely disintegrated in the air; and the wreckage was radioactive." The problem was that no evidence has ever surfaced to substantiate any of these claims.

Project Sign Investigates

Officials from the Air Force's Project Sign began investigating the tragic crash. One reporter noted that "the people on Project Sign worked fast on the Mantell incident." They realized they would be flooded with a ton of queries from the press and knew they had to come up with a quick answer to the tragedy. They quickly found it… or so they thought.

Several weeks before Mantell was killed, an Air Force (AF) F-51 was scrambled to chase a UFO that turned out to be the planet Venus. This was the answer from AF officials since "there were similarities between this sighting and the Mantell incident. So…, the word 'Venus' went out."

Sometime in 1952, USAF Captain J. Edward Ruppelt (who later wrote his own UFO book) joined the fray. As the head of Project Blue Book, he conducted another so-called investigation of the Mantell incident. He spoke with Dr. J. Allen Hynek, then an Astronomer at Ohio State University and scientific consultant to Projects Sign and Blue Book. Hynek had given Sign officials the Venus explanation back in 1948, "mainly because Venus had been in the same place in the sky that Mantell's UFO was observed." By 1952, however, Hynek drew back on this explanation because the planet wasn't bright enough to be seen by Mantell and others since "a considerable haze was present that would have further obscured the planet in the sky."

The Skyhook Explanation

Now that he was forced to reject Venus as an explanation for the sighting, Ruppelt knew he had to search around for another explanation. Hynek had also suggested that the object could have been a U.S. Navy Skyhook weather balloon. A number of these balloons had been released into the sky. Ruppelt bought the explanation. What wasn't explained was how a Skyhook balloon could travel at an estimated 500 m.p.h.

The balloons constituted a secret project that was functioning at the time of Mantell's crash. They were constructed from reflective aluminum and were about 100 feet in diameter. Since the project had a **SECRET** label, neither Captain Mantell, Colonel Wood or the other observers would have been able to identify them as such. A number of Skyhook balloons had been launched in Clinton County, Ohio, about 150 miles north of Fort Knox, but this answer was rejected by serious, more objective investigators. The balloons could not have traveled at anywhere near the great speeds the UFO was capable of reaching. Francis Ridge—who I had worked with when he was the head of NICAP's Indiana subcommittee and who is now the founder and webmaster of the excellent NICAP website—told me that a UFO had been reported around the area where Mantell had chased the object that led to his death.

The base commander, Colonel Guy Hix, said he used binoculars to view the object, which "appeared to have a red border at the bottom" and remained still for a full ninety minutes! Other witnesses at the Clinton County Army Air Field in Ohio said the UFO had the appearance of a flaming red cone trailing a gaseous green mist and was in sight for about thirty-five minutes. An observer at Lockbourne Army Air Field in Ohio said: "Just before leaving, it came to very near the ground, staying down for about ten seconds, then climbed at a very fast rate back to its original altitude, 10,000 feet, leveling off and disappearing into the overcast... Its speed was greater than 500 m.p.h.... in level flight!"

A Follow-Up Investigation

An in-depth follow-up investigation of the Mantell case was conducted by crack investigators from those involved with the NICAP website, including Francis Ridge and Barry Greenwood. As the editor of *Just Cause* during the first quarter of 1994, long-time researcher and investigator Barry Greenwood, the co-author of *Clear Intent: The Government Coverup of the UFO Experience*, wrote an article that helped to clear up some of the misconception concerning the case.

"On January 7, 1948, a series of UFO incidents took place over central Kentucky," Greenwood reported. "Beginning about 1 PM, reports came to the police about a strange object over Elizabethtown, Kentucky. Additional reports from the towns increased concern, so the state police contacted Fort Knox military police to advise them of a circular object 250-300 feet in diameter, moving westward."

Fort Knox police then told authorities at nearby Godman Field about the sighting. Personnel at Godman Tower described the object as being like a "parachute with the bright sun shining on top of the silk." One observer said the object appeared to be round and considerably whiter than the clouds in front of it and it could be seen through the cirrus clouds. Another observer said it reminded him of "an ice cream cone topped with red."

The object appeared to remain stationary in the sky for around eleven hours. Also, witnesses spotted a flight of four P-51 aircraft in the area that were "ferrying grounded aircraft from Marietta Army Air Base in Georgia to Standiford Air Field in Kentucky." One of the pilots was Captain Thomas Mantell.

The NICAP Conclusion

"The picture presented of Mantell chasing a Skyhook balloon to his death with the region filled with IFO [identified flying objects] reports is false," Fran Ridge reported. "There were UFO reports in the region... Mantell didn't just go above 14,000 feet and violate regulations. He was asked to investigate and knew what he was doing. If he had oxygen problems that resulted in anoxia and passing out, it was due to a problem, not him going hell-bent-for-leather after a pinpoint of light in the afternoon sky... The biggest balloon available that day was too far away to be a factor. The case was covered up and declared as unsolved, and was still unsolved and had shook up the Air Force as late as 1952."

Ridge concluded his report of the investigation with: "Thanks to this tremendous effort of these persistent researchers, the case has been stunningly blown wide open after over 70 years."

A Young Hero

Thomas Mantell was a personable young man with great prospects ahead. He was born on June 30, 1922, in Franklin, Kentucky, and died near there in 1948. He graduated from Male High School in Louisville. On June 16, 1942, he responded to the "Remember Pearl Harbor!" cry and joined the U.S. Army Air Corps. He finished flight school a year later. Then he was transferred overseas to the 440th Troop Carrier Group. He was among those in the group who parachuted members of the 101st Airborne Division into Normandy, France, to help clear the way for history's largest amphibious assault during the D-Day operation on June 6, 1944.

As a result of his service abroad, the young Mantell received a number of awards, including the Distinguished Flying Cross, a World War II Victory Medal, the American Campaign Medal, a Distinguished Unit Citation, and the European-African-Middle Eastern Campaign Medal with two stars. After the war, he joined the new Kentucky Air National Guard on February 16, 1947. He became a F51D Mustang pilot assigned to the 165th Fighter Squadron.

Following his death, Thomas Mantell's body was returned to Louisville for burial in the Zachary Taylor National Cemetery. On September 29, 2001, the Simpson County Historical Society unveiled a historical marker in honor of Mantell in his hometown of Franklin.

The Garrison Wood Story

E. Garrison Wood also had a distinguished career in World War II and beyond. He was born on July 6, 1915, in Salem, Virginia. He graduated from Salem High School and completed his education at Roanoke College and Florida Southern College. He graduated from the NABAC School of Banking at the University of Wisconsin. For many years, he was a member of the Exchange National Bank (currently the Bank of America) in Winter Haven, Florida.

In 1964, Wood joined the Financial General Corporation in Washington, D.C. Later, he became a member of the U.S. Army Corps of Engineers until his retirement. During the expanded World War II era, he served for eight years as a B-24 bomber pilot. He flew sixty-five combat missions with the 376th Heavy Bomb Group in Europe.

"That was hell, Gordon," Wood told me over the phone. "Were you ever in a war?"

"No," I replied. "I was in the Army stationed at Fort Belvoir in Virginia, where I was the Medical Librarian. I was fortunate, I guess...."

"Yes, you're damned right about that," the Colonel replied. "General Sherman was right when he said 'war is hell.' I can attest to that."

For his service abroad, Wood was honored with several awards, including the Distinguished Flying Cross with one Oak Leaf Cluster, the Air Medal with Seven Clusters, the Distinguished Unit Citation and Ten Battle Stars. And he was given the award of Honorary Member of the former Royal Yugoslav Air Force. Following World War II, he continued with his military service as an Air Base Commander on both Saipan and Iwo Jima in the Pacific. Later, he left the service as a Lieutenant Colonel to pursue his civilian banking career.

Wood retired in Lynchburg, Virginia, but later lived with his wife, Jean, in Fairfax, Virginia. His final home was in Braselton, Georgia, where he passed away at 2:30 p.m., on November 23, 2010.

CHAPTER TWENTY-TWO

The Wood River Junction and Spanish Peakes UFOs

Shortly following my interview with Colonel Wood, there were at least three detailed sighting reports in and around the Wood River Junction section of Bradford, Rhode Island, from the end of January to March 1, 1973, that arrived at our UFOR headquarters home in Hollywood.

On an unspecified evening in late January, an eight-year-old boy said he saw a "flying saucer" dotted with blue and green lights hovering over his family's farm field. He called for his mother and brother to come outside, but they reportedly did not believe him or comply with his request to "come and see."

UFO Over Nuclear Reprocessing Plant

On the evening of February 5th or the early morning of the 6th, Kenneth ("Ken") and Ann Gardner—area residents with their home on nearby Shumunkanuc Hill in Charlestown overlooking a nuclear reprocessing plant and power lines outside Bradford—spotted "a strangely lit" circular UFO. Ken Gardner—a Navy veteran who was familiar with most conventional aircraft—said it was not like something with which he was familiar.

A few days later, a young couple who lived near Dunns Corners said they had been watching a strangely-lit object for about a week during the evening hours that approached them from the south and headed toward Bradford.

The Fallon Reports

It was 11 p.m., Friday, February 9, 1973. In her report to UFOR, Mrs. William E. ("Eddy") Fallon of Bradford said she "was just dozing off when my husband, who was just coming to bed, suddenly mentioned that there was a bright light outside. By the time I got my eyes open, it had already vanished."

The next day, shortly before 6:30 p.m., February 10, Eddy Fallon left home to pick up his daughter who was visiting with a friend.

"I was watching TV," Mrs. Fallon stated in her report, "when, minutes later, I heard a car tear into the driveway and shortly [there was] a banging at the living room window with Eddy shouting at me to come out on the back porch. I ran out... and immediately caught sight of two very large, wide bright lights or... a series of lights blending together. We watched it slowly disappear... low over a ridge...."

Back home, Eddy said that, only minutes after he left the house, he saw that the road and area to his right were bathed in light. Looking up, he observed a series of white lights that appeared to be on a solid object hovering over a marsh. Then the object tilted and started upward. Fallon said he estimated the round UFO to be about thirty feet in diameter with a dome at its center and a revolving platform around that. There were also bright white lights around the perimeter. Eddy said that the lights looked to him to be arranged like a sidewalk that was spinning in space.

"I Was Getting the Hell Out of There!"

On the top of the object was what appeared to be a dome. He estimated that the UFO was about 200 feet away from him. He apparently watched it until it disappeared from view. Then he quickly backed up his car and sped away from the area of the strange encounter.

"I was getting the hell out of there!" he exclaimed. "I admit it.... I was scared as hell! I just had the feeling that, if I stayed around, something bad would happen. I had a family to protect!"

Following his encounter, Mrs. Fallon called Ann Gardner, a friend, who had reported seeing a similar object four days earlier.

"I saw it flying over my house!" Mrs. Gardner shouted out. "I suddenly got damned scared of it!"

During the day on March 12, Thomas Gariepy, a reporter for the Providence, Rhode Island, *Bulletin*, said he observed through his field glasses at about a quarter of a mile ahead what he described as a bright white light surrounded by numerous flashing red lights. The object was heading slowly toward the northeast near Shumancanuc. Later that night, it was also seen near Route 112 in Carolina.

The Spanish Peakes UFO

In June 1974, Marty and I (along with my stepson, Jay Triche) decided to relocate to Albuquerque, New Mexico, with the idea of managing some property Marty owned in the little town of Belen in the scrub-brush area of the state not far from Socorro, where Police Officer Lonnie Zamora had his encounter with a landing saucer and its occupants in April 1964 (see Chapter Four).

Soon after we settled into a house in a trendy new community on the desert mesa just outside town, we met a select group of local residents who were interested in forming a UFOR New Mexico Subcommittee. They were particularly impressed by our years of working with Major Keyhoe, who held a special place in their minds and hearts. They brought along the Major's fifth and final UFO book, *Aliens From Space* (1973). The men were also fans of my own books, *Mysteries of the Skies: UFOs in Perspective* (1968) and *Strange Effects From UFOs* (1969).

The subcommittee was quickly formed with an impressive group of well-qualified investigators. Meanwhile, I also took on the additional task of becoming the New Mexico State Director of the Mutual UFO Network with the late Walter Andrus as its President.

Our new home was also in the middle of the spot where the annual

International Balloon Festival was held. On a picture-perfect day soon after Marty, Jay and I had settled in, hundreds of multicolored hot air balloons from the festival festooned the sky with brilliant bright colors for miles around. One of the balloon pilots even managed to crash his craft into our back yard, but he was unhurt and apologized for being an uninvited guest. We invited him to "drop in" any time while encouraging him not to fall out of the balloon before hitting the sandy terrain. Some time before the festival concluded, there were several reports of strange objects seen in the sky, but no official reports were apparently made.

Reilly and the Four Horsemen

Not long after the festive balloons left the crowded sky over Albuquerque, the subcommittee gave us our first New Mexico sighting report from a most reliable witness. Bruce J. Kennedy was the Field Investigator.

The witness—Francis ("Frank") C. Reilly, age sixty-seven at the time of his sighting—had unusually impressive credentials. He had attained his Bachelor of Science degree from the prestigious Notre Dame University in South Bend, Indiana. While there, he was the star tackle on the Notre Dame Football Team during the late 1920s and was one of the team's famed Four Horsemen. He later earned Master of Science degrees in both pharmacy and biochemistry from the University of St. Louis.

Following his schooling, Reilly spent four years as a Captain in the U.S. Army Air Corps, where he piloted B-24 bombers and various transport type aircraft. After he left the Air Corps, Frank worked for Cutter Aviation and Trans World Airlines, then retired as a pharmacist from the Sandia Drug Company. He was an expert at recognizing many types of aircraft in the sky.

The DC-3 Cargo Encounter

Bruce Kennedy interviewed the witness and later sent his report, dated December 19, 1974, to our new location in Los Angeles after our sudden move there:

In late August 1952, Frank was piloting a DC-3 cargo aircraft enroute from Chicago... to Albuquerque.... Following a refueling stop in Denver..., [he] was flying south at 8,000 feet on a southerly heading.... At approximately 10:15 p.m., the aircraft was flying over the Spanish Peaks in south-central Colorado.

Mr. Reilly suddenly noticed a chartreuse-colored object approaching his craft at a high rate of speed. The [UFO] was flying at the same altitude as the DC-3 and was closing in on a flight path perpendicular to that of the aircraft [as it was] coming from the west. The witness first feared that it may [have been] a meteor on an inevitable collision course with his aircraft. [He] immediately proceeded to transmit the international distress signal ("Mayday") over the radio....

At that time, the witness noticed the radio was not functioning even though the dial was in the 'on' position. A quick check of the instrument panel revealed that the plane's compass was spinning violently and many of the meters were going 'haywire,' swaying from side-to-side. Following a futile effort to send a radio transmission, [Frank] looked out the canopy just as the object suddenly stopped its rapid forward motion and began to slowly fly alongside the aircraft about 100 feet from the right wing. Mr. Reilly realized with astonishment that he did not know what the object was....

Frank glued his eyes on the solid UFO, which was considerably larger than his DC-3. He estimated it to be at least seventy-five feet in diameter and twenty-five feet high. He said he would be "damned" if he would get any closer.

The "Fast Escalator"

Kennedy continued his report:

> After keeping pace with the witness's plane for approximately two minutes, the object suddenly veered without banking to the right about 200 feet. [It] then rose at a thirty-degree angle at a high rate of speed until it was no longer visible.... On its ascent, the unidentified object seemed as though it was on a fast 'escalator' [since] it did not bank [during its climb].... The witness experienced increased cardio-respiratory activity and much emotional stress during the traumatic event. Mr. Reilly found that the aircraft's instrument panel had returned to normal and the radio was once again in operating order. The rest of the flight was uneventful....

Bruce Kennedy was impressed by Reilly's account and his honest reporting of the sighting:

> Upon cross-questioning, his answers accurately coincided with [the] facts he had stated in his narrative. Several of his fellow members in the Albuquerque Lions Club vouched for Mr. Reilly's honesty, psychological stability and "level-headedness" as well as admitting they had never heard him speak of the sighting prior to that time. One individual, a lawyer, stated he would never hesitate to have Mr. Reilly give testimony in a court of law [due to] his high integrity.

> This investigator was indeed impressed by Mr. Reilly's frankness and he gave every indication that he was telling the truth. The witness indicated that, although he had been a B-24 pilot during World War II, he had never seen anything like the above-mentioned object before or after his sighting.

During the sighting, however, the pilot "experienced increased cardio-respiratory activity and much emotional distress," Kennedy added in his account to UFOR.

CHAPTER TWENTY-THREE

Flying Saucers Pace Trains

As time continued to pass on the mesa, the flurry of sighting reports kept coming into our home at a fast clip.

Two UFOs that made a sideways leap in space, then jumped back to their original positions, were seen by the crew of a Southern Pacific freight train near Canby, California, at about 4:45 a.m. on an unknown day in May 1954.

Melvin Carmichael, fireman; Glenn Head, brakeman; S.P. Oliver, engineer; another brakeman and a crewmember were descending a long grade when they observed two large stationary lights in the sky.

"By God, they're flying saucers!" Oliver exclaimed.

"It sure as hell looks like it!" Head retorted. "What are they doing following us?"

"Maybe we'll see some of those little green men!" Carmichael piped in with a somewhat uncomfortable laugh. "Hell, we could go for a ride in a flying saucer!"

The "Fat Cigars"

In a letter to a UFOR investigator, Carmichael said the objects looked like fat cigars, but were slightly tapered at the rounded ends.

"They appeared to be about two miles ahead of us," Carmichael wrote, "about 1,200 feet above the ground. The larger of the two lights appeared to be about the same length as the diameter of the full moon. The other light was approximately half that size. The lights were white with a row of seven orange-colored 'windows' across the bottom, with another row of three or four above them."

A "Sidewise Leap" in Space

Then the larger UFO made a sidewise leap in space to a point about twenty miles to the left of their original location. The second object followed only a split second later. Five or six seconds after that, they jumped back to their original location.

The train approached the UFOs and passed underneath them. They were cut from view by a large hill east of Canby.

"The lights maintained the same relative position to each other," the fireman stated. "When I first saw them, the smaller light was roughly 200 feet above the larger and slightly to the left. After they had made their sideways move and returned to the same place, their relative positions were the same as before."

The Block-Long UFO

Following the Canby, California case, another train-pacing report came into our UFOR office.

A tremendous UFO—the diameter of which was estimated to be one city block long and which quickly blocked out the sun and sky—paced a train traveling through Washington State from 2:30 to 3:30 p.m. on an unspecified day in 1955. Richard Marell, one of the many witnesses, sent an account to a UFOR investigator, who forwarded to our home office an account of the incident.

According to Marell, the object paced the train, at one time as close as twenty feet. Witnesses reported that the saucer was a dull blue-gray color and appeared to be constructed of three sections molded together. The bottom had what appeared to be windows about six feet in diameter with rounded corners. The windows were indented approximately three feet into the fuselage. Marell said he saw a wall on the other side of one of the windows.

A "Frosted Light Bulb"

"The second elevated (middle) section contained slits approximately ten feet in length and four feet wide," the investigator's report stated. "These were also recessed back into the fuselage about three feet. The smaller uppermost section of the UFO was the only place where illumination was observed. Mr. Marell compared this 'bubble' with that of a 'soft glow or frosted light bulb.'"

The witness said he thought he could detect movement of some kind within this glow, but was not certain. He was positive, however, that he was being watched. He also became frightened and began to wonder if he would get back home safely.

Occasionally, the UFO would alter its position, dipping one edge, then the other. Marell said the object sped away from the train faster than anything he had ever seen.

"I was really scared," Marell remarked. "I don't mind admitting it. Damn! It *had* to be something from outer space!"

An "Angel's Hair" Connection?

Soon after the sighting, the train stopped at a small depot where some men—apparently town officials—questioned the 150 or so passengers who were comparing notes on what they had seen. Marell also noticed a spider web-like substance that "was very much like cotton candy" fall to the ground after the encounter. Could this have been another example of the "angel's hair"-like substance that had been reported in a number of encounters with UFOs from around the world? The investigators felt it may well have been.

There have also been a number of other times when crewmembers and passengers on board trains around the world have encountered UFOs.

A Screaming Noise

At 6:30 a.m., April 28, 1954, forty-five miles west of Geelong, Victoria, Australia, A.E. ("Ted") Smith, 26, the train engineer, and Colin Beacon, 23, the fireman, spotted a huge dark blue round object that was estimated to be up to a whopping 1,500 feet in diameter.

As the startled men watched, the UFO emitted a loud, eerie scream-like sound. Then it swooped down close to the locomotive. Suddenly, it swerved up, hovered overhead, careened around the sky, then rose up out of sight.

UFO on Railroad Tracks

Marius Dewilde, 34, a metal worker, heard his dog frantically barking outside his home in Quarouble, France, on September 10, 1954. He ran outside and was startled to see a dark object sitting on the railroad tracks.

Dewilde was even more startled as he saw what appeared to be two small drawf-like creatures heading toward the UFO. He called out for the creatures to stop, then suddenly found himself paralyzed and unable to move as a strong orange beam of light was projected at him.

The frightened witness said the creatures appeared to be a little more than three feet tall, were bulky, and wore what resembled dark-colored diving suits. The French Air Force and police reportedly investigated the case.

U.S. Senator Spots UFO in U.S.S.R.

At 7:10 p.m., October 4, 1955, U.S. Senator Richard B. Russell, Jr. (D-GA), the Congressional Armed Services Committee Chairman, was traveling on a Soviet train in the Transcaucases region southwest of Baku, U.S.S.R., when he saw the first of two discs take off from near the tracks. Russell said it quickly rose and passed over the train.

The shakened senator ran out of his compartment to alert Ruben Efron, his interpreter, and Colonel E.U. Hathaway, his aide. All three men saw both that object and a second UFO that was round and also shaped like a disc.

Later, a U.S. Air Force intelligence report labeled **TOP SECRET** said: "One disc ascended almost vertically at a relatively slow speed, with its outer surface revolving slowly to the right to an altitude of about 6,000 feet, where its speed then increased sharply as it headed north. The second flying disc was seen performing the same actions...." The take-off area was about one-to-two miles south of the rail line.

It was believed that the report was written by Lieutenant Colonel Thomas Ryan after he interviewed Senator Russell and his companions on October 13 following their arrival in Prague, Czechoslovakia.

White Lights Pace Train

At 3:10 a.m., October 3, 1958, at an undisclosed location in central Indiana, a Monon Railroad freight locomotive was crossing Clinton County when a formation of four odd white lights crossed ahead of the train. Then the objects turned and traversed the full length of the train. The flying objects were observed by the entire crew.

After they passed the back of the train, the objects swung around toward the east, then rapidly turned around and followed the locomotive with what appeared to be coordinated motions. The UFOs followed the train until the conductor shone a bright light on them. This caused the objects to briefly speed away. They returned quickly, however, and continued pacing the train.

The total time the objects were in sight by the train crew was about one hour and ten minutes. Finally, they moved away to the northeast and disappeared with a sudden burst of speed.

Train Crew Spots Humanoids

A train conductor, Enrique R. Galimberti, and an unidentified crew member spotted two bright multi-colored lights about 120 meters away from the railroad tracks near Estacion Casalengo, Santa Fe, Argentina, at 3:30 a.m., April 20, 1967. The conductor reasoned that it might be a fire and quickly applied the brakes to bring the train to an abrupt halt. With lightening-like speed, both he and the crewman grabbed fire extinguishers, jumped from the locomotive, and began carefully approaching the area.

As the men drew near, they saw that the lights were moving around in a circular motion. Behind the lights, they spotted what appeared to be a square metallic object over three meters in width and about the same in height. The aerial craft had several lighted windows around its edge. There was also what looked like a rotating wheel at the front that emitted multicolored flashes of light.

It was what they saw circling the object that startled and frightened the two crewmen. What they described as several short humanoid figures were walking around the UFO. The bareheaded figures wore what appeared to be gray shining uniforms and both were carrying what resembled rifles on their shoulders.

Galimberti and his crewmember scrambled back on board the train and sounded the locomotive's horn in an effort to elicit any reaction from the figures, but there was none. Salvador Pomidor, another railway worker, said he saw what looked like a square metallic object on the ground in the same location.

"I don't mind telling you that those little green men, or whatever they were, scared the shit out of me!" Galimberti remarked.

UFO Plays Tag With "The Cabot"

About half-a-year later, in the northern latitudes, a popular Canadian National Railways train known as "The Cabot" was rolling and clattering along the tracks in the Wentworth Valley of Nova Scotia, Canada, between Halifax and Moncton, on October 25, 1967. Raymond Putnam, the rear brakeman, decided to open the upper half of the train door on the left side of the last car to let some refreshing air inside. Then, as the train passed Wentworth Station, he looked up and spotted a UFO just over the top of some trees.

What the hell is that? he wondered. *A flying saucer?*

Putnam watched in fascination as the object emitted a green vapor-like substance that was billowing from the top. Meanwhile, the UFO was pacing the train. Raymond strained his eyes to keep watching the object, but it gave off such a terrific light that he had trouble looking directly at it. He used both his hands to shield his face while he struggled to peer through the narrow slits of his fingers.

The flying visitor continued to pace the train. At times, it broke off and swooped upwards to the tops of the mountains. Then it would come back to it as the train clacked through more moderate terrain. As the UFO slowly drifted away, it seemed to bank like an airplane at about a forty-five-degree angle.

As the alarmed brakeman continued to watch, a jet plane at high altitude suddenly swooped down and converged on the object. The plane quickly approached from behind the train. This caused the UFO to level out as a short thin exhaust line issued from behind it. As this was happening, the object began to elongate its size into what appeared to be a cigar-shaped cloud, then a long cloud. The UFO sped away with the jet in pursuit. Putnam said that he and two other witnesses watched the aerial phenomenon for thirty-five minutes.

The "Birthday Cake" Disc

About a year later back in the United States, a train engineer known only as "Howard" was sitting in his locomotive cab on the switch track at 3:20 a.m., October 21, 1977, less than four miles north of Fostoria, Ohio, when he saw what at first appeared to be a shooting star that quickly descended into a field. Then it slowly came toward him at an altitude of only about sixteen feet and stopped on the opposite side of the tracks.

Frightened, Howard grabbed his cab radio and called out to his conductor, who was seven or eight car lengths down the track.

"Donald!" he screamed. "Come up to the engine! Hell, man, we've got a goddamned UFO up here!"

Now, the aerial visitor had moved to within two car lengths of the railroad track. It looked much like a birthday cake and appeared to be a disk about ninety feet in diameter and forty-five feet high. The object was lit up like a Christmas tree with what looked like banks of nine vertical tubes separated by a dark void space. There were short horizontal tubes that ran over the tops and bottom of these voids. The slightly tilted disk was rotating in a counter-clockwise manner. The UFO itself glowed yellow with blue, electric-like energy arcs that seemed spread around the disc in a clockwise direction.

Now, Harold quickly turned on his train cab headlight for a two-second count, then switched it off. The UFO did the same thing, as if responding. Then it dimmed down. After observing the train yard for twenty-two minutes, it started spinning faster and faster and got as bright as it had earlier. Suddenly, it took off up and to the northwest until it looked like a yellow star.

"I don't mind telling you that that thing scared the living crap out of me for a minute or two there!" Harold admitted. "It was not something I would want to have happen again."

Huge UFO Zaps Train in Bolivia

Several years later, again in the far south, a flying saucer frightened the crew and passengers on board a diesel train comprised of fourteen cars. The witnesses saw an enormous, blinding cloud of light over Ventilla, Bolivia, on March 10, 1983. The huge UFO flew toward the train, changing color from a bright white to a glowing orange. The passengers, who were rudely awakened, became terrified and screamed in terror. Their terror increased when a yellow ray of light struck the locomotive and stalled the engine.

"I tried to start up the engine, but it was dead," said Sixto Churaz, the Engineer.

Fifteen minutes later, the engine suddenly came to life again as the object began to move away from the train. A combination of railroad officials, local police and University of Qruro experts confirmed that a UFO had paralyzed the train and that it was not a mechanical breakdown.

Strange Object Hypnotizes Train Crew

Nearly two years later, a freight train comprised of a locomotive and seventy cars driven by the engineer, "Orlov," and his assistant "Mironov," was paced by a UFO from Petrozavodsk and Suoyarvi to Kostomukshain in the Soviet Union beginning at 2:35 a.m. in February 1985.

As the train roared through Essoila Station, Orlov noticed some strange object behind the trees moving parallel with the train. It emitted a bright ray of light toward the ground and then drew it back in. Mironov appeared to be unable to speak for a moment as he saw the ball cross the railway and started moving 30-50 meters ahead of the train.

Orlov immediately attempted to stop the engine and slammed on the brakes to avoid collision with the bright ball, but the train would not stop. The two witnesses later said they felt as if they were hypnotized while they stared at the mysterious object, a regular geometric form of about four meters in diameter that moved silently above the surface as if it was drifting.

As the train approached the station in Novye Peski, Orlov called a woman on duty, who went out to meet the approaching train. The woman said she was surprised to see the shining ball followed by the vibrating object looking like an upturned basin. It seemed that the ball might hit the station, but it suddenly separated from the diesel locomotive and passed around the building.

Immediately after the object passed the switch, it immediately rushed to the train. The locomotive twitched heavily and the men were thrown against the windshield. As the train stopped near Zastava, the ball disappeared behind the forest.

Orlov frantically ran from his cab to examine the wheels. As soon as he carefully walked around the locomotive, he felt some strange force press against him. A first, he was unable to move, frozen in mid-stride.

When he was able to function again, he ran toward the cab, but the train started off and kept on moving for some time until the shining ball disappeared behind the forest. Those involved in the incident experienced a strong nervous shock. The witnesses estimated that the UFO followed the train for one hour and twenty minutes.

The Angel's Hair Cigar

In the years to follow, UFOs of all possible shapes and descriptions continued to seemingly harass train crews and passengers around the world. At 3 a.m. on an unspecified morning in August 1996, twelve workers were loading coal on a railway terminus in Hay Point, Queensland, Australia, when they suddenly spotted a mist-shrouded cigar-shaped craft floating above them. They watched as a cloud of web-like material fell from the UFO. Immediately, all their equipment failed, causing the coal train to lose its compressed air.

"Near the middle of the cigar was a bubble-like protrusion with rectangular observation windows," Gary, one of the workers, reported. "I saw shadows standing in the view-ports, looking down at the facility. A dull hum came from the UFO and, when it passed directly above us, the radio went wild. Everyone started shouting at once.... The craft dropped sheets of a cobweb-like substance. When they tried to touch the stuff, it turned into a watery liquid. After a minute or so, the thing flew away. The train still had no compressed air and they had to recharge it before work could go on."

The cobweb-like substance is not an uncommon phenomenon in UFO sightings. It is referred to as "Angel's hair" and is described as "a sticky, fibrous substance reported in connection with UFO sightings.... It has been described as being like a cobweb or a jelly." One theory is that Angel's hair is formed by ionized air sleeting off an electromagnetic field surrounding a UFO.

CHAPTER TWENTY-FOUR

Bizarre Alien "Claim Jumpers" and the Happy Camp Sightings

In 1976, at our home in the beautiful Beachwood Canyon area of Hollywood, California, I received an extraordinary report from UFO investigator Paul Cerny. I had worked with Paul back in the NICAP days when he was the head of our California Subcommittee and knew him to be a highly reliable and truthful individual. Cerny was now the Western Regional Director for the Mutual UFO Network (MUFON). Two years before I received Paul's report, I had been MUFON's New Mexico State Director.

Paul reported that a series of UFO sightings and other strange happenings had plagued the residents of the mountain location near Happy Camp, California, from late October 1975 through April 1976. The sightings were mixed with an occasional close encounter involving alien craft or menacing humanoid figures.

"At the height of the flap in this remote forested and low mountainous region, some of the reports were so bizarre as to be unbelievable," Cerny said in his report to UFOR. "I hesitate even to mention them except for the absolute insistence of several of the main witnesses that these incidents did occur."

Cerny also told me that he and a friend, Tom Gates (head of the Space Science Center at Foothill College in the San Francisco bay area and MUFON's West Coast Astronomy Consultant) made "a spectacular observation" of their own. Paul didn't provide details on the sighting, but he added that he and Gates were also special investigators for Dr. J. Allen Hynek's Center for UFO Studies.

Events leading to the series of sightings were called to Cerny's attention by William Murphy, MUFON State Section Director for Shasta County at Redding, California, "who alerted our bay area group and did some of the investigation."

* * *

The first sighting of real interest occurred on October 25, 1975, by Steve Harris, 19, and Stan Gayer, 24, lumber mill electricians. The men did a lot of hunting and back road exploring in the area and were completely familiar with the surrounding environment.

That night, Steve and Stan were in a flat-topped area known as the "Saddle" by the local folk. It was then a parking area about 100 feet wide by 350 feet long. At about an hour after dark, the men saw a large red "star" in the northeastern sky. There was also a second object in the opposite direction.

Meanwhile, the object in the northeast disappeared. Then the young men saw a reddish-orange light take off from an area below and to the right of them. The UFO rose straight up and out of sight in only a few seconds. This was a rather startling sight in the eerie darkness of the mountain terrain.

"We were pretty shook up about that thing, whatever it was," Stan remarked. "Hell, we were just scared!"

The area of the sighting was sparsely covered with brush, occasional trees and old logs. The size of the object was difficult to determine because of its speed. Nothing could be seen other than the bright orange light making its rapid departure up and out of sight.

After they had calmed down, the men drove their Ford Bronco to the spot from where they saw the orange light take off. This location became known as "the landing site." Other area residents also had similar experiences at this location.

The witnesses examined the area with their flashlights and came upon what appeared to be packing material that was formed into a package about a foot in diameter and four-to-six inches high, as if someone had poured it out of a pail. The two men were certain this material was left there by the strange object. *(Author's note: This "packing material" package echoes the material found after the landing in Roswell, New Mexico. See Chapter Thirty-Two.)*

The material was later analyzed by Dr. Richard F. Haines, a physicist from Los Altos, California. An instrument known as an Energy Dispersive Analysis of X-Rays, Model 608, was used for the tests. The results indicated that the material was a form of vermiculite which was not common to the area, but which had been found earlier by the witnesses.

The vermiculite pile was also examined later when an extremely high-pitched noise was heard, causing one of the observers to grab for a .30-m caliber carbine rifle off the hood of the Ford Bronco. The loud screeching sound came from over the embankment down toward the canyon below and seemed to be only forty-to-fifty feet away. Steve said it sounded electronic, similar to a microphone feedback.

"There's Eyes, Big Eyes!"

At the back of the car, Stan was lighting up the area with a powerful quartz-iodine hand spotlight. He pointed the light toward the sound.

"There's eyes? There's eyes, big eyes!" he suddenly screamed.

Only a set of large eyes was visible. The distance between the pair of eyes and the witnesses was estimated at thirty-to-forty feet. The eerie eyes appeared to be silver in color with a slightly pale blue tinge at about two-and-a-half inches in diameter at an estimated eight inches apart. No body or shape was seen, but the trees and brush in the area were brightly illuminated around and above the object or creature. The eyes then appeared to turn sideways and away, as if whatever it was went retreating back down the embankment.

The witnesses saw that the eyes made a steady ongoing motion as if the figure behind them was walking normally. It appeared like the eyes were floating. They seemed to be highly reflective with no pupils or other recognizable eye-like features.

Steve and Stan later said that they had the distinct impression that the creature had come up the slope and was watching them as they inspected the ground at the site. They considered firing the rifle at the creature, but thought better of it.

Steve said they could not see anything within five feet around and below the penetrating eyes. Their powerful spotlight had a 200,000-candle power strength, but the light was blanked out in that area. It was almost as if the strange intruder didn't want to be seen.

What does this scary little bugger want? the men wondered nearly in tandem.

Then the creature disappeared down the embankment. The two men scrambled to get to their Bronco. They jumped in, turned the ignition, and the engine started on the flat ground. But the car would not move! All four wheels were spinning and throwing off rock and dirt. It was almost like they were partially suspended above the ground, just enough for a forward movement. After about half-a-minute, the car bolted forward as if being released by an invisible force and one wheel went into a ditch. The resulting jolt damaged the rear universal joint, which had to be repaired later. Now thoroughly shaken by the weird encounter with the threatening eyes, the witnesses sped back to town.

A Second Encounter

That same night there was still another encounter with the creature. After Steve and Stan returned to town, they told their story to a friend, Helen White, 63, who insisted they take her back to the scene of the sighting.

"I have to see this thing, whatever it is," she remarked. "Who knows what this thing is? Is it some sort of real humanoid-like creature? Maybe we really have an intruder from far out into space. *Dammit, we've got to go back!"*

The feisty Helen jumped into their car with another young friend, Rick Pool. They quickly returned to the spot and began to shine the light around the same area where the creature had been spotted.

Helen quickly and nervously got her Polaroid camera and flash attachment ready, but nothing happened. Steve then grabbed his rifle.

"If there is anything around here, this should wake them up!" he shouted.

Steve fired several times into the air and the loud rifle cracks reverberated down the mountainside. Almost immediately, there was a loud, strong and frightening *wow-wow-wow* sound behind them.

The group turned quickly around in the direction of the eerie sounds and observed three forms about thirty-to-thirty-five feet away. The figures appeared to be about five feet tall, "vaguely in the form of a human, but [had] a dark non-reflecting form with a glow around the edges or outlines." No eyes were seen.

The creatures were casually moving around, but remained in a small area. Even with the bright light that was shining on them, all the witnesses could see was a bare glowing outline. It was as if the moving forms were absorbing the illumination. Occasionally, the whole form would slightly glow, but no other details were observed.

"Helen, get the picture!" Steve yelled several times.

But Helen just stood there staring, wide-eyed and apparently unable to react. She seemed to be frozen with awe and fright. Steve grabbed her and shook her in an attempt to get her to respond. The question of whether or not her mind may have been manipulated by the creatures came up later.

"Jesus, Help Me!"

Steve continued trying to persuade Helen to take a picture, but she seemed frozen to her spot.

"Do you feel weight on you?" she asked in a heavy, labored tone of voice. "I feel like something is choking me! *Jesus, help me!*"

Suddenly, Stan and Steve also began to feel a choking sensation. Later, Steve remarked that it felt as if his clothes were getting heavy on him and it was very difficult to breathe, as if the oxygen was being depleted from the air. There was no odor.

Steve theorized that the incident could have been something resembling a directed mass hallucination. Well after the encounter with the creatures, he still felt he was having extreme difficulty breathing. His attention kept being drawn back to the incredible incident. He reported that the eerie, seemingly unearthly forms moved slowly around in what was believed to be a thirty-foot area. Steve thought that this may have been because they were aware that Stan Gayer was standing near the Bronco with a loaded 30-06 rifle. The witnesses then decided they should quickly leave the area.

As their vehicle climbed to the top of the hill where they could begin their descent down the mountain, they looked back to the spot and saw a glowing orange-reddish disc-shaped object—which they estimated to be about forty feet in diameter—rise up from near where they were and follow them all the way down the curved and bumpy road to the highway. Then it left them and sped away.

The UFO—which at times appeared to resemble a ball of fire—stayed within about 150 feet over the observers and off to the right above the trees.

Steve, Stan and Helen arrived back in town shaken but with no noticeable ill effects.

The Encounters Continue

Sightings around the Happy Camp area continued and averaged between five and ten witnesses each. On the evening of February 7, 1976, Tom Gates and Paul Cerny were again on the mountaintop with Helen White, who was in her small pickup truck while Tom was with Paul in his station wagon. At times, however, all three witnesses sat in Helen's truck keeping a steady watch in the near-freezing weather with some snow on the ground. Then Paul and Tom took off on their own, but kept in touch with Helen via C.B. radio.

At midnight on that moonless evening, they saw nothing. Disappointed, they decided to drive back down to their motel room. They started out, but stopped at a turnout area near where Helen had suddenly stopped with her pickup heading away from the lookout tower. Cerny and Tom stopped about thirty feet from the pickup where Helen was listening to the radio. Then Tom and Paul suddenly spotted an orange glow behind the dip in the ridge that went down to the right of the tower. The scene reminded them of a forest fire without the accompanying smoke.

"A few seconds later, with increased glow intensity, a large rectangular-shaped object rose slowly up from behind the ridge, exposing itself in its apparent entirety," Cerny proclaimed in his report to UFOR. "Then, after a couple of seconds, it slowly lowered itself back down out of sight… the glow remaining…. It then rose up a second time, repeating the first performance, taking a second look at us."

Once more, the UFO rapidly disappeared while the witnesses waited for it to appear again. Helen, however, did not see it because she was busy tuning her radio.

The "Incomparable" UFO

"The object… was the most brilliant, deep vivid orange color of glowing substance I have ever seen," Cerny remarked. "It was indescribable [and] incomparable to anything that I had ever observed before."

The MUFON investigator said the triangular UFO had a very deep, brilliant orange sheen close to pure red. It also had rounded corners.

"What impressed me the most was its brilliance," Cerny said in a tone that almost resembled an elegy. "The rays of brilliant orange illumination were emanating and streaking out in every direction from the object as bright light would shimmer off of crystal."

While Cerny was in a state of near exhilaration, Tom had grabbed his binoculars and had them "glued on target." He saw what he said was "a slight yellow area in the center." Their distance from the object—which was about forty feet wide—was estimated to be three quarters of a mile.

The next morning, the observers returned to the saddle site, but they did not see anything unusual. Although there were other reports, none could match what Paul Cerny and his companions saw.

Were the strange creatures visitors from another planet, perhaps far out in our solar system or beyond? Cerny seemed to think it was a real possibility. So did I.

The next report I received from Paul Cerny served to throw another whole new dimension into the ever-growing mixture of flying saucer encounters and many of those who reported them.

The Hard-Rock Claim UFO

For Clinton and Jane Chapin, of Redding, California, mining their hard-rock claim for gold—as they had done for the past four decades—was no longer a routine task for them in the rugged Trinity Mountains near Redding, California. Both were seventy-five years old and, after two encounters with UFOs that left them ill and produced some intriguing physical evidence, they undoubtedly wondered whether or not to abandon their life's work and return to a more civilized security.

"The mine location is in the bottom of a hilly wooded canyon with each side averaging about forty-five degree slopes," Cerny stated in his report to UFOR. "The height to the top is approximately 3,000 feet from the canyon bottom, where a small dirt road and stream share the base of the canyon. At the mine location, the canyon bottom flattens out varying fifty to eighty feet in spots.... In summer, it is very hot and dry. In the winter, it gets quite cold with some snow and ice. In October, it is bordering on the cold side."

On October 30, 1969, the couple arrived at the mining site. As they slowed to a stop, they saw a rattlesnake in the middle of the road. Strange.... They seldom saw the reptiles at that time of year. It was too cold. As they left the car, they somehow "felt" the answer: "It was stifling hot... in this immediate area where back down the road, it had been quite chilly." Grabbing his shovel, Clint killed the snake. It was about 10 a.m.

The Volkswagen Egg

Cerny continued his report:

> At this point, they were both aware of something moving in the brush about sixty feet away to the east and off to their right where there was a flattened area of mine tailings. Suddenly, an egg-shaped object with a flat bottom about the size of a Volkswagen rose up off the ground a few feet, then took off like a shot up the canyon, swaying but not striking small trees as it went. It raced up the canyon 600-700 feet, then zoomed upward at about a fifty-to-sixty degree angle and was out of sight, all within two-to-three seconds! The shape was described as half an egg.... There were no lights, windows or protrusions visible. The object appeared to be cream in color to Jane and light gray to Clint. No noise was heard.

The stunned observers cautiously approached the landing site. Again, Cerny explained what was happening:

> They discovered an oblong or oval depressed spot measuring approximately ten feet in diameter in the mixture of dirt and rock of the tailings that were scattered out in a flat area. The depression varied from an inch to two inches deep. They felt the ground in the depressed area,

expecting to find it hot, but, to their surprise, it was as cold as the ground around them. They also found that the depressed area was slightly discolored in appearance from the surrounding ground. After the UFO had left, the stifling heat in the area suddenly diminished and the temperature... seemed to return to normal—on the cool side.

Outside the circle, toward the dirt road, lay a small, conical pile of unusual-looking sand measuring eight-to-ten inches across that had not been present the preceding day. The prospectors scooped it up and took it home with them.

The "Glob" of Metal

The California researcher described to UFOR what happened two days later:

They discovered an unusual glob of heavy metal lying on the ground tailings about eight feet away from the sand pile and two feet outside the depression ring. It had not been there the day before the UFO was sighted.... The glob is about half the size of the average man's fist, rounded on top with stubby protrusions on the bottom. The object weighs about a pound. The rounded top appears to have been burned somewhat. We thought of a possible meteorite explanation, but ruled that out after talking to astronomy consultant Tom Gates and others. The glob was resting gently on top of the ground as if placed or lightly dropped there.... Analysis tests were run in two highly equipped and qualified laboratories, which cannot be named for security reasons...

According to the analysis, the metal glob contained mostly copper, tin, and lesser amounts of iron, chrome, silver, thorium, and a small amount of silicon. The main metals indicated the material may have been brass.

"However," Cerny continued, "these metals are also alien to the Chapin mining claim minerals with the exception of silver and iron. How they got there and why is an unsolved mystery."

Since the witnesses were reluctant to part with the glob, it had to be drilled "to secure inner metallic chips for our analysis.... The interior appears... to resemble brass, but it is quite hard to drill and the chips are quite brittle, unlike ordinary brass." Analysis of the chips was conducted by a skilled scientist in the metallurgic field using sophisticated laboratory analysis equipment and an electron microscope. This procedure produced printouts of the X-ray fluorescence process.

Notations on the analysis stated:

> *The puzzling thing about the glob of metal is the variety of metals all molded into one mass. For what purpose? Alloys are common, but usually consist of just two or more metals of more equal amounts, not as many or the odd combination this specimen has.... The 'glob' appears to have been heavily plated in some sort of heavy plating bath as the exterior appears to be dull gunmetal colored.... Another odd thing about the metallic content of the 'glob' was that the greater percentage of the mass was copper, yet the assay of the minerals extracted from the mining operation itself indicates only .05% copper.*

"Bring the Gun!"

More than seven years after the first encounter, the Chapins were terrorized again by the same or a similar UFO. At about eleven o'clock on the cold morning of December 29, 1976, the elderly couple left their car at the mining site and again felt some heat, but it was not nearly as intense as during the 1969 experience. Perhaps another UFO was in the area, they reasoned. As Clint walked over to the wall area beyond the creek, Jane stood near the car with a .38 pistol strapped to her belt.

"Jane, bring the gun!" Clint yelled with a frightened voice. *"Jesus Christ, here we go again!"*

Downstream—in the brush and about eight feet west of where the alien craft had rested seven years before—was a UFO very similar to the earlier object, but with a difference. This object seemed to have a pockmarked appearance to its surface similar to the exterior of an orange. Almost immediately, the craft rapidly ascended to about 100 feet altitude and emitted some kind of ray or force-field.

Suddenly, Clint felt a violent blow and was knocked hard back against the wall, striking his head as he fell. Jane crumpled to the ice road, injuring her leg. The barrel of her gun was plugged with mud.

The husband and wife were unconscious for twelve to fifteen minutes. As Jane regained consciousness, she discovered that she was cold and wet, drenched in her own urine.

"The goddamned thing scared the piss out of me!" Jane lamented while tightly clutching her gun.

The UFO had disappeared. The Chapins painfully managed to get into their car and slowly drove home to Redding.

Some time later, the couple examined the site, but discovered no physical evidence. This indicated to them that the object may have been suspended slightly off the ground.

"A Dynamite Trap"

"The Chapins are very angry and intent on revenge for what the device did to them," Cerny said in his report to me. "They went so far as to plant a dynamite trap with a weight-tripping gadget in hopes of blowing up the UFO if it came back. They were encouraged by the local sheriff to abandon this idea and remove the explosives in case some innocent person or large animal might accidentally trigger it off. The Chapins tend to blame their present poor health on the UFO.... Jane has a ruptured stomach membrane, which she attributes to the incident. She lost twenty-four pounds from December to February."

On October 17, 1977, the Chapins again experienced an indication of heat in the canyon at the mine site, saying they felt sick and vomited, but did not see any UFO.

"A mysterious aspect to this sighting has recently surfaced in that the Chapins said they were visited by some mysterious scientists who were highly interested in their experience and the mining materials, asking that their identities not be disclosed," Cerny concluded. "According to the Chapins, they were flown out of state to an extensive laboratory facility where they were medically examined and treated in conjunction with their UFO experience and the mineral samples examined as well. However, the couple would not say where they were taken or by whom."

CHAPTER TWENTY-FIVE
Incident in Colusa

Paul Cerny continued his flow of credible and extraordinary sighting reports into our UFOR headquarters.

Bill Pecha, 39, a heavy machine mechanic, was known by his family and friends as a husky, healthy, fearless individual who possessed a keen mind and photographic memory for remembering intricate details. He also had perfect eyesight. All of these highly stable mental and physical attributes were severely put to the test at about 12:45 a.m., September 10, 1976, outside his residence in Colusa, California.

The mechanic had flicked some popcorn into his mouth as he watched an early-morning television movie. Then, as he reached for a drink, the TV set and his air conditioning unit "suddenly went dead." Bill figured that a circuit breaker had probably "kicked out from a short." He went outside to check. As he turned the corner of his mobile home, he became increasingly aware of a static electricity effect on his body. He was horripilating. The hair on his head, arms and chest stood straight up. His head hair also audibly snapped and appeared to sling off crackling sparks that danced around in the air of his home. It nearly resembled a Frankenstein monster effect.

Huge UFO Over Barn

As Pecha looked up at the clear full moon, he was startled to see a huge circular UFO that was hovering about fifty feet over the barn and one corner of his home. He watched in stunned amazement for an estimated five minutes as he felt his accelerated, even pounding heartbeat.

The witness estimated that the diameter of the object was about 150 feet. *This is a big sucker*! he thought.

The dome of the UFO had what appeared to be vertical ribbed sections. There were concave surfaces between each section that reminded him of an old-fashioned glass lemon juice squeezer. The gray dome had a slight peak or point which looked to Pecha like mildly rough and porous slag. The craft's edges and rotating perimeter reminded him of stainless steel. A smaller section that was around a large diameter light source at the bottom of the saucer rotated in a counterclockwise direction at a slower pace than the rim. Six appendages that were three-to-four inches in diameter hung six-to-eight feet from the bottom of the object and gave the appearance of a loosely dangling heavy flexible conduit with frayed ends.

"The more I looked, the more details I was picking up on," Pecha said later. "These flexible-type cables hung down and this light like an upside down ice cream cone came out of the bottom, but only so far down and the beam of light never touched the ground. It was almost as if this thing knew I was there...."

Rapid Spins

Bill said that, as soon as he stepped out of his house, the strange craft began moving over the field behind his home. The appendages were immediately retracted into the bottom, which was rapidly spinning clockwise while the smaller part at the bottom was in a counterclockwise spin. Two fierce-looking claw-like hook arms on the bottom were also retracted. As this was happening, a small door opened on each side just above the arms and a light seemingly mounted on a curved piece of tubing protruded out and slightly downward. The lens area looked like many glass cubes clustered together. The two sidelights emitted a bluish-white beam.

"I was horrified by what I was seeing," Bill later remarked. "It scared the hell out of me! I had never seen anything like it!"

As the UFO backed up toward the home of Slim Davis and his crop dusting airfield a half-mile away, a large red light at its front came on. Meanwhile, the large light on the bottom center intensified to a bright white cone-shaped beam downward which reached only half-way to the ground and stopped in mid-air. The UFO maneuvered around over Davis' home and airplane hanger, lighting up everything.

Objects Over High-Voltage Power Lines

Then, suddenly, Bill spotted two more similar objects that were an estimated seventy feet in diameter hovering over the 500,000-volt power lines that were a couple hundred yards behind the Davis airfield. These objects were constructed like the larger UFO and had two small lights on either side with blue light coming from them.

"Each of the little ones was shining a blue light on the metal towers near them and the entire towers were glowing blue," Pecha stated. "Inside those shafts of blue light, however, was a darker, jerky stream of blue light that seemed to be flowing toward the UFOs, as if they were drawing electricity from the wires."

The two craft seemed to be almost resting on the lines, each one between two power poles but separated by one span section between the poles. Then, suddenly, with sparks flying, a power blackout of the surrounding area occurred.

My God! the thoroughly frightened Pecha thought. *Did those damned objects cause the power to go out?* He knew he was looking at something incredible.

Bill made a beeline for his home, yelling for his wife: *"Lenda! Lenda! Get the hell out here! You've gotta see this! No! Stay inside!"*

Pecha crashed through the doorway of his now blacked-out mobile home, ran to the back window and peered outside. He could see that the UFO was now hovering over Davis' home, with its large bottom light illuminating the area.

Dogs React

Lenda Pecha ran to her husband and grabbed his arm, squeezing it tightly. Then they watched as the mysterious object suddenly shot off at an incredible speed toward the foothills about twenty miles away. Bill reported that the aerial craft covered this distance in only two-to-three seconds while it illuminated the tops of the hills for a second or two. Then the UFO quickly reversed and, at an incredible speed, sped back to hover once more over Davis' home while simultaneously lighting up the area. It also caused his dogs to react. They were howling and barking in an unusual manner.

"Everywhere around the immediate countryside, all the lights were off, ranch yard lights and the whole town was in darkness except for the moonlight and the UFO," stated then MUFON Western States Director Paul Cerny, who led the investigation and sent a report to UFOR.

"What the Hell...?"

By now, Bill Pecha was sweating. *What the hell was this thing going to do next?* he wondered. He began to have real concern for the safety of his family (his two children, who were eight and ten years old, were still asleep). Bill turned away from the window. At about the same time, he watched as the two objects over the power lines suddenly broke away at the same time. Then they shot up and out of sight at a tremendous speed.

Pecha grabbed his wife and they both quickly ran to where their children were sleeping, awakening them. Then the TV set and air conditioner resumed functioning. The family jumped into their pickup truck. Pecha raced backwards out of the driveway with the lights deliberately turned off.

The mechanic rammed his foot onto the accelerator and sped off, reaching speeds up to ninety miles-per-hour as the object closely paced the truck. The UFO would appear on one side, then cross over and appear on the other side of the truck within a few hundred feet. Bill slammed on the brakes as he reached a friend's house. Les and Gayle Arant rushed outside to join the Pechas as, in a state of pure astonishment, they witnessed the UFO, which was now over the edge of town again, but somewhat higher in the sky. Then the flying object rapidly climbed at an angle and disappeared toward Sacramento.

Additional Witnesses

Elaine McGowen, an employee at the Sheriff's Department, also saw the same or a similar large object. So did young Fred Harris, 17, who had gone to the sheriff a few minutes before the Pecha family sighting to report that he and his mother had seen a strange object in the sky west of their home, directly in line with the Pecha home to the west.

"I'm really bad on how large things are, but it was really a very large object," Fred's mom reported. "The whole bottom was a massive, brilliant white light and the top of it was dark in the middle.... You could definitely see the whole outline of the object. I don't know if this was from the light being so bright and throwing [off] a glare so I could see the outline of the top or because the type of metal it was made of, but it was very clear that the outline of the dome was there."

PG&E Pipes In

The next day, Pacific Gas and Electric (PG&E) Company officials announced that the nine-minute blackout the night before was of "undetermined nature." They said that all of Colusa County and some adjoining areas were affected.

There was also some physical evidence. Many of the leaves on the tops of the trees around the Davis home and airfield were turning brown, as if they were heated or scorched.

"One small pear tree and a nearby lilac bush are beginning to have a number of blooms appearing," Cerny reported. "This tree and bush have never bloomed this time of year (late October) before.... The pear tree was slightly scorched or damaged on one side."

For my wife, Marty, and I, the Pecha case was another remarkable example of strange, unknown flying objects interacting with Planet Earth and the individuals residing on it. Our work together at NICAP and in our several UFOR locations constituted one of the remarkable highlights of our life together.

CHAPTER TWENTY-SIX

UFO Zaps a Car in Georgia and Jimmy Carter

One of the most interesting reports UFOR received during its first year of operation came directly from R. Conway Jones, a Supervisor of Consumer Sales for a large bank in Georgia. At the time, I believed it to be what I described as "the first of its kind" because a UFO apparently made a deliberate attempt to "zap" a car and succeeded. Jones told his story under his byline for UFOR's *U.F.O. Research Newsletter*:

> Collecting past due accounts is a thankless job. At the end of a long day, one is more than ready to head for home.
>
> On Friday, November 22, 1968, I made my last call about one mile south of the intersection of Highway 253 and State Route 91. I left this house just after 8 p.m. The night was clear and stars were visible.
>
> I drove to the intersection and turned right toward Newton, Georgia, on Route 91. I proceeded toward Newton for about three miles until I crossed the Notchaway Creek Bridge. As I crossed the bridge, I noticed my radio suddenly faded to complete static and the sound died away. I topped a slight rise in the road and started into a long, gradual curve to the left.
>
> About 100 feet in front of me and fifty to seventy-five feet above the road, I saw an oval-shaped body of light directly over the road. It

was yellowish-white and about fifty feet in diameter. There were no defined edges or appearances of a metallic surface. A beam of light was emitted from the main body of light, which struck the front of my car. My first reaction was to accelerate and speed under the object. However, when I attempted to do this, I found that my car had completely ceased functioning. I then applied the brakes, quickly coming to a halt. Even though the light from the object illuminated the entire road in front of my car, I was aware that my lights had also gone out. I sat in amazement and made no attempt to do anything except look at the object in astonishment.

After what seemed to be two or three minutes, the beam of light was slowly retracted in a way uncommon to any light ever witnessed by me. It was slowly withdrawn with the end of the beam quite visible until it had all been retracted into the main body of light. At this time, the object changed to a bright reddish-orange, fire-like color and very rapidly ascended. In about twenty to thirty seconds, it was completely out of sight, traveling straight upward.

I leaned forward and watched this object ascend. When I sat back in my seat, I discovered that my car was again running and the transmission was still in drive. My lights were shining brightly and my radio once again resumed playing.

The only physical sensation I experienced was a "tingling" all over. This could possibly be due to over-excitement from fear.

I reported this occurrence to local law enforcement personnel and it has been investigated by the U.S. Air Force, NICAP, the Aerial Phenomena Research Organization (APRO) and many others. However, to date, no one has even ventured to guess or attempted to "explain away" this sighting.

Prior to [my sighting], I did not really believe UFOs existed nor did I concern myself with them... However, now I am fully convinced that this is a very real problem and should be thoroughly studied.

The Jimmy Carter Sighting

About six weeks after the Conway Jones incident, James Earl ("Jimmy") Carter—the man who was to become Georgia's most renowned and respected citizen and who two years later became the governor of the state and later president of the United States—reported a UFO sighting of his own while in Leary, Georgia. The sighting is believed to have occurred on January 6, 1969.

It was two years before the peanut farmer would become the governor. He was in Leary to give a speech before members of the local Lions Club. Not long after the encounter, Carter filed his sighting report with NICAP and one or two other UFO groups. I read the Carter NICAP report while I was there in late 1969.

Around 7:15 p.m., a guest called Jimmy's attention to an object that appeared to be about thirty degrees above the horizon west of where he was standing. He later said the object had a clear white glow and was as bright as the moon. As he looked on, the UFO seemed to he heading toward him. Then it stopped just beyond some pine trees. The object changed color to blue, then red, then black, then white before receding out of sight.

A "Green Light" in the Sky

"There was about twenty of us standing outside a little restaurant, I believe, a high school lunch room, and a kind of green light appeared in the western sky," the future president remarked. "That was right after sundown. It got brighter and brighter, and then it eventually disappeared. It didn't have any solid substance to it. It was just a very peculiar-looking light. None of us could understand what it was."

Later, in an interview as late as 2005, President Carter described what he saw again: "All of a sudden, one of the men looked up and said: 'Look over in the west!' And there was a bright light in the sky. We all saw it. Then the light got closer and closer to us and then it stopped. All of a sudden, it changed color to blue and then changed to red, then back to white. We were trying to figure out what in the world it could be. Then it receded into the distance."

Carter admitted that he was puzzled by the strange object. He said he didn't really believe it was a visitor from space because of his knowledge of physics.

Ufologists Robert Sheaffer and Allan Hendry believed it may have been a misidentification of Venus, which was near maximum brilliance in the sky. Carter, however, disagreed with that assessment because he said "he was an amateur astronomer and knew what Venus looked like."

No Government Cover-Up

When he was asked, Jimmy said that he knew of no government cover-up of possible extraterrestrial visits to earth and rumors that the C.I.A. had refused to give him information about UFOs when he became president were not true.

At least one official observer said he had been working on an Air Force project that probed the upper atmosphere by releasing glowing chemical clouds by rockets from Elgin Air Force Base's rocket range in Florida as a possible explanation for Carter's sighting. Some of these sodium and barium clouds were supposedly visible to those on the ground. However, there was apparently no known tie-in to these chemical clouds and what Carter actually observed in the Georgia sky.

During his 1976 Presidential campaign, Carter told reporters that, if he was elected to the highest office in the land, be would demand what he described as "a policy of openness" about UFOs and the people who reported them.

"One thing is for sure," he remarked, "I'll never make fun of people who say they've seen unidentified objects in the sky. If I become President, I'll make every piece of information this country has about UFO sightings available to the public and the scientists."

"The UFO President?"

Jimmy Carter was soon designated by ufologists as "the UFO President." There was hope that, at last, the man occupying the highest office in the land would set the record straight about the government's role in the UFO phenomenon. Despite his pledge, however, once Carter was elected, "he distanced himself from disclosure, citing 'defense implications' as being behind his decision."

Major Donald E. Keyhoe would have been happy if Carter had fulfilled his promise to release all the government's UFO information to the public, but it was not to be. Keyhoe and other dedicated ufologists would just have to keep trying to pry open the tight government lid on UFO reports and landings. As of this writing in June 2017, that has not yet happened and is not likely to occur anytime soon. As Keyhoe told me before I left NICAP, he had no doubt that the government knew the secret of the UFOs, but everyone involved had been sworn to secrecy. By whom?

Beings from another solar system? Or… government officials who knew the truth but were determined to keep that deepest of secrets away from the world's population?

No one knows, but many, including myself, would like to find out. It would be the scoop of the century.

CHAPTER TWENTY-SEVEN

From A Witness in the Light to a Housebound UFO

Shortly before our move to New Mexico in 1974, my wife and I received a UFO sighting report from Mrs. Agnes M. Wehrle, a resident on South Pine Street in Zeigler, Illinois. At about 3 a.m. on October 5, 1973, the retired jewelry department manager was awakened from a sound sleep by what she described as "a bright light in the hallway leading to the kitchen, bathroom and back storage room." She thought she may have left a light on, but quickly realized that the glaring very bright light she saw could not be coming from inside her home.

Agnes jumped out of bed and quickly saw that the back storage room was very bright. But she soon realized that the extreme brightness could not be coming from inside her home.

A Witness "Bathed" in the Light

"Maybe there was a fire somewhere on the back street," Wehrle stated in her report to UFOR.

Agnes was bathed in the bright light that seemed to envelope her. It was almost as if the light were wrapping itself around her. She then noticed that her back yard was as bright as day.

Wehrle cautiously opened her door and stepped out into the back yard where she saw a large disc-shaped object hovering at an estimated sixty feet over some trees about 400 feet away. The almost laser-like light seemed to strike her in the face.

"The light was so bright that I could… stand to look at for only less than a second," the witness continued. "It burned my eyes *so* bad. I kept trying to see. Then I would cover my eyes for a while and try to see again. I kept this up for about fifteen minutes."

Wehrle said the round UFO had blue lights surrounding it, but the bright white light was larger and much brighter than the blue lights.

Optical E-M Effects

Agnes continued her report to UFOR:

> *My eyes burned so bad [that] I could hardly see. After a couple of days, I decided to see a doctor, who said the fluid was dried out of my eyes. He gave me drops to put in my eyes, which I still use. My eyes were very bad at the time I first saw him, but they are better now…*
>
> *My doctor said a lot of people won't mention these [unknown objects in the sky] because of what people will say. And that is the reason I didn't want to say anything about it. I was afraid people wouldn't believe it and would think I was some kind of a nut. But my relatives and friends said I should report it.*

Agnes said her next-door neighbor saw the object as well, but did not report it to the local newspaper. She added that another woman also spotted the unknown aerial craft and was "going to the same doctor that's taking care of my eyes."

The "Made of Glass" UFO

Several months after the Agnes Wehrle encounter, another report came into our UFOR headquarters office from Paul Cerny, the Northern California State Director for MUFON. It was nearly 11 a.m., April 6, 1974. Christine Ezell Johnson, 52, a sales clerk, and her husband were driving south through some spotty fog on Highway 280 near Foothill College in the vicinity of Los Altos, California. Suddenly, the sun broke through the fog and was shining on the surface of a very bright silver metallic-like UFO that sent lightning-like reflections into the fog-enshrouded area.

Mrs. Johnson reported that the object was about 200 feet from the highway. Her husband's attention was drawn to several children who were playing with kites on the side of the highway. She asked him to stop because heavy traffic took all of his attention. As they slowed down, the object suddenly darted forward, heading northwest for a short distance. Then, without stopping, but with a kind of quiver, it changed direction and increased its speed. It went up at a very sharp angle and vanished at a fantastic speed.

"I've never seen anything so huge in all my life," Christine remarked. "It seemed like when the sun hit [the object], there were sparkles… streams."

The cigar-shaped UFO had a reflecting surface and was an estimated 300 feet long and fifty feet in diameter. Both sides were slightly rounded. At the time the object quivered and changed direction, there may have been a sound of wind.

Christine said she got the feeling that "the object was not of this earth."

Meanwhile, numerous sightings of other strange objects in the skies continued coming into our headquarters office.

No April Fools Joke

What Mrs. Ruth A. Ziegenfuss, 60, and her granddaughter, Donna, 15, saw in the sky over Aquashicola, Pennsylvania, at 8:30 p.m., April 1, 1977, was no April Fool's joke. Donna, a student at nearby Palmerton High School, was visiting her grandmother. That visit would not only be the highlight of her visit, but also one of the highlights of her life.

The incident occurred as Ruth and Donna were traveling from the Lower Towamensing to the Little Gap sections of the town. Only minutes after starting their trip, they suddenly saw a small dome-shaped UFO that appeared to be metallic with three bright lights on the bottom.

"Oh, Mammy, that looks weird!" Donna exclaimed.

The "Crackling" Radio

"First, it appeared to be stationary, with very bright lights glaring in our direction," Ruth stated in her report to UFOR on June 26, 1977. "It hovered directly above our car as though [it was] following us for about two miles. Then, all of a sudden, it was directly above our car, its bright lights glaring inside our car. The radio started crackling very loudly, so Donna turned it off."

Ruth said the object appeared to be about twice as big as her car. It had a dome with three very bright lights on it.

"I didn't know what to do!" she admitted, frightened. "My granddaughter began to scream."

Ruth said the UFO appeared to be only ten-to-fifteen feet above her automobile and it looked like it was coming "right down on my car... Then it disappeared in about three seconds near the Trachsville Bridge."

Zeigenfuss and her granddaughter were badly frightened by the close encounter.

"I never before saw anything like it, nor will I ever forget what I saw that night," Ruth remarked in her report to UFOR.

Strange Object Hovers Over House

The UFO sighting reports continued to keep me busy. My desk was overflowing with them as I struggled to sort out the incidents worthy of further investigation and those that were more easily explained as some kind of earthly phenomenon.

At 10:20 p.m., February 26, 1979, Mrs. Rose Marie Julig—a bookkeeper and accounts payable employee at the Midwest Printing Company in Minneapolis, Minnesota—had a startling sighting of a UFO from her home in nearby Columbia Heights. There were two additional witnesses: Sue Arent, of McGregor, and Lee Hoff, from Cottage Grove. The event lasted for an estimated twenty-five minutes in the vicinity of Rose Marie's home at 4340 Benjamin Street, Northeast.

In her report to UFOR, Rose Marie said the UFO traveled over the roof of her home at a very slow pace. Then it stopped in front of her window and hovered there for a while. When the object left, it sped very, very fast over the roof of the house.

During the sighting, Mrs. Julig said her poodle "disappeared out of the room and hid under our bed. He didn't make a sound as I ran through the house.... This is very unusual as my dog barks all the time and especially when anyone runs through the house. He only hides under the bed when he is frightened, which is very rarely. My cat sat still in a corner and didn't move."

UFO on Collision Course With House

Rose Marie sent me her account of the sighting along with a similar report she gave to MUFON:

We were sitting in the living room watching the news on TV. I happened to glance out the window behind me when I first noticed a very, very bright object (light) in the sky. It was coming from the east....

We watched the bright light moving very slowly toward us. It came closer and closer and then turned slightly toward the north.... Then we noticed [that] the bright white light was actually two lights.... We also noticed two small red blinking lights in the back. Then [the UFO] made a forty-five-degree angle turn towards us and [it] looked like it was going to hit the house....

The next minute, it was approximately twenty feet above the house. [It was] slightly tilted. It came to a complete stop.... A portion of it was overlapping the right side of the window, so we could see it very clearly. It [had] a big, flat, solid, gray bottom [and] stayed there for about one minute before it left in an upward direction and went towards Northeast Minneapolis.... We did not hear any noise until it left. When I ran to the back door and opened [it], I heard a soft hum.

We watched it hover over... Minneapolis for a short while and the bright light was still shining in our direction. Then it moved slowly toward [the downtown area].... We watched it for awhile... before it disappeared.

On March 1, Rose Marie called Dr. J. Allen Hynek's Centers for UFO Studies (CUFOS) in Evanston, Illinois. She spoke with Hynek's colleague, Dr. Allen Hendry, who "was very interested in my story" and requested more information from Sue Arent, who was with Rose Marie during the sighting. Back home at UFOR headquarters, I never heard back from Mrs. Ziegenfuss as to whether or not CUFOS had followed through with their sighting.

CHAPTER TWENTY-EIGHT

Flying Disc Causes Physiological Effects

During the summer of 1975—while living with my wife, Marty, and stepson, Jay, in a home on Beachwood Canyon directly under the famed HOLLYWOOD sign in Los Angeles—I read of a report that fascinated me. It involved a flying saucer that caused severe physiological effects to the main witness. Mrs. Terri Smith, 19, saw the object with her cousin Imelda Lugo, 12, and Manuel and Frances Lugo, her uncle and aunt, within the city limits of Gilroy, California, sixty-three miles south of San Francisco, on August 10, 1975.

I located Terri Smith's phone number and interviewed her on August 13 about the unusual and frightening sighting. She reported that she was driving Imelda home when they spotted a bright, gray, metallic, oval-shaped UFO that emitted a humming noise. It had three large, long legs extending from the bottom.

"Hey, Terri, it looks like a spacecraft!" Imelda exclaimed in an excited state. "It's a flying saucer! Wow! Maybe it's going to take us to another planet!"

Frightened Witnesses

Almost immediately, Terri began feeling uneasy, as if she was becoming disoriented. She slowed the panel truck down near El Cerrito Way and Wayland Lane. She and Imelda became frightened and huddled against each other as the UFO came very close to the truck.

"There were green, red and tiny little white lights on the legs and around the disc part," the witness told me in a still frightened state. "I paced the object with my car a little distance. It became brighter and had a light blue haze around it. It moved slowly and turned as I turned the van around. Then it seemed to be coming down on the van, lowering itself to just over the treetops."

Mrs. Smith parked in front of her uncle's home, at which time it seemed like the UFO was coming down on them. Imelda was in hysterics as Terri ran inside to alert her aunt and uncle. Mr. and Mrs. Lugo quickly scurried outside.

"It'll Get You!"

"I ran outside in my nightgown thinking that maybe there was something or someone after them," Frances Lugo remarked. "They told me not to go outside. They said: 'It'll get you!'"

As Frances frantically ran out of the house, the UFO was hovering just above the treetops near Carmel Street and El Toro Way.

"It was a gray-colored disc with small lights all around it," she explained. "Two huge, recessed headlights were shining."

Jose Lugo also rushed outside. He saw the object moving slowly toward the north. Suddenly, it accelerated and disappeared in the sky at a terrific speed.

Witness is "Spaced-Out"

As Terri Smith paced the object, she felt "spaced-out and light-headed." She added that she had a feeling that occupants (which she did not see, only "felt") were inside the UFO and wanted to take her and her cousin inside the craft.

"I really felt there were humanoid-like occupants inside that flying saucer," Terri told me. "They wanted to assure us that everything was all right—that there was nothing to fear. It was like a psychic thing. It seemed like the thoughts of these space beings were coming across to me, that they wanted to say something to me that would be good for all of us, for everyone on earth. I must admit that I was scared at first, but later thought the occupants of that spacecraft had good intentions. Still, for some reason I can't explain, I was frightened and still am."

I could clearly feel Mrs. Smith's anxiety as I spoke to her over the phone. She added that, immediately after the sighting, she felt nauseous. This feeling persisted on-and-off throughout the next day (August 11). But that was only the beginning.

Physiological Effects

"The following evening [August 12], while taking a shower, I noticed a scratch along a vein on the back of my left hand with a hole bigger than a pin prick," Terri elaborated. "The hole apparently opened up while I was showering and blood squirted out of it. I was scared.... Had the aliens done this? Were they experimenting with me? Jesus, what was going to happen next? *Was I going to be kidnapped on board a flying saucer?!*"

By the next morning (August 13), the scratch had mysteriously disappeared, but the inflammation around the hole and the hole itself remained. She said Cousin Imelda had an identical wound on the back of her right hand. Both of these irregularities occurred after the sighting and neither witness had any real idea that made sense as to how they originated.

"UFO Believers"

Terri Smith said that, after their encounter with the flying object, both she and her aunt were UFO believers. But Terri had not done any extensive reading on the subject and had not pursued it. Now, however, she was not so sure. At first, she admitted, she thought I might have been a "kook" out to exploit her somehow, but was convinced otherwise following the lengthy telecon. She told me that Judy Mann, an investigator for APRO, and a Professor from Berkeley (probably Dr. James Harder, an

APRO investigator and consultant) and four of his students interviewed her. She was also informed that the Gilroy Police Department had sent a report of the sighting to CUFOS.

Also investigating the incident was the always reliable Paul Cerny, who had worked with me on a number of cases. When he arrived, he said the Lugos were still shook up.

Other area residents also spotted the same or a similar object. Robert Bluemmer, 42, and his wife said it had a red and blue light at its center and made what they described as flitting motions.

A Horticulturist's Nightmare

At about the same time I received the account of the Terri Smith sighting, I was also sent a report from Mrs. Doris R. Fickelsher, a horticulturist from Angola, New York.

It was an unusually hot and sultry night in the early morning hours of June 12, 1968. Doris was star-gazing on the porch of her Gowans Road home while two of her children were sleeping beside her covered with light blankets.

Everything was still and quiet until 3 a.m. when a large pulsating light that Doris estimated to be about sixty feet in diameter slowly approached her property. The witness watched with growing enthusiasm and saw that the metallic-gray UFO looked like it had curved windows and an internal red light that flashed to green, then back to red. It resembled two inverted soup bowls with curved windows at the front. It appeared to be heading straight for both her home and the residence of her neighbor on the other side of her driveway.

"Our dog was whining and acted frightened," the witness told me in her report. "The cats also ran from the porch acting very frightened. It was unusual for these animals to act in this manner unless they were physically threatened."

Doris said she was not really alarmed until the object reached the middle of the field and descended to an estimated 200 feet above the ground on her property. She suddenly felt she was in the middle of a nightmare. She ran inside and grabbed her flashlight as the UFO slowly descended toward the open field in front of her property. As it descended, the trees seemed to be vibrating and its branches were bent down toward the ground. At the same time, the children's blanket was mysteriously blown off of them. The children, however, were not injured.

Mrs. Fickelsher shone the flashlight on the UFO, apparently causing the object to ascend so quickly straight up that it seemed to vanish from the very air itself.

Doris was so frightened that she tried rising from her seat on the porch, but her legs would not support her. She forced herself to move enough to enable her to wake her children and scurry them into the house.

In the days and months that followed, the witness said that the sighting was what launched her into the study of the UFO phenomenon and "I have been in search of answers since then."

CHAPTER TWENTY-NINE

Flying Saucers Pace Planes

In our Beachwood Canyon home in Hollywood, my wife and I continued to receive UFO reports from our erstwhile investigator, Paul Cerny. One that caught my immediate attention involved a professional photographer and his wife. It was one of several reports we received involving flying objects that paced airplanes.

It was April 11, 1977. The giant Boeing 747 jet had just taken off from Los Angeles International Airport (LAX) for the next leg of its journey to San Francisco International. Fred Svihus, a professional photographer, and his wife, Eva, had window seats just behind the left wing of the aircraft.

At about eight a.m., the plane was flying at approximately 20,000 feet altitude in the vicinity of Vandenburg Air Force Base near Lompoc, California. Svihus was filming the jet's flap action and the clouds with his Bolex movie camera at the standard eighteen frames per second.

"My God! What's That?"

"My God! What's that?" Eva Svihus suddenly yelled. "Do you see it, Fred?"

"Yes, I'm filming it!" her husband exclaimed.

Four oval, glowing objects in echelon formation sped by at an estimated five-to-seven miles distance and slightly lower than the aircraft. They flew in the opposite direction from the jet.

"Svihus continued to 'pan' the... objects as they went past his window, being careful to steady the camera and holding it as close to the plexiglass window as possible without touching the lens shell to it....," stated Cerny in his report to UFOR. "The objects... continued on out of sight behind the airliner. As the UFOs were just about out of sight, he watched as they suddenly broke formation and scattered.... Reflections were ruled out due to the closeness of the lens to the window and the fact that the UFOs were very obviously against a clear blue sky with the sun shining on them from the opposite side of the airplane where the observers were seated."

Cerny added that most of the passengers disembarked at LAX, and none of the few remaining travelers observed the phenomenon. There was some indication, however, that the plane's crew may have seen the UFOs.

Shooting the "Unknowns"

"The UFOs were exposed on thirty-two individual frames of the film," Cerny continued. "Near the Los Angeles airport..., Mr. Svihus shot out a few frames of the moon as it was visible in the early morning sky... It was interesting to compare the size of this two-thirds full moon... to the later shots of the 'unknowns,' which appeared to this observer as about one-third to one-quarter the size of the moon in comparison."

The UFOs were in view for only four-to-five seconds.

"The position of the four objects with respect to one another seemed to remain relatively the same with only a slight deviation noted in repeated viewing of the film," Cerny wrote. "Under photographic analysis..., any deviation of the positions of the objects should be more prominent and can be measured."

The Hallstrom Incident

More than eight months later, at about 12:35 p.m. on New Year's Day, January 1, 1978, Floyd P. Hallstrom and Jim Victor took off from the airport in Oxnard, California, heading for Browns Field in San Diego. Victor was delivering the Mustang II he had sold to a customer and Hallstrom—piloting a Cessna 170A—went along to return his friend to home base.

Hallstrom was a commercial pilot with a helicopter rotary wing and single engine land aircraft rating. He had been a pilot since 1941, prior to America's entry into World War II.

Hallstrom flew directly toward LAX while Victor, in the faster plane, hugged the coastline, flying over Pepperdine University's beautiful campus with a clear view of the Pacific Ocean in Malibu, then on to Point Mugu. The sky was crystal clear.

At 1:07 p.m., Floyd was flying over downtown Santa Monica, bordering the coastline. He was cruising at an altitude of approximately 7500 feet.

"I could observe traffic and buildings on the ground extremely clear," he remarked.

From "Out of the Haze"

Hallstrom peered ahead, looking for Victor, when he saw what he described as "a spot coming out of the haze." It was probably Jim, he reasoned, but… *No, it couldn't be.* The thing was coming toward him. Maybe it was a passenger helicopter out of LAX. But, this, too, he quickly discounted. Then, "all of a sudden, I was able to make out the complete form of a saucer shape or round object" at an estimated 6,000 feet altitude. The UFO was to the left of his aircraft at a distance of one-half to three-quarters of a mile.

The pilot quickly honed in on the object and saw it very clearly. It was about thirty feet in diameter and resembled a complete half sphere on a small land base measuring about three feet thick. The dome was an estimated twenty feet in diameter and the entire object was about fifteen feet high. There were sixteen-to-twenty evenly spaced oval-shaped windows around the base of the sphere. The dimensions of the windows looked to be about eighteen by twenty-four inches. The surface of the UFO looked like nickel or highly polished steel or chrome.

The object disappeared in a line over the distant Hollywood Hills. Hallstrom had observed it for approximately one minute.

An "Overwhelming Urge"

In a preface report on the incident dated February 15, 1978, Idabel Epperson—a long-time Los Angeles-based UFO investigator and stalwart friend of both NICAP and UFOR—said that, as the object passed under his plane, Floyd had a sudden overwhelming urge to meet with the pilot of that spaceship and wished fervently for the UFO to return and lead him to a landing place where they could meet and talk. Hallstrom flew over the city of Downey—around twenty miles from LAX—a few minutes later.

At 1:17 p.m., the same or a similar object described as a rotating metallic spheroid was seen over Downey flying in the opposite direction from where Hallstrom saw his UFO disappear.

Floyd quickly radioed Victor in the Mustang ahead. With his friend accompanying him, he reported the incident to the Federal Aviation Administration (FAA) at both Browns Field and Oxnard.

"Inexplicable Incidents"

But the story did not end there. For some weeks after the sighting, Hallstrom was plagued by a series of inexplicable incidents, including emotional upheavals, physiological reactions, insomnia, and disturbing dreams.

A few nights after the encounter over Santa Monica, Hallstrom and his wife, Gwen, were awakened by a noise that seemed to be coming from inside the bedroom itself, according to Mrs. Epperson, who said the couple searched but found nothing. Then they heard a high-pitched humming sound. Hallstrom rushed outdoors but saw nothing.

That same week—on three different mornings shortly before dawn—Floyd observed a light hovering over his house. He said it was definitely not light from a conventional aircraft.

"Disquieting Dreams"

"The most puzzling and disturbing of all was the change that had come over Hallstrom himself," Epperson remarked in her preface report:

> He told me that he had a very uncomfortable pressure in his head that he never had before. He also had trouble sleeping and some nights he did not sleep at all.... This was a new experience for him... When he did sleep, he had disquieting dreams, mostly about UFOs and aliens. This, too, was a new experience. Previously, he was not even aware he was dreaming. In spite of all of this, he still maintained that he would go with the aliens willingly if they came after him. When I asked him why, he answered: "Because they have superior intelligence and we have much to learn..." We have talked with Mr. Hallstrom from time-to-time by phone since his sighting. Our conversation with him [on February 13] was very encouraging. He is feeling very much himself again and [was] 'back to normal,' as he put it.

A tape recording made by Hallstrom on January 14 confirmed that he had been suffering.

A *"Very Disturbing"* Event

"[The incident] has very definitely affected my emotions, my work, my home life and the people around me...," he explained. "I am a very difficult person to live with at this time. It seems to me that this incident has attacked me subconsciously. I can only describe this feeling, the way it affects me emotionally, is in a manner the same as you have when you have lost a very dear friend.... It gets stronger as time goes by.... It is affecting my sleep.... It seems... my mind... always wanders back to this flying saucer incident, and it certainly is very disturbing to me."

On January 4, only three days after the sighting, Hallstrom wrote a letter to Defense Secretary Harold Brown, asking that the American public be informed of what he called "the truth about UFOs." Copies of the letter were sent to California congressional and state lawmakers.

Prior to his sighting, Hallstrom had had an impressive seventeen-and-a-half career in the U.S. Navy, commencing with the outbreak of World War II for America. He served as an aircraft mechanic and a combat air crewman on all types of aircraft. Additionally, he was squadron maintenance chief and assisted in training combat air crewmen. He also served with several commanders-in-chief of the Atlantic Fleet and became thoroughly trained in all phases of aircraft. Over the years, he had obtained a reputation as an honest individual and a highly qualified aviator.

"A Thoroughly Honest Man"

"I know Floyd Hallstrom to be a thoroughly honest man and an eminently qualified observer," wrote Philip D. Terry, Director of Airline Sales for a large corporation, on January 16. "I believe him and he is convinced he saw what he describes."

Dennis Leatart investigated the incident for APRO.

"Of the ten or eleven years I have been researching UFOs, this is the most outstanding and remarkable case of all…," Leatart stated in his report. "I found Mr. Hallstrom to be a very highly intelligent man… who, in no uncertain terms, knows what he saw was real, physical and something not made on this earth."

CHAPTER THIRTY

The Humming UFO and Sightings in Pennsylvania and Maryland

UFO sighting reports continued to come into UFOR's home headquarters in Hollywood. One of these events occurred at 8:30 p.m., April 1, 1977. But it was no April Fool's joke.

Mrs. Ruth A. Zeigenfuss, 60, of Aquashicola, Pennsylvania, and Donna, 15 (her granddaughter), were returning to Ruth's home when they spotted a large UFO that caused electro-magnetic (E-M) effects and badly frightened the two witnesses. Ruth described the event in her report to UFOR:

> ...We saw these terrific bright lights in the sky. I mentioned it to my granddaughter and she said: "Oh, Mammy, that looks weird!" We continued to drive for about two miles, seeing these lights all the time.... Then, all of a sudden, there it was directly above our car, its bright lights glaring into our car. The radio started crackling very loudly, so Donna... turned it off.
>
> [The UFO] was about twice as big as my car, but round with a dome and there were very bright lights on it. I didn't know what to do. I was scared. My granddaughter began to scream. She was really scared!
>
> We thought it was going to come right down on my car. It looked like it wasn't more than ten or fifteen feet from the roof of my car. It was very light out that night (moonlight) and we could see it very well. It

seemed to be dark gray in color and kept hovering over our car for about one-half mile. Then, all of a sudden, it disappeared and was gone in about three seconds. I never before saw anything like it. Nor will I ever forget what I saw that night. I even began to think I might be kidnapped by alien beings from another planet outside our solar system... But, somehow, I don't think that beings from outer space mean to harm us...

The Humming, Vibrating Cigar

Less than a year later, at about 3:30 a.m., February 4, 1978, Mrs. Claire Semaza—a City of Orange, California, resident—was awakened in her bedroom by a weird noise that sounded as though a mob of people were humming. She felt like the strange sound was eerily vibrating its way into her body and mind. The inexplicable event seemed to hold her down. She couldn't get her physical body off the bed. Fifteen-to-twenty minutes later, the humming intensified to such an extent that Claire began to feel a burning sensation in her ears.

Meanwhile, a neighbor, Mrs. Dorothy Pascl, and Mrs. Semaza's two children—Donna, 14, and Eric, 11—were also awakened by the unusual, strange and loud humming noise. The sound rapidly grew so strong with such a piercing, penetrating sound that the Semazas thought something was about to land on their roof or crash through the window.

While still clad in their nightclothes, Claire and her two children raced out into the front yard of their two-story apartment complex. Then they caught a glimpse of something toward the south-southeast. They observed what they described as an oval or cigar-shaped object just above some trees an estimated two blocks to one-half mile away.

The Smoke Layer

"The sky above [the UFO] glowed in one area with a pinkish color and, a little further away, to the left, was a hot, clear red color," stated Willard D. Nelson, a local UFO investigator, in his report on the incident to UFOR. "Below and around the object was a layer of haze or 'smoke,' gray in color.... The object was slowly rising, leaving the smoke layer behind. It was a dark shape, but it had two bright red lights, one on each end of the oval, with several smaller bluish-white lights swung horizontally between the two reds. The red lights cast shafts of light downward and outwards, looking like shafts of sunlight from a sunset.... Rising higher, it flashed a brilliant white light on and off for perhaps three seconds and then... shot off, ascending toward the left, higher and higher to the southeast."

Dog Goes "Bananas"

During the sighting, Susie—the Semaza female dog—went "bananas" for about half-an-hour. She had given birth to her first litter of puppies two days earlier.

"There she was with seven puppies to protect, and she must have felt that extreme danger threatened," wrote veteran UFO investigator Idabel Epperson in her account of the incident. "The cozy box that she and the puppies occupied was on the ground floor. She carried a puppy upstairs and tried to hide it in a couple of places—the last place she tried was under the bed—but that didn't satisfy her. She took the puppy out from under the bed and hid it behind the drapes. This was the right place, she thought, so she carried the rest of the puppies one-by-one upstairs and hid them all behind the drapes."

The "Patchwork Quilt"

At 5:45 a.m., neighbor Dorothy Pascl rose early to do some shopping at the nearby all-night Albertson's Market. After arriving there, she glanced skyward and was startled to see what appeared to be cloud-like, pinkish-red patches resembling a patchwork quilt that was apparently left by the UFO. The size of the glowing patchwork area was roughly guessed to be 300 feet long by fifty feet high. By about 6:15, the patches had dissipated.

Dorothy did not see the actual unidentified object. Mrs. Semaza and her children experienced a heightened sense of excitement and some fear during the sighting.

Marylanders Report Sightings

Two and a half months after the Hallstrom encounter, Maryland residents reported sightings in April 1978. John Lutz, President of Odyssey Scientific Research Association in Baltimore, sent his team's investigatory report to UFOR.

At 4:30 a.m., April 23, Mr. and Mrs. Charles White were driving about eighteen miles east of the rugged mountainous Cumberland area when they spotted an oval-shaped UFO approximately forty-to-sixty feet long and twenty feet high. It hovered over a ravine around 500 feet east of Route 40 and was an estimated 250 feet above the bottom of the ravine.

The witnesses stopped and placed a red emergency flare on the road in an effort to prevent a possible collision with another vehicle. Then they watched in amazement as the UFO rose slowly to an altitude of approximately 1,000 feet, then flew east while slowly gaining altitude and was lost to sight after passing over an adjoining mountain.

The Whites stated that the object first looked like new sand-blasted gray cast iron, rigid, possibly metal, whose outline appeared luminous, but fuzzy, or indistinct as it slowly rose into the air. It had a sky-blue color and became brighter as it gained altitude. No sound was detected.

Forty-six hours later—at 2:15 a.m., April 25—Robert Steven Hake was driving south on I-83 between Hereford and Shawn Roads just north of Baltimore when he saw an object that was approximately fifty feet in diameter with three large rectangular windows and a white light. It also had a small tower or dome on top with several revolving red lights. There were silhouettes or outlines of two occupants within the strange object.

Object Swoops Down on Car

"At one point…," Lutz stated in his report, "the UFO swooped down to almost road level and approached the witness' vehicle in a head-on collision course until, at the last moment, the object suddenly gained altitude and went over the 1976 Ford Maverick."

The unknown flying craft ascended until it finally appeared as a bright star. Hake flagged down a state highway patrol car containing Trooper Joel Connelly. The lawman also saw the object, which now looked like a brilliant star that was resting directly under the moon and between two smaller stars. Connelly then drove on to McCormick Avenue and turned his patrol car's bubble light on, but the strange star never approached.

Connelly arrived at his barracks about fifteen minutes later, but when he looked up toward the moon and stars again, he noticed that the moon and the two smaller stars were there, but the bigger one in the center had disappeared.

CHAPTER THIRTY-ONE

From NASA to a Silver UFO

My office desk inside our home in the Beachwood Canyon area of Hollywood continued to be piled high with UFO information and sighting reports from around the world. I was particularly interested in the possibility that the National Aeronautics and Space Administration (NASA) could have an interest in collecting and maintaining a continuing compendium of UFO sightings. This piqued my attention because I was well aware that then-current President Jimmy Carter had reported his own saucer sighting (see Chapter Twenty-Six).

Looking out of my window at our tree-enshrouded pool, I perused the latest communication from one of my contacts, Howard Benedict, an Associated Press writer. His eye-opening lead said that President Carter wanted NASA to consider reopening the government's probe of unidentified flying objects. Was the man once touted as The UFO President serious? I wondered…. This was after he had promised to make all the UFO information available, but didn't. It made serious investigators sit up and take notice. I began to wonder if the government had known for a long time that at least some of the bona-fide UFO reports involved contact with alien beings. Keyhoe, Dick Hall and I had come to that conclusion back in the NICAP days. And Jim McDonald had considered it the most likely hypothesis.

"Give Me One Little Green Man"

Meanwhile, Dave Williamson, NASA's Assistant for Special Projects, immediately sounded a negative drumbeat in his response to Benedict's article:

> We're not anxious to do it because we're not sure what we can do. It's my personal opinion that it's not wise to do research on something that is not a measurable phenomena. Spending public money for such research is questionable.
>
> There is no measurable UFO evidence such as a piece of metal, flesh or cloth. We don't even have any radio signals. A photograph is not a measurement... .
>
> Give me one little green man—not a theory or memory of one—and we can have a multi-million-dollar program. It's a scientific dilemma. How do you prove something that doesn't exist?
>
> It's like the Loch Ness monster revisited. Everyone sees it, but there is no physical evidence.

Williamson was the head honcho of a number of so-called technical experts who were charged with recommending the steps NASA could take concerning a White House request that it establish a UFO panel of inquiry. (This afforded me a brief glimmer of hope that the nation's Chief Executive might be serious about reopening a national inquiry of credible saucer reports.) The idea was that such a panel would take up where the Air Force left off ten years ago when it closed its UFO investigation group, Project Blue Book.

Williamson was charged with making his recommendation to Robert A. Frosch, the NASA Administrator, who would formulate his own decision and pass it on to Dr. Frank Press, the President's Science Adviser. Press shot back his own missive to Frosch, suggesting that NASA should become the government's focal point in what would be called "a national revival of interest" in UFO sighting reports. Frosch responded by pointing out that a panel of inquiry would cost a lot of money. He suggested that his technical staff make a study to see if it was justified.

An Upsurge of Letters

Press also admitted that his office had received an upsurge of letters, especially from young people asking about UFOs. And Williamson said he expected even more interest because of a popular new film, Steven Spielberg's blockbuster *Close Encounters of the Third Kind* (1977). No question about it. This fine film was making the rounds and stirring up a great deal of more interest in the overall UFO phenomenon.

Meanwhile, I had written to Frank Press, asking if the government was really debating a serious investigation. He fudged on that, but admitted that he had been receiving an influx of letters asking about UFOs, but he didn't have enough staff members to handle the deluge of inquiries. He asked NASA to take over this task. A NASA official played down the number of daily letters, saying the average was only two or three letters a day. He speculated that Press might have acted because some of the letters demanded that Carter fulfill his campaign promise to investigate UFOs. A White House spokesman concurred, saying he vaguely recalled Carter making the pledge but could not pinpoint the time or place.

"The See-Saw Effect"

Now began a brief period I called "the See-Saw Effect," hardly a remote thing when dealing with government officials. First, the *National Enquirer* had gotten into the act with the story, informing its millions of readers about the possible NASA involvement. This intrigued me because I knew that the *Enquirer*, usually regarded as an inaccurate scandal sheet, had taken a different tack on the UFO problem and was actually reporting on the phenomenon in a fair, objective, and accurate manner. At NICAP, we had often remarked that some of the *Enquirer* stories were considerably more accurate than many of the mainstream press accounts.

On October 18, 1977, I wrote Dr. Press again, citing the *Enquirer* story and offering to make myself and the UFOR files "available to any qualified government investigator looking into this intriguing phenomenon." I received a Halloween-dated later from Stanley D. Schneider, Assistant to the Director, Executive Office of the President, Office of Science and Technology, who was responding for Dr. Press.

The *National Enquirer* is "Correct"

"What you read in the *National Enquirer* is essentially correct," he admitted. "NASA has been asked to determine… whether they should undertake to sponsor a new investigation of the UFO phenomena."

Schneider closed by saying he would forward my letter to NASA for their response. Shortly after that, I received a letter from O.B. Lloyd, Jr., NASA's Director of Public Services. He said that: "No decision has been reached on whether NASA will take a new and continuing investigation of aerial phenomena…. If it is determined that NASA will assume the full UFO investigative function, we will be back in touch with you."

Flash ahead another two weeks…. I wrote Lloyd back thanking him for his letter. I also remarked that I understood that Dr. Richard Henry at NASA was in charge of a UFO inquiry. Therefore, some kind of "preliminary study must be underway. Can you confirm this? Is there any timetable on this study? Will NASA make a recommendation to the President and/or his science adviser regarding a continuing UFO investigation?"

To-and-Fro Missives

The to-and-fro missives continued. In a letter dated December 6, I heard from Dr. Henry, NASA's Deputy Director of Astrophysics Division, Office of Space Science. Answering for Lloyd, he made the following points:

- "The letter to NASA's Administrator from the President's science adviser… did not mention President Carter's name."

- "I am not in charge of an UFO inquiry, nor is anyone at NASA."

- "To my knowledge, NASA does not have files of UFO reports... other than the piles of material people have been sending me... since word of Dr. Press' letter was released" and "I don't know what the 'special suspense file' is."

- "To sum up, absolutely nothing is happening at NASA on UFOs except that a few of 'us bureaucrats' are trying to help our Administrator, Dr. Frosch, arrive at a sensible and good response to Dr. Press' request."

The Greenwood Take

Barry J. Greenwood is a crack UFO researcher and investigator who I knew from the NICAP years. He is the co-author with Lawrence Fawcett of *Clear Intent: The Government Coverup of the UFO Experience* (Prentice-Hall, Inc., 1984). Barry graciously agreed to give me a summation of his scholarly take and added his comments on the most highly publicized crash-and-retrieval case of all... the Roswell, New Mexico, incident in July 1947 (see the next chapter):

> *It is a possibility that the 1977 inquiry to NASA may have been the event that started the ball rolling on the beginning of the modern version of Roswell. Between 1947 and 1978, there was little comment about Roswell in the national press. A few brief mentions in UFO literature, including an inclusion in a 1967* Look Magazine *UFO special issue, can be found, but, in the main, it had been overlooked as a significant event. Then, after the NASA offer of a multi-million dollar investigation into UFO crash artifacts and/or bodies, in very short order, people began to surface with reports of saucer artifacts and bodies at*

Roswell, New Mexico. Leonard Stringfield, who had begun to collect rumors of crashed retrievals in the mid 1970s, alluded to the Roswell report in his Abstract 18 of the first Status Report he had written on April 5, 1978, a few months after Major Jesse Marcel surfaced. Prior to that time, there was nothing collected by Stringfield on the story.

It is puzzling that, in the previously cited dead zone of Roswell saucer news, not a single of the estimated 400 witnesses now having contributed to the narrative had spoken out then. This included the 1952, 1967, 1965-1967, and 1973 sighting waves, when cover-ups and dramatic saucer reports were often front-page news. There wasn't a peep, even in the local press where scoops are sought to enhance local reporting reputations. Not even an anonymous Letter to the Editor.

Only from 1978 on do we see a great push to tell all on this. By then, however, the trail was quite cold and, in terms of documentation, it was ice cold after more that three decades. Narratives were—as they always still are regarding crashed disc reports—virtually the only evidence of the events.

At this point, the matter seemed pretty much closed. The last I heard about a possible NASA involvement came from respected UFO researcher and investigator Idabel Epperson, who wrote: "If the U.S. goes back to the same old cover-up system…., we are going to look pretty silly." Amen to that!

The Silver Spaceship

Meanwhile, the stream of reports continued to flow onto my crowded office desk. The lone witness of one of these sightings was Marie Louise Schmidt, 62, a self-employed secretary from Rockwood, Michigan. She told me her story:

On April 29, 1978, at about 11:45 p.m., as I was watching television..., I was attracted to a row of very bright lights, white and amber, across my picture window. [The object] was going very slow... I judge about three miles an hour and the sound [it emitted] was like a very low hum....

As it was going by, I took a very good look at it. It was right up to the window and it was so huge that I could only see the side of it.... As it was gliding by, I was more curious to see how it was made. The row of lights were on the bottom and across the back. I did not see the front or the far side....

Above the lights, the spaceship was silver and, as it was passing by, I seen [sic] a door and on each corner were large knobs. The knobs were cushioned. I was anxious to see windows, but there were none....

I also noticed [that] it was built in one piece. There were no seams or rivets. The only seam was the door. Then, when I seen [sic] the tail section, I was surprised, for it was shaped in a large scroll, as you see in my drawing.... This design was so weird that I was sure it came from outer space. I watched it going west and I understand that two women from Carlton also seen [sic] it the same night. Their description seems the same, only they didn't mention the tail section....

The lights were so intense, especially the back lights. The one in the center was a lot larger than the one on the side.... Since I looked direct into it, it seems like my eyes water a lot and [I] need stronger lens. It was like looking into the sun.

My tree in the front yard was budding out and, after a few days, I noticed the buds were dried and I wondered if the UFO had damaged it. My family was going to chop it down. I mentioned [that] it may come back and it did.

The "Large House" UFO

Marie added that, as she looked out her window, the UFO resembled a large house that was flying by. She hunched herself over in a frightened state as the object glided over the treetops in a kind of up-and-down movement and side-to-side and it would creak and make sort of a giggling noise.

The witness added that staring at the white light had weakened her eyes. Also, the tree in her front yard had burned leaves after the object flew over it. And Marie heard her neighbor's dog frantically barking during the encounter with the unwanted intruder.

CHAPTER THIRTY-TWO

UFO "Retrievals of the Third Kind" and the Incident at Roswell

Speculation that the bodies of alien beings from crashed UFOs are being held by the U.S. government is hardly new. Since the publication of Frank Scully's book *Behind the Flying Saucers* in 1950 containing a story in which a saucer allegedly crashed near Aztec, New Mexico, in 1948, such reports have periodically surfaced.

The Scully account has been pretty much proven to be a hoax, and similar stories over the years have come from individuals with less than honest and impressive credentials. No serious researcher gave the reports any credence.

Len Stringfield: A Well-Known Factor

Then along came Leonard ("Len") H. Stringfield in early 1978. He was well-known to researchers and serious ufology students as a reliable individual not prone to wild, unsubstantiated claims. He was a friend of Major Donald E. Keyhoe, longtime head of NICAP, and his credentials were impressive. I briefly met Len once in the NICAP office around 1968 and was impressed by his no-nonsense knowledge of UFOs.

By 1978, Len was the author of several highly regarded UFO books, including *Situation Red: The UFO Siege*. His friend Keyhoe had penned the Foreword. He was also the Director of Civilian Research, Interplanetary Flying Objects (CRIFO) and published *ORBIT*, a monthly newsletter.

More than twenty years earlier, in 1957, he had been the Public Relations Adviser for NICAP. From 1967 to 1969, Stringfield was the Early Warning Coordinator for the University of Colorado UFO Project headed by Dr. Edward U. Condon. In 1978, he became the UFO Research Advisor to Grenada Prime Minister Sir Eric Gairy.

"UFO Crash Retrievals"

Stringfield was also active in generating real interest in UFOs within the august body of the United Nations. And he continued to publish his own Status Reports on what he considered to be "UFO crash retrievals" until his death on December 18, 1994, following a long battle with lung cancer.

I was grateful to receive from Len his lengthy paper, "Retrievals of the Third Kind: A Case Study of Alleged UFO Occupants in Military Custody," dated April 5, 1978. To his credit, he was the first to admit that there were flaws in the report and that much more research needed to be done. Most of the real names of witnesses and informants were not used and some of the information was fragmented and second or third hand. Exact dates were few, but there was enough solid material from a reliable, well-respected researcher to raise some real questions and possibly insure additional investigation.

ETs and a "Cosmic Watergate"

As I opened the report and began reading it, I became quickly convinced that, if even one of Stringfield's many informants was telling the truth, then maybe the Air Force did, indeed, have proof that at least some UFOs are extraterrestrial and Stanton Friedman's coined phrase "cosmic Watergate" would take on a new meaning. When I continued reading the report, I began thinking that—despite the lack of more detailed information and investigation—Len may just have the most startling and important UFO paper to date. If it proved to be authentic, it would provide an earthquake-like jolt to not only establishment science, but to more than a few serious researchers who had turned away from the ET theory. But…

The operative word here is "maybe."

One of the most incredible aspects of Stringfield's research was that there were more than fifty sources who bore information relative to retrievals and storage of alien craft and/or the deceased alien humanoids allegedly recovered from the craft. Len selected twenty-two of these sources for the paper. Following, in chronological order, are capsule-sized accounts of most of those selected sources.

From New Mexico to Wright-Patterson Air Force Base

- *Summer 1947.* Near Roswell, New Mexico. This report was an early version of the famous retrieval case when a UFO was allegedly recovered in Roswell with humanoid bodies on or around July 2, 1947. A witness identified only as a Major "J.M." (Jesse Marcel) investigated an unidentified object that was said to explode in the air and rain fragments of metal and other material over a square mile area. The fragments "could not be bent or broken." No occupants were seen.

- *1948. Northern Mexico.* A Provost Marshal at Carswell Air Force Base (AFB) near Fort Worth, Texas, participated in the recovery of a metallic disc ninety feet in diameter approximately thirty miles south of the Texas-Mexico border across from Laredo. His job was to cordon off the crash site. On board the object was a single dead humanoid four feet six inches tall, hairless and hands with no thumbs. An Air Force Captain observed the UFO in flight while it was reportedly being tracked on radar at 2000 miles-per-hour. It executed a ninety-degree turn and flew east over Texas. The captain alerted a fellow pilot and both flew to the crash site where they were sworn to secrecy. A U.S. Navy intelligence officer reportedly saw the UFO being loaded onto military trucks.

Todd Zechel, Research Director of Ground Saucer Watch and a former National Security Agency employee, interviewed both the main witnesses.

- *1952. Edwards AFB, California.* A radar specialist saw a UFO descending on his radar screen. The object was confirmed crashed and the witness was told not to mention the incident to anyone. The UFO was more than fifty feet in diameter with a row of windows around its center. Its metallic surface was in a burned-blackened condition. The radar specialist was told that the craft contained dead humanoids that were four-and-a-half feet tall. He also heard that the UFO was held for a short time in a hangar at the base, then was shipped to Wright-Patterson Air Force Base (AFB), Ohio, the home of Project Blue Book, the official UFO debunking entity.

- *1952. Wright Patterson AFB, Dayton, Ohio.* In what is believed to be a separate case than the one immediately above, a civilian security guard allegedly saw a tractor hauling a tarpaulin-covered craft into a tight security area at the base. He also observed an alien body allegedly recovered from the UFO, which crashed somewhere in the southwest.

A "Crudely-Made" Movie

- *Spring 1953. Fort Mommoth, New Jersey.* A radar specialist with a secret security clearance and his colleagues were summoned to the base theater to view a special, crudely-made film with no title or credits. A desert scene was shown with a silver disc containing a domed top and an open door at the bottom firmly embedded in the sand. The object was fifteen-to-twenty feet wide and the door was two-and-a-half feet wide and three feet high. The interior of the UFO was apparently seen, showing only a panel with a few simple levers. Then the scene shifted to two tables with two bodies on one table and another body on the other. The small humanoids looked mongoloid with disproportionally large heads, small noses and mouths and eyes that were shut. Their skin was leathery and ashen-colored. Each body was encased in a tight-fitting suit. The select audience was asked to think about the movie, but was warned not to relate its contents to anyone. Two weeks later, an intelligence officer told the main radar specialist to "forget the movie you saw; it was a hoax." The officer also warned the specialist not to mention the film to anyone else. Shortly thereafter, the specialist heard from security officers that a UFO had crashed somewhere in New Mexico and had been recovered along with its occupants the year before.

- *April 1953.* Air Force Major Daly (real name), a metallurgist at Wright-Patterson, was flown blindfolded to what was described as a hot and sandy undisclosed site to examine a crashed UFO. The silver, metallic craft was twenty-five-to-thirty-feet in diameter and contained metal that was determined *not to be native to earth*. Its entranceway was four-to-five feet high and two-to-three feet wide. Daly saw no bodies.

Engineer Sees Crashed UFO, Alien Body

- *May 21, 1963.May 21, 1953. Near Kingman, Arizona.* Fritz Werner (a pseudonym)—a Project Engineer on an Air Force contract with the former Atomic Energy Commission at the Nevada Atomic Proving Ground—was whisked under strict security conditions to the location of an oval UFO with unfamiliar metal that had impacted twenty inches into the sand. The object was about thirty feet in diameter, with an entranceway around three-and-a-half feet high and one-and-a-half feet wide. Werner's job was to determine, from the angle and feet of impact into the sand, how fast the vehicle's forward and vertical velocities were at the time of impact. Someone else looked inside the car and saw two swivel seats, an oval cabin, and an unspecified number of instruments and displays. The engineer peered inside a nearby tent and saw the body of the UFO's only occupant. It was about four feet tall and had a dark brown complexion. The corpse wore a silver, metallic suit and a skullcap. The engineer and the others present had to take an oath of secrecy. On June 7, 1973, Werner, a member of the American Association for the Advancement of Science, signed an affidavit in the presence of Raymond E. Fowler, Research Director for MUFON and former head of the NICAP Massachusetts Subcommittee. Werner also told Fowler that, in 1953, the Air Force believed, even knew, that UFOs were real, but they did not know how to handle the situation. Some questions subsequently have been raised about this report.

- *1953, Near Dutton, Montana.* Cecil Tenney (real name) observed a silver, cigar-shaped object that was obviously in trouble. It pulsated and belched out fire and smoke for seven or eight minutes. Then there was an explosion and the road was littered with balls of fire. A state highway patrolman also saw the UFO in distress and was given Tenney's name. That evening, Tenney was grilled for thirty minutes and signed a statement swearing him to secrecy. On his way out, he saw men carrying bags with bulges shaped like the protruding limbs of bodies.

- *1955. Wright-Patterson.* During the 1940s and 1950s, a woman known only as "Mrs. G." worked in the Foreign Materials Division with a top security clearance rating at the base. She was assigned to cataloguing incoming UFO material, including items from the interior of a recovered object. Mrs. G. observed two humanoids preserved in chemicals being moved from one room to another. They were four-to-five feet tall with large heads and slanted eyes. The witness told her story years later while dying of cancer, reasoning that "Uncle Sam can't do anything to me once I am in my grave."

Four Burned Alien Bodies Recovered

- *1957. Southwestern United States.* Lieutenant Colonel "T" said a UFO was tracked to the point of its contact with the ground at an undisclosed location. The area was roped off and the National Guard was summoned in order to maintain maximum security. Four badly burned bodies were recovered from the object. The aliens were about five feet tall, had large heads and wore silver suits that were not damaged by the heat, but were fused to their flesh. The bodies were sent to Wright-Patterson AFB and placed in a deep freeze morgue at −120 degrees.

- *1962. Near Holloman AFB, New Mexico.* Military jets were scrambled as a UFO was tracked on radar. The object experienced difficulty in flight and crashed in the desert. The round craft was sixty-eight feet in diameter and thirteen feet high. Two dead occupants forty-two inches high and clad in one-piece suits were found and transported to a major medical university for tests. The UFO was shuttled to an undisclosed military base where it was studied in an attempt to learn its method of propulsion. (Robert D. Barry, Director of the 20th Century UFO Bureau, said his sources included an intelligence agent and a scientist).

- *December 1964. Fort Riley, Kansas.* At two a.m. on an undisclosed day, Private First Class "A.K." was ordered to patrol an area where a large UFO rested on the ground and was told by a Major General to shoot if anyone tried to force their way to the craft. The object was thirty-five-to-forty-eight feet in diameter and twelve-to-eighteen feet high. It was round and had an aluminum-like surface. Surrounding the center of the craft was a black band made up of squares, each jutting out about ten inches. No occupants were seen.

Nine Alien Bodies

- *1966. Wright-Patterson.* "J.K.", a military intelligence officer, reported seeing nine alien bodies in deep freeze at the base. While viewing the corpses, he was told that thirty bodies were held in preservation at that time at the air base. He was also informed that the UFO containing the bodies was at the base and that other downed UFOs were in custody at Langley AFB in Virginia and McDill AFB in Florida. During his tour of duty (1966-1968), J.K. heard of five UFO crashes in the tri-state area of Ohio, Indiana and Kentucky. One incident reportedly involved the retrieval of three alien bodies.

- *1967. Wright-Patterson.* James Mitchell, a civil service electrician with a top-secret clearance, obtained an eight-by-ten black-and-white glossy photograph showing two men holding up a body about three-and-a-half feet tall against a desert background. The entity's oversized head was pear-shaped and it wore a metallic-like suit. Slits indicated the eyes and mouth. Mitchell said that, during early morning exercises in the Arizona desert, members of a military unit saw a group of aliens near a landed craft. There was a brief skirmish in which one alien resisted. The creature was given an injection, causing its death. The other occupants fled to their craft, which quickly took off. The entity's body, preserved in ice, was shipped to Wright-Patterson.

A TOP SECRET Report

- *1968. Nellis AFB, Nevada.* According to a **TOP SECRET** report revealed by Major General "T" (same as above), a large UFO hovered over Nellis for three days, during which time three smaller craft were emitted from it. One of the craft landed on the base grounds. A colonel and a security detachment rushed to investigate as a humanoid emerged from the craft. Then a light beam was aimed at the colonel, who was instantly paralyzed. The UFO quickly joined the mother ship, which left the area. (Springfield reported he obtained additional corroborative information about the incident from an unidentified intelligence source).

- *1973. Wright-Patterson.* A military pilot observed five crates on a forklift inside a hangar. Three of the crates contained the bodies of humanoids from a UFO that had allegedly crashed in the Arizona desert. The occupants were approximately four feet tall with large, hairless, narrow heads, brown skin, open eyes and small mouths. They wore tight-fitting suits and were lying uncovered on a special fabric to prevent freeze-burn from the dry ice that was packed beneath. One of the entities was apparently a female. The pilot, who was sworn to secrecy, learned that one creature was still alive when the military team arrived at the site. Unsuccessful attempts were made to save its life by administering oxygen. The UFO was also shipped to Wright-Patterson.

Three Bodies With Large Heads

- *1973. Wright-Patterson.* Air Policeman Carl S. was driven blindfolded to a secret room containing ranking officers and scientists. On a table he saw what he was ordered to guard: three bodies around three feet tall with large heads and off-white or cream-colored skin. The bodies were lying on refrigerated tables.

- *Spring 1973. Wright-Patterson.* Len Stringfield allegedly reported that a source at the base told him that military personnel had carried into a certain area on the base several litters with little alien bodies from an undisclosed location.

Area 51

The place known as Area 51 located in the Nevada desert has long been rumored to house alien extraterrestrial craft, some with ET bodies. The **TOP SECRET** location serves to keep intact secrets the U.S. Government may not want its citizens to know about. It has been rumored that this was near where the saucer that reportedly crashed with three alien bodies aboard in July 1947, near Roswell, New Mexico, was retrieved. For days, the story goes, government officials were involved in the recovery of the saucer and its deceased occupants and whisked them away to the area now known as Area 51.

Some UFO enthusiasts have argued that the Area 51 mountain site was the perfect place to draw attention away from the true site of the government alien archives located about fifteen miles away from there.

Here, government officials would be better hidden away to develop their own devices and weapons partially based on what was learned from the crashed saucers and their alien bodies. It was also reported that Jan Harzan, Executive Director of MUFON, believed that close to ten percent of the UFO reports his organization received could be studied with the aim of recreating the alien technology with the ultimate goal of the U.S. Government improving its own scientific advancement.

Crash-and-Retrieval Cases Revisited

The steady march of crash-and-retrieval cases complete with the recoveries of alien bodies continued. The Alien Bodies Recovered website has listed the following cases with few details and no comments on whether or not competent investigations were performed:

- *February 13, 1948.* Aztec, New Mexico. Twelve bodies recovered.
- *July 7, 1948.* Mexico, south of Laredo, Texas. Three bodies.
- *September 10, 1950.* Albuquerque, New Mexico. Three alien bodies.
- *1952.* Specific date unknown. Spitzenbergen, Norway Two bodies.
- *August 14, 1952.* Ely, Nevada. Sixteen bodies.
- *April 18, 1953.* Somewhere in Arizona. One body.
- *June 19, 1953.* Laredo, Texas. Four bodies.
- *July 10, 1953.* Johannesburg, South Africa. Five bodies.
- *October 13, 1953.* Dutton, Montana. Four alien bodies.
- *May 5, 1955.* Brighton, England. Four bodies.

- *June 12, 1962.* Holloman Air Force Base, New Mexico. Two bodies.

- *November 10, 1964.* Fort Riley, Kansas. Nine bodies recovered.

- *October 27, 1966.* Somewhere in Arizona. One body.

- *1966-1968.* Five separate crashes in Indiana, Kentucky and Ohio allegedly yielded three bodies.

- *July 18, 1972.* Morocco. Three bodies.

- *July 10, 1973.* Somewhere in Arizona. Five bodies.

- *May 12, 1976.* Australia. Four bodies.

- *April 5, 1977.* Somewhere in Ohio. Eleven bodies retrieved.

- *June 22, 1977.* Arizona. Five bodies.

- *August 17, 1977.* Mexico. Two bodies.

- *November 1988.* Afghanistan. Seven bodies.

- *1989.* South Africa. Two extraterrestrial beings were reportedly found alive.

- *July 1989.* Siberia. Nine living extraterrestrials retrieved.

Incident at Roswell

The most famous and well-known crash-and-retrieval case on record is the famed incident at Roswell, New Mexico, sometime between June 14 and July 4, 1947, when something crashed in the desert. One article from *Time* Magazine reported that rancher W.W. ("Mac") Brazel came across wreckage that was scattered over a 200-yard area that consisted largely of rubber strips, tinfoil, wooden sticks, Scotch tape, other tape with a floral design and what he described as a rather tough kind of paper. Brazel discovered this debris on July 14 as he was making his rounds at the J.B. Foster sheep ranch, about eighty-five miles northwest of Roswell.

At first, Mac didn't think very much about what he had found. He returned to the site with his wife and two children and brought some of the debris back home with him.

A Crashed Flying Saucer

On July 7, Brazel told Roswell Sheriff George Wilcox that he may have come upon the site of a flying saucer that had crashed to earth. The Sheriff then phoned Roswell Army Air Field, headquarters of the 509th Bomb Group, and notified Major Jesse Marcell, the group intelligence officer.

Along with Counterintelligence Corps Officer Sheridan Cavitt, Sheriff Wilcox picked up Mac Brazel and drove out to the ranch. They picked up the debris, which weighed only about five pounds, and placed it in the trunk of Marcel's Buick.

On his way back to Roswell, Marcel stopped at his home to show off the booty. He awakened his son, Jesse, Jr., 10, and showed him some tinfoil, plastic, beams or struts that appeared to be metallic. There were also weird markings that resembled hieroglyphics. Jesse, Jr., saw that his dad was excited and remembered him uttering the words "flying saucers."

"We Have… a Flying Saucer"

A short time after the debris was gathered, Walter Haut, the Press Officer at the 509th Bomber Group, said that the Group Commander, Colonel William Blanchard, issued an order that he put out a press release. The Colonel also allegedly remarked: "We have in our possession a flying saucer. The thing crashed north of Roswell, and we've shipped it all to General [Roger] Ramey, Eighth Air Force at Fort Worth."

The press release immediately caused a sensation. On July 8, the front page of the *Roswell Daily Record* had the following headline emblazoned across its front page: **"RAAF CAPTURES FLYING SAUCER ON**

RANCH IN ROSWELL REGION." Somehow, the word quickly spread around the globe and press enquiries poured in from all over the world. No question about it. This was *BIG* news at the time!

An Empty Saucer?

Almost as quickly as the word about the incident spread around the world, it was debunked by the Air Force. General Ramey and Warrant Officer Irving Newton released what they hoped would be the definitive word: what Brazel found were the remains of a high-altitude weather balloon.

The following day, the *Daily Record* was quick with another front-page headline: **"GENERAL RAMEY EMPTIES ROSWELL SAUCER"**

The "Cosmic Watergate"

For thirty-one years, the Roswell incident quickly faded from the public consciousness. Then, in 1978, Stan Friedman, a former nuclear physicist whom I knew from my NICAP days and who called New Brunswick, Canada, home, was in a Baton Rouge, Louisiana, television station waiting for an interview spot. He was told that Jesse Marcel, who was then retired and living near the station, had once handled the wreckage of a UFO. And he still held to the belief that the debris he found was from an extraterrestrial source.

Friedman's antenna immediately stood at full attention. After he interviewed Marcel and some others involved with the incident, he came up with his often quoted belief that there was a cover-up of "cosmic Watergate" proportions. This reportedly led to the first of more than two dozen books on the Roswell case alone: *The Roswell Incident,* by Charles Berlitz and William L. Moore, in 1980.

A Crash-and-Retrieval Team

Fast-forward ten years to 1988. Members of Dr. J. Allen Hynek's Centers for UFO Studies (CUFOS) in Chicago assembled a crash-and-retrieval team and sent it to Socorro to discover the crash site, recover any remaining debris, and interview still-surviving witnesses.

Three years later, the book *UFO Crash at Roswell*, by Kevin Randle and Don Schmitt, a CUFOS investigator, was published. They had little doubt that the government had recovered the remnants of a UFO in Roswell and had taken possession of its crew, several little alien bodies. This was apparently backed up by Glenn Dennis, 22, a mortician, who remarked that officials at the air base had asked him about the availability of child-size coffins and procedures for embalming bodies that had been exposed to the weather for a number of days.

It was also reported that a badly frightened Army nurse said she had worked with doctors who were performing autopsies on strange-looking, small bodies. She was allegedly quickly transferred off the base to an unknown location in England. Later, she reportedly lost her life in a plane crash. The reader should bear in mind, however, that these are the observations of Randle and Schmitt and the reports have not been independently confirmed as fact.

Beware the Corso Story

In 1997, only a year before his death, retired Colonel Philip Corso caused a volcanic stir when his book, *The Day After Roswell: A Former Pentagon Official Reveals the U.S. Government's Shocking UFO Cover-Up* was published. During World War II, the Colonel was a military officer. When he was on active duty in the Korean War, he was assigned to General of the Army Douglas McArthur's staff at the Army intelligence office. Corso was also a member of the National Security Council during the administration of President Dwight D. Eisenhower. During the 1960s, he secured a spot in the Pentagon as the Chief of Foreign Technology in Army Research and Development, where he said he was reportedly in charge of the Roswell files.

The Colonel allegedly reported that there were four ETs that were four-and-a-half feet tall. They had grayish-brown skin, four-fingered hands and oversized bald heads. Two of them were still alive when they were found. Another tried to escape, but was allegedly shot by nervous soldiers. Still another was clinging to life, but was quickly dying when he arrived at Roswell Army Air Field in the back of an Army truck.

Corso added icing to the ET cake by saying that other retrieved UFOs were kept at Edwards Air Force Base (AFB) in California, and Nellis AFB in the location known as Area 51 in Nevada. And he said it was President Truman who gave the go-ahead to establish an ultra-secret MJ-12 program (more on this later). He also reportedly said that the primary purpose of the Star Wars program was to prepare for war against the extraterrestrials in case of an invasion.

Corso also allegedly said that he was given pieces from the Roswell wreckage with orders to determine whether or not any of the material could be used as a weapon. He added that he was directed to harvest possible UFO technology from the wreckage and farm it out to U.S. corporations. He said that just about everyone wanted to be in on the Army's Roswell technology.

As amazing as this may sound, little of it can be backed up with real history or documentation that Corso could have brought into the light with him through the years. One sure thing gleaned from a reading of his book is how he has Zelig-like placed himself into significant historical developments as the Reagan Star Wars effort, the Cuban missile crisis of 1962, the Warren Commission inquiry into the Kennedy assassination and other major events as if he had been a major player in each of these historical developments. And his endorsement of the MJ-12 allegations is telling. This is something the reader will see is replete with problems.

The Roswell Story Continues

As the reports continue, the debris retrieved from the crash site was flown to the Air Materiel Command headquarters at Wright Field, Ohio, where Lieutenant General Nathan E. Twining was the commander. On July 7, General Twining flew to the Alamogordo Army AFB. The following day, July 8, he was reported to have been at Kirtland AFB and had talked to the press about flying saucers not being a product of the armed forces. On July 11, General Twining left New Mexico.

Allegations of these events continued to more forward at a fast pace in their retelling as General Curtis LeMay was said to have sent Lieutenant General Laurence C. Craigie, Chief of the Research and Engineering Division at Headquarters Army Air Force, to investigate the site of the saucer crash. Then LeMay allegedly immediately met with President Harry Truman.

Debris and Body Recovery

Additional men were allegedly directed to the field of debris at the Foster ranch and were assigned to assist in cleaning it up. Soldiers pushing wheelbarrows moved across the field, tossing in the debris. When the wheelbarrows were filled, the soldiers took the debris to collection points. Then the debris was loaded into covered trucks to be driven into Roswell. Here, the reader should note how this part of the story was dramatically expanded from the original five pounds of debris that was reported in 1947.

It was claimed that several flights carried debris and bodies to apparently undisclosed locations. In 1978, one individual, Pappy Henderson, reportedly told his close friend, John Kromschroeder, that he had flown wreckage from a crashed saucer out of Roswell and on to Dayton. Richard Hall, the late NICAP Assistant Director, observed: "I think a very strong case can be made that the basic reasons they succeeded in the recovery right under the noses of the populace and the base personnel are (1) the remote locations, and (2) the tightly knit and controlled nature of the base traditions and operations. On top of that, the blatant use of threats of violence to keep people silent is well-established, and that sure as hell is not good planning. Apparently they got away with it only because of who and where they were."

Such opinions were common within certain factions of the UFO community at the time and were basically accepted at face value.

The Blanchard Tour

Colonel William Blanchard, the Roswell Army Air Field Commander, reportedly took one or more individuals to a B-29 hangar at the base that was under heavy guard. In the hangar, there was, allegedly, a small egg-shaped object about fifteen feet long and about six feet high with a metallic surface.

Apparently, one witness reported seeing what he described as "a couple of bodies under a canvas tarpaulin. Only the heads extended beyond the covering..." The occupants' heads appeared to be larger than normal.

Debris Images on Film

Barry Greenwood continues his well thought-out account:

> There was also a report that "pieces of the wreckage" were taken to the office of General Ramey and were replaced with "the remains of a weather balloon and radar kite." This was what the rumor mill provided. The more familiar debris images were photographed in Ramey's office, overseen by J. Bond Johnson of the Fort Worth Star-Telegram, responding to a wire dispatch in his newsroom about the incident. The pictures appeared in the late editions of newspapers on July 8 and the next morning editions.
>
> These photos became the subject of dispute years later when it was claimed that an image showing General Ramey holding a piece of paper in his hand was a **TOP-SECRET** message describing the news of the crash and bodies in a military teletype. Various attempts to de-

cipher the paper yielded very subjective results about so-called "victims," "wreck," and other allusions to the debris being unusual. The visible words were extremely blurred and have not submitted to modern photo analysis very well.

On the other side of the coin, one attempt to decipher it suggested that the paper is actually a newsroom wire dispatch describing the Roswell information in a journalistic style that was handed to Ramey and held in plain view. It was certainly more plausible than thinking the general would hold an alleged **TOP-SECRET** document openly in his hand while a civilian photographer was snapping an image of what would have been a grievous security violation. That translation also suggested that the text includes a misspelled "Haught," meaning Walter Haut, the Roswell Army Air Force Base spokesman who briefed on the story very early in a news cycle.

The press reported the misspelling widely supporting J. Bond Johnson's original version of how he handed it to Ramey.

Other reports had as many as five bodies that were recovered and taken to the base hospital for examination. The bodies, along with some debris from the crash site, were claimed to have been flown to Andrews Army Air Force Base in Washington, D.C.

This newly refurbished incident at Roswell was now a linchpin leading to more retro-assertions about the Roswell follow-up, namely…

The TOP SECRET MJ-12 Report

On the heels of the new retelling of Roswell that began in 1978, rumors of something called "Operation Majestic 12" (MJ-12) was said to be a **TOP SECRET** operation whose operatives were responsible only to the President. It was allegedly established on September 24, 1947, under an Executive Order signed by President Truman.

The purpose of MJ-12 was to investigate the crash of the alien spacecraft near Roswell. Documents associated with it are said to have confirmed that the American government was extensively involved in the retrieval of a crashed ET craft, including the occupants. Assorted documents released from non-official sources were directly on-target target to create a lingering firestorm among UFO investigators. As promising as this sounded, there were serious problems with the story and particularly with the documents themselves.

No government agency accepted responsibility for them. One document was said to have been found at the National Archives in Washington, D.C., but this was in no context with other paperwork in the same archives box. It was, in fact, found b*etween* folders instead of *in* one.

The other key documents were mailed to an associate of the prime MJ-12 proponent, William Moore, on a roll of film sent from Albuquerque, New Mexico. This happened to be where another associate of Moore, Sergeant Richard Doty, was stationed at Kirtland Air Force Base. Doty was known to be involved in dubious activities related to UFOs while he was within the Air Force as an Office of Special Investigations (OSI) agent. This included document forgery. Moore and Doty were known to have been involved in creating a fiction novel with the core of the MJ-12 story outlined before the debate became public.

The controversy over this persisted from the early 1980s until 1989, when Moore admitted to being an unpaid government agent who, in addition to disseminating questionable MJ-12 papers, fed false information to Albuquerque businessman Paul Bennewitz that helped to cause him mental distress over his UFO beliefs. It was later succeeded by a second version of MJ-12 claims by someone else, Tim Cooper, who claimed to have over 4000 secret documents that were leaked to him partly via his post office box being stuffed with them. Sans envelope or postage! The provenance for all this is sadly lacking.

CHAPTER THIRTY-THREE

The Syracuse UFO Flap

Robert ("Bob") Barrow was pissed.

"Things are insane here!" he exclaimed in his July 1978 letter I received at my home in Hollywood, California. Bob—a UFOR investigator from Syracuse, New York—sent me the details of a series of UFO sightings from a multitude of witnesses in and around that area of New York State. He said that, within a fifty-mile radius of Syracuse, residents had reported many sightings of unknown objects in the sky from November 1977 through May 1978.

The sighting characteristics included objects that shook a house, were tracked on radar, caused E-M effects, paced cars, lit up surrounding areas, frightened witnesses, and produced possible physiological effects. Barrow personally investigated the March 30 and April 29 sightings and sent his reports to UFOR.

Meanwhile, Bob was decrying the lack of local law enforcement cooperation, specifically the Onondaga County Sheriff's Department and the local police department. He added: "Higher-ups have been very hush-hush about the UFO activity and law enforcement people have been ordered not to discuss their sightings publicly."

UFO "the Size of a House"

The myriad of sightings apparently began in Plymouth, about fifty miles southeast of Syracuse, on November 23. Thomas ("Tom") Colledge, a veal farmer, had lived on his land with his wife, Mary, and their children for seven years. He had crawled into bed at about 12:45 a.m. when he and Mary heard a tremendous roaring sound. Hand-in-hand, they quickly jumped out of bed and ran to their bedroom window, where they expected to see a low-flying or disabled jet plane. What they saw instead was a huge, arrowhead-shaped object about the size of a house. The brightly glowing UFO was an estimated eighty feet long and fifty feet wide.

"The whole house was shaking," Colledge reported. "It wasn't like any kind of aircraft I had ever seen. At first, I was so engrossed in admiring it that I didn't immediately realize how strange it was…. The damned thing lit up my whole back yard. I thought it was going to crash into my barns, but it flew over them. It put out a mercury vapor lamp in the process. Jesus, I was scared! I didn't know what the hell we were dealing with! Good God Almighty!'"

The Cross-Shaped Object

Mary was apparently as stunned and confused as her husband by the strange object. She said the UFO hovered for a few seconds and was covered with flashing and streaming red and white lights. She added that the lights appeared to form a cross as it drew away.

"It was more like a rocket taking off from Cape Kennedy," Mary added. "We could see the bottom and back of it…. It was really pretty."

"It looked like one of those Delta wings that the Air Force was trying to develop after World War II," Tom continued. "It was silver or metallic in color. Red lights were turning around it. I could see an orange glow coming out of what looked like circular turbines on the back of it. The flying object scared us, but it was really beautiful to look at."

The strange craft, which was visible for twenty-to-thirty seconds, flew in a straight line over a nearby hill. And the loud roar could still be heard for a few minutes after it had disappeared from view.

The Travers Experience

Ten minutes later, at the other end of town, Mr. and Mrs. Tom Travers and their sixteen year-old son were watching television when they heard an extremely loud noise that sounded like an entire squadron of Air Force jets over the house. They saw and later described apparently the same object that the Colledges witnessed. Travers, a boiler repair technician, observed it from a slightly different angle and explained what he observed.

"I saw what looked like two or three rows of windows running around the front of it," he told me. "They were lit up from the inside by what looked like some kind of fluorescent light…. The thing was as big as my house—maybe eighty feet from front-to-back. It looked like a solid mass to me, and it was shaped like a manta ray. *Wow!* I mean, it was really something unreal!"

The couple's son ran outside and saw the mammoth UFO pass over their house. He described it as being triangle-shaped, adding that it was much louder than a jet. The bottom had two gigantic white lights shining down from the front of it. The boy could see reddish-orange flames coming out of the back of it.

The witnesses felt that the object was searching for something since it flew at a slow pace and never went higher than about 150 feet off the ground.

There were a few other area sightings during the next several months, but it was not until the end of March that the UFOs returned *en masse*.

The Lobello Sighting

Linda and Donald Lobello lived directly across the street from Brenda Edwards and her live-in babysitter Diane McGuire, south of Syracuse on Kramer Drive. Other witnesses included a Syracuse police officer. On an evening during the last week of March, they all saw a glowing object, which didn't look or behave like a star.

"I didn't believe in UFOs until that night." McGuire admitted. She watched with her friends and neighbors and saw what she described as "a glowing diamond or oval-shaped object with a cross-shaped pattern of blinking red-green-blue-yellow-and-white lights."

UFO Parries With a Helicopter

On the evening of March 29, a UFO sporting flashing and multicolored lights was seen by a group of housewives and other residents of the south side of Syracuse. Police quickly dispatched a helicopter and patrol cars to investigate.

The first policeman on the scene was Edgar Prue. He observed the strange object through binoculars as the police helicopter tried to approach it.

"I tried to play it down, but I knew it was something unexplainable," Officer Prue remarked. "It traveled away from the helicopter in a rapid backward movement and then it just disappeared. It was a really weird thing."

The Pompey Road Encounter

At 10:15 pm., March 30, Joseph LaBella, a Brockport College student, was traveling west on Pompey Center Road in nearby Pompey in his 1976 Ford LTD when he observed a very brilliant light in the distance behind him. He said it was an oval-shaped object with what appeared to be a panel of blinking Christmas lights running horizontally around it. At first, he thought it may have been a car with only one headlight functioning or a motorcycle. He noticed that there was some static on his FM car radio as he unsuccessfully attempted to dial in a station.

"Looking up and around in amazement, he instantly noticed, in a field on the driver's side, at a distance of thirty-to-fifty yards, an object pacing his car....," Barrow stated in his report. "The object seemed... about the size of a train's boxcar... and had lights in abundance. There was a row of many bright white lights along the side in the middle.... The top and bottom each had rows of duller blue-white lights in a panel, going all the way across.... Suddenly, the UFO ascended so fast that it caused its lights to blur. The lights reminded him of a Christmas tree."

The badly frightened witness sped home after a brief stop at a shopping center to get his bearings. His parents found that he was extremely upset and in need of strong cups of coffee and calming words.

Meanwhile, a number of other people in the area spotted flashes of light from the UFO. About twenty-five residents of the northern and western parts of the county reported seeing strange lights and objects in the sky that night.

Passenger Plane Passes Under UFO

Six days later—shortly after 10 p.m., April 5—Dennis Kiteveles, 33, a police dispatcher from Van Buren, and his family were visiting his wife's sister and brother-in-law next door when their oldest son, Denny, 11, looked out of a window and spotted an object in the sky behind the house. He said it was a revolving, oval-shaped UFO with red, blue, green and yellow flashing lights around the middle over the Baldwinsville-Van Buren area. It hovered over the woods, then appeared to rock back and forth and, at times, would move in a rectangular-shaped pattern.

Meanwhile Kiteveles' wife, Linda, 29, said that a passenger plane passed under the UFO as it made its approach to Syracuse. The couple's son saw two flashes of white light that came from the UFO and arced to the ground. At the same time, the lights in the home went out.

An Unholy Howl

Only minutes after the strange object was sighted, the Kiteveles' coonhound began furiously barking. Then the bark turned into a strange, terrifying howl.

"It was completely different from his normal howl, like he was in pain," the dispatcher recalled. "Then I looked out the window and saw this object hovering about 2,000 feet from the house. It was very large and roughly oval in shape. It had to be bigger than a 747 jumbo jet and looked like two pie tins, one on top of the other. It had recessed lights around the mid-part and they were flashing like the lights of a theater marquee. This was nothing like a plane!"

Dennis and his family lived directly in the flight path of nearby Hancock International Airport.

"When I realized it wasn't a plane, my first reaction was fear," Kiteveles admitted. "I was scared, really scared. I thought maybe I might be abducted on board the damned thing!"

Spinning Like a Top

Suddenly, the UFO began spinning like a top. This movement appeared to dim and blur the lights. As it started to slow down, the witnesses focused on the colors (red, blue, green, and yellow) of the lights spaced around the alien visitor's middle. The top of the object was still spinning when Kiteveles put in an urgent call to the Sheriff's Department and told them what had happened. A dispatcher there said he would authorize sending a helicopter to get a closer look at the eerie UFO. After a search, Sergeant Paul Zemenz, the helicopter pilot, returned to home base. He said he could find nothing out of the ordinary during his search. He did say that he contacted the Hancock Airport. Officials there admitted tracking a UFO on their radar screen around four or five miles from Kiteveles' home.

"Yes, I can confirm that on April 5 we were in communication with a sheriff's helicopter pilot and, at that time, there was an unidentifiable target showing on our radar," Tom Hable, Deputy Chief of the Federal Aviation Administration's (FAA) control tower operation, reported back.

"There's a Plane Near It!"

While Kiteveles was on the phone giving the sheriff's dispatcher directions to his home, his wife, Linda, frantically yelled out: "There's a plane near it!"

"As the plane was coming toward the UFO, all the bright lights of the object suddenly went out," she remarked. "And when the plane, a landing passenger jet, got underneath the object, a high-intensity beam of light shot out of one end of the UFO."

The next morning, Linda discovered something strange.... There had been a brief power outage during the night, but the electric clocks in their home had not only somehow not lost any time, but had *actually gained over three minutes!*

The Blackouts

A Niagara Mohawk spokesman reported that there were two brief, consecutive interruptions in power at 10:15 p.m. along the company's 115,000-volt line between the Long Branch substation north of Liverpool and the Mortimer substation south of Rochester. And a New York State Gas and Electric Power Corporation spokesman said that around 3,000 homes in the Jordan-Elbridge area had briefly lost service. Both utilities were tied into the Mortimer substation.

Meanwhile, the Niagara Mohawk officials at first said they had no idea what caused the blackout, which occurred at 10:12 p.m. in the villages of Jordan and Warners as well as in several other locations. It was explained away as a bad insulator on the terminal to that line. At 12:34 p.m. the next day (Thursday), another outage occurred. This time Niagara Mohawk blamed the loss of power on a damaged porcelain insulator at Mohawk's Longbranch substation on Lake Shore Boulevard, about a mile and a quarter from the Kiteveles home.

Sometime during all this action with the UFO, the pilot of an incoming aircraft said he observed the power blackout but did not see the UFO. A police helicopter crew, however, did report seeing two flashes of light and the blackout. Also, controllers at Hancock Field reported that an unidentified blip appeared on their radar screens.

The Vietnam Veteran's Experience

At about the same time as the Kiteveles sighting, Jan R. Bowles, a Vietnam veteran, and his girlfriend were driving on Route 31 in nearby Cicero, New York. When Bowles rounded a corner, he saw that his companion had a shocked and puzzled look on her face.

"What's wrong?" he asked.

"There….," his nervous companion uttered as she nervously pointed out of the windshield.

Jan immediately noticed a tubular object hovering above the trees on the left side of the road. It had four bright white lights that were shining directly down toward the ground. Meanwhile, two cars had passed him, but their occupants didn't appear to have observed the object.

"When we pulled off the side of the road, the object started moving," Bowles explained. "When the first car went by, the object dipped and turned and looked toward the second and third car. When they went by, it just started moving slowly, horizontally alongside the car at fifty or sixty yards away at about treetop level."

UFO Scans Ground

When Bowles and his companion first saw the UFO, it was only about ten feet above the treetops and was just sitting still there. The object emitted four lights toward the ground as if it was scanning the territory.

Then the object began to move, making a short drop. It turned toward the witnesses, facing the other cars. Suddenly, it changed direction toward the left, slowly enough so the witness could have walked along with it. The entire sighting lasted from three-to-six minutes.

Jan Bowles was a Vietnam serviceman who was familiar with all types of aircraft. As the object made its turn, he saw red and blue lights. He also said that the thrashing sound like sticks on the trees that may have been clicking appeared to be coming from under the UFO.

Jan said the object's maneuvers convinced him that it was either manned or computerized because it made a quick drop and a quick sharp turn.

"I've never seen an aircraft operate like that," he remarked.

The Dump Truck Object

The veteran had parked his car across the street from a dump truck and estimated that the UFO was considerably larger than the truck. At first, the object moved very slowly, at an estimated three-to-five miles per hour. When it disappeared, however, it just shot up into the air and was gone. When it was first seen, it was an estimated seventy-five feet in the air. Then it suddenly dropped to about fifty feet above the ground.

The next day, Bowles returned to the area of the sighting in an attempt to determine where the object came from. The veteran and his companion thought it may have approached from a swampy or flat-wooded area.

Bowles said that, at first, he was very reluctant to report the sighting since he was involved in a legal matter and didn't want to convey the impression that there was anything wrong with his credibility by observing what others might refer to negatively as a "flying saucer." Bowles reported his sighting to Barrow.

Jan Bowles spent three years (1966-1969) in the U.S. Army. A year of that time was spent in North Vietnam. He also was a student at Onandaga Community College, where he took courses in early childhood education and was currently attending Syracuse University, working for a degree in early childhood education and psychology.

A Parapsychology Devotee

Jan had also been a devotee of parapsychology for twelve years and had lectured in the field. At the time of his sighting, he was operating a group known as Unity is Seen In Open Minds (UISIOM).

Bowles freely admitted that there was still another reason why he was reluctant to report his sighting... He said that having a UFO sighting along with his work with parapsychology might make him suspect to some people.

An Earlier Sighting

Barrow also told me that Bowles had another UFO sighting on an unspecified date about five years ago on Canal Road in Canastota, New York. He was driving with a woman companion when she pointed out a cigar-shaped object containing four lights that was facing the car. Bowles quickly slammed on the brakes and the UFO also came to an abrupt halt an estimated thirty feet in front of the car and near some trees dotting the Erie Canal.

The shaken couple drove slowly forward while the object moved back. When they went back, the object advanced forward. Again, the witnesses stopped and the object also stopped. It suddenly moved away down the canal. A car approached behind the witnesses and the object suddenly shot straight up and disappeared.

Investigator Barrow questioned the witness about his thoughts on UFOs.

"The universe holds life both less and further advanced than us," Bowles responded. "If more advanced, that life could certainly find it possible to travel here. If other planetary life isn't making contact, then something else is making these realities take shape."

The Psychic Phenomena Card

Barrow was obviously impressed by the main witness.

"I find the witness' involvement in psychic phenomena quite important here and felt it was relevant to pursue this aspect a bit more," Barrow wrote me. "He feels every person has the ability to be psychic, although the environment holds us back from using our minds' full potential. He does believe he has the ability to cause certain things by using his abilities.... When pressed on the issue, Bowles did note that for two or three days after the sighting, he felt detached from the realities of earth...."

Bowles was apparently positive that there was something coming from there to here. It gave him the feeling that there was other life in the universe and that fact was going to be known soon. It was a psychic feeling.

"The positive reality was that this was the second time I've seen something very similar and it moved," he said. "It did some weird things. It's not a vehicle I know from Earth...."

Bowles added that he believed he had the ability to feel life forms when they are present. He said he tried to do so in connection with the object, but he detected no life forms.

As far as Bob Barrow knew, none of the other witnesses were involved with parapsychology. But Bowles certainly was. The veteran said that, whenever he drives at night, he has a feeling of awe when he thinks of the sighting and the strange object. It was almost as if he was expecting the UFO to make contact with him again. Bowles said with marked emphasis: "I was *meant* to see it! And it was *meant* to see me! Damned if it wasn't!"

Close Encounters

Bowles added that he had seen Steven Spielberg's cinematic epic, *Close Encounters of the Third Kind* (1977) about a week before his sighting. He had joked about it with his companion in the car who had not seen the film.

"If this is a promotional stunt for *Close Encounters*, it's superb!" Bowles gushed. "Hell, I would climb aboard that beautiful spaceship anytime! Think of what we might learn from the occupants!"

The witnesses added that their sighting looked like somebody had taken a scene right out of the movie and performed it there before their eyes. They thought the whole thing was going to turn out to be a big publicity stunt and they just happened to pick Syracuse to do it in.

"My impression of Mr. Bowles [age 29] is that he is sincere about his experience and is sensitive about his own and others' reactions to it," Barrow concluded in his report. "He is not enthusiastic about getting publicity.... We probably have here a good example of the sort of reports that exist in quantity in central New York... reports that may never be located due to local official ridicule and some press disinterest."

The UFO and "Mr. T"

Still another encounter with a UFO that happened on or about April 5 involved an anonymous witness calling himself "Mr. T", 24. It was about 8:45 p.m. and the sky was dark. In his report to UFOR, Robert Barrow wrote:

> The witness was driving home from a night class at Onandaga Community College, Syracuse… towards his home in nearby Skaneateles. He was on a stretch of road bordered by forest-land on either side, though he recalls something like an old-fashioned lumber mill on the opposite side of the road…. He suddenly noticed it was very bright to the left of me, where the woods are, and I looked over and there was a big orange disc just over the treetops…. It was like in the corner of a lot…. I looked away because I had to watch the road. I looked back again and it was gone…. In a matter of seconds, the back of the car lit up and got really bright. I drove on for about two or three more miles and it was gone. An orange light came in through the back window and was the same color as the object…. The orange light was almost… bright enough to read by.

The "Long and Slim" Disc

The witness said he was driving slowly at about fifteen miles per hour and only saw the object for a few seconds. He described it as long, slim and disc-shaped. The UFO was well defined (clear and sharp) against the very dark sky. It first appeared in his rearview mirror. The huge orange-colored disc appeared to be as tall as a two-story house. Its orange glow lit up the trees and ground at first, then the road.

Barrow said the witness was not a heavy reader of UFO books and had not seen *Close Encounters of the Third Kind*. He had a Graphic Arts college degree and was not into studying psychic phenomena.

A Return Visit

On the evening of April 6, Baldwinsville was again visited by a UFO. Just after seven o'clock, William Colton and Robert Waltz were driving home when they observed a bright ball of white light that was quickly heading west. Then it suddenly stopped in mid-air and remained motionless. A few minutes later, the light went out and a series of red, green and blue flashing lights came on. Then, the men said, the object suddenly disappeared.

Around an hour later—at the opposite end of the county—six boys and two girls were riding bicycles in Southwood when they saw three lights in the southern sky. The lights hovered over the Southwood water tower hill, lighting it up like daytime before it quickly disappeared.

The following evening, Paul Cunningham and four friends observed a UFO they estimated to be as large as an airliner. It had an orange outline and was over Onondaga Hill. Near Syracuse, Cunningham snapped a photograph with his Polaroid camera. A policeman also reportedly saw the unknown object.

L-Shaped Object Paces Car

At 1:12 a.m., April 29, a married couple (who wished to remain anonymous) were driving in Syracuse when they had a feeling that there was something overhead. Looking up, they saw a roughly L-shaped antenna-like structure that paced them at fifty-five miles per hour for about a minute.

The object sported lights," Barrow wrote in his report. "It looked like an upside down L… and had a top light of bright white…, a center blinking red light and a bottom bright light of white. The man states that he had a feeling that his stomach was 'pulling towards the roof of the car.' The UFO sped off to the south and, at a distant point…, stayed in one spot, yet moved back and forth.… The object was, perhaps, four-to-five car lengths long."

The elongated section of the UFO was about fifty feet long and the shorter section extended out at a forty-five degree angle towards the longer piece, which was about twenty-five feet long.

Disc Flies Over Car

At 11:45 p.m. the following Wednesday, May 3, Bobby Barrows, 15, a ninth grade student at Cazenovia Central High School, had been baby-sitting for Debbie Ballway, an employee at a local restaurant. Debbie was driving Bobby to his home very close to where she lived. After dropping him off, she returned to her own residence and parked in the driveway with the car motor still running.

Suddenly, Debbie observed a disc-shaped fluorescent UFO with colored lights at the top and a bright white light on the bottom that emitted a humming, whistling sound approximately a mile south of Cazenovia. The huge UFO approached from the south. Then it slowly flew over Ballway's car and sped away to the north. She heard what she described as "a *shsh-shshshshing* sound."

The witness said the object was motionless at first. Then it came slowly over her car and quickly sped away to the north. She added that the UFO was saucer-shaped and had a fluorescent white light at its bottom along with red, blue and yellow lights along its upper half.

Meanwhile, Bobby, who was in the bedroom of his own home nearby, rushed to his window and watched the object for several minutes. He said the colored lights on the flying saucer were red in front and back and yellow on both sides. The bright white light was shining down. Both Debbie and Bobby said that it took the object between three and five minutes to move what appeared to be less than 200 yards. Then it picked up speed tremendously and disappeared.

CHAPTER THIRTY-FOUR

UFOs Cavort Over Pittsburgh

UFOs continued their appearances across the United States....
It was a moonless, unusually clear star-strewn night in the sky over Pittsburgh, Pennsylvania, on March 1, 1978. At 10:15 p.m., Glenn A. Ricci, 22, an independent construction contractor from Morningside, was driving with his girlfriend—Claire A. Gallery of Stanton Heights—south on Fox Chapel Road when Claire pointed out a large bright light that was traveling overhead.

Ricci pulled over to the side of the road and stopped his car. Despite the unusually cold weather, he turned the radio and heater off and rolled the windows down. The witnesses stared intently at the object for a few minutes.

Glenn said the object appeared to have two very powerful lights scanning the skies directly ahead of it. He roughly estimated it to be between one and three miles away.

"A Large Awkward Object"

"We saw an outline of a large awkward object with bright lights," he said in his report to UFOR. "As the craft continued to move, it came closer.... Then, from another direction, came a smaller object.... This craft flew through the sky at *such* a speed... I couldn't believe it! I wondered if it could have been man-made. It appeared to be long and thin with flashing blue and silver-colored lights. *It was a hell of a thing!*"

The silver light turned to more of a bright white color, which lit up the area very much like daylight. The lights operated in a very quick sequence. Then, Ricci said: "In a near flash, I watched it do a 180-degree turn around and head toward the larger object, which was nearly directly ahead of us." The smaller UFO sped toward the larger object with such ease and maneuverability that it never appeared to slow down. The craft disappeared over a large nearby hill.

Ricci quickly started his car and drove up the hill on Delafield Road, hoping for a better view, but he and Claire could not spot the strange craft. Glenn parked the car at the Highland Park Reservoir and scanned the sky again. It took less than a minute before the larger object once again appeared from the general direction of downtown.

The "Massive" UFO

The UFO appeared to be coming in from downtown Pittsburgh and got bigger and bigger as it approached them from the west. Ricci described it as "massive."

"It just hung there nearly overhead...," he remarked. "It seemed to be constructed of metal of some sort... The lower side... appeared to have steel grating along its underbody... It shone a very bright light down on us...."

"Do you think they are watching us?" Claire asked with more than a hint of concern in her voice.

Glenn said there was a definite outline of light around the car as if there was a spotlight on he and Claire in a darkened room.

"The underbody appeared to have panels with light coming from behind them," he continued. "There were also a few scattered [smaller] lights on the bottom... In the middle of the ship there was a cylinder-type protrusion extending downward and inside the cylinder [there were] three triangular lights with their ends butted together, forming a fourth triangle... These lights were flashing [in sequence] continuously."

"Oh, My God!"

Then the UFO descended and hovered over the Highland Park Reservoir at an estimated altitude of about 2,000 feet.

"Oh, my God!" Claire exclaimed in her report to UFOR. "What will we do if it lands?"

After Glenn and Claire watched the object for an estimated three minutes, it started to move, slowly at first and then, all of a sudden, it was gone while emitting a low kind of hissing sound. Ricci told UFOR that he estimated the object to be larger than the reservoir.

"I mean, it was *huge*!" he exclaimed. "It seemed to cover the whole sky! I don't mind telling you that I was scared as hell!"

After the sighting, Ricci had to reevaluate his thinking about strange objects in the sky.

"I Just Didn't Believe…"

"At that time, I was very hesitant to acknowledge that it was a UFO…," he told us. "Then I just didn't believe in any such things… I am a very skeptical person.… But now, I don't know.… Regardless of what anyone may say, I know what I saw! I am now a true believer in the actual existence of these aerial phenomena. Maybe someday we will know what they are. Are they beings from outer space? Hell, I don't know, but they *are* something we can't explain!"

Pittsburgh police and other agencies reportedly received more than 300 calls that same evening from witnesses who saw unidentified objects over and around the city. According to one local paper, Ricci described the larger UFO as being bigger than a football field or about the size of the reservoir.

The Golden Balls Triangle

Residents of Pittsburgh continued to see UFOs over the city skies well into the 21st Century. MUFON has posted a number of these sightings on its Witness Reporting Database. The names of the witnesses are not revealed.

At about 4:50 p.m., November 16, 2012, a man was driving west on Interstate 422 from Johnstown to Pittsburgh when he spotted "a glowing ball to my left moving in the same direction as me." Then he saw another glowing ball. The two objects appeared to join together and were also joined by a third flying ball.

"They stayed in a triangular formation and hovered a few miles in front of me for… six-to-ten minutes…," the witness reported. "I pulled over and got some pictures… While the objects were hovering, [a] flame or light was coming out of the bottoms, making them resemble jellyfish… After ten minutes or so, they faded from sight."

UFOs Over a Power Plant

The observer continued driving and soon saw the objects hovering over what appeared to be a nuclear power plant. This could have been either the Bettis Atomic Power Laboratory—a U.S. Government-owned research and development facility in Pittsburgh—or the Beaver Valley Power Station near Shippingsport.

As darkness approached, the witness saw several military jet planes approaching from the west "heading towards where I had seen the objects by the plant." The pilots, however, apparently did not pursue the objects, which, the witness said, initially moved independently, then joined up and hovered in formation. After the UFOs disappeared, the driver and several other motorists pulled over to the side of the road and took pictures.

Top-Speed Cigar

At 2 a.m., April 12, 2014, an unidentified female witness and her husband were driving on Highway 79 near Pittsburgh when they suddenly noticed a cigar-shaped object in the sky. It was traveling at an incredibly fast speed.

The aerial object looked to be whitish underneath, like a mist. It headed toward the west and quickly disappeared.

"I have never seen anything move that fast ever," the witness reported. "I live near an airport in Ontario, so I see many different kinds of airplanes and helicopters."

UFO Changes Colors

A male witness in Pittsburgh was on the front porch of his house welcoming his wife home at approximately 8:05 p.m., September 17, 2014, when he saw a bright, sharp white light moving at a high rate of speed from the northeast to the east.

"I then turned my head to look at it and it was stationary for about ten or fifteen seconds and then descended quickly changing colors to red," the man remarked. "Then it ascended quickly to almost where it started, then turned blue and shot ten degrees to the southeast and stopped."

The witness pointed to the object, shouting to his wife to observe it as it headed toward the south. It slowly changed colors again and rapidly descended.

"That was the last I could observe it because it went behind a tree and I lost track of it…," the observer remarked.

Flying Triangle "Like a Living Creature"

An unidentified male witness was on Level 5 of the Third Avenue parking garage in Pittsburgh at an undisclosed time on Friday, April 14, 2017. As he looked west over the Ohio River, he "suddenly saw this black triangle-shaped craft with two red lights hovering above some buildings west of where I was standing… At first, I thought it might be a drone, but, as I kept looking at it, there were no propellers on it. The craft changed shape from a triangle to a diamond.…"

Then the aerial object changed its shape from a triangle to a diamond. It began moving up and down, then jerked ahead in a straight line. The object was pure black with two red lights in front and two blue lights in the back.

The witness said the UFO "gave me an uneasy but exciting feeling. The way the object moved effortlessly in the sky looked to me like a living creature. The red lights in front looked more like eyes than lights that gave me an uneasy feeling that it was looking at me. All of a sudden, it turned around and took off out of sight."

CHAPTER THIRTY-FIVE

The AATIP Program

As Christmas 2017 was quickly approaching, news headlines blared around the world that the U.S. Government had been funding a secret investigating unit it called the Advanced Aerospace Threat Identification Program (AATIP) that ran for a reported five years from 2007 to 2012 at a cost of $22 million. A crack team at *The New York Times* broke the news of the well-hidden effort.

What was termed a "shadowy program," parts of which remained classified, was proposed by Senator Harry Reid (D-Nevada), who resigned from Congress earlier in 2017 after serving a term as the Senate Majority Leader. Robert Bigelow—a longtime Reid friend, and his aerospace research company located in Las Vegas—received the go-ahead to run the program. According to news reports, Bigelow "is currently working with NASA to produce expandable craft for humans to use in space."

The Bigelow Outlook

In May 2017, Bigelow appeared on CBS' highly-rated, long-running television program *60 Minutes* and said that he was "absolutely convinced" that UFOs have been surveying the earth and that aliens do exist. The AATIP program, Bigelow added, produced documents that described sightings of aircraft that seemed to move at very high velocities with no visible signs of propulsion, or that hovered with no apparent means of lift.

Bigelow also gave the order to his company officials that his buildings had to be modified so they could be used for "the storage of metal alloys and other materials" that were supposedly "recovered from unidentified aerial phenomena." *[Author's note: This one statement appears to offer confirmation that the U.S. Government has recovered evidence that aliens from space have crashed-landed on American soil.]* It was also reported that some of the material was being studied so "scientists can try to figure out what accounts for their amazing properties." And researchers studied individuals who reported that they had experienced physical effects from encounters with the objects and examined them for any physiological changes. AATIP personnel also took reports from military service members who had reported UFO sightings.

The report also indicated that there was some speculation that Area 51 was being used to store possible aliens from space along with the alien spacecraft. This supposedly included the debris discovered by Mac Brazel at the site of the Roswell UFO crash in July 1947. (See Chapter Thirty-Two.)

As Bigelow geared up for the project and began hiring qualified individuals for the AATIP, he searched for experts in such areas as biological cognitive interaction, forensic pathology, and electromagnetic (E-M) fields.

Along the way, Bigelow decried the fact that the United States was "the most backward country in the world on this issue. Our scientists are scared of being ostracized and our media is scared of the stigma. China and Russia are much more open and work on this with huge organizations within their countries." And he said that smaller countries like Belgium, France and England, along with such South American countries as Chile, are also more open to studying the phenomenon.

"They are positive and willing to discuss this topic rather than being held back by a juvenile taboo," he remarked.

Extraordinary Discoveries

By the year 2009, Senator Reid reportedly believed that the program had made such extraordinary discoveries that he argued for heightened security to protect it.

"Much progress has been made with the identification of several highly sensitive, unconventional aerospace-related findings," he said in his letter to William Lynn III, a Deputy Defense Secretary.

Reid requested that the AATIP be designated as a "restricted special access program" limited to only a few need-to-know officials. His request, however, was denied.

"There's a Whole Fleet of Them!"

Those involved in the program also reportedly studied videos and documents that showed encounters between UFOs and American military aircraft. One of these documents, released in August 2017, involved a white oval UFO the size of a commercial airplane that was chased by two Navy F/A-18F Super Hornet fighter jets from the U.S.S. *Nimitz*, an aircraft carrier about 100 miles off the coast of San Diego, California, at about 12:30 p.m. on November 14, 2004.

Commander David Fravor and Lieutenant Commander Jim Slaight were on a training mission when a Navy cruiser, the U.S.S. *Princeton*, radioed them that the ship's radio had been tracking a mysterious aircraft at an altitude of 80,000 feet when it hurtled toward the sea and stopped at about 20,000 feet.

Both Fravor and Slaight were ordered to investigate. Fravor radioed back that the UFO was hovering about fifty feet above the churning water. The oval object appeared to be forty feet long. It was described as "jumping around erratically."

"I Want to Fly One"

Commander Fravor said that, when he got closer, the craft suddenly sped away "like nothing I've ever seen." He described it as "a white Tic Tac, about the same size as a Hornet… with no wings." He added that the UFO was "hanging close to the water." It also reportedly shadowed the actions of Fravor and the other pilots. Then it vanished from sight.

"As I get closer, as my nose is starting to pull back up, it accelerates and it's gone… faster than I'd ever seen anything in my life…," Fravor remarked. "I have no idea what I saw. It had no plumes, wings or rotors and outran our F-118s.... I want to fly one."

Program officials also amassed a collection of video and audio recordings of reported UFO incidents. These included "footage from a Navy F/A-18 Super Hornet showing an aircraft surrounded by some kind of glowing aura traveling at high speed and rotating as it moves." Meanwhile, the various Navy pilots were trying hard to understand what their eyes were seeing.

"There's a whole fleet of them!" one pilot excitedly announced.

Reid also managed to elicit the support of fellow Senators Ted Stevens, a Republican from Alaska, and Daniel K. Inouye, a Hawaiian Democrat, for the program. However, both men are now deceased. Stevens passed away in 2010 followed by Inouye two years later.

The Elizondo Effect

The top honcho of the program was Luis Elizondo, a military intelligence official who ran the endeavor from his office on the fifth floor of the Pentagon's C Ring area. He reported that, even though the program appeared to have been shut down, "the only thing that had ended was the effort's government funding." He said he continued working with the U.S. Navy and the C.I.A. until October 2017, when he angrily resigned as a protest against what he described as as excessive secrecy and internal opposition.

"Why aren't we spending more time and effort on this issue?" he asked Defense Secretary Jim Mattis in his resignation letter.

There were also reports that Elizondo joined with Christopher K. Mellon, a former official from the Defense Department, and others in a new commercial venture called To the Stars Academy of Arts and Science. They plan to use the Academy to raise money for UFO research.

In a recent interview, Elizondo remarked that he and his government colleagues had determined that the phenomena they had studied did not seem to originate from any country on earth.

"That fact is not something any government or institution should classify in order to keep [it] secret from the people," Elizondo stated.

John Glenn Pipes Aboard

Harry Reid said he discussed the UFO problem with acclaimed Astronaut and Senator John Glenn from Ohio, who passed away in 2016.

Glenn reportedly told Reid that he thought the federal government should be taking UFOs seriously and should also be talking to military service members. This would primarily be pilots who reported that they had seen aircraft they could not identify or explain. But… the sighting reports "were not often reported up the military's chain of command… because service members were afraid they would be laughed at or stigmatized."

Senator Stevens, who had been an Army Air Force pilot who flew transport missions over China during World War II, said he had been waiting to have his hand in the UFO phenomenon since he was in the Air Force. He added that he was once "tailed by a strange aircraft" which followed his plane for miles.

As of this writing on New Year's Eve 2017, there is enough evidence to determine that the AATIP continues with the aid of secret private funding. This also continues to raise the inevitable question: "Are getting closer to proving that the Earth has been under surveillance by outer-space beings for untold centuries?"

As of February 11, 2010, the Bigelow Aerospace Advanced Studies (BAASS) program through the National UFO Reporting Center, U.S. Department of Transportation, Federal Aviation Administration, has posted a telephone number (877) 979-7444 and e-mail address Reporting@baass.org for those who want to report UFO sightings. As of this writing on April 15, 2018, the telephone number and e-mail address are still up and operating.

The eyes-to-the-skies drama continues…

EPILOGUE

Celebrity Quotes

A large number of prominent people have seen UFOs or offered their opinions about them. Following (in alphabetical order) are some of these individuals:

- **Muhammad Ali**, world-famous championship boxer: "If you look into the sky in the early morning, you see them playing tag between the stars."

- **Monsignor Corrado Balducci**, Vatican Curia, theologian who was said to be close to the pope: "There are already numerous considerations which makes the existence of these beings into a certainty we cannot doubt… Extraterrestrials are not demonic. They are not due to psychological impairment. They are not a case of entity attachment, but these encounters deserve to be studied carefully… Extraterrestrial contact is a real phenomenon. The Vatican is receiving much information about extraterrestrials and their contacts with humans from its embassies in various countries, such as Mexico, Chile and Venezuela." The Pope reportedly charged Monsignor Balducci with studying reports of UFOs sent in from Vatican embassies around the world.

- **David Bowie**, Singer and Musician: "They came over so regularly, we could time them. Sometimes they stood still, other times they moved so fast it was hard to keep a steady eye on them."

- **James Earl ("Jimmy") Carter**, U.S. President (1977-1981): "I don't laugh at people any more when they say they've seen UFOs. I've seen one myself." (See Chapter Twenty-Six).

- **Gordon Cooper**, Astronaut: "For many years, I have lived with a secret… I can now reveal that every day in the USA, our radar instruments capture objects of form and composition unknown to us."

- **Air Chief Marshal Lord Dowding**, Commander of the Royal Air Force Fighter Command during the Battle of Britain in World War II: "I am convinced that these objects do exist and that they are not manufactured by any nations on earth."

- **Mikhail Gorbachev**, the last head-of-state in the Union of Soviet Socialist Republics (USSR): "The phenomenon of UFOs does exist, and it must be treated seriously."

- **Professor Stephen Hawking**, world famous physicist: "Of course it is possible that UFOs really do contain aliens, as many people believe, and the Government is hushing it up."

- **Anthony Hopkins**, Best Actor Oscar recipient for *Silence of the Lambs* (1991): "It's really a mathematical certainty that we are not alone. It would be a joke to think we're the only ones in the universe… We can be safely and mathematically [certain that there] must be millions and millions of forms of civilizations… and that some of them are advanced… I think it was Einstein who said that it is possible that we have been visited by superhuman [beings that] exist in a different space-time continuum. Otherwise how could they get here from [a solar] system that is four and a half light years away?"

- **Robert Klein,** Comedian: Summer 1957. Klein—from Kent, Connecticut—was fifteen years old. He and about twenty-five other young campers were playing baseball when they spotted "six cigar-shaped objects [at] extremely high altitude. They were in formation, one right behind the other, traveling between the cloud layers… They were just coasting along…"

- **General of the Army Douglas MacArthur**: In 1995, MacArthur said: "The next war will be an interplanetary war. The nations of the earth must someday make a common front against attack by people from other planets. The politics of the future will be cosmic, or interplanetary."

- **Sarah McClendon,** White House Press Correspondent and Dean of the White House Press Corps, from her press release distributed on March 30, 1998: "The real danger to the U.S. and perhaps this whole planet is [that] the government has placed such a heavy blanket of secrecy upon this issue… Those in government who have knowledge showing UFOs are identifiable feel the subject cannot be discussed by those in the know without serious repercussions. Others are afraid their friends and co-workers will think they are crazy if they even so much as insinuate that UFOs are identifiable as manned craft from outside the earth. This particularly applies to newspaper editors and publishers, reporters and analysts. Thus the U.S. is denying itself the chance to learn more about UFOs or to encourage research despite the fact that the U.S. stands to gain from such discussions…. Not publicized but true is that the Clinton Administration, soon after coming to office, had many briefings on the subject. Laurance Rockefeller provided the information for the President and Mrs. Clinton. Others provided documents and verbal briefings to presidential advisors… and Vice President Albert Gore…. Hundreds of others who work or have worked in secret defense and scientific agencies are willing to swear under oath that alien craft are repeatedly penetrating our airspace. *(Author's note: "When I recently discovered this missive from Sarah McClendon, I was blown away by it. Sarah, now deceased, had been my main sponsor to the National Press Club during the time that I was a member of the White House Press Corps from 1971 to 1974. Dan Rather was my secondary sponsor. My interactions with both McClendon and Rather were covered in my book* Connections: A Lifetime Journey Through the World of Celebrity *(2017), also published by BearManor Media.)*

- **Dr. Herman Oberth**, a father of modern spaceflight: "It is my thesis that flying saucers are real and that they are spaceships from another solar system… I and my colleagues are confident that they do not originate in our solar system"

- **Ronald Reagan**, U.S. President (1981-1989) on his UFO sighting while Governor of California aboard a Cessna Citation aircraft: "I looked out the window and saw this white light. It was zigzagging around. I went up to the pilot and… said to him: 'Let's follow it!' We followed it for several minutes. It was a bright white light. We followed it to Bakersfield [California], and all of a sudden to our utter amazement it went straight up into the heavens. When I got off the plane I told Nancy about it."

- **Mel Torme**, Singer: Around 2 a.m. one night in 1953, Torme was outside his apartment building walking his dog in Manhattan when he saw a "red light in the sky over the East river… It moved faster than my eyes could follow it, before stopping dead in its path… Then it did lazy hoops, almost like a figure-eight. It made a few more circles and went zap again to another part of the sky." Torme said his dog was "rooted still to the ground, shaking and seemingly transfixed by the UFO." Two decades later, Tracy Torme, Mel's son, wrote the screenplay for the movie *Fire in the Sky* (1978), starring James Garner and based on the famous Travis Walton abduction case.

- **Dennis Weaver**, Actor: "I think there is a lot of evidence that we've made contract."

- **Sigourney Weaver**, Actress, star of *Alien* (1979) and *Avatar* (2009): "We are not alone in the universe. I think there is a department in our government which is exclusively dedicated to quashing reports about aliens. And that's so unfair…"

Capsule UFO Sighting Reports (1975-2018)

- *January 1, 1975.* 6:25 a.m. Quintanaortuno, Spain. A luminous pale-yellow cone-shaped UFO was seen by four soldiers in a car at a military base. It rapidly descended and hovered over the vehicle. Then the object's light went out. A short while later, four more objects showed up. They formed a row, then shot out jets of white light downward.

- *January 5, 1975.* 2:30 p.m. Brownstown, Illinois. Young David Mahon, 15, was taking pictures of his dog behind his house when he heard a loud drone-like sound and quickly spotted a black disc flying overhead. He snapped five photos, then rapidly found himself being lifted up. He passed out and regained consciousness in a small compartment with a row of orange, blinking lights around it. Less than a minute later, he lost consciousness again and woke up near his home. He had been gone for about an hour.

"Humanoid-Like Creatures"

- *January 12, 1975.* 2:30 a.m. North Bergen, New Jersey. Witnesses observed ten humanoid-like creatures about three-and-a-half feet tall dig up soil samples for several minutes. The humanoids wore helmets and coveralls. Minutes later, they scrambled back into a domed disc-shaped craft. The UFO emitted a humming noise as it ascended into the sky. There were marks on the ground and the observers said there was interference to their CB radios.

- *February 14, 1975.* Petite-He, Reunion, France. Three humanoids in what looked like protective gear descended from a dome-like disc. A flash of light was emitted and the witnesses were temporarily paralyzed.

- *February 23, 1975.* About 6:30 p.m. Yamahata and Kono, two seven year-old boys somewhere in Japan saw a bright orange UFO flying toward them. They heard a ticking sound. The domed disc that was about six feet high landed on three ball-shaped legs in a nearby vineyard. The boys cautiously went up to the object and saw that it had strange words embossed on its surface. Then a ladder was extended from out of the craft down to the ground, allowing a humanoid-like being an estimated four feet tall to disembark. The creature was dressed in a silver suit and carried what appeared to be a gun. He had dark brown skin and large pointed ears. His very large head had no apparent nose, eyes or mouth. The boys said the creature had what appeared to be three silver fangs that extended from where the mouth would be. Then the witnesses observed another smaller humanoid, who was grasping a control lever in the cockpit. One of the beings touched one of the boys and uttered words that were garbled and resembled a tape recorder that was running backwards. The boy crumbled to the floor in an apparent paralytic state. His companion carried him from the vineyard home on his back. Later, two concrete posts were found pushed over at the landing site.

Humanoids in Texas

- *May 3, 1975.* San Antonio, Texas. No specific time given. Witnesses observed a Saturn-shaped UFO with two humanoids that were seen through the transparent dome. There were also electro-magnetic (E-M) effects to their truck.

- *May 5, 1975.* 9:20 p.m. Pleasanton, Texas. A truck driver spotted a domed disc on the ground. He saw two humanoids inside the dome. Then the witness was struck by a blinding light and his hands went numb.

UFOs Over a Navy Research Platform

- *July 15, 1975.* 2 p.m. Nineteen miles off the coast of Panama City, Florida, in the Gulf of Mexico. Two brothers (a recent officer with the U.S Army and an electronics engineer) were fishing near the U.S. Navy Undersea Warfare Manned Research Platform when they spotted two UFOs fly in from the west. The metallic-looking objects that appeared to be as big as a Boeing 727 airplane stopped and hovered over the facility for an estimated ten minutes. Then they flew together toward the southeast. Once again, they returned to hover over the platform. A short time later, they suddenly shot upwards and quickly disappeared. At the same time, two Air Force F-4 jets roared overhead and veered obliquely upward in what appeared to be hot pursuit of the UFOs.

- *July 31, 1975.* No time specified. Loxton, South Africa. A witness saw an oval-shaped craft with a couple of occupants. Then a light from the UFO struck the witness in his face. He suffered from vomiting and a nose-bleed. Physical traces were also discovered at the site.

Aliens in New Mexico, France and Virginia

- *August 13, 1975.* 1:20 a.m. Near Alamagordo, New Mexico. A man named Moody, 32, was speeding through the desert when he observed a metallic disc. A high-pitched sound was emitted from the object and his car stalled and wouldn't start. Later, Moody had a lapse of time or memory with a loss of one-and-a-half-hours. He also recalled being abducted by two Grey aliens that were about four feet, eight inches tall. They had large eyes and heads with slit-like mouths and wore tight-fitting coveralls. The witness said he was laid on a medical examination table. Telepathy was apparently used.

- *August 22, 1975.* 11:30 p.m. St. Omer Pas-de-Calais, France. Two young men were on their newspaper delivery route between Boulogne and Lille on their motorbike when they were followed by an aerial vehicle. They also noticed a light shining on a field. The witnesses stopped and saw that an oval-shaped object had landed. It was illuminated by a yellow-white light emitted from inside the object. Outside the UFO they could see two humanoid forms an estimated two meters tall standing side-by-side. The figures quickly headed toward the men. Badly frightened, the two Frenchmen rapidly rode off on their motorbikes.

- *September 3, 1975.* Nighttime. Manassas, Virginia. Melinda Chow embarked from her bus when she spotted an orange disc that was glowing above some nearby treetops as it descended. She emerged from the clearing and saw the UFO sitting on what appeared to be stilts some 200 feet away. A humanoid-like figure about five feet tall was walking around the disc. The occupant had long skinny legs, very short arms, and a face that seemed to occupy about half the height of his body. His skin appeared to be leathery and gray in color. He walked around in a bouncing, hopping motion. Chow ran to her home terrified.

Disc Zaps Witnesses in Brazil

- *October 25, 1975.* 6-7 p.m. Sao Gondolo do Amarante, Ceara State, Brazil. A man was reportedly struck by a blue light beam from a disc-shaped object. He apparently died from the hit. Several other observers said they had also been attacked and were terrified by the experience. Some even said that a blue light had paralyzed them. [This is one of the very few cases in which a death was possibly caused by a UFO.]

- *November 11, 1975.* No specific time noted. Freeze Out Lake, Montana. An employee with the Montana Fish and Game Department reported seeing a light that was flying directly behind a B-52 bomber. The witness used his riflescope for a better look and saw that the object was pacing the aircraft. It briefly attached itself to the B-52, then detached itself and climbed out of sight. An investigation by Sheriff Pete Howard of Chouteau County revealed that, as the object was attached to the B-52, the plane's radar equipment failed to function.

Physiological Effects in Brazil

- *December 17, 1975.* Nighttime. The city of Americana in Sao Paulo, Brazil. A boy, Salles de Andrade, 16, saw an intense beam of light while he was walking home. He woke up the next day in a thicket 28 kilometers away. He could not recall how long he had been missing, but he did have headaches and strange marks on his forehead and arms.

- *November 29, 1980.* 5 a.m. Alan Godfrey, an on-duty police officer, claimed to have been abducted by an alien spacecraft in Todmorden, West Yorkshire, England. At the same time, a strange luminescent object was spotted by other police officers.

"England's Roswell"

- *December 25 and 26, 1980.* Rendlesham Forest in Suffolk, England. This incident later became known as "England's Roswell." [See Chapter Thirty-Two.] It is considered by many to be the most famous and most reported UFO event to have happened in Britain. Rendelsham was the location of two bases leased by the U.S. Air Force in Britain during the Cold War. On Christmas night, "a blazing light in the forest" brought security forces from RAF-Woodbridge out to investigate what they believed to be a downed plane. Three officers followed the path of the blazing light and watched as a triangular craft landed. They drew close to the object and inspected it. It appeared to have strange symbols on the side that looked somewhat like Egyptian hieroglyphics. The officers reportedly spent approximately forty minutes making notes and observing the UFO. Then they watched it take off at an extraordinary speed as it moved through the trees and disappeared. The same or a similar object returned to the same spot two nights later. This time, the witnesses saw a beam of light from the object that came down to the ground. They inspected the area where the UFO had originally been sighted and found significant radiation readings. Also, nearby tree branches had been broken. Then the frightened observers saw a bright orange-red light approach them from between the trees. It came very close to one witness, then receded into a farmer's field. Suddenly, the light appeared to explode and the object disappeared. But that wasn't the end of the encounters. The witnesses also saw multicolored objects to the north" One of the UFOs sped rapidly overhead, then stopped and sent down a laser-like white beam. Then, as quickly as it appeared, it disappeared.

Hudson Valley's "Floating City"

- *March 24, 1983*. V-shaped lights in the Hudson Valley. This suburban area, about one hour's drive north of New York City, was the scene of more than 5,000 UFO sightings from 1982 through 1986. It was perhaps one of the biggest clusters of UFO reports ever. This particular night, however, stands out because of the sheer number of reports. In excess of 300 residents called a local organization's hotline that night. They reported seeing a large V-shaped array of lights that moved slowly and nearly silently across the sky. Some of the observers even got close enough to the enormous object to label it as big as "a floating city." At 7:30 p.m., Hunt Middleton, a local resident, said he saw a row of seven extremely bright lights. He said: "They were all blinking on and off and were red, blue, green and white.... The lights were stationary. It was just hovering in the sky." The startled witness said he watched the object for five minutes. By the time Middleton had gotten his family to come outside, however, the UFO had disappeared.

- *August 12, 1983*. Alfred Burtoo, 77, was quietly fishing on the Basingstoke Canal in Great Britain when "a UFO landed nearby. Two humanoid beings beckoned him onto their disc-shaped vehicle and he was medically examined by English-speaking creatures." Burtoo, however, said he was rejected by the alien creatures because he was too old.

The Alien on Ilkley Moore

- *December 1, 1987*. A man calling himself Philip Spencer (not his real name), a retired policeman, said he snapped a picture on Ilkley Moore in England of what he claimed was an alien creature. Then he saw a white-colored craft leaving the area. The photo of the object was examined by Kodak Laboratory experts at Hemel Hempstead and "they decided that the object was not superimposed." Later, under hypnosis, Spencer claimed to have been abducted and medically examined.

Cattle React in Great Britain

- *March 1993*. The meterorlogical officer at the Royal Air Force Shawbury site in Great Britain allegedly saw a huge, triangular-shaped craft fly slowly over the base. Suddenly, it shot "a beam of light at the ground while emitting a low-frequency humming sound." Then the UFO rapidly picked up speed and flew away to the horizon many times faster than a military jet. On that same night, an unidentified couple saw a

UFO over a field hundreds of miles away. Investigating, they observed that, while the UFO had gone, all the cows that were standing silently in the middle of the field were facing each other in a perfect circle.

- *July 3, 1996.* Beach, North Dakota. An unidentified witness and her two sons were driving on a dirt line road when they saw a circular-shaped UFO with six legs hovering over a fence row. The witness said her sons saw what looked like shadowy figures moving about in the windows of the object. A few minutes later, it began ascending while the frightened boys dove under the vehicle. The object then went straight up and disappeared.

The Phoenix Lights

- *March 13, 1997.* The Phoenix Lights. Thousands of people in Arizona and Nevada were among those looking at the Hale-Bopp Comet. At 8:30 p.m., many of those observers spotted a huge V-shaped object outlined by seven lights. Police departments in Phoenix, Tempe, Glendale and other Arizona cities saw something that would change their lives. Sue, Kevin and Aaron Walton said it looked like what they described as "a boomerang several football fields wide." At 10 p.m., what was described as a "stunning set of lights" appeared and were filmed on video. Mike Cristen spotted eight or nine lights that formed a gentle arc. He estimated the lights to be as much as five miles wide. Four months later, members of the Maryland Air National Guard said they had been in town at the same time as part of their winter deployment. They were conducting night training exercises over the Barry Goldwater Range 180 miles from Phoenix and dropped flares. Few people however, believed that explanation.

- *June, 1997.* Nicole (last name redacted), 38, a television journalist from Munich, Germany, said that, during a vacation in Hawaii, she looked out of her bathroom window and saw a round object with a dome-like structure at the top land on a nearby hill. Then a flashing white light came from the UFO and a figure emerged down an invisible stairway. It stopped after two steps. "I had the feeling that he detected me....," the witness explained. "I panicked…, ran into the bedroom… and hid in the bed."

UFO Abducts Elk

- *February 25, 1999.* Shortly before noon, three forestry workers were planting seedling trees in the Washington State mountains when they saw a small, disc-shaped UFO drift over a nearby ridge to the south and descend into the valley to the north. Eleven other co-workers also spotted the object. They saw the UFO head toward a herd of elk. As the animals scattered, the object moved directly over a lone elk and seemed to lift it off the ground. The UFO then disappeared with the animal.

- *July 14, 2001.* UFOs over and near the New Jersey Turnpike. An off-duty police officer was among the multiple witnesses who watched amazed as an array of yellow lights flew in formation in suburban New Jersey near New York City late in the evening. Shortly after that incident, at about 12:30 a.m., Carteret Police Lieutenant Dan Tarrant got a call from his nineteen-year-old daughter who was outside with friends and had seen strange lights in the sky. Tarrant stepped outside and and said that "what he saw was astounding." There were sixteen golden-orange colored lights, several in a V-type formation. Other lights were scattered around the V. He said that the mysterious lights flashed across the sky for about ten minutes, then faded one-by-one into the darkness.

- *November 7, 2006.* O'Hare International Airport, Chicago, Illinois. United Airlines pilots and other personnel reportedly observed a saucer-shaped UFO over an airport terminal before it shot straight up and disappeared.

The "Dudley Dorrito"

- *November 28, 2007-December 13, 2011.* During more than a four-year period, a large number of witnesses from Great Britain's West Midlands area apparently had multiple nighttime sightings of a silent, black triangular-shaped object in the skies. The local press had fun dubbing the UFO the "Dudley Dorrito."

- *January 8, 2008.* During the evening, about forty local residents of Stephensville, Texas—including Police Officer Lee Roy Gaitan and an amateur civilian pilot—watched a UFO hover over the farming community for approximately five minutes before it streaked away into the night sky. Gaitan said he was walking to his car when he saw a luminous object that reminded him of pictures of erupting volcanoes suspended 3,000 feet in the air. Another witness estimated that the UFO was about a half-mile wide, about a mile long, and bigger than a Wal-Mart.

A "Large as a House" UFO

- *April 30, 2008.* 9 p.m. Trumbull, Connecticut. While taking his dog for a brief walk, a man noticed an enormous elongated disc with red and green flashing lights that was hovering over the field directly next to his house. He watched it for approximately ten minutes, then put his dog into the house. The observer said the object was over Trumbull High School. After he called the police, he and other observers watched it for another ten-to-twelve minutes. Then the UFO moved toward the Agricultural Science School and the nearby animal pasture. It descended close to the ground as it moved on. Then it flew up to treetop level and disappeared. The witness said the object was as large as a house.

- *May-September 2008.* Istanbul, Turkey. During a four-month period, an evening guard at the Yeni Kent Compound made a series of videotapes of one or more nocturnal objects totaling two and a half hours. Officials at the Sirius UFO Space Science Research Center said the videotapes constituted the most important images of a UFO ever filmed.

- *June 8-20, 2008.* Numerous sightings occurred in North Wales, United Kingdom. One encounter involved a police helicopter that followed a UFO over Cardiff, near MOD St. Athan and the Bristol Channel. In a separate and most dramatic incident, numerous witnesses saw that the helicopter was nearly struck by a UFO before the pilots decided to pursue it. Hundreds of other witnesses throughout Wales saw unexplained flying objects on the same or preceding days.

UFOs in South Africa and England

- *February 27 and March 6, 2009.* Middleburg-Witbank, South Africa. Dual formations of orange-red objects were seen by many witnesses and video was recorded by some of the observers as the UFOs traveled from Middleburg to Witbank sixteen miles away. At 9:51 p.m., the first formation of seven UFOs was spotted. After being in sight for a while, they eventually disappeared behind some clouds. At 8 p.m. on March 6, twenty-three of the objects were observed.

- *September 10, 2009.* In the Glen Road area near Lennoxtown, Great Britain, three individuals in a car were reportedly struck by a brilliant light beam. The startling encounter lasted for two-to-three minutes.

- *February 26, 2011. 8 p.m.* Doncaster, England. A witness and his daughter were in their garden when they saw a a cluster of thirty to forty small star-like lights with a hint of blue that seemed to have dropped straight down from the sky. The lights formed a boomerang shape. Then the "boomerang" moved slowly away in the eastern sky.

- *May 11 and June 15, 2011.* Tierpoort, near Pretoria, South Africa. An estimated twenty silent, orange lights with consistent luminosity were observed as they traveled faster than a commercial aeroplane over Tierpoort. On June 15, seven of the objects returned and were photographed as they crossed the sky in a single file over Tierpoort.

SOS and Horseshoe Objects

- *May 29, 2012.* 3:23 a.m. Two friends were star-gazing when they spotted a light moving across the sky at a high rate of speed at an undisclosed location in Great Britain. One of the witnesses tracked it with his binoculars. "I shined SOS at the object," he remarked. "The object flashed a light back at my friend and I. The object shined a light at us four separate times while moving across the sky." Then the UFO quickly disappeared from view.

- *April 25, 2013.* 9:22 p.m. Aquadilla, Puerto Rica. A Customer and Border Protection Caribbean Air and Marine Branch DHC8 maritime patrol craft was on routine patrol when a UFO was spotted as the aircraft was taking off. It was seen by the aircraft captain and the Aguadilla Airport radar operator. It was also tracked on radar. It was believed the object may have contained smugglers and the crew followed it. The UFO circled the airport, then flew toward the ocean. When it was first seen, it was horseshoe-shaped. Then it changed to a spherical shape as it approached the ocean. The object skimmed the surface of the ocean, then disappeared below the surface.

- *July 13, 2013.* A pilot at the controls of an Airbus A320 had a close encounter with a UFO that passed extremely close to the cockpit while he was flying at 34,000 feet above Berkshire, England. There was no time to make an evasive maneuver, causing the Captain to duck as he believed a collision was imminent.

Lights Over Prince Edward Island and Colorado

- *June 4, 2014.* Late evening. Kensington, Prince Edward Island, Canada. John Sheppard was extinguishing a bonfire when he spotted unusual lights in the sky over the Gulf of St. Lawrence. He activated his cell-phone and filmed twenty-two minutes of the sighting. The Mutual UFO Network (MUFON) later dubbed it a confirmed sighting. The Canadian Broadcasting Company covered the event.

- *October 3, 2014.* Breckenridge, Colorado. Police officers received a number of reports of UFOs over the city. The objects remained still for up to fifteen minutes. Then, there was a flashing and the objects took off across the mountain ridge.

The Fairlee Arrow

- *October 30, 2014.* About 7:45 p.m. Fairlee, Vermont. While heading north on Route 5 toward town, a driver spotted just above the town's street lights, a triangle-shape of soft orange lights that came on all at once, then faded out one-by-one, disappearing completely. It was like a large arrow pointing northward. The witness drove out to the public beach and began walking on the sand when he saw what looked like a north-bound jet very high up in the sky. Suddenly, half a dozen orange disc lights came downward one after another, then disappeared quickly.

- *November 11, 2014.* Alborz, Iran. A plane passenger reported observing a fast-moving, round UFO that zoomed under the jet and disappeared.

The Piscataway Triangle

- *July 31, 2015. 9 p.m. Somerville, New Jersey.* A man and some close friends were driving on Route 287 toward Piscataway when they spotted a triangular form with three circular light objects. As soon as they saw the object, the circular light at the tip of the triangular formation moved away very fast. The driver said the incident "scared the living crap out of me!!!"

- *December 31, 2015. 11:55 p.m. Fairbanks, Alaska.* The witness was driving near the University of Alaska farm fields when he saw five objects rise from the west at near-ground level and move across the highway at an altitude of 300-400 feet. They appeared to be under independent control. Each of the UFOs seemed to be emanating a red/yellow glow or pulse that remained constant. The witness doubled back on the highway when he spotted three new craft similar to the first five that also flew over the roadway. Then the objects gained altitude and spread out, headed east, then climbed higher and disappeared.

The Anchorage Orbs

- *December 31, 2016. 6:36 a.m. Anchorage, Alaska,* was also the site of another UFO sighting exactly one year later. An unidentified witness reported: "Three hours after witnessing one large, bright, orange orb traveling south-southwesterly over mid-town Anchorage, I sighted… three identical orbs a few miles… above the Ted Stevens International Airport…. [They] were moving around in separate, oblong paths at casual speeds, with… one or another momentarily breaking away from its path to perform a zig-zag or to move somewhat farther afield, and every few minutes all of them slowly dimming and returning to full brightness. After about twenty minutes…, they simultaneously dimmed out for good as a routine aircraft was making its approach from the Chugach Mountains."

- *December 31, 2016.* 11 p.m. Fuquay, North Carolina. A witness reported "bright lights moving around my property, shadows moving, orbs, glowing eyes" every night for about two weeks. The observer said he had a video with humanlike figures.

Saucers in Australia

- *February 16, 2017.* 5:30 p.m. Dee Why Beach, New South Wales, Australia. A witness named "Pete" was walking on the beach with his two-year-old daughter when he saw a glowing orange-colored object that was shaped like a fat saucer. The UFO entered a cloud, then reemerged from it and quickly disappeared.

- *March 8, 2017.* 6 a.m. Mooney Money, Australia. A woman named "Sarah" said she was traveling on the train to Sydney when she spotted an orange light over the Mooney Money Bridge that straddled the Hawkesbury River. The UFO was orange and round like a perfect sphere. It then started morphing into, like a jelly rounded object, less perfect and changed colours to reddish then back to the orange sphere and then shot off so quick west toward Singletons Mill.

Objects Over Newcastle and Redland Bay

- *April 23, 2017.* Around 9:45 p.m. Newcastle, New South Wales, Australia. A witness named "Andrew" had just gotten out of his car when he observed a dark object so large that it blocked his view of the stars as it passed by. The UFO was boomerang-shaped. Eight-to-ten dim lights were seen along the leading edge. About ten seconds later, the object just drifted away and disappeared into the darkness.

- *May 29, 2017.* Approximately 9:45 p.m. Redland Bay, Queensland, Australia. A woman named "Brooke" said she was asleep in bed when she heard a loud noise. Rushing to her window, she saw a massive UFO with multi-coloured blue, red, green and yellow lights. Brooke ran to another part of the house where she could see the bay. The UFO had stopped and was hovering over the water. Then it turned a full ninety degrees and began moving slowly to the south. A few seconds later, it shot off south at a very fast pace, disappearing in a few seconds.

Incidents in New South Wales

- *July 23, 2017.* Approximately 3:00 p.m. South Avalon, New South Wales, Australia. While halting for a traffic light, a man and his girlfriend spotted an odd-looking triangular shaped object that was about the size of a car with no visible wings or propellers. The UFO was "just hanging there and not moving." The craft appeared to be metallic and had five corners. Then it suddenly disappeared in the blink of an eye.

- *July 25, 2017.* About 3:45 a.m. Campsie, New South Wales, Australia. A man named "Pat" said he was awakened by his wife, Robyn, who was looking out the window of their bedroom. The couple heard a low frequency throbbing/hum/pulsating sound in the bedroom. They saw a roundish disc-shaped glow which flew above and past the house.

UFO Hovers Near Copper Mine

- *August 29, 2017.* Afternoon. Pima Company Copper Mine south of Tucson, Arizona. While flying over the open-pit copper mine at about 35,000 feet altitude, two witnesses saw a saucer-shaped disk at low altitude hovering near the mine.

- *November 25, 2017.* Newhall, California. A large red UFO was seen hovering over Sierra Highway that changed position and colors within milliseconds.

- *November 27, 2017.* Cherry Valley, Massachusetts, A cigar-shaped object flew from over nearby woods only twenty feet over a house before it disappeared.

- *January 28, 2018.* Evening. Las Vegas, Nevada. Steven Barone shot a video of four white lights maneuvering in the sky.

Flying Objects Over Phoenix

- *February 24, 2018.* Phoenix, Arizona. Two pilots on a Phoenix Air Learjet and an American Airlines jet saw a strange object pass over their planes. "I don't know what it was," said one of the pilots. "It wasn't an airplane."

- *April 3, 2018.* Evening. Heywood, Manchester, United Kingdom. A family member used an IPhone to capture a photograph of a disc-shaped UFO while the family dog barked loudly. At one point, the object seemed to be turning into a light ring.

- *April 11, 2018.* Phoenix, Arizona. An unidentified witness saw and photographed several purple beams and other strange orb-like lights that were "dancing in the skies."

References

A.D.M., Information on Peter Killian UFO Sighting of Feb. 24, 1959, as in possession of CSI Research Section, Feb. 28, 1959.

A,D,M., Letter to L.E. Baney, Wayne, New Jersey, May 23, 1959.

Advanced Aviation Threat Identification Program. From *Wikipedia*, the free encyclopedia @ http://en.wikipedia.org/wiki/Advanced_Aviation_Threat_Identification_Program/.

"A Flying Saucer Spotted in Gilroy." *San Francisco Chronicle*. August 13, 1975.

Aliens—Everything You Want-To-Know. Alien Bodies Recovered @ www.aliens-everything-you-want-to-know.com/AlienBodiesRecovered.html.

Marie Anderson, Believe It or Not.... *The Shelley Pioneer*, December 7, 1967.

"Another UFO Sighting Reported." Monroe, Michigan, *Evening News*, May 4, 1978.

"Are UFOs real? Famous people who believed." *The Telegraph*, November 8, 2017.

Associated Press. "Mystery Object Puzzles West Texas Areas." *Alamogordo Daily News*, November 4, 1957.

Associated Press, "2 Saucer Men Didn't Talk English." *The Seattle Times*, November 3, 1967.

Babylon Observer Report: "J. Edgar Hoover's Quest For UFOs," May 19, 2008 @ http://dubroom.blogspot.com/2008/05/Babylon-observer-report-j-edgar-hoovers.html.

J. Balter, Acting Commissioner of Police, Government of Western Australia, Police Department, East Perth, W.A. Sighting report letter to NICAP, Washington, D.C., February 20, 1968.

William P. Barrett, *The Real Story. Roswell: Inconvenient Facts and the Will to Believe*, by Karl T. Pflock. *Crosswords Weekly*, Albuquerque, New Mexico, June 28, 2001.

Robert Barrow, Aerial Phenomena Research Organization (APRO) Field Investigator, Strange Light Follows and Shines Into Car. Taped interview with witness, August 23, 1978.

Robert Barrow, APRO Field Investigator, "A Close Encounter of the Second Kind Near Syracuse, New York, August 21, 1978."

Robert Barrow, APRO Field Investigator, Syracuse, New York. Letter to Gordon Lore, President, UFO Research Associates (UFOR), Hollywood, California, May 31, 1978.

Joseph A. Bauer, M.D., "A Surgeon's View: Alien Autopsy's Overwhelming Lack of Credibility." Special Report. *Skeptical Inquirer*, January 1996.

Noel J. Becar, San Mateo, California. Report on Unidentified Flying Object(s) to NICAP, Washington, D.C., June 29, 1967.

"Floyd Bennett." From *Wikipedia*, the free encyclopedia @ https://en.wikipedia.org/wiki/Floyd_Bennett.

Hubert Beyer, "2 Support Local Man's UFO Report." *Winnipeg Free Press*, May 23, 1967.

Hubert Beyer, "U.S. UFO Expert In Winnipeg." *Winnipeg Free Press*, June 5, 1967.

Hubert Beyer, "UFOs: At Least 'Cause For Concern.'" *Winnipeg Free Press*, July 3, 1967.

David Birkan, "Canadian UFO Sightings Show Dramatic Increase." *NOW*, Toronto, Ontario, Canada, July 7-13, 1994.

Heidi Blake, "UN 'to appoint space ambassador to greet alien visitors.' A space ambassador could be appointed by the United Nations to act as the first point of contact for aliens trying to communicate with Earth." *The Telegraph*, February 22, 2010.

Ted Bloecher, NICAP Staff, Washington, D.C., Letter to C. Reed Hicks, Idaho Falls, Idaho, August 26, 1968.

Lloyd C. Booth, as told to Glenn D. Kittler, "I Shot a Flying Saucer." *Male*, September 1953.

Lloyd C. Booth, Conway, South Carolina. Letter to Albert Baller, Greenfield, Massachusetts, March 8, 1953.

Melvin Carmichael, Klamath Falls, Oregon. UFO report to NICAP, Washington, D.C., May 29, 1972.

Horace Carter, "Booth Still Says He Shot It; Odd Death Of Cows Linked With Horry's 'Flying Egg.'" *The Charlotte Observer*, February 15, 1953.

"Jimmy Carter UFO Incident." From *Wikipedia*, the free encyclopedia @ https://en.wikipedia.org/wiki/Jimmy_Carter_UFO_incident.

Sean Casteel, "The Profound UFO Encounters of Celebrities, Pop Stars and the World's Most Famous Prize Fighter, Muhammad Ali—Part Two," July 5, 2015. Spectral Vision. Exploring the World of the weird and Unknown @ https://spectralvision.wordpress.com/2015/07/05/.

Lucinda Cawley and Gerry Hunt, "Spinning UFO Eludes Police Copter After Power Blackout Hits Area." *National Enquirer*, August 23, 1978.

Paul C. Cerny, Northern California State Director, Mutual UFO Network (MUFON). UFO Sighting Report, Los Altos, California, sent to Gordon Lore, President, UFO Research Associates (UFOR), April 6, 1974.

Ralph Chapman, 'Flying Saucer' Sightings Still Get Air Force Study. *New York Herald Tribune*, March 1, 1959.

Heather Chisvin, "'I Was Burned by UFO.'" *The Winnipeg Tribune*, May 22, 1967.

Heather Chisvin, "Experts May Probe Man's UFO Claim." *The Winnipeg Tribune*, May 23, 1967.

Ted Cilwick, "Identified UFO spotter sorry now that he went public." Norwich, New York, *Evening Sun*, April 6, 1978.

Esther Clark, "Two Phoenix Pilots Claim Sighting UFOs In Skies." *Phoenix Gazette*, March 21, 1969.

Jay Cochran, Assistant Director, FBI Technical Services Division, Washington, DC. Letter to Stanley Schneider, Assistant to the Director, Office of Science and Technology Policy, Executive Office of the President, Washington, D.C., June 15, 1977.

Helene Cooper, Ralph Blumenthal and Leslie Kean, Glowing Auras and 'Black Money': The Pentagon's Mysterious U.F.O. Program. *The New York Times*, December 16, 2017 @ www.nytimess.com/2017/12/16/us/politics/pentagon-program-ufo-harry-reid.html.

Helene Cooper, Leslie Kean and Ralph Blumenthal, 2 Navy Airmen and an Object That 'Accelerated Like Nothing I've Ever Seen." *The New York Times*. December 16, 2017 @ www.nytimes.com/2017/12/16/us/politics/unidentified-flying-object-navy-html.

Richard Corliss, "Autopsy or Fraud-topsy? A documentary about a purported alien stirs the liveliest debate of any home movie since the Zapruder film." Show Business, *Time*, November 27, 1995.

William ("Bill") Curry, Sports Editor, *The Clearwater Sun*, Florida. Report on Unidentified Flying Object(s) sighting sent to NICAP, Washington, D.C., November 25, 1967.

Keith Darnay, "N.D.'s Connection to UFOs." *The Bismarck Tribune*, June 25, 2012.

Peter B. Davenport, Director, National UFO Reporting Center, and Robert A. Fairfax, Director of Investigations, Mutual UFO Network, for the Washington State, "Elk Abduction in Washington State." National UFO Reporting Center Case Brief, February 25, 1999.

Patrick DeFrancisco, "Retired Army intelligence officer reveals his close encounters." One Man's View. Allentown, Pennsylvania, *Morning Call*, August 28, 1997.

"Do Our Oceans Harbour Alien Crafts? What Are All The Strange Reported Sightings At Sea?" Me Time For the Mind @ www.metimeforthemind.com.

Elizabeth L. Douglas, Titusville, Florida. Report on Unidentified Flying Object(s) form sent to NICAP, Washington, D.C., July 30, 1967.

Stephanie Dube Dwilson, Advanced Aerospace Threat Identification Program: 5 Fast Facts You Need to Know. Heavy.com, December 19, 2017.

"EAA's Noel Becar," *Sport Aviation*, March 1967.

The Editors of Publications International, Ltd., "Ronald Reagan Sees a UFO." How Stuff Works @ https://science.howstuffworks.com/space/aliens-ufos/ronald-reagan-ufo-htm.

Idabel Epperson, Chairman, NICAP Los Angeles Subcommittee. Letters to Richard Hall, Assistant Director, NICAP, September 24 and 25 and October 7, 1965.

Idabel Epperson, Chairman, Los Angeles NICAP Subcommittee, Letter to Gordon Lore, NICAP Assistant Director, Washington, D.C., November 30, 1967.

Idabel Epperson. Letter on possible NASA involvement in UFO investigations to Gordon and Marty Lore, UFO Research Associates, Hollywood, California, December 3, 1977.

William E. Fallon, Wood River Junction, Rhode Island. UFO Sighting Report Form sent to UFO Research Associates, Washington, D.C., July 11, 1973.

Mrs. William E. Fallon, Wood River Junction, Rhode Island. Letter to Gordon Lore, President, UFO Research Associates, Washington, D.C., March 11, 1973.

"The FBI and UFOs. Flying Flapjacks, Saucers and Saw Blades, April 6, 2010." The Federal Bureau of Investigation @ https://archives/fbigov/archives/news/stories/2010/april/ufos_040610.

Doris R. Fickelsher, Founder and Director, Allied Saucers Association, Angola, New York. UFO Sighting Report and Letter to Gordon Lore, President, UFO Research Associates, Washington, D.C., April 15 and May 3, 1971.

W.P. Fisher, Major General, USAF, Director, Legislative Liaison, Department of the Air Force, Washington, D.C. Letter to Howard W. Robison, Member of Congress, 37th District, New York, May 6, 1959.

W.P. Fisher, Major General, USAF, Director, Legislative Liaison, Department of the Air Force, Washington, D.C. Letters to the Honorable Harry Flood Byrd, United States Senate, May 6 and June 8, 1959.

E.G. Fitch, United States Government. "Flying Disks." Office Memorandum to D.M. Ladd, July 10, 1947.

Julie Fitzpatrick, "Encounter, Or Illusion?" *Syracuse Post-Standard*, April 7, 1978.

Donald E. Flickinger, Chairman, NICAP North Dakota Subcommittee #1 in Minot. Sighting Report Letters to NICAP, Washington, D.C., both dated December 15, 1968.

"Flying Saucer Photo a Hoax," *San Jose Mercury*, October 27, 1965.

"'Flying Saucer' Seen Saturday." Monroe, Michigan, *Evening News*, May 5, 1978.

Don Frost, "She Claims UFO Sighting: 'No Light Like That From This Earth.'" *The Southern Illinoisan*, October 9, 1973.

John G. Fuller, *Incident at Exeter: Unidentified Flying Objects Over America Now*. G.P. Putnam's Sons, New York, 1966.

John G. Fuller, *The Interrupted Journey: Two Lost Hours "Aboard a Flying Saucer."* The Dial Press, New York, 1966.

Gladys Fusaro, Huntington, New York, Report of Telephone Conversations Between Mrs. Gladys Fusaro and Mrs. Peter Killian, Saturday, February 28 and March 16, 1959.

Gladys Fusaro, Huntington, New York, Report of Telephone Conversation Between Captain Peter Killian and Mrs. Gladys Fusaro, March 20, 1959.

Gladys Fusaro, Huntington, New York, Reports of Telephone Conversations Between Gladys Fusaro and Captain and Mrs. Peter Killian, April 2, 16 and 21, 1959.

Thomas Gariepy, "Wood River Junction Watches Its Saucer." Providence, Rhode Island, *Bulletin*, March 21, 1973.

Nicholas Geranios, The Associated Press, "'Ufologist' catalogs sightings of odd things in the sky." *Register-Guard*, Eugene, Oregon, October 29, 2007.

"Gilroyans see UFO at close range." *Gilroy Dispatch*, August 11, 1975.

Joan Given, "Flying Saucers Change Life of Eden Housewife." *Courier Express*, Buffalo, New York, March 14, 1971.

Walt Glines, "Hectic week follows sightings of UFOs." *Gilroy Dispatch*, August 15, 1975.

"Green men and red men." *Christian Science Monitor*, January 15, 1968.

Barry Greenwood, The Mantell "UFO"--A Smoking Gun, Maybe! *Just Cause, Citizens Against UFO Secrecy*, Number 39, March 1994.

Max Greenwood, Pentagon acknowledges program to investigate UFO encounters: report. *The Hill*, December 16, 2017 @ http://thehill.com/organization/advanced-aerospace-threat-identification-program.

Major Vollie E. Griffin (USAF), Electronic Warfare Officer, Department of the Air Force, Detachment 14, Bismarck, North Dakota. UFO sighting forms of the Bismarck area reports sent to Donald E. Flickinger, NICAP North Dakota Subcommittee Unit #1, December 5, 1968.

Donald J. Griffiths, Schenectady, New York. UFO sighting report to Gordon Lore, President, UFO Research Associates, Washington, D.C., October 26, 1973.

Jim Hadgin, Strange 'Lights' in Sky Make Pilot, Crew Blink. *Long Island Newsday*, February 26, 1959.

Richard H. Hall. From *Wikipedia*, the free encyclopedia @ https://en.wikipedia.org/wiki/Richard_H._Hall.

Richard H. Hall, Bethesda, Maryland. Personal and Confidential Letter to NICAP Board Members, Washington, D.C., December 9, 1969.

Richard H. Hall, Secretary of NICAP. Letter to Major Lawrence J. Tacker, Department of the Air Force, Office of Information Services, The Pentagon, Washington, D.C., March 22, 1960.

Bruce Handy, "Roswell Or Bust. A town discovers manna crashing from heaven and becomes the capital of America's alien nation." *Time*, June 23, 1997.

Linda G. Heath, Mechanicsville, Virginia. UFO sighting report letter to NICAP, Washington, D.C. June 26, 1967.

Rex E. Heflin. Personal report to NICAP, Santa Ana, California, dated on or about Sept. 26, 1965.

Richard C. Henry, Deputy Director of Astrophysics Division, Office of Space Science, National Aeronautics and Space Administration (NASA), Washington, D.C. Letter to Gordon Lore, President, UFO Research Associates, Hollywood, California, December 6, 1977.

Michael Hesemann, "The Alien Autopsy Film-Facts vs. Armchair Research." *Nexus Magazine*, Volume 3, No. 6, October-November, 1996.

Kevin Hickey, "B'ville family reports UFO." *Syracuse Herald-Journal*, April 6, 1978.

Kevin Hickey, "They're Everywhere!" *Syracuse Herald-Journal*, April 7, 1978.

Guy Hottel, Special Agent in Charge of the FBI's Washington Field Office. United States Government Office Memorandum, "Flying Discs & Flying Saucers," to J. Edgar Hoover, Director, the Federal Bureau of Investigation, March 22, 1950.

Ernest Imhoff, "Physicist Reports Speedy UFO." *The Baltimore Sun*, August 3, 1966.

Leon Jaroff, "Did Aliens Really Land? An examination of events in 1947 shows something did happen. But the resulting stories got out of hand and out of this world." *Time*, June 23, 1997.

Whitney Jefferson, "19 Celebrities Who Totally Believe in Aliens." Celebrity @ www.buzzed.com/whitneyjefferson/celebrities-who-believe-in-aliens.

Kent Jeffrey, "Roswell—Anatomy of a Myth." Roswell Homepage, Microsoft Internet Explorer, June 27, 1997.

Kent Jeffrey, Roswell: "The whole story. Time for the truth about Roswell." Center for UFO Studies, June 29, 1997.

Christine Ezell Johnson, San Mateo, California. UFO sighting report letter sent to Paul C. Cerny, Northern California State Director, MUFON, June 21, 1974.

Christine Ezell Johnson. UFO Sighting Report Form, Mutual UFO Network, Inc., sent to Paul C. Cerny, Northern California State Director, MUFON, July 16, 1974.

Lenard Johnson, Constable 2514, Boyup Brook Station, South Western District, Australia. UFO sighting report sent to NICAP, November 1, 1967.

R. Conway Jones, "A Witness Describes His Sighting." *UFO Research Newsletter*, Vol. I, No. 3, June-July 1971.

Peter Jordon, "The Day After Roswell: A Former Pentagon Official Reveals the U.S. Government's Shocking UFO Cover-Up," by Colonel Philip Corso. *UFO Magazine*, July 12, 1997.

Rose Marie Julig, Columbia Heights, Minnesota. UFO Sighting Report Form sent to Walter H. Andrus, Jr., Director, Mutual UFO Network (MUFON), Quincy, Illinois, March 7, 1979.

Rose Marie Julig, Columbia Heights, Minnesota. UFO Sighting Report Form sent to Gordon Lore, President, UFO Research Associates, Hollywood, California, July 5, 1979.

Bruce J. Kennedy, UFO Sighting Report, Field Investigator, New Mexico Subcommittee, UFO Research Associates (UFOR), Albuquerque, to Gordon Lore, UFOR President, August 1974.

Major Donald E. Keyhoe. UFO Researchers and People. "Extraterrestrial Contact, Scientific Study of the UFO Phenomenon and the Search for Extraterrestrial Life" @ www.ufoevidence.org/researchers/detail3.htm.

Major Donald E. Keyhoe, AF Spokesman Ridicules UFO Witnesses, Says Some Are Drunks. Action Follows Airline Pilots' Reports of UFO Formation. *U.F.O. Investigator*, February-March 1959.

Major Donald E. Keyhoe, "Air Force Admits Faulty UFO Investigation." *The U.F.O. Investigator*, May-June 1966.

Major Donald E. Keyhoe, "Congressional Hearings on UFO Problems: Scientists Urge Unbiased National Investigations." *The U.F.O. Investigator*. Vol. IV, No. 7, July-August 1968.

Major Donald E. Keyhoe, "NICAP Calls Colorado UFO Project [a] Failure." Press Release, April 30, 1968.

Major Donald E. Keyhoe, NICAP Director. Letter to The Honorable Lyndon B Johnson, President of the United States, The White House, Washington, D.C., April 30, 1968.

Major Donald E. Keyhoe, "The Truth About the Condon Report." *The U.F.O. Investigator*, January 1969.

Captain Peter W. Killian, American Airlines, Inc., Flight 139. UFO Sighting Report to NICAP, February 24, 1959.

John Thomas King, Bangor, Maine. Letter to Robert Mattingly, North Anson, Maine, March 31, 1966.

John Thomas King, Bangor, Maine. UFO Sighting Report to NICAP, Washington, D.C., March 28, 1966.

Diana S. Knop, NICAP Staff (Sightings). Letter to Robert Watts, Capital Aviation Corporation, Municipal Airport, Bismarck, North Dakota, December 4, 1968.

James J. Koenig, "The inside story on UFOs." The Belleville, Illinois, *News Democrat*, August 8, 2000.

Michael Kostelnuk, "Michalak Describes Radioactive Find Made at UFO Site." *Winnipeg Free Press*, May 21, 1968.

Sandy Larson's Space Mummy. The Iron Skeptic. Mummies from Space @ www.theironskpetic.com/articles/larson/larson.htm.

Dorothy Lewis, "National UFO researcher to probe area sightings." *St. Paul Dispatch*, March 8, 1979.

"Charles Lindbergh, An American Aviator." Charles Lindbergh Biography @ www.charleslindbergh.com/history.

"List of Reported UFO Sightings." *Wikipedia*, the Free Encyclopedia @ http://en.wikipedia.org/wicki/List_of_reported_UFO_sightings.

O.B. Lloyd, Jr., Director of Public Services, National Aeronautics and Space Administration (NASA), Washington, D.C. Letter to Gordon Lore, President, UFO Research Associates, Hollywood, California, November 3, 1977.

Gordon Lore, "Alien 'Claim Jumpers'—Bizarre Encounters." *UFO Research Newsletter*, Vol. V, No. 12, May-June 1978.

Gordon Lore and Harold Deneault, *Mysteries of the Skies: UFOs in Perspective* (Prentice-Hall, Inc., 1968)

Gordon Lore, "A Reported Landing in Spring Grove, Pennsylvania, Saturday, October 16, 1965" (NICAP, 1965).

Gordon Lore, "Huge UFO Paces Train." *UFO Research Newsletter*, September-October 1972, Vol. II, No. 6.

Gordon Lore, President, UFO Research Associates (UFOR), Washington, D.C. Letters to Mrs. Doris R. Fickelsher, Founder and Director, Allied Saucers Association, Angola, New York, April 2 and May 12, 1971.

Gordon Lore, President, UFOR, Hollywood, California. Letter to O.B. Lloyd, Jr., Director of Public Services, National Aeronautics and Space Administration (NASA), Washington, D.C., November 18, 1977.

Gordon Lore, President, UFOR, Hollywood, California. Letter to Dr. Frank Press, Director, Office of Science and Technology Policy, The White House, Washington, D.C., October 18, 1977.

Gordon Lore, President, UFOR, Hollywood, California. Letter to Mrs. Ruth Ziegenfuss, Aquashicola, Pennsylvania, June 11, 1977.

Gordon Lore, "Photographer Films UFOs From Plane Window." *UFO Research Newsletter*, Vol. V, No. 10, February-March 1978.

Gordon Lore, "Pilot Incident, Animal Reaction Are the Main Characteristics of California Reports." *UFO Research Newsletter*, Vol. V, No. 11, March-April 1978.

Gordon I.R. Lore, Jr., and Harold H. Deneault, Jr., *Mysteries of the Skies: UFOs in Perspective*. Prentice-Hall, Englewood Cliffs, New Jersey, 1968.

Gordon Lore, Jr., President, UFO Research Associates, Bethesda, Maryland. Letter to Mrs. William E. Fallon, Wood River Junction, Rhode Island, May 18, 1973.

Gordon Lore, "New Witness Discovered in Mantell Tragedy." *UFO Research Newsletter*, Vol. I, No. 2, May-June 1971.

Gordon Lore, "NICAP Position Paper." National Investigations Committee on Aerial Phenomena (NICAP), Washington, D.C., April 1968.

Gordon Lore, *Strange Effects From UFOs*. (NICAP, 1969).

Gordon Lore, President, UFO Research Associates, Washington, D.C. Letter to Douglas J. Griffiths, Schenectady, New York, October 23, 1973.

Gordon Lore, "Train Crew Observes Maneuvering Objects." *UFO Research Newsletter*, August-September 1972.

Gordon Lore, UFO Scorches Highway. *The U.F.O. Investigator*, Vol. III, No. 12, March-April 1967.

Robert J. Low, "Some Thoughts on the UFO Project." Memorandum to E. James Archer and Thurston E. Manning, University of Colorado UFO Project, Boulder, Colorado, August 9, 1966. This memorandum would later be labeled "The Trick Memo."

Marius Lubbe, Director, Creative Minds Computer Schools, "UFO Over Pretoria, South Africa," August 28, 1996.

Victor Mackie, "Manitoba Sightings Cited." *Winnipeg Free Press*, July 29, 1967.

Victor Mackie, "UFO Probe Due." *Winnipeg Free Press*, July 21, 1967.

Major General M. M. Magee, Chief of Staff, North American Air Defense Command, Colorado. Letter to the Honorable James B. Utt (R-CA), House of Representatives, Washington, D.C., November 9, 1965.

Prarthito Maity, "Top 10 sightings after 2000" @ www.ibtimes.com/top-10-ufo-sightings-after-2000-294357.

"Mantell UFO Incident." From *Wikipedia*, the Free Encyclopedia @ https://en.wikipedia.org/wiki/Mantell_UFO_incident.

Mrs. Robert L. Mattingly, North Anson, Maine, Letter to Major Donald E. Keyhoe (USMC-Ret.), Director, NICAP, Washington, D.C., March 28, 1966.

Clark C. McClelland, Co-Chairman, NICAP Florida Subcommittee Unit 3, Indian River City, Florida. Summary of Elizabeth L. Douglas sighting report, July 20, 1967, sent to NICAP, Washington, D.C., July 30, 1967.

Clark C. McClelland, Co-Chairman, NICAP Florida Subcommittee Unit 3, Florida Operations, Indian River City, Florida. Letter with sighting reports sent to Richard H. Hall, NICAP, Washington, D.C., August 11, 1967.

Clair A. McDevitt, "Davenport highlights various UFO sightings." *Daily Record*, Roswell, New Mexico, July 7, 2000.

"James McDonald, a Cloud Physicist, Leading Scientific Defender of U.F.O. Existence, Dies," *The New York Times*, June 16, 1971.

Dr. James E. McDonald, Institute of Atmospheric Physics, The University of Arizona in Tucson. Letter to Miss Isabel Davis, NICAP, Washington, D.C., October 9, 1967.

Dr. James E. McDonald, Institute of Atmospheric Physics, The University of Arizona in Tucson. Letters to Richard H. Hall, Assistant Director, NICAP, Washington, D.C., October 5 and 14, 1966.

Dr. James E. McDonald, "Are UFOs Extraterrestrial Surveillance Craft?" *UFO Research Newsletter*, Vol. 1, No. 9, December 1971-January 1972.

Dr. James E. McDonald, "UFO Sightings Over Buckskin Mountains, Arizona," March 17, 1969.

Dr. James E. McDonald, UFO Report to Gordon Lore, Vice President, NICAP, May 9, 1969.

"Professor James McDonald, physicist, UFO buff." The *Washington Daily News*, June 15, 1971.

James McDonald. "Physicist, Investigator Of UFOs." *The Washington Post*, June 17, 1971.

Peter McLintock, "Weird Rivals For Manipogo." Manitoba *Globe and Mail*, June 3, 1967.

Lex Mebane, Administrative Vice-President, Civilian Saucer Intelligence of New York. Letter to Captain Peter Killian, American Airlines pilot, Hicksville, New York, March 14, 1959.

Anne Midgette, "Aliens Abduct City's Identity." *Wall Street Journal*, September 3, 1997.

Clay T. Miller, Chief Photographer for *The Register*, Santa Ana, CA. Letter to NICAP dated December 31, 1965.

David Miller, "Are We Being Watched by UFOs?" *Sunday Star*, July 8, 1984.

Peter M. Millman, National Research Council of Canada, Radio and Electrical Engineering Division, Ottawa, Canada. Letter to Gordon Lore, Assistant Director, NICAP, December 5, 1968.

Robert Monell, "UFO's in Central New York." *The Syracuse New Times*, May 21, 1978.

Shirley M. Moody, Mechanicsville, Virginia. Report on Unidentified Flying Objects(s) sent to NICAP, Washington, D.C., July 19, 1967.

"SS *Morgantown Victory*. Victory Ship built by the U.S. Maritime Commission during World War II" @ www.usmm.org/victoryships.html.

Chris Morris, Navy Pilot Describes UFO Sighting: "A White Tic Tac" the Size of a Plane. *Fortune*, December 19, 2017 @ http://fortune.com/2017/12/19/navy-ufo-stories/.

Richard D. Moss, Long Prairie, Minnesota. Letter to NICAP, Washington, D.C., December 2, 1968.

National UFO Reporting Center Transcript, "UFO Events Over Arizona, March 13, 1997."

National UFO Reporting Center, "Transcription of Interview with Beach, North Dakota, UFO Witness, July 3, 1996."

"New Mexico UFO Landing Report" prepared by the New York Investigative Subcommittee of the National Investigations Committee on Aerial Phenomena (Jose A. Cecin, Chairman), May 7, 1964.

News Desk, Former Pentagon official claims aliens visited Earth. Luis Elizondo was ex-chief of the $22 million 'Advanced Aerospace Threat Identification Programme', *The Express Tribune,* January 14, 2018.

1948, "The Death of Thomas Mantell." *UFO Casebook* @ www.ufocasebook.com/Mantell.html

NUFORC Home Page @ www.nuforc.com.

Jan Overall. Letter to Frank (last name unknown), January 11, 1966.

Bob Peel, "Cazenovians Report 'UFO'", *Syracuse Post-Standard,* May 12, 1978.

Pentagon Blows the Lid: The Advanced Aerospace Threat Identification Program. The Project Avalon Forum. Chronicles of the human awakening… where science and spirituality meet @ http://projectavalon.net.

John Picton, "Beware of Flying Saucers, UFO Watcher Warns." *Toronto Star,* September 6, 1981.

Henry W. Pierce, "UFO Group Asks Residents [to] Report All Area Sightings." *Pittsburgh Post-Gazette,* March 3, 1978.

Henry W. Pierce, "UFO Tale Told; Reports Compared." *Pittsburgh Post-Gazette,* March 4, 1978.

Paul Pihichyn, "UFO Sighting in Manitoba." *Winnipeg Free Press,* April 6, 1968.

Doris Piris, "UFOs Plague Coulterville Residents." *Tri-County Shopper,* August 23, 1967.

Nick Pope, "Top 10 UFO incidents in the UK." *The Telegraph,* May 26, 2017.

Bruce Posner, "UFO Sightings Told By Metroland Men." *Knickerbocker News-Union Star,* Albany, New York, August 14, 1973.

Bob Pratt, "200 See Gigantic UFO Near Pittsburgh." *National Enquirer,* May 30, 1978.

Greg Price, Pentagon Searched For Aliens and UFOs at Harry Reid's Request: Report. *Newsweek,* December 16, 2017.

Ralph Rankow, Photographic Illustrations, New York City. Letter to Richard H. Hall, Assistant Director, NICAP, Washington, D.C., September 30, 1965.

Ralph Rankow, Photographic Illustrations, New York City. Report to NICAP, October 29, 1965.

Recent public disclosure of a $22 million military program investigating UFOs. Kiwi Farms @ https://kiwifarms.net/threads/nyt-publicly-discloses-advanced-aerospace-threat-identification-program.3.

Glenn A. Ricci, Pittsburgh, Pennsylvania, UFO Sighting Report to Gordon Lore, President, UFO Research Associates, Los Angeles, California, April 14, 1978.

Charles Richards, United Press International, Day Lead UFO, Socorro, New Mexico, April 27, 1964.

C. Reed Ricks, Idaho Falls, Idaho, UFO Sighting Report to NICAP, Washington, D.C., November 13, 1967.

C. Reed Ricks, Idaho Falls, Idaho, UFO Sighting Report to Ted Bloecher, NICAP, Washington, D.C., August 22, 1968.

Francis Ridge, NICAP Site Coordinator/Nuclear Connection Project, "The 1975 UFO Chronology." NICAP UFO. National Investigations Committee on Aerial Phenomena @ www.nicap.org/Chronos/1975fullrep.htm.

Francis Ridge, Roswell & The Wave of '47: Too Many Coincidences. NICAP. National Investigations Committee on Aerial Phenomena @ www.nicap.org.

"Rumanian Sightings Revealed." *The U.F.O. Investigator*, June-July 1969, Vol. IV, No. 12.

"Says He Observed and Shot 'Flying Saucer.'" *The State*, Columbia, South Carolina, February 8, 1953.

Marie Louise Schmidt, Rockwood, Michigan. Letter and UFO Sighting Report Form sent to Gordon Lore, President, UFO Research Associates, Hollywood, California, August 8, 1978.

Stanley D. Schneider, Assistant to the Director, Executive Office of the President, Office of Science and Technology Policy, Washington, D.C. Letter to Gordon Lore, President, UFO Research Associates, Hollywood, California, October 31, 1977.

David A. Schroth. Letter to Gordon Lore, UFO Research Associates, September 30, 1976.

Rob Schwarz, UFO Sightings 2018-This Year's Reported Encounters With Unidentified Objects. Stranger Dimensions @ www.strangerdimensions.com/featured/ufo-sightings-2018/.

"SC Man Tells of Studying Hovering 'Flying Saucer,' Shooting Into It." *The State*, Columbia, South Carolina, February 7, 1953.

"SS *Morgantown Victory*: Three in Crew of GAA Ship Tell of Sighting of 'UFO.'" *Sealift Magazine*, June 1966, Vol. XVI, No 6, Washington, D.C.

Dawn Stover, "50 Years After Roswell." *Popular Science*, June 1997.

Strange unidentified flying object over Manchester, UK, 3-April-2018, Latest UFO Sighting. UFO Videos & News About Extraterrestrials @ www.latest-ufo-sightings.net.

Major Lawrence J. Tacker (USAF), Executive Officer, Public Information Division, Office of Information Services, Department of the Air Force, Office of the Secretary. Letter to Mr. Fred A. Kirsch, UFO Research Committee, Akron, Ohio, March 19, 1959.

Major Lawrence J. Tacker (USAF). Letter to Mr. Richard Hall, Secretary NICAP, Washington, D.C., March 24, 1960.

Bill Tillottson. "It Was Something But No One Knows What." *The Bismarck Tribune*, November 27, 1968.

"The Truth About the FBI-UFO Memo? Harry Truman Did Not Like J. Edgar Hoover." *The UFO Partisan* @ http://ufopartisan.blogspot.com/2011/04/truth-revealed-by-fbi-ufo-memos-truman.htm.

"UFO Evidence. Scientific Study of the UFO Phenomenon and the Search for Extraterrestrial Life." UFO Quotes: "Celebrities and Others" @ www.ufoevidence.org/documents/doc1745.htm.

"UFO Reported In Wood River." Westerly, Rhode Island, *Sun*, February 7, 1973.

"UFO Sightings and Related Events (1980-1990)." UFOR @ www.ufor.asn.au/sightings/

"UFOs and Dead Alien Bodies Are Being Stored But Not in Area 51" @ Disclose.tv@www.disclose.tv/news/ufos_and_dead_alien_bodies_are_being_stored_but_not_in_area_51/138853.

"UFOs and the Church. Testimonies of UFOs by Famous Christians" @ www.logos-christian.org/sightings/.

"UFOs And The Guy Hottel Memo." Federal Bureau of Investigation (FBI), March 25, 2013 @ www.fbigov.news/stories/Ufos-and-the-guy-hottel-memo.

"UFOs Sighted Near Bismarck." *The Forum*, Fargo-Moorhead, North Dakota, November 27, 1968.

Unidentified Flying Object Report, Socorro, New Mexico, 24 April 1964. United States Air Force Statement on Socorro, New Mexico Case, June 8, 1964.

Unidentified Flying Object, Socorro, New Mexico, From Strategic Air Command, Albuquerque 62, New Mexico, to Director, FBI, April 25, 1964.

United Press International, "Flying Saucer, Midgets Land on Car, Pair Says." *San Diego Evening Tribune*, November 3, 1967.

United States Air Force Projects Grudge and Bluebook Reports 1-12. Published by The National Investigations Committee on Aerial Phenomena (NICAP), Washington, D.C., 1968.

Dr. Vasil Uzunoglu, Annapolis, Maryland, UFO Sighting Report to NICAP, Washington, D.C., August 9, 1966.

Gary Valtenuta, *The Majestic-12 documents*. UFO News: a National and World Report. *North Seattle Journal*, Lynnwood, Washington, August 12, 2000.

Chris Vernon, "The Truth Is Out There." *This Week*, Lindsay, Ontario, Canada, February 10, 1996.

"Was the Death of Dr. McDonald A Suicide?" The Corvallis, Oregon *Benton Herold*, August 19, 1971.

Robert K. Watts, Chief Pilot, Capital Aviation Corporation, Bismarck, North Dakota. Report on Unidentified Flying Objects sent to NICAP, December 7, 1968.

Walter N. Webb, Boston, Massachusetts. UFO report letter sent to Richard H. Hall, Assistant Director, NICAP, Washington, D.C., May 23, 1959.

Mrs. Agnes M. Wehrle, Zeiger, Illinois. Letter to Gordon Lore, President, UFO Research Associates, Washington, D.C., February 11, 1974.

John Wenz, "Why So Many People Are Reading This Old FBI Memo About UFOs." *Popular Mechanics*, January 7, 2016 @ www.popularmechanics.com/technology/a18874/fbi-Ufo-file-guy-hottel.

Don West, "Expert: UFO was no phony." *San Jose Mercury*, August 15, 1975.

Bill Wilkerson, "Levelland 'Flaming Thing' Brings World Knocking At City's Door." *Lubbock Morning Avalanche*, November 4, 1957.

Weyland Yutani, J. Edgar Hoover UFO Memo. "The Army Retrieved Crashed Disc." *Unacknowledged, The Informer*, October 3, 2013.

"What the FBI's UFO Memo Shows About American Intelligence," *Wired*, April 3, 2013.

Jack B. Wilhelm, Air Traffic Controller, Bismarck Airport, North Dakota. Report on Unidentified Flying Objects sent to NICAP, Washington, D.C., December 5, 1968.

Jack B. Wilhelm, Air Traffic Controller, Bismarck Airport, North Dakota. Letter to NICAP, Washington, D.C., December 12, 1968.

"In Memory of E. Garrison Wood, July 6, 1915-November 23, 2010." Diuguid Funeral Service & Crematory, Lynchburg, VA @ www.memorialsolutions.com/sitemaker/sites/Diugeil/memsol.egi?user_id=383045.

Roy W. Woodward, Goldsworthy Mining Ltd., Finucane Island, Port Hedland, Western Australia. UFO sighting report to T.M. Olsen, UFOIRC, November 5, 1967.

William Yardley, Frederick I. Ordway III Dies at 87. NASA Official Helped Shape 'Space Odyssey.' *New York Times*, July 13, 2014.

Index

Numbers in **bold** indicate photographs

A

Acker, T.F. 177
Adamski, George 43
Advance 71
Advanced Aerospace Threat Identification Program (AATIP) 375-379
Aerial Phenomena Research Organization (APRO) 9, 11, 40, 147, 152, 198, 298, 311-312, 320
Aguadilla Airport 398
Air Force Bluebook Reports 137-145, 254
Air Force Grudge Reports 137-145, 254
Air Force Office of Scientific Research (AFOSR) 148
Air Force Public Information Division 30
Air Materiel Command 351
Air National Guard 89, 141
Air National Guard Fighter Group 253
"A.K.," Private First Class 342
Alamagordo Army Air Force Base 388
Alamo Dam 154
Albuquerque Lions Club 266
Aldrich, Jan 236
Ali, Muhammad 381
Aliens from Space; The Real Story of Unidentified Flying Objects (1973) 245, 263
Alvarez, Jose 15
American Airlines 21, 24, 25, 26, 28, 29, 403

American Association for the Advancement of Science (AAAS) 340
American Institute of Aeronautics and Astronautics (AIAA) 229, 230, 233
Anderson Air Force Base 141, 177
Anderson, Third Mate Richard M. 65, 67
"Andrew" 402
Andrews Army Air Force Base 92, 95, 353
Andrus, Walter 263
Angel's Hair 269, 276
Angelucci, Orfeo 43
Annapolis Valley 195
Anton, St. 162
Arant, Gayle 294-295
Arant, Les 294-295
Area 51 344-345, 350, 376
Arent, Sue 306, 308
"A Reported Landing in Spring Grove, Pennsylvania…" 53-63
"Are UFOs Extraterrestrial Surveillance Craft?" 229-233
Arges 162
Armstrong, Mary Louise 125
Arnold, Kenneth 3, 79, 134
Ashcroft, Art 45
Associated Press (AP) 30, 41, 327
Atkinson, Colonel Ivan C. 148
Atomic Energy Commission (AEC) 339
Aveling, R.O. 174
Aztec, New Mexico 335, 345

B

Baker, Jr., Dr. Robert M.L. 127, 129-130
Balducci, Monsignor Corrado 381
Ball, Norman 63
Ballen, Lloyd 17,
Ballway, Debbie **222**, 368
Baltimore, Maryland xv, xvi, 5, 93, 95, **222**, 324, 325
Baney, L.E. 31
Banner, Captain Frederick William 72-73
Barnes, Rita 171
Barrow, Robert ("Bob") 355, 358, 363-367
Barrows, Bobby 368
Barry, Bob 53, 54, 56-57
Barry, Robert D. 342
Basingstoke Canal 392
Beacon, Colin 270
Beall, E.V. 94
Beallsville Hospital 183
Beaver Valley Power Station 372
Becar, Noel J. 110-116
Begay, Willie 168-171, 172
Behind the Flying Saucers (1950) 335
Bell, Alphonzo 128
Bell, Alvin 131
Benedict, Howard 327, 328
Bennewitz, Paul 354
Berliner, Donald 60
Berlitz, Charles 348
Berson, F.A. 185
Bethurum, Truman 43
Bettis Atomic Power Laboratory 372
Big Marsh 167
Bigelow Aerospace Advanced Studies (BAAS) 379
Bigelow, Robert 375-376
Bismarck Air Traffic Control Tower 133
Bismarck International Airport 131

Bison Northern States Power Plant 133
Bitu, Valercu 160
Blackwell, Sergeant Quinton 252
Blanchard, Colonel William 347, 352-353
Bluemmer, Robert 312
Blumen, Dr. William 118
Boeing 49, **219**, 315, 387
Booth, Lloyd C. 163-167
Bowie, David 381
Bowles, Jan R. 361-365
Braun, Dr. Wernher von 97
Brazel, W.W. ("Mac") 346-347, 348, 376
Brew, Charles 184-185
"Brooke" 402
Brooks, Angus 188-189
Brooks, William 63
Broughman, Kathleen 186-187
Brown, Harold 89, 319-320
Brown, T. Townsend 236, 237
Bruns, Edward A. 81-82
Bryan, Colonel Joseph III 89, 235, 236, 237, 240, 245
Bryant, Larry 168
Buckskin Mountains 153-155
Bunescu, Ion 157
Burtoo, Alfred 392
Butcher, Harold 185-187
Butcher, Robert 185-187
Butcher, Mrs. William 185-187
Butcher, William, Jr. 185-187

C

"Cabot, The" 272-273
Cape Hatteras 71, 75
Carmichael, Melvin 109-110, 267-268
Carpenter, Corporal Lee 95
Carpenter, Dean 178
Carr, Robert Spencer 108

Carswell Air Force Base 337
Carter, Dr. Lauris S. 87
Carter, President James ("Jimmy") Earl 124, 151, 299-301, 327, 329, 330, 382
Carvalho, Bernard J.O. 236
Casalengo, Estacion 271
Cass, Blake 241, 246
Cavitt, Sheridan 347
Center for UFO Studies (CUFOS) 278, 308, 349
Central Intelligence Agency (C.I.A.) 26, 235, 236, 237, 240, 241, 245, 300, 378
Cerny, Paul 277-278, 283-289, 291, 294, 295, 304, 312, 315-316
Chapin, Clinton 284-289
Chapin, Jane 284-289
Chapman, Ralph 30
Charleston Evening Post 3, 4
Chavez, Sam 34, 42
Chow, Melinda 389
Christiansen, Pearl 197-198
Churaz, Sixto 274
Civil Aviation Agency (C.A.A.) 166
Clarke, Arthur C. 97-99
Claunch, Robert S. 65, 66-67
Cleaver, Marshall 108
Clem, Sheriff Weir 16, 17, 18
Clements, Lieutenant Albert 253
Clinton County Army Air Field 252, 256
Clinton, First Lady Hillary 383-384
Clinton, President William ("Bill") Jefferson 383-384
Close Encounters of the Third Kind (1977) 99, 329, 365, 366
Cloud Gap 36
Coca, Dumitru 158
Coca, Mrs. Dumitru 158

Cohen, Alvin 5-7
Colledge, Mary 355-356, 357
Colledge, Thomas ("Tom") 355-356, 357
Collins, Mrs. Robert 83
Collner, J.D. 145
Colton, William 367
Columbus, Christopher 68
Commonwealth Scientific and Industrial Research Organization 185
Condon, Dr. Edward U. 117-120, 122, 123, 125-126, 149, 150, 151, 152, 153, 231, 237, 336
Connections: A Lifetime Journey Through the World of Celebrity 240, 384
Connelly, Joel 325
Constantinescu, M. 161
Cooper, Gordon 382
Cooper, Tim 354
Corso, Colonel Philip 349-350
Cotsci, Vasile 159
Cozens, Charles 178-179
Craigie, Lieutenant General Laurence C. 351
Crawford, Sue 95
Cristen, Mike 393
Crowder, Clifton 60-61, 63
Cunningham, Paul 367
Curry, William 107-108
Cutezatorii 162

D

Daily Citizen 198
Daily Press 30
Daly, Major 339
Daniel Guggenheim Fund for the Promotion of Aviation 242
Davis, Isabel 166-167
Davis, Kevin 196

Davis, Slim 292-295
Day After Roswell, The: A Former Pentagon Official Reveals the U.S. Government's Shocking UFO Cover-Up 349-350
Dearborn Observatory 60, 91, 120
Dee, James John 25, 31
Demler, John H. 181-183
Dennis, Glenn 349
De Andrade, Salles 390
De Rochefort, Nicolas 236
Dewilde, Marius 270
Doris 71
Dorsey, Captain James A. 187
Doty, Sergeant Richard 354
Dougall, Magistrate W.K.C. 201
Douglas, Elizabeth L. 101-103
Douglas, Ingrid 103
Douglas, Steven 103
Dow Air Force Base 83
Dow, John 198-20 1
Dowding, Lord 382
Dowling, Officer Frank L. 93-95
Dr. August Raspel Memorial Award 113
Druffel, Ann **216**, 228, 233-234
Drummond, Roscoe 91
DuBarry, John 243
"Dudley Dorrito, The" 395
Duplantis, Lynn 144-145

E

Edenton, USS 75
Edmonds, Captain C.H. 50
Edmonds, Roy 63
Edwards Air Force Base 350
Edwards, Brenda 357
Efron, Ruben 270
Einstein, Dr. Albert 382
Eisenhower, President Dwight D. 349
Elgin Air Force Base 300
Elizondo, Luis 378-379
Elmes, Claude L. 201
El Toro Marine Station 49
Emmons, Earl 107
England's Roswell 390-391
Epperson, Idabel 46-47, 50-51, **221**, 318-319, 323, 332
Everell, James 69
Evers, Ed 46-47
Experimental Aircraft Association 112

F

Fache, Able Seaman 66, 67
Fallon, Mrs. William E. 262-263
Fallon, William E. ("Eddy") 262-263
Fargo Air Field Control Tower 134
Fausse, Captain Ernest M. 191
Federal Aviation Administration (FAA) 131-132, 133, 177, 178, 318, 360, 379
Federal Bureau of Investigation (F.B.I.) 34, 36, 37, 38, 40
Fickelsher, Doris R. 312, 313
Field, The 166
Fink, Richard 7
Fire in the Sky 385
Firestorm: Dr. James E. McDonald's Fight for UFO Science 228, 233-234
Fischer, John ("Jack") 133
Fisher, Major General W.P. 30
Fitch, E.G. 36
Flickinger, Donald E. 131-133, 135
Flying Saucers: A Modern Myth of Things Seen in the Skies 9
"Flying Saucers Are Real, The" 244
Flying With Lindbergh 243
Fort Belvoir, Virginia 259

Fort Knox, Kentucky 251, 256, 257
Fort Lee Fire Department 62
Fort Mommoth 338-339
Fort Riley, Kansas 342, 346
Fort Worth Star-Telegram 352
Foster, J.B. 347, 351
Fournet, Dewey 236
Fowler, A.J. 14
Fowler, Raymond E. 180, 340
Francis, Bruce 183
Franklin, Joe 77-79, 81, 126
Franklin, Paul 198-201
Franklin, Sir John 71
Fravor, Navy Commander David 377-378
Freedom of Information Act 38, 137, **219**
Freedom of Information Committee 138
French Air Force 270
Friedman, Stanton ("Stan") **220**, 336, 348
Frosch, Robert A. 328-329, 331
Fry, Daniel 43
Fuller, John G. 77-78, 79-81, 126
Fusaro, Gladys 27-28, 29, 30

G

Gabrian, Captain Benjamin 161
Gairy, Prime Minister Sir Eric 336
Gaitan, Police Officer Lee Roy 395
Galimberti, Enrique R. 271-272
Gallegos, Orlando 39-40
Gallery, Claire A. 369
Gardner, Ann 261, 263
Gardner, Kenneth ("Ken") 261
Gariepy, Thomas 263
"Gary" 276
Gates, Tom 277-278, 283, 286
Gayer, Stan 278-282
Gheorghiu, Virgil 158-159

Gilroy Police Department 312
Gladfelter, P.H. 57
Glenn, Senator John 379
G., Mrs. 341
Godfrey, Alan 390
Godman Field, Kentucky 251-252, 257
Gorbachev, Mikhail 382
Gore, Vice President Albert ("Al") 384
Gorman, George F. 134
Gow, Jeffery J. 186-188
Gray, John 47
Great Falls Air Force Base 133
Ground Observer Corps (GOC) 6-7
Ground Saucer Watch 338
Gruver, Eugene 58
Guinn, Virginia A. 194
Gutierrez, Pedro 68

H

Haas, C.J. 187
Hable, F.A.A. Deputy Chief Tom 360
Haines, Dr. Richard F. 279
Hajacos, James 62
Hake, Robert Steve 324-325
Hale-Bopp Comet 393
Hall, Richard ("Dick") H. xvii, 1-2, 3, 5, 7, 13, 21, 30, 33, 40-41, 43, 46, 47, 48, 53, 54, 58, 59, 60, 86, 91, 92, 109, 117, 119, 124, 127, 129, 143, 149, 152, 172, 227, 228, 229, 235, 237-239, 245, 327, 351
Hall, Dr. Robert L. 127, 129
Hallstrom, Floyd P. 316-320, 324
Hallstrom, Gwen 318
Hammon, Bob 170
Hammon, Willard 170-171
Hammond, Lieutenant 253
Hanbury Hall 174

Hancock International Airport 360
Happy Camp, California 277-289
Harder, Dr. James A. 127, 129, 311-312
Harper, Corporal Tom 171
Harris, Fred 295
Harris, Steve 278-282
Hartmann, Kenneth 7
Hartranft, J.B. 238
Harzan, Jan 345
Hathaway, Colonel E.U. 270
Haut, Walter 347, 353
Haver, Ed 107
Hawecki, Henry C. 188
Hawking, Professor Stephen 382
Head, Glenn 109, 267
Heflin, Rex E. 45-51, **206, 207**
Helder, Robert 144
Henderson, "Pappy" 351
Hendry, Dr. Allan 300, 308
Hennessey, Julian A. 189
Henry Grinnel Expedition, The 71
Henry, Dr. Richard 330-331
Her Majesty's Coastal Service 195
Herman Review 82
Highland Park Reservoir 370, 371
Hill, Barney 79-81, 135
Hill, Betty 79-81, 135
Hillenkoetter, Admiral Roscoe 236-237, 241, 244, 245
Hix, Colonel Guy 252, 256
Hobana, Ion 157, 158, 160, 162
Hoff, Lee 306
Holloman Air Force Base 341, 346
Holmes, Chief Justice Oliver Wendell 1
Hoover, J. Edgar 36-39
Hopkins, Sir Anthony 383
Hottel, Guy 37, 38
"Howard" 273-274

Howard, Sheriff Pete 389
Hunter, Earl 168
Hynek, Dr. J. Allen 34-35, 40, 41, 42, 60, 90, 91, 120-122, 127, 128, **217**, 233-234, 255-256, 278, 308, 349

I

Ilkley Moor, England 392
Incident at Exeter: The Story of Unidentified Flying Objects Over America Now 77-78
Interrupted Journey, The: Two Lost Hours "Aboard a Flying Saucer" 78, 79-81
Inouye, Senator Daniel K. 378

J

James, Cecil 198
Jardine, Gary 196
Jefferson, Thomas 121
Jim Williams River 154
"J.K." 342
"J.M.," Major 337
Johnson, Christine Ezell 304-305
Johnson, J. Bond 352, 353
Johnson, President Lyndon B. 123
Jones, R. Conway 297-299
Jones, Reverend Elwell 165-166
Jones, Ray 17
Journal of Space Flight, The 166
J.P.A. 70
Julig, Rose Marie 306-308
Jung, Dr. Carl 9-11, **224**
Just Cause 240, 257

K

Kaeburn, Dr. Leslie 98-99
Kane, Dr. Elisha Kent 71-72
Katchen, Leon 60, **212**
Kennedy, Bruce J. 264-265, 266

Kennedy Space Center 103
Kentucky Highway Patrol 251
Ketchum, H.B. 166
Keyhoe, Major Donald E. xiii, xiv, xvii,
   2, 3, 9-11, 21, 29-32, 47, 77, 81, 86,
   87-89, 91, 97, 98, 112, 114, 116,
   117, 118-120, 122, 123, 124-127,
   128, 143, 149, 152, 153, 157, 168,
   172, **202**, **203**, **224**, 229, 235-237,
   238-239, 240, 241-247, 263, 301,
   327, 335
Killian, Captain Peter W. 21-32
Killian, Mrs. Peter W. 21-32
King, John 82-85
King, Mrs. William 193
King, William 193
Kingsbury, David 39
Kinsey, Ian 195-196
Kirshner, Robert 55, 58
Kirtland Air Force Base 40, 351, 354
Kiteveles, Dennis 359-361
Kiteveles, Denny 359-361
Kiteveles, Linda 359-361
Klason, Willis 82
Klein, Robert 383
Knopp, Diana 157
Kono 386-387
Kromschoeder, John 351-352
Kubrick, Stanley 97-99

L

LaBella, Joseph 358
Ladd, D.M. 36
Lady of the Lake 72-73
LaGate, Edna 31
Lake Erie 24, 25
Lake Havasu 153-154
Langley Air Force Base 342

LaPaz, Dr. Lincoln 42-43
Larson, Jackie 135-136
Larson, Sandy 135-136
Leatart, Dennis 320
LeBailly, Major General E.B. 89
Le Bourget Field 242
Lee, James 18
LeMay, General Curtis 351
Levelland Police Station 14
Levelland, Texas 13, 14, 15, 16, 17, 18, 19
Lindbergh, Colonel Charles 114, 116,
   202, **203**, 242, 243
Lloyd, O.B., Jr. 330
Lobello, Donald 357-358
Lobello, Linda 357-358
Loch Raven Reservoir 5-6, 7
Lockbourne Army Air Field 252, 256
Long, James 17
Long John Program 25
Look Magazine 126, 331
Lore, Gordon 54, 80, **210**, **212**, **215**, 239
Lore, Martha ("Marty") D. 228, 229,
   251, 263, 264, 296, 309
Lorenzen, Coral 40, 147, 198
Lorenzen, James 147, 198
Los Angeles International Airport
   (LAX) 315, 316, 317, 318
Low, Robert 118, 122, 123, 124
Lubbock Lights 13, **204**
Lugo, Frances 309-312
Lugo, Imelda 309-312
Lugo, Jose 310, 312
Lugo, Manuel 309-311
Luke Air Force Base 142-143
Lusby, Joan 53, 54
Lutz, John 324, 325
Lycoming College 121
Lynn, William III 377

M

MacIntyre, William ("Bill") 235
"Made of Glass" UFO 304-305
Magee, Major General M.M. 49
Mahon, David 385
Malone, Richard 104-106
Malstrom Air Force Base 132
Mann, Judy 311
Mann, Mrs. Claude 171
Manning, Thurston E. 125, 148-150
Mantell, Captain Thomas F., Jr. 251-258
Marcell, Jesse, Jr. 347
Marcell, Major Jesse, Sr. 347
Marcoux, Rudolph C. 86
Marell, Richard 268-269
Marietta Army Air Base 257
Mariner, Dr. Allen S. 172-173
"Marsh gas" 120
Martin-Bus, Barry 201
Martin, Norman 61
Martin, Ronald 16
Maryland Air National Guard 393
Massachusetts Bay Colony 69
Mattis, Jim 378
McAndrew Air Force Base 140-141
McClelland, Clark C. 101, 102, 103
McClendon, Sarah 383-384
McDill Air Force Base 342
McDonald, Betsy
McDonald, Dr. James E. 81-82, 93, 117, 119, 124, 125-127, 128-129, 137-138, 143, 144, 147, 149, 150, 152, 153, 154, 155, 166-167, 178, 179, 182-183, 184, **214**, **215**, **216**, 227-234, 240, 327
McGowen, Elaine 295
McGuire, Diane 357-358
Mebane, Lex 23, 25-27, 32
Mellon, Christopher K. 378
Meloney, John 191
Middleton, Hunt 391-392
Mihail Kogalniceanu Airport 161
Milakovic, Doris 174-175
Milakovic, Milin 174-175
Miller, Clay T. 50
Minot Air Force Base 132-133, 134-135
Minot City Police 133
Mintz, Daniel H. 241, 245, 246
"Mironov" 275-276
Mitchell, James 342-343
MJ-12 350, 353-354
Monon Railroad 271
"Moody" 388
Moody, Sergeant 35
Moody, Shirley M. 100-101
Moore, Harold 167-168
Moore, William L. 348, 354
Moss, John 137, 138-139
Mount Rainier 3, 79, 134, 243
"Mr. Swamp Gas" 60
"Mr. T" 366
MUFON Witness Reporting Database 372
Murphy, William 278
Mutual UFO Network (MUFON) 246, 277, 278, 284, 294, 304, 307, 340, 345, 372, 399
Muza, Mark 167-168
Myers, Dan 54
Myers, Dwight 53-59, **208**
Myrick, Albert 178
Mysteries of the Skies: UFOs in Perspective 77, 80, **209**, 263

N

Nagen, Joan 194
NASA's Marshall Space Flight Center 97

National Aeronautics & Space Administration (NASA) 87, 97, 120, 129, 231, 327-334, 375
National Enquirer 329, 330
National Investigations Committee on Aerial Phenomena (NICAP) 1-2, 3, 5, 9, 13, 19, 21, 29, 30, 31, 33, 35, 39, 40, 41, 43, 45, 46, 47, 48, 50, 53, 54, 56, 57, 59, 60, 61, 65, 77, 78, 81, 82, 83, 87, 88, 89, 91, 92, 93, 95, 97, 98, 99, 100, 101, 102, 103, 105, 106, 107, 108, 109, 111, 112, 117-118, 119, 120, 122, 123, 124, 126, 128-129, 131, 132, 136, 137, 138, 139, 143, 144, 145, 147, 149, 151, 152, 153, 157, 158, 162, 163, 166, 168, 172, 173, 175, 176, 177, 178, 179, 180, 181, 183, 185, 186, 187-188, 189, 190, 191, 192, 194, 196, 197, 198, 201, **202, 205, 209, 210, 211, 212, 213, 214, 219, 221, 225,** 227, 235-239, 240, 245, 251, 254, 256, 257, 277, 296, 298, 299, 301, 318, 327, 329, 331, 335, 336, 340, 348, 351
National Press Club 245, 384
National Security Agency (NSA) 338
National Security Council 349
National UFO Reporting Center 379
Nellis Air Force Base 343, 350
Nelson, Willard D. 323
Nevada Atomic Proving Ground 339
New Mexico State Police 34
New York Herald Tribune 30
New York Times 147, 375
Newton, Irving 348
Niagara Falls Air Force Base 187
"Nicole" 394
Niculescu, Alexander 161

Nixon, Stuart 235, 237, 238, 245
Norris, Peter 185
North American Air Defense Command (NORAD) Center 49
North American Aviation 46, 47
North American Treaty Organization (NATO) 73
Northwestern University 60, 90, 91
Notchaway Creek Bridge 297
Notre Dame Football Team 264
Notre Dame University 264

O

Oakland International Airport 113
Oakland, Simon 78-79, 126, **215**
Oberth, Dr. Herman 384
O'Brien, Dr. Bryan 87
O'Connor, Bob 25
Odyssey Scientific Research Association 324
Office of Science and Technology 330
Office of Special Investigations (OSI) 354
Official Secrets Act 73
O'Hare International Airport 395
Ohio Bureau of Criminal Investigation 184
Ohling, Captain 71
O'Leary, Terry 135-136
Oliver, S.P. 109, 267
Onondaga County Sheriff's Department 355
"Operation Blue Book" 8-9
Operation Mainbrace 73
"Operation Majestic 12" see MJ-12
ORBIT 335
Ordway, Dr. Frederick ("Fred") III 97-99
Orion 22, 23-24, 25, 30, 32
Orion's Belt 23-24
Orlansky, Jesse 87
"Orlov" 275-276

P

Pacific Gas and Electric Company (PG&E) 295-296
Pakowhai Power Station 199
Palo Duro Canyon 18
Panorama Magazine 157
Paranteau, Betsy 193-194
Parapsychology 363, 365
Parham, Beauford E. 176-178
Pascl, Dorothy 322, 324
"Pat" 403
Patrick Air Force Base 139
Patuxent Naval Air Station (PAX River) xiii, xv, 65
Patuxent River xiii, xvi
Paul, Captain J.M. 196
Paun, Dr. Adina 162
Paz, Dr. Lincoln La 35, 42-43
Peabody Conservatory of Music xv, 1, 5
Pearl Harbor 74, 243, 258
Pecha, Bill **223**, 291-295, 296
Pecha, Lenda 293, 294
"Pedigreed Piddlin' Pup in Ten Piddles and a Puddle, The" 1
Pelchy, Elaine 191-194
Pelchy, Mrs. Oliver 192
Pentagon, The 139, 236, 243, 349, 378
Pepperdine University 317
"Pete" 401
Petrie, Captain Glynn 65-67
Pflock, Karl T. 194
Phoenix Lights, The 393-394
Pima Company Copper Mine 403
Pingree, Beverly 31
Pomidor, Salvador 272
Pool, Rick 281
Porter, Dr. Robert W. 87
Portland Underwater Defense Station 189
Powers, William 60
Press, Dr. Frank 328-330, 331
Preston, Royal Navy Lieutenant Tom 73-74
Prince Georges County Police Department 93, 95
Project Blue Book 47, 89, 90, 134, 231, 254, 255, 328, 338
Project Grudge 254
Project Saucer 254
Project Sign 255
Providence (Rhode Island) Bulletin 263
Prue, Edgar 358
Puncas, N.D. 31
Purdy, Ken 243-244
Putnam, Raymond 272-273

Q

Quinn, Mrs. Elaine 171-172
Quintanella, Major Hector 47

R

RAF Boulmer 75
RAF Woodbridge 390
Ramey, General Roger 347, 348, 352-353
Randle, Kevin 349
Rankow, Ralph 48-49
Rather, Dan 384
Read, Arnold 179
Reagan, President Ronald 124, 151, 350, 384
Redcliffe Power Station 198-199
Reeves, Jack 133
Register, The 50
Reid, Senator Harry 375-379
Reilly, Francis ("Frank") C. 264-266
Rendelsham Forest 390
Report on Unidentified Flying Objects, The 138

Resolute 71
"Retrievals of the Third Kind: A Case Study of Alleged UFO Occupants in Military Custody" 336-337
Ricci, Glenn A. 369-371
Richards, Charles 41
Richmond News-Leader 121
Ricks, C. Reed 168-169, 172
Ridge, Francis L. 256, 257-258
Ringstead Bay 189
Ripley, Ben 153-155
Rivers, E. Mendel 87, 89
Roach, Franklin 118
Robinson, Bill 107
Robinson, Wiley 145
Robison, Howard W. 30-31
"Robyn" 403
Rockefeller, Laurance 383
Roosevelt Field 242
Roswell Army Air Field 347, 350, 352
"Roswell Captures Saucer On Ranch In Roswell Region" 348
Roswell Daily Record 347, 348
Roswell Incident, The 348
Roswell, New Mexico 36, 38, **220**, 279, 331-332, 337, 344, 346-348, 349, 350-354, 376, 390
Rouland, Mrs. Sharon 187
Roush, J. Edgar 126, 128, 130, **221**
Royal Air Force
Royal Air Force Fighter Command 382
Royal Air Force Middle East Command 188
Royal Air Force Shawbury 392
Royal Yugoslav Air Force 259
Ruppelt, Captain Edward J. 73, 138, 255-256
Rush, Dr. Joseph 118

Russell, Senator Richard B., Jr. 270-271
Ryan, Lieutenant Colonel Thomas 89, 271

S

"Saddle, The" 278, 284
Sagan, Dr. Carl 87, 127, 129
S., Carl 344
Salaz, Joe 14
Salt Lake Tribune 41
San Jose Mercury 47
Santa Maria 68
"Sarah" 401
Saucedo, Pedro 14
"Saucers or Stars?" 30
Saunders, Dr. David R. 118, 119, 125
Scheaffer, Robert 300
Schmidt, Marie Louise 332-333
Schmit, Ladislau 160-161
Schmitt, Don 349
Schneider, Stanley D. 330
Scientific Study of Unidentified Flying Objects 117, 147
Scott, Professor William A. 118
Scully, Frank 335
Sealift Magazine 65
Seat Pleasant Police Station 94, 95
Secretary of the Air Force's Office of Information 139
"See-Saw Effect, The" 329-330
Semaza, Claire 322-324
Sheppard, John 399
Sheridan, Dan 177
Simon, Dr. Benjamin 79, 80
Simpson County Historical Society 258
Sirius UFO Space Science Research Center 396
Six-Mile Canyon 42
60 Minutes 375-376

Slaight, Lieutenant Commander Jim 377
Slater, Herman L. 153-155
Small, Philip 5-7
Smith, A.E. ("Ted") 270
Smith, Terri 309-312
Smith, Officer William L. 94
Smithsonian Astrophysical Satellite Tracking Program 42
Smithsonian Contributions to Knowledge 72
Snake River Valley 171
Socorro, New Mexico 33, 34-35, 40-41, 42, 43, 45, **217**, 263, 349
Solomons Island xiii, xv, 1
Southern Pacific Railroad 109, 267
South Hill Police Department 62, 63
Space Science Center 277
Spanish Peakes 263-265
Spargo, Alexander Roy 106, 107
Spencer, Philip 392
Spirit of St. Louis, The 242
Sport Aviation 113
Spring Grove Elementary School 54, 57, 58
Spring Grove Junior High School 54
Springhill Record, The 196
Sprinkle, Dr. R. Leo
S.S. Morgantown Victory 65-68
Stallion Site 43
Standiford Air Field 257
Stanford, Ray 40
Star Wars Program 350
Stefan, Batsa 159
Stefanescu, Captain Nicolae 162
St. Elmo's Fire 19
St. Leo's Cemetery 180
Stevens, Senator Ted 378, 379
Storia, Cornelia 158-159
Storia, Vasile 158

St. Petersburg Independent, The 107
Strand, Lieutenant Colonel Howard 89
Strange Effects from UFOs 163, 263
Strategic Air Command (S.A.C.) 36
Strickling, Ward 184
Stringfield, Leonard ("Len") H. 332, 335-337, 344
Sullivan, Walter 147-148
Sulsberger, Sheriff F.L. 183-184
Svihus, Eva 315-316
Svihus, Fred 315-136
Swart, Captain 70

T

Tacker, Major Lawrence J. 30
Tapping, Hugh 179
Taradale Police Station 199
Tarrant, Police Lieutenant Dan 394-395
Ted Stevens International Airport 400
Tenney, Cecil 340
Tennyson, Lord Alfred 81
Terry, Philip D. 320
Thompson, Will 133
Time Magazine 346
"Three Jacks, The" 133
Titusville Police Department 103
"T," Lieutenant Colonel 341
"T," Major General 343
Tolson, Clyde 36
Torme, Mel 384-385
Torme, Tracy 385
Tortorell, Dan 198
Tossie, Guy 168, 170-171, 172
To the Stars Academy of Arts and Science 378
Towson Police Department 7
Towson State College 7
Trachsville Bridge 306

Trans World Airlines 264
Travers, Tom 357
Travers, Mrs. Tom 357
Triche, Jay 263
"Trick Memo," The 124
Trinity Mountains 284
Trinity Site 41
Trotier, Joseph 132-133
True Magazine 243
Truman, First Lady Bess 37
Truman, President Harry S. 37-38, 350, 351, 353
"Truth About the Condon Report, The" 153
20th Century UFO Bureau 342
Twining, Lieutenant General Nathan E 351
2001: A Space Odyssey 97-99

U

UFO Crash at Roswell 349
U.F.O. Investigator, The 31, 88, 122, 152, 157
"UFO President, The" 301, 327
UFO Research Associates (UFOR) 43, 251, 261, 262, 263, 266, 267, 268, 277, 283, 284, 286, 291, 294, 296, 297, 303, 304, 306, 307, 308, 316, 318, 321, 323, 324, 330, 355, 366, 369, 371
U.F.O. Research Newsletter 439, **218, 219, 221, 222, 223, 224**, 251, 297
UFOR New Mexico Subcommittee 263
UFO Scientific Board of Inquiry 128
UFOs? Yes! Where the Condon Committee Went Wrong 125
Unicorn Coffee House 1
Union of Soviet Socialist Republics (U.S.S.R.) 270-271, 382
United Airlines 26, 31-32, 395

United Nations (UN) 81, 121, 128, 229, 336
United Press (UP) 174
United Press International (UPI) 41, 49
Unity is Seen in Open Minds (UISIOM) 363
University of Alaska 400
University of California 127
University of Colorado 117, 125, 148, 231, 336
University of Colorado UFO Project 336
University of Maryland 93
University of Qruro 275
University of St. Louis 264
University of Wisconsin 259
U.S.A.F. Space Systems Division 50
U.S. Air Force 3, 4-5, 19, 21, 23, 24, 25, 26, 30-31, 32, 34-36, 37, 38, 39, 46, 47, 48-49, 50, 60, 73, 83, 85, 87, 88-90, 91, 92, 93, 95, 112, 117-118, 120, 121, 122, 123, 129, 132, 133, 134, 137-139, 144, 145, 148, 149, 152, 153, 167, 178, 187, **219**, 231, 237, 243, 251, 254, 255, 258, 271, 298, 300, 315, 328, 336, 337, 338, 339, 340, 346, 347, 348, 350, 351, 353, 354, 356, 357, 379, 382, 387, 390
U.S. Army xvi, 1, 34, 36, 41, 72, 164, 167, 198, 252, 256, 257, 259, 347, 349, 350, 351, 352, 353, 363, 383, 387
U.S. Army Air Corps 254, 258, 264
U.S. Army Corps of Engineers 259
U.S. House Committee on Government Operations 138
U.S. Maritime Commission 65
U.S. Naval Academy 236, 241
U.S. Navy 7, 72, 108, 129, 145, 166, 196, 256, 261, 320, 337, 377, 378, 387

U.S. Navy Undersea Warfare Manned Research Platform 387
U.S. News and World Report 2
U.S. Park Police 94
U.S.S. Franklin D. Roosevelt 73
U.S.S. Nimitz 377
U.S.S. Princeton 377
U.S.S. Tiro 74
U.S. Weather Bureau 142
Utt, Congressman James B. 49
Uzunoglu, Dr. Vasil 92-93

V

Vage Refinery 158
Vallee, Dr. Jacques 90, 233-234
Vandenburg Air Force Base 315
Vatican, The 381
Vega, Alberto 39-40
Venus xv, 43, 255, 256, 300
Victor, Jim 316-317, 318
Victoria 69
Victorian Flying Saucer Research Society 185
Vietnam War 235, 361, 362, 363
Vigil, Captain Martin E. 39-40
Voice of America 236

W

Wallace, William L. 180-181
Wallace, Mrs. William L. 180-181
Walton, Aaron 393
Walton, Kevin 393
Walton, Sue 393
Walton, Travis 385
Waltz, Robert 367
Ware, Dr. Willis H. 87
Watts, Jack 132
Weaver, Dennis 385
Weaver, Sigourney 385

Webb, Walter N. 13-14, 16, 19, 41-43, 173, **217**
Wehrle, Agnes M. 303-304
Wellington Channel 71-72
Wells, Gregory L. 183-184
Wells, James E. 183
Wells, Mrs. James E. 183
Werner, Fritz 339-340
Wertheimer, Michael 118
Westinghouse Research Laboratories 178
WGCB Radio 53, 54, 57
Wheeler, Jim 14
White, Charles 324-325
White, Mrs. Charles 324-325
White, Helen 280-282
White House 38, 328, 329, 383
White House Press Corps 383, 384
White Sands Proving Grounds 34, 35
Wilbur, George 114
Wilcox, Sheriff George 347
Wilhelm, Jack 133-134
Willemoes 73
Williams, Frank 16
Williams, Police Chief Bill 62
Williams, Ted 98
Williamson, Dave 328-329
Winfrith Atomic Station 189
Winthrop, Governor John 68-69
Wolf, Dr. Norman S. 173
Wood, Flight Lieutenant A.M. 75
Wood, Lieutenant Colonel E. Garrison 251, 259
Wood, Jean 259
Wood River Junction 261
World War I 113
World War II 65, 115, 118, 158, 167, 188, 243, 254, 258, 259, 266, 317,

320, 349, 356, 379, 382
Wright Brothers 68
Wright Field 351
Wright, Newell 15
Wright Patterson Air Force Base 35, 337-338, 339, 341, 342, 343-344
Wright, Robert 144

X
X, Mr. 172

Y
Yamahata 386
Yarrow, Peter 1
Yates, Captain A.D. 31
Yeni Kent Compound 396

Yolder, Captain Richard T. 41

Z
Zacchini, Mario 144
Zachary Taylor National Cemetery 258
Zamora, Lonnie 33-36, 39, 40-43, 45, **215**, 263
Zechel, Todd 338
Zemenz, Police Sergeant Paul 360
Ziarul Scuntea Magazine 157
Ziegenfuss, Donna 305-306
Ziegenfuss, Ruth A. 305-306, 308
Zmeuranu, Gregore 158

About the Author

GORDON LORE began his professional writing/editing career as Vice President of the National Investigations Committee on Aerial Phenomena (NICAP, then the world's largest UFO organization) in the mid-1960s. He was responsible for heading a large scientific network of subcommittees that lent its expertise toward solving one of the primary mysteries of the 20th century and beyond. He played a prominent role in a day-long Congressional hearing on UFOs in September 1968. Lore was an uncredited scientific advisor to the late director Stanley Kubrick on his seminal science fiction film, *2001: A Space Odyssey*, in 1967, which celebrated the 50th year of its release in April 2018. He is also the senior author of *Mysteries of the Skies: UFOs in Perspective* (Prentice-Hall, Inc., 1968), the first-ever book based entirely on the early history of UFOs, and the sole author of *Strange Effects From UFOs* (NICAP, 1969). He edited *UFOs: A New Look,* the *UFO Investigator* and the *UFO Research Newsletter.* He wrote and edited hundreds of published articles on one of the most mysterious scientific puzzles of all time.

His book, *The Earle Family of NEWFOUNDLAND and the Birth of a Canadian Atlantic Province* is now available as a Nook Book on the Barnes & Noble website. This work, with the title *The Earle Family of Newfoundland and Labrador,* was also published in book form on July 1, 2015, by DRC Publishing in St. John's, Newfoundland and Labrador. Gordon also has his book entitled *The Priest of Kali: A Novelized Biography Based on the Life and Spiritual Ecstasies of Sri Ramakrishna*

(2017) posted on the Amazon Kindle Book site. His book *Connections: A Lifetime Journey Through the world of Celebrity* (2017), is now available from BearManor Media at www.bearmanormedia.com or from Gordon. lore@gmail.com.

Gordon also became a writer-editor in the public utilities field as a White House and Congressional Senate/House Gallery correspondent and National Press Club member. He was in the Oval Office of the White House in 1972 when President Richard M. Nixon signed the Environmental Protection Agency legislation that would further protect the air and water quality in the United States and its territories.

In 1975, Lore became the Editor of *The Rockwell News*, Rockwell International's employee newspaper, and wrote about numerous topics from the Apollo program, the Space Shuttle and nuclear energy. From 1992 to 2012, he was a prominent writer-editor in the kidney disease and renal transplantation arena. His hundreds of published articles on this topic led to his being recognized as a nominee for the prestigious first Medal of Excellence (known as the Nobel Prize of the renal care field) from the American Association of Kidney Patients (AAKP). One of the articles he solicited resulted in the formation of a dialysis clinic in the only hospital on the island country of Belize, leading to his AAKP recognition.

Lore has also written and published on a number of other issues, including the spiritual, the occult and the early history of aviation. He is particularly known among his colleagues as never having missed an editorial deadline in his entire 55-year career.

Gordon may be reached at (661) 255-7155 and Gordon.lore@gmail.com.

www.ingramcontent.com/pod-product-compliance
Lightning Source LLC
Chambersburg PA
CBHW070220240426
43671CB00007B/708